Munkman on Damages for
Personal Injuries and Death

Munkman on Damages for Personal Injuries and Death

Eleventh edition

Gordon Exall, BA (Warwick)
of Lincoln's Inn, Barrister

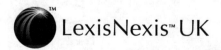

United Kingdom	LexisNexis UK, a Division of Reed Elsevier (UK) Ltd, Halsbury House, 35 Chancery Lane, LONDON, WC2A 1EL, and 4 Hill Street, EDINBURGH EH2 3JZ
Argentina	LexisNexis Argentina, BUENOS AIRES
Australia	LexisNexis Butterworths, CHATSWOOD, New South Wales
Austria	LexisNexis Verlag ARD Orac GmbH & Co KG, VIENNA
Canada	LexisNexis Butterworths, MARKHAM, Ontario
Chile	LexisNexis Chile Ltda, SANTIAGO DE CHILE
Czech Republic	Nakladatelství Orac sro, PRAGUE
France	Editions du Juris-Classeur SA, PARIS
Germany	LexisNexis Deutschland GmbH, FRANKFURT, MUNSTER
Hong Kong	LexisNexis Butterworths, HONG KONG
Hungary	HVG-Orac, BUDAPEST
India	LexisNexis Butterworths, NEW DELHI
Ireland	LexisNexis, DUBLIN
Italy	Giuffrè Editore, MILAN
Malaysia	Malayan Law Journal Sdn Bhd, KUALA LUMPUR
New Zealand	LexisNexis Butterworths, WELLINGTON
Poland	Wydawnictwo Prawnicze LexisNexis, WARSAW
Singapore	LexisNexis Butterworths, SINGAPORE
South Africa	LexisNexis Butterworths, DURBAN
Switzerland	Stämpfli Verlag AG, BERNE
USA	LexisNexis, DAYTON, Ohio

© Reed Elsevier (UK) Ltd 2004

A CIP Catalogue record for this book is available from the British Library.

ISBN 0-406-96009-7

9 780406 960092

Typeset by Doyle & Co, Colchester
Printed by the Cromwell Press, Trowbridge, Wilts

Foreword to the eleventh edition by The Rt Hon Lord Justice Kennedy

Everyone of my generation who undertook personal injury litigation, must feel indebted to John Munkman, not only for his excellent book on Employers Liability but also for this slimmer book which in every edition has clearly set out the principles of the law relating to damages for personal injuries and death. Even if it did not give a detailed answer to a particular problem, it never failed to point the reader in the right direction. Such a book does, however, need to be kept up to date, and if the present editor had not accepted John's invitation not only personal injury lawyers but also others who for one reason or another come into contact with this area of the law would all have suffered. Some of the chapter headings indicate all too clearly why a new edition is now needed – for example the growing importance of care claims (chapter 11); instructing experts: a massive change in culture (part of chapter 18) and provisional damages (chapter 19). The new editor has wisely retained John's aim to be both concise and comprehensible, as well as comprehensive, and it seems to me that he has more than justified John's choice of his successor.

Preface to the eleventh edition

Whilst cases are regularly returned inside chambers it must be rare for authorship of a book to be selected on a similar basis. It is with some trepidation that I have accepted John's invitation (expressed in a codicil to his will) to take over the writing of his text on damages. It is a book that has commanded my respect for many years. It was recommended as compulsory on my first day at work as an articled clerk; it was equally useful when I took up practice at the Bar.

In taking up the challenge I have had to consider what makes this book important and unique. When John wrote the first edition in 1956 it was one of the first attempts to set out the law of personal injury damages in a coherent format. It must have come as a ray of light to practitioners struggling to come to grips with what was a new and developing subject.

In some ways the modern practitioner is need of the same ray of light. The problem for the personal injury lawyer today is not that they are faced with a dearth of material on the subject, but with a glut. Each of the major works on personal injury is in four volumes and there is a daily barrage of new material on damages which arrives on the desktop, or on the computer screen.

This mass of information can have profound practical effects. For those involved in the modern world of personal injury damages there are serious problems in telling the wood from trees.

The aim of this book is to set out the major principles of damages relating to personal injury and death in a succinct and comprehensible manner. Whenever possible I have followed John's practice of citing the crucial parts of judgments in full. There are, however, major changes. I have carried out extensive revision to the text, many new chapters are added and the format of the book has changed extensively. I hope to have kept the central Munkman principle of being concise and comprehensible.

When completing a new edition John always paid tribute to the Butterworths (now LexisNexis UK) staff and I have come to understand why. As ever, I must thank my family for their patience in the preparation of this text. However, the greatest tribute must go to John Munkman himself.

John was a legal scholar of the highest order. However, he was not just an expert lawyer. In addition to his practice at the bar he had a wide range of experience. He had qualified as a solicitor in 1939 and took his Bar exams in the Far East whilst serving in the Air Force. Even at the end of his life he was regularly travelling, climbing, reading and writing. He was an accomplished athlete and mathematician. He was interested in politics, international affairs and was, perhaps, the last practising member of the bar to have seen active service in the Second World War. His ambition in life had been to be a Spitfire pilot; ironically his health (eyesight) let him down.

It is, however, as a legal writer that John will be remembered. In addition to writing texts on personal injury and damages John also wrote books on quasi contract, tax law and a brilliant book on principles of advocacy. The breadth of his legal knowledge was a boon to his colleagues. I was privileged to be in chambers with John for eight years and it is clear his intellect, sharp judgment and patience with the numerous members of the bar who sought his advice are still sorely missed.

Needless to say, any errors in this text are my own. Like my predecessor I welcome correspondence on any issues relating to the text.

Gordon Exall
Zenith Chambers
10 Park Square
Leeds
March 2004

Preface to the first edition

I was first invited to write a book on damages for personal injuries (with special reference to quantum) as long ago as May 1953. The invitation arose out of an article in the Law Journal, which attracted some interest at the time. In that article I drew attention to the difference in approach which follows from the fact that damages are now usually assessed by a judge sitting alone, and not by a jury. Juries do not give reasons for their decisions, and it does not greatly matter if the verdict of one jury is widely different from the verdict of another in a similar case. Juries are allowed to be capricious, but judges are not: they have to act on reasoned principles, even if they do not state them, and marked disparities between awards for the same type of injury would give rise to criticism. Therefore, by degrees, the principles of the law have been restated, and at the same time there has been a growing tendency to treat awards in comparable cases as useful guides and illustrations.

But at that stage, three years ago, I declined the invitation to write at length on the subject, partly because I did not want to write any more legal books, and partly because it would have been premature to do so: there were not enough decided cases to illuminate the principles of law, and very few useful illustrations of quantum were available.

Law year, however, when the invitation was renewed, I felt that, if I could throw some new light on the subject, I was no longer justified in refusing merely for reasons of personal inconvenience. The material available had greatly increased in the meantime, largely because the All England Law Reports had made it their policy to report occasional cases on damages, though much of the material is still contained in newspaper cuttings and is often (but not always) less reliable and complete than law reports.

The aim of this book, as finally planned, is twofold. First, to give a complete statement of the principles of law on the assessment of damages for personal injuries (including damages on death); secondly, to frame a broad classification of the type of cases which arise, and to offer typical illustrations of awards which can be used as general guidelines in comparable cases. By a fortunate coincidence, the case of *Waldon v War Office* was heard in the Court of Appeal as I was finishing the text, and the views expressed in that case were exactly in accordance with the opinions I had previously formed. It cannot be said too often that awards on quantum are never more than illustrations and guides. They are not leading cases or authorities: yet they may be of great value, especially in the settlement of claims.

In conclusion, I am sorry that I cannot reply to enquiries about the details of any of the illustrations cited. I have done my best to extract what is relevant out of data which are often imperfect, and the extracts contain everything which is known to me and is relevant.

John Munkman
Leeds
August 1956

Contents

Appendix II

Table of statutes

Paragraph numbers in **bold** type indicate where the legislation is set out in part or in full

Table of statutory instruments

Paragraph numbers in **bold** type indicate where the legislation is set out in part or in full

Table of cases

PARA

B

PARA

PARA

PARA

PARA

I

J

PARA

PARA

PARA

PARA

CHAPTER 1

Damages in general

1.1 'The aim of compensatory damages is to restore the plaintiff to the position he or she would have been in if the relevant tort (or breach of contract) had not been committed. In other words, an injured plaintiff is entitled to compensation for the past, present and future losses that are consequent on his or her actionable personal injury. The application of this principle to pecuniary losses is relatively straightforward. This is not the case, however, in relation to non-pecuniary loss, since money cannot restore a broken limb or renew a shattered frame. The award of damages is a monetary remedy, and non-pecuniary losses are losses which are "not susceptible of measurement in money." They are such that, by definition, they cannot be measured by reference to the market.'[1]

1   *Damages for Personal Injury: Non-Pecuniary Loss* (Law Com no 140) para 2.1.

1.2 Few practitioners have time to reflect on the basic principles of compensation, still less to consider its historical and jurisprudential roots. However, an understanding of these basic principles gives a major advantage to anyone involved in a claim for personal injury.

DAMAGES ARE COMPENSATION IN MONEY

1.3 When one person causes harm of any kind to another person – whether it is personal injury, damage to property, or financial loss – the normal remedy which the law gives (if it gives a right of action at all) is a right to recover damages. Damages are simply a sum of money given as compensation for loss or harm of any kind. The law on the nature of damages has been stated from time to time in somewhat varying terms by eminent judges; for example, by Viscount Dunedin in *Admiralty Comrs v SS Valeria (Owners)* [1922] 2 AC 242 at 248, HL:

'The true method of expression, I think, is that in calculating damages you are to consider what is the pecuniary consideration which will make good to the sufferer, as far as money can do so, the loss which he has suffered as the natural result of the wrong done to him.'

That is to say, you give compensation which is estimated to be the *equivalent* of that which has been lost. This basic point is one that underlies the vast majority of claims for personal injury.

1.4   An alternative statement of the law is by Lord Blackburn in *Livingstone v Rawyards Coal Co* (1880) 5 App Cas 25 at 39:

'where any injury is to be compensated by damages, in settling the sum of money to be given ... you should as nearly as possible get at that sum of money which will put the person who has been injured ... in the same position as he would have been in if he had not sustained the wrong.'

1.5   This looks rather at the cost of restoration or repair. Both these cases were about damage to property. Now property can generally be replaced, if destroyed, or repaired, if damaged. In applying Lord Blackburn's words to personal injuries, or indeed to property if it is unique and irreplaceable, it must be recognised that the primary rule is compensation. The rule that compensation is measured by the cost of repair, or restoring the original position – restitutio in integrum – is a derivative or secondary rule, which applies only if and so far as the original position can be restored. If it cannot, the law must endeavour to give a fair equivalent in money, so far as money can be an equivalent, and in that way 'make good' the damage. Lord Morris of Borth-y-Gest said in *Parry v Cleaver* [1970] AC 1 at 22, [1969] 1 All ER 555 at 564, HL:

'To compensate in money for pain and for physical consequences is invariably difficult but ... no other process can be devised than that of making a monetary assessment.'

MEANING OF COMPENSATION

1.6   The word 'compensation' is derived from a Latin root, 'compensare', meaning 'weigh together' or 'balance'. The fundamental principle is to 'give to each person that which is their *right*'. This is essentially a matter of equality or balance. If someone owes a debt, it must be paid back. If he infringes a right, he must pay the equivalent in money of the injury or damage sustained.

DAMAGES ARE NOT PUNITIVE

1.7 It is an essential element of the vast majority of personal injury and fatal accident cases that damages are not punitive. The aim is to compensate and not to punish. As Lord Goddard said in *British Transport Commission v Gourley* [1956] AC 185 at 208, [1955] 3 All ER 796 at 805, HL:

'Damages which have to be paid for personal injuries are not punitive, still less are they a reward. They are simply compensation ...'

It has also been said:

'There is nothing punitive in calling on a defendant to pay that which the law says is a just recompense for the injury the plaintiff has been caused.'[1]

(There are some exceptions to the basic rule which are examined in chapter 5.)

1   *Parry v Cleaver* [1970] AC 1 at 33, [1969] 1 All ER 555 at 574, HL, per Lord Pearce.

UNIVERSALITY OF THE REPARATION PRINCIPLE

1.8 Most actions for damages for personal injuries are founded on tort, such as negligence, breach of statutory duty or assault; but sometimes they are based on breach of contract, for example, the failure of a shipping or railway company to carry passengers safely. In these cases too the same principle is applied:

'the common law says that the damages due either for breach of contract or for tort are damages which, so far as money can compensate, will give the injured party reparation.'[1]

From this leading principle that damages are compensation – but compensation in terms of money – a number of consequences follow, and three things require special mention.

1   *Admiralty Comrs v SS Susquehanna* [1926] AC 655 at 661, HL, per Viscount Dunedin.

DAMAGES MUST BE FULL AND ADEQUATE

1.9 The necessity that damages should be 'full' and 'adequate' was stressed by the Court of Queen's Bench in *Fair v London and North Western Rly Co* (1869) 18 WR 66, 21 LT 326. In this case the plaintiff was a clergyman aged 27, earning £250 a year and with good prospects. He was involved in a railway accident and sustained a spinal injury which resulted in paralysis of the lower limbs and impairment of the senses. The jury awarded to him £5,000 general damages. £5,000 would represent a very large sum in 1869, more than £100,000 today. Nevertheless the court declined to order a new trial on the ground that the damages were excessive.

1.10 In *Rushton v National Coal Board* [1953] 1 All ER 314 at 316, CA, Singleton LJ said:

'Every member of this court is anxious to do all he can to ensure that the damages are adequate for the injury suffered, so far as they can be compensation for an injury, and to help the parties and others to arrive at a fair and just figure.'

1.11 In *Heil v Rankin* [2000] PIQR Q187 at Q199, Lord Woolf MR stated:

'The court's approach involves trying to find the global sum which most accurately in monetary terms reflects or can be regarded as reflecting a fair, reasonable and just figure for the injuries which have been inflicted and the consequences they will have ...'

DAMAGES ARE NORMALLY ASSESSED ONCE AND FOR ALL

1.12 The common law rule was that damages were assessed once and for all, and compensation was given not only for loss and injury which had already accrued, but also for loss and injury which might develop at a future date. For example, in a personal injuries case, future loss of earnings or profits was estimated; and any risk that the claimant's condition might deteriorate had to be taken into account at that time. If serious injuries supervened unexpectedly, a second action could not be brought. Where damages resulted from one and the same cause of action, they had to be assessed once and for all. Lord Reid said in *British Transport Commission v Gourley* [1956] AC 185 at 213, [1955] 3 All ER 796 at 808, HL:

'... damages must be assessed as a lump sum once and for all, not only in respect of loss accrued before the trial but also in respect of prospective loss.'

1.13 Therefore, under the common law rule, if there was a possibility of epilepsy developing at a later date, the chances had to be estimated and taken into account: *Jones v Griffith* [1969] 2 All ER 1015, [1969] 1 WLR 795, CA. Lord Diplock said in *Mallett v McMonagle* [1969] 2 All ER 178 at 191, HL that:

'in assessing damages which depend on its view as to what will happen in the future or would have happened in the future ... the court must make an estimate as to what are the chances that a particular thing will or would have happened ...'

1.14 This is different from an inquiry into past events, where the court must decide one way or the other whether a thing happened or not and act on a preponderance of probability. In the case of future uncertainties, it simply values the chances, which means in practice that if there is a possibility of a future deterioration or loss which may or may not occur, it will be valued on a *percentage* basis according to the extent of the risk.

1.15 It is still the normal rule that damages are assessed once and for all to include present and future consequences of the injury. But the Administration of Justice Act 1982, s 6 and consequent rules of Court makes it possible for rules of Court to authorise the assessment of damages in two stages if there is a risk that the claimant will develop a serious disease or a serious deterioration in his condition. Where this is permitted, damages will be assessed in the first instance without taking the risk into account at all, but may be given at a later stage if the disease or deterioration actually occurs. The Administration of Justice Act 1982, s 12 makes a similar change in Scots law. (For further details see chapter 19 below.)

DIFFICULTY AND UNCERTAINTY OF ASSESSMENT DOES NOT PRECLUDE AN AWARD OF DAMAGES

1.16 There are many losses apart from personal injuries which cannot easily be expressed in terms of money. If a rare porcelain vase is shattered or a family heirloom destroyed, the article itself cannot be replaced and probably has no market value. So, too, if an arm is lost, or a person is deprived of the sense of smell, there is no market value for the personal asset which has been taken away, and there is no easy means of expressing its equivalent in terms of money.

1.17 Nevertheless a valuation in terms of money must be made, because otherwise the law would not be able to give any remedy at all. In *The Mediana* [1900] AC 113 the plaintiffs were deprived of the use of a lightship, but sustained no pecuniary loss as another lightship was kept in reserve. Yet it was held that the plaintiffs were entitled to substantial damages for the loss of the use of their ship for a period, and Lord Halsbury LC answered the objection that assessment was too uncertain in the following terms (at 116–117):

'Of course the whole region of inquiry into damages is one of extreme difficulty. You very often cannot even lay down any principle upon which you can give damages; nevertheless, it is remitted to the jury, or those who stand in place of the jury, to consider what compensation in money shall be given for what is a wrongful act. Take the most familiar and ordinary case: how is anybody to measure pain and suffering in moneys counted? Nobody can suggest that you can by any arithmetical calculation establish what is the exact amount of money which would represent such a thing as the pain and suffering which a person has undergone by reason of an accident ... But, nevertheless, the law recognises that as a topic upon which damages may be given.'

1.18 Similarly Goddard LJ said in *The Ceramic (Owners) v The Testbank (Owners)* [1942] P 75 at 80, [1942] 1 All ER 281 at 283, a case which concerned the apportionment of blame between two ships involved in a collision:

'It is no doubt true that one cannot apportion blame with anything approaching mathematical accuracy; but that is a familiar difficulty in cases where the damages are at large. In an ordinary accident case, there is no yardstick by which the court can measure the amount to be awarded for pain and suffering or ensuing disability.'

1.19 It has been held in numerous cases that uncertainty in the quantification of damage does not prevent an assessment, provided that some broad estimate can be made: see, for instance, *Hall v Ross* (1813) 1 Dow 201, HL (damage to fishery); *Chaplin v Hicks* [1911] 2 KB 786, 80 LJKB 1292, CA (loss of chance of theatrical engagement); *Carson v Willitts* [1930] 4 DLR 977, 65 OLR 456, Ont SC (App Div) (loss of chance of striking oil through failure to make additional borings). In actions for personal injuries, the court is constantly required to form an estimate of chances and risks which cannot be determined with anything like precision: for example, the possibility that the injury will improve, or deteriorate, or the possibility of improved earnings if the accident had not occurred: see *Fair v London and North Western Rly Co* (1869) 18 WR 66, 21 LT 326.

1.20 Obviously, the law will disregard possibilities which are slight or chances which are nebulous: otherwise, all the circumstances of the situation must be taken into account, whether they relate to the future which the claimant would have enjoyed apart from the accident, or to the future of his injuries and his earning power after the accident. (See chapters 6 and 10 below.)

1.21 The fundamental principle of the law of damages can be summarised as follows: damages are compensation for an injury or loss, that is to say the full equivalent in money so far as the nature of money admits; and difficulty or uncertainty does not prevent an assessment.

CHAPTER 2

Overview of the types of damages in personal injury cases

QUANTIFICATION

2.1   There are two basic issues in relation to the quantification of damages in personal injury cases:

(1) What are the items of loss and injury for which compensation is given?

(2) How are those items quantified, or reduced to terms of money?

Items of loss for which damages are given

2.2   In general, damages are given for every kind of injury and damage caused by an unlawful act, and for all consequential loss and expense. The items of loss and damage vary from one type of case to another. In a case of personal injuries, for example, loss of earnings, pain and loss of the enjoyment of life are all relevant factors.

2.3   There are some types of loss, however, which are not free from difficulty. For a long time it was disputed whether damages could be recovered for nervous shock and supervening neurosis unaccompanied by physical injury; and damages cannot always be recovered for mere discomfort and inconvenience, or for humiliation and injured feelings. (See chapter 7 below.)

2.4   Some items of loss may be too 'remote', ie too far removed from the original accident. Suppose, for instance, that bad medical advice is given, which makes the injury worse. Is the cost of the mistaken treatment recoverable? And are damages recoverable for the aggravation of the injury? This type of problem turns on whether, in the eyes of the law, the defendant was the cause of the loss in question, and is therefore properly a question of liability and not part of the law of damages. Nevertheless a summary of the law of remoteness of damage is given in chapter 3 below – which, however, makes no pretence to be complete.

Quantifying the loss

2.5   Where the loss is in itself of a financial character, such as loss of wages or profits and medical expenses, the assessment of the damages is primarily a matter of arithmetic. The claimant is entitled in principle to full indemnity.

2.6   Where the loss is not of a financial character – like the loss of an arm – and cannot be measured in financial terms, the court must nevertheless make a broad estimate in terms of money, and will be guided by awards made in comparable cases.

The two main elements in damages for personal injuries: personal loss and pecuniary loss

2.7   In every case of personal injuries, there are two main factors which have to be taken into account in assessing the damages.

2.8   On the one hand, there is the personal injury itself, ranging from the loss of a limb or other part of the body to slight cuts or bruises, and involving not only pain and hardship, but also the loss of the pleasures of life. On the other hand, there is the financial loss.

2.9   Cockburn CJ distinguished these two factors in *Fair v London and North Western Rly Co* (1869) 18 WR 66, where he said:

'In assessing [the] compensation the jury should take into account two things; first, the pecuniary loss [the plaintiff] sustains by the accident; secondly, the injury he sustains in his person, or his physical capacity of enjoying life. When they come to the consideration of the pecuniary loss they have to take into account not only his present loss, but his incapacity to earn a future improved income.'

2.10   This broad distinction between personal loss and pecuniary loss runs through all the cases: see, for example, the leading cases in the House of Lords, *British Transport Commission v Gourley* [1956] AC 185, [1955] 3 All ER 796, HL and *H West & Son Ltd v Shephard* [1964] AC 326, [1963] 2 All ER 625, HL.

Quantifying the financial loss

2.11   In estimating the financial or pecuniary loss, the court must first form an opinion, from the evidence and probabilities in the case, of the nature and extent of the loss. Thus in the case of loss of earnings, the court must first decide what the claimant would have been earning if the accident had not happened, allowing for any future increase or decrease in the rate of earnings. Then it is necessary to decide how long the loss will continue – whether there is incapacity for life, or for a shorter period. Finally, an estimate must be made of the amount (if any) which the claimant can still earn in future, notwithstanding his disability.

2.12   Similarly, if medical and nursing expenses are claimed, the court must find as a fact what expenses have already been incurred, and must estimate from the evidence the expenses which will be incurred in future.

2.13   These findings of fact are the essential starting point, although judges do not invariably express their precise and detailed conclusions. When many factors are uncertain, it is sometimes best to look at the facts in a broad perspective.

2.14   But, once the extent of the financial loss has been ascertained, it is not in doubt that the claimant is entitled to a full indemnity. Therefore, when proof is given of the amount of wages lost and the expenses incurred up to the date of the trial – the 'special damages' – the claimant is entitled to the exact figure. The principle of law is well expressed in a case from New Zealand:[1]

> 'Where in an action for general damages for personal injury, apart from the imponderable elements, the question of financial loss is involved, it is the duty of a jury to make the money situation after the injury, as far as possible, coincide with what it was before, so that the injured party's money prospects are disturbed to the least possible extent.'

1   *Shelton v Viles* [1939] NZLR 14.

Quantifying the personal loss

2.15   When we turn to the assessment of the personal loss – the loss of a limb, or an eye, or the endurance of pain and discomfort – it is at first sight an entirely different problem. Different it certainly is, and more difficult: but the difference is not so profound as is sometimes suggested, and the difficulty is no greater than many others which the law is able to resolve.

Damages for the injury *are* compensation

2.16 There are dicta in the older cases which suggest that damages for the injury itself, as distinct from the financial loss entailed, are not compensation at all, but a kind of solatium, a sympathetic payment admitted to be less than is really due. If this were right, damages would be by nature wholly discretionary, and it would be left to the judge or jury to decide, in an arbitrary manner, how far the amount should fall short of adequacy. They could take into account, for example, the fact that a paralysed and unconscious claimant is incapable of enjoying the money, and perhaps also the ability of an average defendant to pay. An argument on these lines was addressed to the House of Lords in *H West & Son Ltd v Shephard* [1964] AC 326, [1963] 2 All ER 625, HL. To some extent this argument prevailed with Lord Devlin in his dissenting speech, but it was rejected by the majority of the House. Lord Morris of Borth-y-Gest, for instance, said (at 348, 633):

'I consider that it is sufficient to say that a money award is given by way of compensation and that it must take into account the actual consequences which have resulted from the tort.'

And he continued a little later:

'If damages are awarded to a plaintiff on a correct basis it seems to me that it can be of no concern to the court to consider any question as to the use that will thereafter be made of the money awarded.'

He added that 'there may be items which will only be awarded if certain needs ... are established' such as nursing, medicine and transport for a crippled person. These, of course, come under the heading of financial loss and are a different matter.

The claimant need not be conscious of the loss

2.17 The main point actually decided in *H West & Son Ltd v Shephard* [1964] AC 326, [1963] 2 All ER 625, HL was that a plaintiff is entitled to substantial and not merely token damages for being deprived of the joys of life, although by reason of prolonged unconsciousness there is little or no distress about the loss. It was not in dispute that a plaintiff who was aware of the situation would have substantially more because of the mental distress. The point of the decision is that damages are not 'consolation money'. They are given for the harm actually sustained.

2.18   In *Lim Poh Choo v Camden and Islington Area Health Authority* [1980] AC 174, [1979] 2 All ER 910, HL, the House of Lords adhered to the principle laid down in *H West & Son Ltd v Shephard* [1964] AC 326, [1963] 2 All ER 625, HL and said that if the law were to be changed it should be changed by Parliament as part of a comprehensive review of the law of damages.

The value of the injury

2.19   In principle, damages for the injury itself are intended to be like all other damages: an equivalent in money – so far as the nature of money admits – for the loss sustained. The problem for the court, therefore, is to place a *fair value* on the lost limb or eye, or whatever the injury is. This does not mean that you value a leg or eye in isolation; it means that you value the totality of the harm, positive and negative, which the loss has entailed, the loss of the good things of life and the positive infliction of pain and distress. Lord Reid said in *Baker v Willoughby* [1969] 3 All ER 1528 at 1532, HL:

> 'A man is not compensated for the physical injury; he is compensated for the loss which he suffers as a result of that injury. His loss is not in having a stiff leg; it is in his inability to lead a full life, his inability to enjoy those amenities which depend on freedom of movement and his inability to earn as much as he used to earn or could have earned ...'

2.20   While these various effects are different from one case to another, nevertheless a typical injury such as the loss or impairment of a leg has much the same effects on the majority of mankind, so apart from earning capacity one would expect rather similar damages for the loss of the same limb. It is this consideration which justifies the establishment of a standard range of damages for a particular type of injury.

Assessing the value of the injury

2.21   This matter is dealt with in detail in chapter 8 below. In essence the courts look to awards of damages which have been made by other courts in comparable cases. In *Bird v Cocking & Sons Ltd* [1951] 2 TLR 1260, CA, Birkett LJ said (at 1263):

> 'Although there is no fixed and unalterable standard, the courts have been making these assessments for many years, and I think that they do form some guide to the kind of figure which is appropriate ... when, therefore, a particular matter comes for review, one of the questions is, how does this accord with the general run of assessments made over the years in comparable cases.'

2.22 In *Rushton v National Coal Board* [1953] 1 QB 495 at 501, [1953] 1 All ER 314 at 317, CA, the same learned judge brought out the point that a social element is involved in the valuation:

> 'It is useful to look at comparable cases to see what other minds have done, and so to gather the general consensus of opinion as to the amount which a man in a certain state of society ought to be awarded.'

2.23 This principle of having regard to awards in comparable cases has been carried much farther since those tentative first approaches. It was approved by the House of Lords in *H West & Son Ltd v Shephard* [1964] AC 326, [1963] 2 All ER 625, HL and also by the Judicial Committee in *Singh (infant) v Toong Fong Omnibus Co Ltd* [1964] 3 All ER 925, [1964] 1 WLR 1382, PC, where an award was set aside as being too much 'out of line with a discernible trend or pattern of awards in reasonably comparable cases'. In the latter case (an appeal from Singapore) it was added that comparison should be made with cases 'in the same jurisdiction or in a neighbouring locality where similar social, economic and industrial conditions exist'. This brings out the point that we are concerned with a social estimate in which the courts are the mouthpiece of society at large: as Sachs LJ put it in *Jones v Griffith* [1969] 2 All ER 1015, [1969] 1 WLR 795, CA 'the views of reasonable men in general and of judges in particular', or as Salmon LJ said in *Fletcher v Autocar and Transporters Ltd* [1968]1 All ER 726 at 750, CA:

> 'the damages awarded should be such that the ordinary sensible man would not instinctively regard them as either mean or extravagant, but would consider them to be sensible and fair ...'

2.24 In *Ward v James* [1966] 1 QB 273 at 275, [1965] 1 All ER 563 at 574, CA, Lord Denning MR said:

'... the award of damages in personal injuries cases is basically a conventional figure derived from experience and from awards in comparable cases.'

The word 'conventional' (also used by Lord Morris of Borth-y-Gest in the House of Lords and Judicial Committee cases mentioned at para 2.23 above) does not or should not mean that the amount is arbitrary, but rather that it is arrived at by general custom and agreement.

2.25   Again, Lord Diplock said in *Wright v British Railways Board* [1983] 2 All ER 698 at 699, HL:

'Any figure at which the assessor of damages arrives cannot be other than artificial and, if the aim is that justice meted out to all litigants should be even-handed instead of depending on idiosyncrasies of the assessor, whether jury or judge, the figure must be "basically a conventional figure derived from experience and from awards in comparable cases".'

2.26   Further, comparable figures are a guide and a tool, not the essence of the award: they are always open to review by the court. Lord Diplock went on to say ([1983] 2 All ER 698 at 705–706[1]) that to establish guidelines, including the approximate range of awards for particular types of injury, is very much within the province of the Court of Appeal; that although guidelines are not inflexible, they should not be varied too frequently or they will cease to be useful, but they should be adjusted automatically for inflation. Guidance is now published by the Judicial Studies Board (see appendix I). This should now be looked at first of all as the primary source. (See chapter 8 below.)

1   *Wright v British Railways Board* [1983] 2 AC 773, [1983] 2 All ER 698, HL.

CHAPTER 3

Remoteness of damage and causation

REMOTENESS OF DAMAGE: PRACTICAL DIFFICULTIES

3.1 On the face of it, damages are given for all the consequential loss and expense which flows from the injury. It is possible, however, for the damage to be too 'remote', ie too far removed from the wrongful act of the defendant. Alternatively it can be argued that the defendant's breach has not *caused* the loss.

3.2 Remoteness of damage is a confusing subject, not because it is difficult in itself, but because, like an archaeological site, it has been overlaid with successive theories which are inconsistent with one another. It is closer to questions of liability than to the assessment of damages, because, in ultimate analysis, the question is whether the defendant's act *caused* the loss or expense which is in question. Nevertheless, it helps to include here a brief account of the law.

REMOTENESS IN PRACTICE

3.3 Questions of remoteness arise in practice in two different ways. First, it may be argued that the accident itself was too remote from the defendant's act. For example, in *SS Singleton Abbey v SS Paludina* [1927] AC 16, 95 LJP 135, HL, two ships were cast adrift from their moorings in harbour through the action of the defendant ship, and subsequently came into collision while they were still, in a sense, in a position of danger, yet were able to navigate as free agents. It was held (as Lord Sumner put it at 26) that the defendant ship had 'merely created the occasion' for the collision and was not liable for causing it.

3.4 Secondly, it may be said that, although the accident was caused by the defendant, some of the consequential loss or expense was not. This sort of question is liable to be raised in personal injury cases, for example, where some mistake is made in the course of the medical treatment.

3.5 These two forms of the problem of remoteness are not distinguished in the authorities, and in principle the law is the same in both cases. But in practice, where the defendant is admittedly responsible for the injury, the court will be reluctant to exclude consequential loss and expense of a reasonable character: see, for example, *Rubens v Walker* 1946 SC 215, Ct of Sess (cost of mistaken medical treatment).

ISSUES OF REMOTENESS IN CASES OF NEGLIGENCE OR BREACH OF STATUTORY DUTY

3.6 In both these cases, unlike many torts, it is a necessary part of the cause of action that the breach of the duty of care or other duty should result in damage. The question is, what type of damage? And, if there is some limitation, does it extend to consequential damage, or is consequential damage of any kind recoverable if there is at least some primary damage to support the cause of action?

Statutory duty

3.7 With regard to breach of statutory duty, it has long been held that when a statute is intended to give protection against harm of one kind, it does not give a right of action when breach of the statute results in harm of a different kind: *Gorris v Scott* (1874) LR 9 Exch 125, 43 LJ Ex 92 (sheep swept overboard from ship owing to absence of pens required as safeguard against disease). But statutes to protect workers against accident are normally construed as giving protection against injury generally: *Grant v National Coal Board* [1956] AC 649, [1956] 1 All ER 682, HL (action lies for failure to support roof not only where injuries caused by fall itself but also where due to collision with fallen debris).

Negligence

3.8 In cases of negligence the duty is to take reasonable care against harm which a reasonable man would foresee as likely. His duty to take care is in proportion to the degree of risk.

3.9 It was formerly considered that once negligence is established, liability extends to all its consequences. Foreseeability, it was said, is the test for liability but not for compensation: *Re Polemis & Furness Withy & Co* [1921] 3 KB 560, 90 LJKB 1353.

The Wagon Mound *decision*

3.10 This view was held to be wrong in *Overseas Tankship (UK) Ltd v Morts Dock and Engineering Co Ltd, The Wagon Mound* [1961] AC 388, [1961] 1 All ER 404, PC, where the Judicial Committee of the Privy Council, in an appeal from Australia, decided that there is liability only for the type of damage which, because it was a foreseeable type of damage, gave rise to a duty of care. So where oil had been negligently spilt in Sydney harbour, causing slight foreseeable damage by fouling a slipway, the defendants were not liable for consequential damage (held not to be foreseeable, as the oil was not in itself inflammable) when the oil was set on fire by molten metal falling on cotton waste and burnt a wharf.

3.11 This case caused much controversy, largely because the judgment was in sweeping terms which suggested that all existing law on whether damage is caused by some accident should be superseded by the test of 'foreseeability'. Now that the dust has settled, it is clear that *The Wagon Mound*[1] has a more limited effect. It establishes an equivalent, in actions for negligence, to the rule in *Gorris v Scott* (1874) LR 9 Exch 125, 43 LJ Ex 92 for breach of statutory duty. Just as the duty to fence in sheep to prevent disease could not be stretched to a duty to prevent them being washed overboard, so a duty of care to avoid foreseeable damage of one type cannot be invoked to recover for damage of another type which was not foreseeable and therefore gave rise to no duty. This does not mean that a strained view should be taken of what is foreseeable, or that pedantic distinctions should be made between different 'types' of damage.

1   *Overseas Tankship (UK) Ltd v Morts Dock and Engineering Co Ltd, The Wagon Mound* [1961] AC 388, [1961] 1 All ER 404, PC.

No liability for negligence not of a foreseeable type

3.12 So in an action for negligence there is no liability for damage which was not of a foreseeable type within the scope of the duty of care: on the other hand, there is liability for damage of a foreseeable type notwithstanding that (perhaps owing to a claimant's special vulnerability) it is more extensive than expected or spreads in an unexpected way; nor is it necessary that the manner in which the damage is caused should be foreseen: *Smith v Leech Brain & Co Ltd* [1962] 2 QB 405, [1961] 3 All ER 1159, QBD (foreseeable burn on lip, in pre-cancerous condition, turned to cancer); *Hughes v Lord Advocate* [1963] AC 837, [1963] 1 All ER 705, HL (injury by burns from lamp foreseeable, caused by unforeseeable explosion of lamp); *Rowark v National Coal Board* [1986] CLY 42 (sprain to wrist foreseeable: tenosynovitis within the risk though it affected the tendon).

What connection is required between the breach and the damage

3.13   This is the true question of remoteness. It is, of course, plain that the damage must be the result or consequence of the tort, which is another way of saying that the tort has caused it or brought it about. But one thing springs from another, and consequences spread out indefinitely like ripples from a pebble thrown into a lake. A line has to be drawn somewhere. Now if *The Wagon Mound*[1] had superseded all the previous law on causation, including many cases decided in the House of Lords, only one question would be asked. Has the accident been *followed* by harm of a foreseeable type? But it is not enough that damage has followed; it must be shown that it was caused by the accident, and caused in a way which was not too remote. It need not have been caused in a foreseeable way, as Lord Reid made clear in *Hughes v Lord Advocate* [1963] AC 837, [1963] 1 All ER 705. So foreseeability cannot be the sole test. Hitherto damage has not been considered remote (in a *causal* sense as distinct from a *liability* sense) if it was either (i) a direct consequence of the accident, ie the automatic physical effects before any new factor intervened or (ii) although indirect, that is supervening at a later stage, it was a foreseeable consequence. The fact that English law accepts a dual test of remoteness appears from the speech of Lord Porter in *Morrison Steamship Co Ltd v SS Greystoke Castle (Owners of Cargo lately laden on)* [1947] AC 265 at 295, [1946] 2 All ER 696 at 709, HL, where he said:

'One method of ascertaining the damages in an action of tort is to ask what loss would a reasonable man anticipate as a result of the wrongful act. To this the *Polemis* case[2] added a further liability, viz, damage consisting of the direct physical consequences of the tortious act, whether they would reasonably be anticipated or not.'

1   *Overseas Tankship (UK) Ltd v Morts Dock and Engineering Co Ltd, The Wagon Mound* [1961] AC 388, [1961] 1 All ER 404, PC.
2   *Re Polemis & Furness Withy & Co* [1921] 3 KB 560, 90 LJKB 1353, CA.

3.14 The test of 'direct' consequences, convenient though it is for a purely mechanical train of events, is not apt to measure human intervention. Indeed it seems correct to say that as soon as a deliberate human act intervenes anything which follows is no longer a direct consequence of the original wrong. Therefore liability in these cases must depend on some other test.

3.15 In general, if the claimant or some other person has acted in a reasonable and predictable way in difficult circumstances created by the defendant, damage resulting from such intervention does not become remote: see, for example, *Haynes v Harwood* [1935] 1 KB 146, 104 LJKB 63, CA, where a policeman sustained injuries through stopping a runaway horse, and such cases as *Steel v Glasgow Iron and Steel Co Ltd* 1944 SC 237, Ct of Sess and *Hyett v Great Western Rly Co* [1948] 1 KB 345, [1947] 2 All ER 264, where workmen took risks – perhaps ill-judged risks – to protect their employer's property.

3.16 A fortiori, inadvertent or automatic actions do not break the sequence of causation: see *Thurogood v Van den Berghs and Jurgens Ltd* [1951] 2 KB 537, [1951] 1 All ER 682, CA and *Scott v Shepherd* (1773) 3 Wils 403, 2 Wm Bl 892.

3.17 In general, if the original damage has left the claimant exposed to risks of misfortune, misjudgment or accident which would not otherwise have arisen, further damage from the materialisation of these risks may be recoverable, unless it was wholly due to the negligence or deliberate act of the claimant or a third party. Where the line should be drawn is a question of fact.

Medical expenses mistakenly occurred

3.18 One important application of this principle is the case where the claimant has incurred expense in following medical advice which proves to be mistaken, as in *Rubens v Walker* 1946 SLT 200, Ct of Sess. Lord Patrick said in that case (at 201):

'It is a reasonable and probable consequence of a wrongdoer's breach of duty that a person hurt will incur expense in following the treatment prescribed by reputable experts employed by him to cure him. Each case must be decided on its own merits.'

3.19   Obviously the situation is quite different where the further damage results from negligence on the part of a doctor, for example – to take an extreme case – if a surgeon amputates the wrong limb by mistake. The damage would then be entirely due to a new intervening factor, not to the original injury.

3.20   In *Robinson v Post Office* [1974] 2 All ER 737, [1974] 1 WLR 1176, CA the plaintiff sustained a minor wound, which was made much worse (encephalitis and brain damage supervened) by an anti-tetanus injection. There was a contest of fact as to whether the doctor was negligent in failing to make a preliminary test injection for special susceptibility. The court decided that there was no negligence, and in any event a test injection would not have revealed the weakness in time. Accordingly there was no novus actus interveniens and the defendants were liable for the full consequences. It seems debatable whether, in any case, mistaken treatment of the original injury even if negligent would amount to a novus actus. This is entirely different from removing the wrong limb: it is within the risk of the original accident, and there is no good reason why both defendants should not be liable.

A second accident

3.21   Another issue which occurs is where there is a second accident, such as a fall in a hospital ward before a fractured leg has united, or a further strain to an injured back while it is still weakened: *Boom v Thomas Hubbuck & Son Ltd* [1967] 1 Lloyd's Rep 491, QBD. In *Wieland v Cyril Lord Carpets Ltd* [1969] 3 All ER 1006, QBD an elderly lady's neck was injured. She was fitted with a surgical collar: shortly afterwards she fell on stairs through misjudgment because the collar had altered the tilt of her bifocal spectacles. The further injuries were held to be within the risk of the original accident: but the judge said it might have been different if the plaintiff had had more time to adjust. In *McKew v Holland & Hannen & Cubitts (Scotland) Ltd* [1969] 3 All ER 1621, 1970 SC (HL) 20 a different view was taken on the facts of the case. The pursuer sustained a minor leg injury which rendered his knee liable to give way. He claimed that, when descending a steep flight of stone steps from the house into the street, the knee had given way suddenly and he jumped (or hurled himself) to the foot of the steps, sustaining a serious heel injury, to avoid toppling head foremost. The House of Lords held that it was an 'unreasonable' act for the pursuer, knowing his weakness, to descend these steps without a stick or helping hand: therefore the sequence of causation was broken from the start of the descent. The opinion was expressed that it would not have been broken merely by the misjudged reaction when the leg gave way.

Adverse reactions of third parties

3.22 Medical complications are not the only risk to which the claimant may be exposed by the injuries. An adverse reaction by other persons – perhaps even an excessive or unreasonable reaction – if reasonably to be expected from the nature of the injuries, is another example. So if a wife or husband is unable to cope with the situation and the marriage breaks up, the personal disadvantage and distress sustained by the claimant are, it seems, admissible consequential losses: but the court has drawn the line at a claim for financial loss following the divorce proceedings, partly on the ground that orders in these proceedings simply divide the property rights which the parties have, so that there is no loss, and partly for reasons of policy: *Pritchard v J H Cobden Ltd* [1988] Fam 22, [1987] 1 All ER 300, CA.

Change in claimant's behaviour as a result of the injuries

3.23 In *Meah v McCreamer* [1985] 1 All ER 367, [1985] NLJ Rep 80, QBD the plaintiff lost control of aggressive sexual instincts through damage to the frontal lobe of the brain, committed a series of rapes and was sentenced to a long period of imprisonment. Damages were given under this head for the imprisonment, but in further proceedings an additional claim for damages paid to the victims of the rapes was held to be too remote, and in any case excluded on grounds of public policy: [1986] 1 All ER 943. Similarly if an injury results in a disturbed mental state, not necessarily amounting to insanity, suicide may be a foreseeable consequence: *Pigney v Pointers Transport Services Ltd* [1957] 2 All ER 807, [1957] 1 WLR 1121, Ct of Sess. It is otherwise where suicide results from brooding over an injury which has not brought about a neurosis or other disturbed mental state: *Cowan v National Coal Board* 1958 SLT (Notes) 19.

NOVUS ACTUS INTERVENIENS

3.24   The chain of causation is broken – as a general rule – by what is described as a novus actus interveniens, that is to say a new and independent cause: *Weld-Blundell v Stephens* [1920] AC 956, 89 LJKB 705, HL; *SS Singleton Abbey v SS Paludina* [1927] AC 16, 95 LJP 135, HL.

3.25   But the intervention of a new cause – whether the act of a third party or the claimant's own act, or even some natural cause – does not necessarily exonerate the defendant. It may be that the risk of such an intervention is one of the very risks against which the claimant was entitled to be protected: thus it is negligent to leave dangerous articles lying about, such as loaded firearms or inflammable substances, and in such a case damage caused by a third party who misuses the articles is not too remote: see *Dixon v Bell* (1816) 1 Stark 287, 5 M & S 198; *Philco Radio and Television Corpn of Great Britain Ltd v J Spurling Ltd* [1949] 2 KB 33, [1949] 2 All ER 882, CA. There are many other cases where the defendant has a duty to foresee and prevent damage arising from the act of a third party, or from the acts of the claimant himself.

The underlying principle

3.26   The principle of law may therefore be stated as follows. Prima facie, a free and deliberate human act is a novus actus interveniens, which exonerates the original wrongdoer from the subsequent damage, although he has created the opportunity for this damage to supervene. But there is no exoneration from further liability when the original wrongdoer ought to have foreseen that the opportunity for harmful intervention by a third party would arise as a natural consequence of his wrongful act and he had a duty to prevent it; nor (as appears from the authorities already cited) when the claimant himself, or his medical advisers, have made a reasonable but possibly mistaken decision in circumstances of difficulty created by the wrongdoer. In all such cases the further damage is a natural and probable consequence of the original wrong.

Unreasonable behaviour by the claimant

3.27   Even within a risk created by the defendant, however, he is not responsible for damage due to the unreasonable behaviour of the claimant himself or, at any rate if it is not a predictable risk, of other persons for whom the defendant has no responsibility. Thus there was no liability to a man whose knee had been weakened in an accident when he imprudently went down steep stone steps without a stick or other help and sustained further injury: *McKew v Holland & Hannen and Cubitts (Scotland) Ltd* [1969] 3 All ER 1621, 1970 SC (HL) 20.

3.28   In one case, a whole family who sustained trivial injuries became subject to a long-term neurosis through the influence of a neurotic mother, and the defendants were held not liable for this aggravation: *McLaren v Bradstreet* (1969) 113 Sol Jo 471, CA.

Effect of a later (unconnected) accident

3.29   The possibility that a second accident may be due to some weakness created by the first accident, and therefore part of its consequences, has already been mentioned.

3.30   *Baker v Willoughby* [1970] AC 467, [1969] 3 All ER 1528, HL raised the converse question whether a later and unconnected accident may terminate or supersede the original accident and cut short the compensation for it, if this has not yet been awarded. The plaintiff's leg had been fractured, leaving some permanent disability and loss of earning power, and some continuing pain with risk of osteo-arthritis. Before the trial his leg was shot by armed robbers and had to be amputated. The Court of Appeal held that damages for the fracture should be given only for the period up to amputation. The House of Lords, however, overruled them and decided that since the plaintiff's earning capacity and enjoyment of life had been diminished permanently by the first accident, he was entitled to damages for this as a continuing loss notwithstanding the greater damage which had made his condition worse. A person liable for the second accident would be responsible only for the increased loss caused by that accident; in particular he would have to compensate for an earning capacity already reduced (Lord Reid at 1533H).

3.31   If the later accident actually *reduced* disability (as could happen, for instance, if the shock terminated a neurotic state, or a badly crippled finger which was no more than an impediment had to be amputated) or if it shortened the period of disability, for example, by causing death, there would be ground for reducing the damages: *Baker v Willoughby* [1970] AC 467, [1969] 3 All ER 1528 at 1534C, HL.

3.32   In assessing the effects of this case and the criticisms which have been made of it by a House of Lords differently composed, it is important to appreciate that an injury has two distinct sets of effects, negative and positive: it takes away capacity for enjoyment and working, but also inflicts the positive evil of pain and discomfort (para 6.8 below). While the deprivation of capacity continued after the second accident in *Baker v Willoughby* [1970] AC 467, [1969] 3 All ER 1528, HL, the pain could not, nor the future risk of arthritis, so damages under these heads were not recoverable (at 1534E): Lord Reid seems entirely right in saying that the negative effects, the loss of earning capacity and enjoyment of life, were a permanent loss qualifying for full compensation, although what was left might be reduced still further.

Effect of a supervening disease

3.33   In the subsequent case of *Jobling v Associated Dairies Ltd* [1982] AC 794, [1981] 2 All ER 752, HL the House held that a supervening illness, which was in no way due to the accident and would have rendered the plaintiff incapable of work in any event, automatically brought to an end any continuing loss due to the accident: and this was so although the disease was in no way present even in incipient form at the time of the accident. However, the decision turned on the underlying assumption that the disease would have supervened in any event. Thus Lord Bridge said (at 767):

'even if the plaintiff had never sustained the tortious injury, his earnings would now be reduced or extinguished.'

and similarly Lord Keith said (at 764):

'it is appropriate ... to recognise that the illness would have overtaken the plaintiff in any event.'

3.34   This is, of course, the normal and natural inference in the case of an illness, unless there is evidence that it was brought on by the injury. But a subsequent accident is a completely different matter. It depends on being at a particular place at a particular time after the first accident, and as the first accident, unless very trivial, would have altered the pattern of the claimant's life and his subsequent movements, it is most unlikely that he would have met with the same subsequent accident in any event. It is therefore thought that *Baker v Willoughby* [1970] AC 467, [1969] 3 All ER 1528, HL is still good law, and that continuing loss of earnings can be recovered unless it is shown that the second accident would have happened in any event, although, for the reasons explained above, there will be no continuing claim for pain and suffering which is superseded by a greater injury. Nevertheless the speeches in *Jobling v Associated Dairies Ltd* [1982] AC 794, [1981] 2 All ER 752, HL contained strong criticism of the reasoning in *Baker v Willoughby* on the assumption that supervening injury and supervening illness can be equated.

REMOTENESS OF DAMAGE: DISTINCTION BETWEEN BREACH OF CONTRACT AND TORT

3.35   There is some difference between the rules of remoteness in actions for breach of contract, on the one hand, and for tort, on the other.

3.36   In an action for breach of contract, the defendant is not liable for *special* damage, ie for damage which would not follow in the ordinary course, unless he has notice of the special circumstances which give rise to this damage: see *Hadley v Baxendale* (1854) 9 Exch 341, 9 Exch 341; *Victoria Laundry (Windsor) Ltd v Newman Industries Ltd* [1949] 2 KB 528, [1949] 1 All ER 997, CA. *Koufos v C Czarnikow Ltd, The Heron II* [1969] 1 AC 350, [1967] 3 All ER 686, HL restates the rule in rather different terms, but does not alter the substance of it, at any rate for present purposes. As a matter of fact, this rule chiefly operates in practice where there is a breach of a commercial contract which results in a loss of profit, for example, where a shipload of wheat has been bought for resale at a special price and is not delivered, or where machinery is required for carrying out a special building contract and is delivered too late. In cases of this sort the defendant is not liable for the special loss of profit unless he contracted in the knowledge that it might be incurred.

Does this apply in personal injury actions?

3.37   There cannot be any scope for the operation of this rule in actions for personal injuries. If the claimant is injured in a railway accident – where the action is founded on breach of contract – his damages are the same as they would be in a motor accident – where the action is founded on tort. Damages for loss of earnings, in both cases alike, will depend upon the earnings the claimant would actually have received but for the accident, and the defendant's lack of knowledge of the rate of earnings is irrelevant. In *Phillips v London and South Western Rly Co* (1879) 4 QBD

406, 27 WR 797 the Court of Appeal rejected the argument that the rule in *Hadley v Baxendale* (1854) 9 Exch 341 applies to such cases.

Damages where there is pre-existing injury or vulnerability

3.38   Where a claimant has some pre-existing weakness which renders him more liable to injury than other persons – such as a thin skull or a tendency to bleed – the defendant is liable for such injuries (assuming he is liable at all) although their extent could not be foreseen: *Smith v Leech Brain & Co Ltd* [1962] 2 QB 405, [1961] 3 All ER 1159, QBD (pre-cancerous condition in lip turned into cancer through burn); *Love v Port of London Authority* [1959] 2 Lloyd's Rep 541 (pre-existing tendency to neurosis, due to weak heart, was triggered off by accident); *Robinson v Post Office* [1974] 2 All ER 737, [1974] 1 WLR 1176, CA (unknown susceptibility to anti-tetanus injection after wound); *Malcolm v Broadhurst* [1970] 3 All ER 508, QBD (husband and wife injured in the same accident, personality changes in husband had worse effects on her because of her previous neurotic condition, but the vulnerability of her part-time job with her husband – because it was the only one which could be combined with housework – was considered too remote); *Hoffmueller v Commonwealth* (1981) 54 FLR 48, NSW, Sup Ct CA; *Brice v Brown* [1984] 1 All ER 997, 134 NLJ 204, QBD (predisposition to neurosis from slight injuries no different from vulnerability to physical injury).

Where the injury has a more serious consequence

3.39   Similarly there is full liability where a particular injury has more serious consequences for a man because of a pre-existing disability: for example, where a man who has lost one eye is made blind by losing the other (*Paris v Stepney Borough Council (No 2)* (1951) 101 L Jo 77, CA) or where a blind man is rendered deaf (*Haley v London Electricity Board* (1965) 109 Sol Jo 295, CA). It is a ground for increasing damages rather than reducing them if a man suffers from ill-health which makes the injuries harder to bear: *Mustard v Morris* [1982] 1 CLY 11, CA (injury to diabetic with bad circulation in leg).

The acceleration of a pre-existing disability

3.40   It is otherwise if disability which would have arisen in any event is merely accelerated. Damages are then given for the period of acceleration, but cease at the point when the disability would have been present in any event. A common example is osteo-arthritis: *Jackson v Holland-America Line Ltd* [1963] 1 Lloyd's Rep 477, QBD. No damages at all were recovered for the acceleration of a surgical operation which had to be performed some time in any event: *Cutler v Vauxhall Motors Ltd* [1971] 1 QB 418, [1970] 2 All ER 56, CA.

Exacerbation of pre-existing damage

3.41 So also if additional damage is caused where pre-existing damage exists, the defendant is not liable for the pre-existing damage as such, but only for the additional damage: *Performance Cars Ltd v Abraham* [1962] 1 QB 33, [1961] 3 All ER 413, CA (motor car already damaged so as to require respraying; further damage did not carry any liability for cost of respraying); *Baker v Willoughby* [1969] 3 All ER 1528 at 1533H, HL. As indicated above, the additional damage may itself be more serious because of the pre-existing damage.

CAUSATION AND ASBESTOS CASES

Asbestosis: a special case

3.42 The principles relating to causation in relation to asbestos exposure were considered in detail by the House of Lords in *Fairchild v Glenhaven Funeral Services Ltd; Fox v Spousal (Midlands) Ltd; Matthews v Associated Portland Cement Manufacturers (1978) Ltd* [2002] UKHL 22, [2003] 1 AC 32. This is a case of some importance but its practical ramifications are primarily confined to cases related to asbestos exposure.

The difficulty with causation and asbestos exposure

3.43 It is not possible for a claimant, who was been exposed to asbestos in the course of employment with more than one defendant, to show *which* particular period of exposure caused the development of mesothelioma. Applying the conventional 'but for' test in these circumstances a claimant cannot show that his mesothelioma arose from the exposure with employer A or employer B.

The solution favoured by the House of Lords

3.44   Lord Bingham, at para 21, laid down six conditions:
(1)   C was employed at different times for differing periods by both A and B;
(2)   A and B were both subject to a duty to take reasonable care or to take all reasonable measures to prevent C inhaling asbestos dust because of the known risk that asbestos dust (if inhaled) might cause a mesothelioma, and
(3)   both A and B were in breach of that duty in relation to C during the periods of C's employment by each of them with the result that during both periods C inhaled excessive quantities of asbestos dust, and
(4)   C is found to be suffering from a mesothelioma, and
(5)   any cause of C's mesothelioma other than the inhalation of asbestos dust at work can be effectively discounted, but
(6)   C cannot (because of the current limits of human science) prove, on the balance of probabilities, that his mesothelioma was the result of his inhaling asbestos dust during his employment by A or during his employment by B or during his employment by A and B taken together.

At para 341 Lord Bingham states that where these six conditions are satisfied then C is entitled to recover against A and B. He made it clear that his decision was confined to findings on this specific set of facts. Whilst the principles may be developed over time his speech was confined to the facts and issues directly before the House.

1   *Fairchild v Glenhaven Funeral Services Ltd; Fox v Spousal (Midlands) Ltd; Matthews v Associated Portland Cement Manufacturers (1978) Ltd* [2002] UKHL 22, [2003] 1 AC 32.

Causation a part of the issue of liability

3.45   Lord Hoffmann observed that causal requirements are just as much part of the legal conditions for liability as the rules that prescribe the conditions of liability.

> 'Once it is appreciated that the rules laying down causal requirements are not autonomous expressions of some form of logic or judicial instinct but creatures of the law, part of the conditions of liability, it is possible to explain their content on the grounds of fairness and justice in exactly the same way as the other conditions of liability.[1]'

The effect of denying causation in the current case would have the effect (except in single employer cases) empty the duty of care of content. In this type of case the law should treat a material increase in risk as sufficient to satisfy the causal requirements for liability.

1   *Fairchild v Glenhaven Funeral Services Ltd; Fox v Spousal (Midlands) Ltd; Matthews v Associated Portland Cement Manufacturers (1978) Ltd* [2002] UKHL 22, [2003] 1 AC 32.

Guarding against encroachment of traditional causation principles

3.46   All of the speeches in *Fairchild*[1] cautioned against a widespread relaxation of the traditional rules of causation. Lord Nicholls, at para 421, stated:

'I need hardly add that considerable restraint is called for in any relaxation of the threshold "but for" test of causal connection. The principle applied on these appeals is emphatically not intended to lead such a relaxation whenever a plaintiff has difficulty, perhaps understandable difficulty, in discharging the burden of proof resting on him. Unless closely confined in its application this principle could become a source of injustice to defendants. There must be good reason for departing from the normal threshold "but for" test. The reason must be sufficiently weighty to justify depriving the defendant of the protection this test normally and rightly affords him, and it must be plain and obvious that this is so. Policy questions will loom large when a court has to decide whether the difficulties of proof confronting the plaintiff justify taking this exceptional course. It is impossible to be more specific.'

1   *Fairchild v Glenhaven Funeral Services Ltd; Fox v Spousal (Midlands) Ltd; Matthews v Associated Portland Cement Manufacturers (1978) Ltd* [2002] UKHL 22, [2003] 1 AC 32.

The limits of the Fairchild principle

3.47   It is important to recognise the limitation of the *Fairchild* case.[1] It is confined to a narrow range of specific cases. The principles will not be extended readily or easily.

1   *Fairchild v Glenhaven Funeral Services Ltd; Fox v Spousal (Midlands) Ltd; Matthews v Associated Portland Cement Manufacturers (1978) Ltd* [2002] UKHL 22, [2003] 1 AC 32.

CHAPTER 4

Mitigation of damages

MITIGATING THE DAMAGES – A MISNOMER

4.1   It is sometimes said that it is the duty of the claimant to mitigate the damages, by doing whatever is reasonable to minimise the loss as far as he or she can.

4.2   It is more accurate to say that the claimant cannot recover damages for an aggravation or prolongation of his injuries which is due to his own wilful act or neglect or where he has failed to take reasonable steps to reduce the losses. The law is summarised in the judgment of Pearson LJ in *Darbishire v Warran* [1963] 3 All ER 310, [1963] 1 WLR 1067, CA:

> 'It is important to appreciate the true nature of the so-called "duty to mitigate the loss" or "duty to minimise the damage". The plaintiff is not under any contractual obligation to adopt the cheaper method: if he wishes to adopt the more expensive method, he is at liberty to do so and by doing so he commits no wrong against the defendant or anyone else. The true meaning is that the plaintiff is not entitled to charge the defendant by means of damages with any greater sum than that which he reasonably needs to expend for the purpose of making good the loss. In short, he is fully entitled to be as extravagant as he pleases but not at the expense of the defendant.'

THE BURDEN OF PROOF

4.3   The burden of proof in establishing a failure to mitigate loss is on the defendant: *Garnac Grain Co Inc v HMF Faure and Fairclough Ltd and Burge Corpn* [1968] AC 1130n, [1967] 2 All ER 353, HL. Further the defendant must clearly set out its case in relation to failure to mitigate loss. (See chapter 18 below on procedure.)

CONSEQUENCES OF FAILURE TO MITIGATE

4.4 There are various consequences of the failure to mitigate:

(1) The claimant cannot recover for losses which he ought to have avoided.

(2) The claimant can recover for losses incurred in attempt to mitigate the damage.

(3) The claimant cannot recover for loss which he has avoided.

(4) If the claimant has not mitigated his losses then damages are based on the losses that would have been sustained had the claimant acted reasonably and mitigated his loss.

COMMON ISSUES OF FAILURE TO MITIGATE LOSS IN PERSONAL INJURY ACTIONS

Failure to return to work promptly

4.5 Issues often arise as to whether the claimant can return to work or should have returned to work at an earlier date. To some extent these are fact specific. However, the parties must remember that the defendant has to establish not only that the claimant is able to return to work, but that there is work available for the claimant to do. There are several Court of Appeal cases that deal with issues relating to employment.

Emblem v Ingram Cactus

4.6 In *Emblem v Ingram Cactus* (5 November 1997, unreported), CA the plaintiff was injured at work. Subsequently he was made redundant for reasons unconnected with the injury. The defendant later offered the plaintiff a job similar to his old job and the claimant refused the offer. The trial judge held that the refusal was reasonable. The Court of Appeal upheld this decision. The defendant had made two offers of employment. The first was made when the claimant was certified as unfit for work. The plaintiff offered no explanation as to why he refused a second offer. The Court of Appeal upheld the judge's decision that it was for him to consider, as a question of objective fact, whether or not the plaintiff could reasonably have refused the offer of employment. The judge identified five features:

(1) The offer was being made on behalf of an employer who was at that time being sued by the plaintiff, and who was at that time denying liability. That placed the offer in a wholly different category from one made by a third party.

(2) The work was to be at the very premises where the plaintiff had suffered his injury and under the supervision of someone who had been in a managerial capacity at the time of the accident.
(3) The work was to be of the same general nature as that in the course of which the plaintiff had been injured.
(4) The plaintiff was not physically capable of undertaking all the work that would have been expected of him.
(5) The plaintiff would have had to wear specially adapted steel-capped boots (the need arising out of the injury).

4.7   Simon Brown LJ expressly supported the first contention:[1]

'It is one thing for a plaintiff to return to work once he has recovered; another to expect him to return after being made redundant following a serious injury when then offered a new job. He does not know, for example, whether or not the employers have changed the system of work which earlier imperilled him and what they might say about that when it comes to the liability trial.'

1   *Emblem v Ingram Cactus* (5 November 1997, unreported), CA.

4.8   The first three reasons set out were said to be proper factors for a person offered re-employment to have regard to in deciding whether or not to accept the offer.

4.9   The Court of Appeal upheld the judge's decision. It dealt robustly with an argument that once the judge accepted the offer was made the burden in some sense shifted. Simon Brown LJ rejected this approach:[1]

'To my mind this is not the correct approach. At that end of the day there was one question, and one alone, for the judge: Had the defendants discharged the burden upon them of showing that, objectively speaking, on the evidence before the court the plaintiff could not have reasonably refused the offer.'

1   *Emblem v Ingram Cactus* (5 November 1997, unreported), CA.

NOT A HIGH BURDEN

4.10   Lord Justice Ward agreed. He stated:[1]

'The judgment must, it seems to me, be reviewed on this basis: firstly, that the onus was on the defendant; secondly, that as the defendant is the wrong-doer, the test of reasonableness is not set unduly highly; thirdly, that reasonableness is to be judged by such objective factors as are capable of being derived from the totality of the evidence; and, fourthly, that the finding is primarily one of fact for the judge to make.'

1   *Emblem v Ingram Cactus* (5 November 1997, unreported), CA.

Staying on the employer's payroll: Froggatt v LEP Intl

4.11   In *Froggatt v LEP Intl* [2002] EWCA Civ 600, [2002] All ER (D) 108 (Apr) the Court of Appeal considered an argument of failure to mitigate loss when the employer had, throughout the period of absence from work, stayed on the defendant's books as an employee (although unpaid). There were advantages to the claimant in staying on the defendant's books because he was getting a prospective benefit from the defendant's pension fund. The disadvantage was that whilst he was technically employed he was unable to obtain retraining. The court upheld the judge's decision that the defendant had failed to show that the defendant had failed to mitigate his loss.

THE ABSENCE OF EVIDENCE FROM THE DEFENDANT

4.12   One feature of the *Froggatt* case[1] was the absence of any evidence from the defendant. Pill LJ observed (at [30]):

'When in circumstances such as the present defendants are seeking to show unreasonableness in the claimant, it is customary to produce evidence, in one way or another, as to alternative employments which are open to him and for which he could have applied. There is a conspicuous lack of any such evidence in this case and in his judgment the judge, understandably in that event, makes no reference to the types of work which would have been open to the claimant, or to his prospects in the Manchester area of obtaining such lighter work. There is no suggestion that the claimant had any technical or clerical skills which would have made him readily suitable for sedentary work of that kind.'

1   *Froggatt v LEP Intl* [2002] EWCA Civ 600, [2002] All ER (D) 108 (Apr).

ADVANCE NOTICE REQUIRED FROM THE DEFENDANT OF AN ALLEGATION TO MITIGATE LOSS

4.13   Chadwick LJ agreed on this point. He described it as trite law that it was for the defendant to establish by evidence the defence of failure to mitigate. He observed at [43][1] that:

'That is to say, it was for the defendant to establish by evidence that
the claimant had not acted reasonably in failing to seek alternative
employment in lighter work.

If it were to be the defendant's case that the judge should have found
that the claimant was fit to undertake light work within one year of
his injury and had acted unreasonably in failing to seek such work
from an alternative employer, it would have made the task of the
judge – and the task of this court on appeal – if that contention had
been identified in some document in advance of the trial so that the
claimant and the judge would know with some degree of specificity
what was the case that the claimant had to meet. That was not done.
There is no indication in the pleadings that any such contention was
going to be advanced.'

(This is considered in more detail at paras 18.12–18.18 and 18.37–18.39 below.)

1   *Froggatt v LEP Intl* [2002] EWCA Civ 600, [2002] All ER (D) 108 (Apr).

Unreasonable attempt to retrain

4.14   In *Benning v TG Motors Ltd* the Court of Appeal considered the
issue of failure to mitigate loss in *TG Motors v Benning* [2002] EWCA
Civ 858. After being seriously injured the claimant started an access course
to train as a teacher. The trial judge regarded this ambition as unrealistic
given the claimant's prior educational qualifications. The judge declined
to award damages for loss of earnings after the date that the claimant
started training. The Court of Appeal found that the judge should have
considered the position had the claimant not started teacher training. If
the claimant has not mitigated his loss this does not mean that he cannot
recover. The true position is that if the injured party has failed to take
reasonable steps to mitigate his loss the damages he may recover from the
defendant are to be measured by reference to what he would have recovered
had he mitigated his loss properly.

4.15   On the facts of that case the evidence as to future employability
was uncertain. However, it was certain that the claimant was at a major
disadvantage in the labour market. For that reason the court awarded
£35,000 on a *Smith v Manchester Corpn*[1]/disability in the labour market
basis.

1   *Smith v Manchester City Council (or Manchester Corpn)* (1974) 118 Sol Jo 597, 17
KIR 1, CA.

An unsuccessful attempt to return to work

4.16   In *Morris v Richards* [2003] EWCA Civ 232, [2003] All ER (D) 385 (Feb) the claimant returned to work after a three-year period of absence and worked at a job which was much better paid than her pre-accident employment. After around six months she left her new job alleging discrimination, and claimed for her loss of earnings after leaving the new job. The trial judge awarded loss of earnings for the period after she left the new job. The defendant appealed arguing that the loss of earnings after the new job were too remote. Schiemman LJ stated (at [16]):

> 'The proper approach in a case such as the present is to start from the now undisputed facts that the defendant was to blame for the injuries suffered by the claimant and that by reason of the defendant's wrongful action she lost the job which she liked and for which she was trained. The fact that she obtained another job and then lost it will not automatically disqualify her from recovering from the tortfeasor damages in respect of the period of the loss of her job ("the period in issue"). The crucial question is whether, in respect of the period in issue, it is just and that she should recover damages from the tortfeasor. If she was at fault in losing her new job then she will have difficulty in recovering for the period in issue. If she was not at fault then in general she will recover. The question whether she was at fault is one which in principle the trial judge should resolve bearing in mind that it was the wrongful act of the defendant which put the claimant in the position of having to find a new job and that therefore she should not be judged too harshly.'

Refusal to undergo a medical operation

4.17   The law as to mitigation and the refusal to undergo medical treatment which could alleviate the situation was considered in detail by the Privy Council in *Geest plc v Lansiquot* [2002] UKPC 48, [2003] 1 All ER 383. In that case the claimant declined to undergo surgery which may have alleviated a back problem. The Council considered its earlier decision in *Selvanayagam v University of the West Indies* [1983] 1 All ER 824, [1983] 1 WLR 585, PC where it was held that the burden of proof was on the plaintiff to prove, on a balance of probabilities, that the refusal to undergo surgery was reasonable. It was held that the *Selvanayagam* decision could not be relied upon as an accurate statement of law. However, it made little difference on the facts of that case. There was nothing in the evidence that suggested it was unreasonable for her to refuse the operation.

4.18 It is now clear that, as with other aspects of the law of mitigation, the burden of proof lies with the defendant.

Car hire

4.19 Although not technically part of the personal injury claim, claims for car hire often accompany personal injury claims, particularly when the claimant is a driver whose car has been damaged. It is not always reasonable for the car hired to be of the same prestigious standard as the car damaged, particularly if the loss of use was for a short period: *Watson-Norie Ltd v Shaw* [1967] 1 Lloyd's Rep 515, 111 Sol Jo 117, CA. Delay by the insurers can justify the hiring of a car for a 20-week period: *Mattocks v Mann* [1993] RTR 13, [1992] 31 LS Gaz R 34, CA.

Mitigation and liability

4.20 In some cases a failure to mitigate loss can be used as a bar to liability. In *Richardson v LRC Products Ltd* (2000) 59 BMLR 185, QBD, Ian Kennedy J, the claimant brought an action after she had become pregnant, allegedly due to the failure of a condom. The judge held that the claimant had not established negligence on the part of the condom manufacturer. He also stated that the claimant had failed to mitigate her losses by failing to take the morning after pill. The claimant knew of the morning after pill but made no inquiries as how it could be obtained. It is settled law, however, that a claimant need not have an abortion to end an unwanted pregnancy: see *Emeh v Kensington and Chelsea and Westminster Area Health Authority* [1985] QB 1012, [1984] 3 All ER 1044, CA.

CHAPTER 5

Special forms of damages

SOME SPECIAL FORMS OF DAMAGES

5.1 Apart from damages of the normal kind – which may be described as compensatory or substantial damages – there are one or two special cases.

Nominal damages

5.2 Nominal damages are given where the claimant's legal rights have been infringed, but he is not able to prove any loss or damage. The amount is traditionally £2, which is intended to show that the claimant has successfully vindicated his rights.

Exemplary or vindictive damages

5.3 Exemplary damages are awarded in an action of tort where the defendant has not only committed a legal wrong against the claimant, but has behaved in an outrageous or insulting manner when doing so. They might be considerably higher than the amount required to compensate the claimant. In part they were intended to punish the defendant, but they were also intended as a solatium for the insult or humiliation which had been suffered. Formerly they were not distinguished from aggravated damages, but new rules were formulated by the House of Lords in *Rookes v Barnard* [1964] AC 1129, [1964] 1 All ER 367, HL and superseded all earlier authorities. As to *aggravated* damages, the jury or judge in assessing the compensation may:[1]

'take into account the motives and conduct of the defendant where they aggravate the injury done to the plaintiff. There may be malevolence or spite or the manner of committing the wrong may be such as to injure the plaintiff's proper feelings of dignity and pride.'

1   [1964] AC 1129 at 1221, [1964] 1 All ER 367 at 407.

5.4   So aggravated damages are really compensation for hurt feelings: *McCarey v Associated Newspapers Ltd* [1965] 2 QB 86, [1964] 3 All ER 947, CA (a libel case). They contain no punitive element.

EXEMPLARY DAMAGES IN PERSONAL INJURY CASES?

5.5   Exemplary damages are now unlikely to arise in personal injury cases not involving government agencies. They have no place in clinical negligence: *Krajl v McGrath* [1986] 1 All ER 54, [1985] NLJ Rep 913, QBD. They were said to be appropriate only for high-handed acts by government servants or against defendants making a profit out of the wrong. They should be awarded even in such cases with restraint, having regard to the means of the parties, and only where there is punishable conduct.

5.6   The most common consideration of exemplary damages is in actions against the police. Guidelines as to how damages should be assessed in these circumstances were given in *Thompson v Metropolitan Police Comr* [1998] QB 498, [1997] 2 All ER 762, CA. In essence the main function of damages in these cases is to compensate the claimant, not to punish the defendant. Exemplary damages should only be awarded where there had been conduct, including oppressive or arbitrary behaviour by police officers, or other agents of the state. The jury should bear in mind that such damages are a windfall for the claimant.

AGGRAVATED DAMAGES

5.7   Aggravated damages usually arise in cases of assault. The aim is to compensate for the additional humiliation and injury to the feelings that an assault can entail. Conversely provocation offered by the claimant to the defendant may reduce the damages for assault: *Judge v Berkeley* (1825) 7 C & P 371n. But damages cannot be reduced below the real amount of compensation for the injury.

UNNECESSARY MEDICAL TREATMENT

5.8   In *Appleton v Garrett* [1997] 8 Med LR 75, 34 BMLR 23, QBD the defendant was a dentist who, motivated primarily by greed, had carried out negligent and unnecessary dental work on his patients. Dyson J held that this was a case of trespass to the person. Aggravated damages were appropriate, but should not be punitive. The purpose of these damages was compensatory. There needed to be a relationship between general damages for pain suffering and loss of amenity and the aggravated damages award. He awarded aggravated damages based on 15% of the general damages award.

THE TRUE PURPOSE REMAINS COMPENSATION

5.9 As the above analysis shows, even in the case of aggravated and exemplary damages the true purpose is compensation. Generally the law discourages damages as a means of punishment.

CHAPTER 6

Damages for personal loss: disablement, pain, suffering and loss of amenity – what is being compensated?

PERSONAL LOSS AS AN ELEMENT IN DAMAGES

6.1 The term 'personal loss' is used here to denote the physical injury, that is, every kind of harm and disadvantage which flows from the defendant's negligence, other than the loss of money or property. It includes the loss or impairment of the integrity of the body; pain and suffering, both physical and mental; loss of the pleasure of life; actual shortening of life; and, at least in some cases, mere discomfort or inconvenience.

THE CLAIM FOR THE PHYSICAL INJURY IS COMPENSATION AND NOT A SOLATIUM

6.2 The central point here is that the damages for the physical injury *are* compensation and not a mere solatium; neither are they a reward or 'winnings'. There are dicta in the older cases which suggest that damages for the injury itself, as distinct from the financial loss entailed, are not compensation at all, but a kind of solatium, a sympathetic payment admitted to be less than is really due. If this were right, damages would be by nature wholly discretionary, and it would be left to the judge or jury to decide, in an arbitrary manner, how far the amount should fall short of adequacy. An argument on these lines was addressed to the House of Lords in *H West & Son Ltd v Shephard* [1964] AC 326, [1963] 2 All ER 625, HL, but it was rejected by the majority of the House. Lord Morris of Borth-y-Gest, for instance, said (at 348, 633):

> 'I consider that it is sufficient to say that a money award is given by way of compensation and that it must take into account the actual consequences which have resulted from the tort.'

And he continued a little later:

'If damages are awarded to a plaintiff on a correct basis it seems to me that it can be of no concern to the court to consider any question as to the use that will thereafter be made of the money awarded.'

He added that:

'there may be items which will only be awarded if certain needs ... are established such as nursing, medicine and transport for a crippled person.'

These, of course, come under the heading of financial loss and are a different matter. (See chapters 11 and 12 below.)

6.3 The main point decided in *H West & Son Ltd v Shephard* [1964] AC 326, [1963] 2 All ER 625, HL was that a plaintiff is entitled to substantial and not merely token damages for being deprived of the joys of life, even though by reason of prolonged unconsciousness, as in the *West* case, there is little or no distress about the loss. It was not in dispute that a plaintiff who was aware of the situation would have substantially more because of the mental distress. The point of the decision is that damages are not 'consolation money'. They are given for the harm actually sustained.

6.4 In *Lim Poh Choo v Camden and Islington Area Health Authority* [1980] AC 174, [1979] 2 All ER 910, HL the House of Lords adhered to the principle laid down in *H West & Son Ltd v Shephard* [1964] AC 326, [1963] 2 All ER 625, HL and said that if the law were to be changed it should be changed by Parliament as part of a comprehensive review of the law of damages.

THE PERSONAL LOSS COVERS MORE THAN PAIN

6.5 In assessing the claim for personal loss there are many factors to be considered. These include the bodily injury sustained; the pain undergone; the effect on the health of the sufferer, according to its degree and its probable duration as likely to be temporary or permanent.

6.6 The personal loss embraces much more than compensation for actual pain.

6.7 The most authoritative pronouncements are now in *H West & Son Ltd v Shephard* [1964] AC 326, [1963] 2 All ER 625, HL where Lord Pearce said (at 365, 643):

'If a plaintiff has lost a leg, the court approaches the matter on the basis that he has suffered a serious physical deprivation, no matter what his condition or temperament or state of mind may be. That deprivation may also create future economic loss which is added to the assessment. Past and prospective pain and discomfort increase the assessment. If there is loss of amenity apart from the obvious and normal loss inherent in the deprivation of the limb – if, for instance, the plaintiff's main interest in life was some sport or hobby from which he will in future be debarred, that too increases the assessment. If there is a particular consequential injury to the nervous system, that also increases the assessment. These considerations are not dealt with as separate items but are taken into account by the court in fixing one inclusive sum for general damages.'

6.8 Most injuries have both negative and positive effects: they take away earnings and capacity for enjoyment which would otherwise have continued; and they positively inflict pain and mental distress and cause extra expense. *H West & Son Ltd v Shephard* [1964] AC 326, [1963] 2 All ER 625, HL clarified a number of important points. It was a case where a young woman was completely paralysed but had little consciousness of her affliction. Arguments were presented that the measure of damages is loss of happiness, so where there is limited awareness of this and the plaintiff would be unable to spend or enjoy the money, damages should be moderate. The House held by a majority:
(1) that substantial damages are due for a serious injury and loss of the enjoyment of life, although there is little or no awareness of the loss;
(2) damages would be greater where there was consciousness of the loss, because this adds mental suffering to the injury;
(3) if life is shortened, damages are proportionate to the *duration* of the loss;
(4) subjective happiness is not the measure of damages;
(5) if the right figure is awarded, the court is not concerned with the use which the claimant does or can make of it; but
(6) the actual needs of the claimant, for example, for nursing, will warrant additional damages as part of the financial loss.

6.9 In general:

'... damages are designed to compensate for such results as have actually been caused ...The fact of unconsciousness ... will eliminate

those heads or elements of damage which can only exist by being
felt or thought or experienced ... not, however ... the deprivations of
the ordinary experiences and amenities of life ...'[1]

1   *H West & Son Ltd v Shephard* [1964] AC 326, [1963] 2 All ER 625 at 633, HL, per
     Lord Morris of Borth-y-Gest.

THE ELEMENTS OF A CLAIM FOR PAIN, SUFFERING AND LOSS OF AMENITY

6.10   The personal loss, then, has a number of elements or aspects. Where
there is permanent injury, the damage to be assessed may include any or
all of the following elements:
(1)   total loss, or impairment, of a limb or other specific part of the body,
      or impairment of the body as a whole;
(2)   the shock of the injury, sometimes followed by neurosis;
(3)   physical pain at the time of the injury, during surgical operations and
      perhaps during the rest of life;
(4)   mental distress;
(5)   inability to look after the bodily needs of life;
(6)   disfigurement, by scars or mutilation; and
(7)   loss of the joys of life, such as sports, recreation, music or the mere
      ability to walk about.

6.11   Where there is no permanent injury or disfigurement, the main
factors are pain and shock and a temporary loss of the enjoyment of life.
Sometimes neurosis supervenes on a minor injury.

6.12   Analysis has been carried to this extent by the courts in order to
estimate the full measure of the loss to the claimant and to ensure that the
damages give adequate compensation for all aspects of the injury.

6.13   Nevertheless, as the speech of Lord Pearce (see para 6.7 above)
shows, these items are no more than elements or aspects of the injury, to
be brought into the scales in assessing a single figure of damages, in which
sometimes one element and sometimes another will preponderate. Judges
may find it convenient on some occasions to separate the various elements,
but more commonly they are all thrown into the balance to arrive at a
single broad estimate.

6.14   In *Heil v Rankin* [2000] PIQR Q187 at Q199, CA Lord Woolf MR
observed that:

'In determining what is the correct level of damages for PLSA [pain, suffering and loss of amenity], it is not usual for the court to attribute differing sums for different aspects of the injury. The court's approach involves trying to find the global sum which most accurately in monetary terms reflects or can be regarded as reflecting a fair, reasonable and just figure for the injuries which have been inflicted and the consequences they will have in PLSA. A sophisticated analytical approach distinguishing between pain and suffering and loss of amenity is not usually required ... We do, however, accept the submissions ... that to consider the individual strands of PLSA can provide a check as to the adequacy of the whole. There can also be special circumstances in a particular case which makes separation necessary.'

The injury itself: loss or impairment of bodily integrity

6.15   Some injuries involve the total loss of a limb or an eye or some other integral part of the body. In other cases there is no total loss, but some degree of impairment, such as a permanent limp or a reduction in the field of vision. In yet other cases, there is impairment of the body as a whole, chiefly as a result of damage to the central nervous system.

6.16   It is clear that substantial damages are due for either (1) the total loss, or the impairment, of a limb or other specific part of the body; or (2) impairment of the body as a whole, irrespective of whether there is loss of earning capacity or amenities: but, of course, these factors make an immense difference to quantum. So Sellers LJ said in *Wise v Kaye* [1962] 1 QB 638 at 651, [1962] 1 All ER 257 at 263, CA:

'The first element ... is the physical injury itself ... the physical injury itself has always ... been a head of claim which has justified and required in law an award of damages according to the extent, gravity and duration of the injury.'

And Lord Pearce said in *H West & Son Ltd v Shephard* [1964] AC 326 at 365, [1963] 2 All ER 625 at 643, HL:

'The practice of the courts hitherto has been to treat bodily injury as a deprivation which in itself entitles a plaintiff to substantial damages according to its gravity.'

6.17   In Scotland, in *Dalgleish v Glasgow Corpn* 1976 SLT 157 at 160, Ct of Sess Lord Wheatley LJ-C said:

> 'Leaving aside the subjective element, namely the awareness of the loss and deprivation occasioned by the injuries, which ... falls properly within the element of pain and suffering, the actual mutilation of the body seems to me to call for damages on a scale commensurate with the nature of the injuries and not simply on a conventional scale which has no real relationship to these injuries.'

In the normal case of, for example, the loss of a leg, a single sum is assessed which comprises damages for loss of integrity and at the same time for pain and suffering and loss of enjoyment of life.

6.18   It frequently happens, however, that substantial damages are given for such injuries as the loss of a part of a finger or of a toe, where there is no loss of future earning capacity and only slight interference with the enjoyment of life.

6.19   In principle, the loss of bodily integrity gives a right to damages even if there is no damage at all to earning capacity or to the enjoyment of life. Thus damages have been awarded for the removal of the spleen, an internal organ which apparently serves no indispensable physiological purpose.

Pain and suffering

6.20   'Pain and suffering' – which is the customary phrase, although it might be thought that pain and suffering are one and the same thing – is recognised by the law as a topic for which damages may be given: per Lord Halsbury LC in *The Mediana* [1900] AC 113 at 116.

6.21   Prospective as well as past suffering must be allowed for. So Greer LJ said in *Heaps v Perrite Ltd* [1937] 2 All ER 60 at 60, 81 Sol Jo 236, CA:

> 'We have to take into account not only the suffering which he had immediately after the accident but the suffering that he will have throughout his life in future.'

6.22   The duration of the pain is important; so, too, is the state of consciousness of the injured person. In *Mills v Stanway Coaches Ltd* [1940] 2 KB 334, [1940] 2 All ER 586, CA the injured person survived for four days only, and during all or most of that period she was unconscious:

accordingly the Court of Appeal reduced an award of damages for pain and suffering to a token sum.

6.23   In the case of minor injuries, such as a broken leg or arm from which the claimant recovers completely, or the everyday case of a claimant who is knocked down by a motor car and escapes with bruises and abrasions, 'pain and suffering' is the main element in damages (plus some allowances for temporary interference with the enjoyment of life).

6.24   In all cases some extra allowance must be made for unpleasant surgical operations, especially where there is a series of skin-grafting operations or where there is an awkward fracture of a bone which necessitates more than one operation to set it properly.

Shock and distress

6.25   Under the heading 'pain and suffering' must be included mental distress – in particular the distress which a permanent cripple must experience because he is constantly dependent upon the care of other persons, or because his enjoyment of life and possibly its duration are cut short: *H West & Son Ltd v Shephard* [1964] AC 326, [1963] 2 All ER 625, HL.

6.26   Shock and nervous disturbance also come under this heading, but damages for nervous shock have had a confused legal history and therefore require separate explanation. (See chapter 7 below.)

Loss of the pleasures or amenities of life

6.27   Damages may be awarded for the loss of the pleasures or amenities of life, either permanently – by the loss of a leg, for example – or temporarily – as by mere detention in hospital or in bed for a period. This is a distinct element altogether from pain and suffering, or from loss of earning power.

6.28   In *Heaps v Perrite Ltd* [1937] 2 All ER 60, 81 Sol Jo 236, CA, the plaintiff had lost both hands, and Greer LJ said that the following facts had to be taken into account (at 61):

> 'the joy of life will have gone from him. He cannot ride a bicycle, cannot kick a football. At any rate, if he can kick a football he cannot catch one. He cannot have any of the usual forms of recreation which appeal to the ordinary healthy man ...'

6.29   In more general terms, Lord Roche said in *Rose v Ford* [1937] AC 826 at 859, [1937] 3 All ER 359 at 379, HL:

'I regard impaired health and vitality, not merely as a cause of pain and suffering, but as a loss of a good thing in itself.'

6.30   In every case of this sort, the personal circumstances of the claimant must form the background of the assessment. If a young man is injured, who, though healthy, has never taken up athletic pursuits, he cannot complain very strongly that he is now unable to do so. On the other hand, a regular rugby player, for example, can properly claim, as an item in the damages, that he has lost even one rugby season through being detained in hospital or restricted by his doctor's orders. So too a sprained ankle may be a serious matter to a runner or jumper whose performance approaches Olympic standards. These, no doubt, are exceptional cases: but the most ordinary person is entitled to compensation if he is deprived of his little strolls with his dog, his work in his allotment garden, or his visits to the club or football ground. Similarly loss or interruption of a holiday may be taken into account: *Ichard v Frangoulis* [1977] 2 All ER 461, [1977] 1 WLR 556, QBD.

6.31   In the case of married persons, injuries which interfere with the normal conduct of life, or prevent sexual relations, may warrant substantial damages on that ground. In the case of a woman, the fact that she is prevented from having children is a serious loss. If, because of the injuries, the marriage breaks down and there is divorce or separation, damages are recoverable for the personal loss, but not for the cost of a divorce settlement, which is considered too remote: *Pritchard v J H Cobden Ltd* [1988] Fam 22, [1987] 1 All ER 300, CA. In *Oakley v Walker* (1977) 121 Sol Jo 619, QBD, where the wife left because of the husband's 'change of personality', damages were allowed for the cost of looking after the children and home help; in *Lampert v Eastern National Omnibus Co Ltd* [1954] 2 All ER 719n, [1954] 1 WLR 1047, QBD the claim was rejected because disfigurement was not the real reason for the husband's desertion (and the judge considered that in any case he was worthless).

An already disabled or injured claimant

6.32   On similar grounds a lower assessment may be justified for a person who is already a permanent invalid without prospects of recovery. For example, the loss of a leg which is already paralysed cannot in the nature of things be compared with a similar loss sustained by a claimant in good health and in the prime of life. But an existing disability or old age often justifies a higher award, for instance, if a bad knee involves almost complete cessation of active life when a younger person would be able to overcome the handicap.

6.33   In *Frank v Cox* (1967) 111 SJ 670, CA the plaintiff was aged 77 years. Sachs LJ stated (at 670):

'I take the view myself that when one has a person in advancing years, in some respects of impairment of movement may perhaps be more serious than it is with a younger person. It is true ... that he has not got as many years before him through which he has to live with this discomfort, pain and impairment of movement. But it is important to bear in mind that as one advances in life one's pleasures and activities particularly do become more limited and any substantial impairment in the limited amount of activity and movement which a person could undertake, in my view, becomes all the more serious on that account.'

6.34   Similarly in *Mustard v Morris* (1981) CA no 374 (unreported) the court considered an argument that damages for the personal injury should be reduced because the plaintiff was already seriously disabled. Watkins LJ stated:

'With respect, I think that argument is misconceived. If a man who is a diabetic and who has arterial disease to the extent that this plaintiff had, is severely injured so that life is much more difficult to bear than otherwise it would have been, a defendant is in my view, quite unable, with justification, to say that a reduction in damages should be brought about. Indeed, an argument to the contrary might well be made. To impose upon a man who, through natural causes, has been made ill to a certain extent, very grave injuries such as were sustained by this plaintiff and which reduces his capacity to bear natural ill health, is in my judgment more likely to increase than reduce damages.'

Loss of leisure

6.35   For example, due to having to work overtime to make the same earnings, is a factor in damages under this heading; so, too, is the loss of an enjoyable or interesting career. (See chapter 10, paras 10.22–10.33 below.)

Shortening of life

6.36 Formerly, damages were given for the loss of expectation of life, that is, for the actual shortening of life by a certain number of years, and damages under this head were capable of devolving to the estate of an injured person on his death. The principle of awarding damages for loss of expectation of life was approved by perhaps the most distinguished House of Lords of recent times, presided over by the great Lord Atkin, on the ground that enjoyment of life over the lost years was something of real value: *Rose v Ford* [1937] AC 826, [1937] 3 All ER 359, HL.

6.37 Damages for loss of expectation of life have now been totally abolished, both for living claimants and for the estates of deceased persons: Administration of Justice Act 1982, s 1(1)(a). But if life has been shortened *and the injured person is aware of it*, the assessment under the head of pain and suffering not only may, but *shall* take into account any suffering caused 'or likely to be caused' by that awareness: see s 1(1)(b). The same rule applies in Scotland: Damages (Scotland) Act 1976, s 9A, as inserted by the Damages (Scotland) Act 1993, s 5.

Disfigurement

6.38 Disfigurement has always been regarded as an important element in assessing damages, especially where a young person is disfigured and their prospects of forming a relationship are impaired.

6.39 Disfigurement generally accompanies rather severe injuries, and it is then difficult to determine how much of the damages is due to the injuries and how much is due to disfigurement.

6.40 Disfigurement is more serious when it leads to loss of a career, or when the claimant is very conscious of the disfigurement and avoids social occasions.

6.41 In fact it seems that in Victorian times the large awards for disfigurement were really based on the loss of prospects of marriage, which was then the career of most women, on which they depended for financial support.

Discomfort and inconvenience

6.42   Discomfort and inconvenience may be regarded as a slight form of pain and suffering. It has been treated in many cases as an admissible item in an action for damages for breach of contract: for example, in *Stedman v Swan Tours Ltd* (1951) 95 Sol Jo 727, CA (inferior accommodation booked by travel agency for holiday); *Bailey v Bullock* [1950] 2 All ER 1167, 94 Sol Jo 689, KBD (negligent failure of solicitors to recover possession of house for plaintiff); *Hobbs v London and South Western Rly Co* (1875) LR 10 QB 111, 39 JP 693 (plaintiff taken by train to wrong town, and had to walk home in the middle of the night); and *Jarvis v Swans Tours Ltd* [1973] QB 233, [1973] 1 All ER 71, CA (£125 awarded for a disappointing holiday).

6.43   It is difficult to conceive that an action of tort would lie for inconvenience alone, but where the action lies on other grounds, inconvenience and discomfort are taken into account in assessing the damages, for example, in *Ichard v Frangoulis* [1977] 2 All ER 461, [1977] 1 WLR 556, QBD (traffic accident disrupted holiday in France).

Disease or illness

6.44   The courts have often had to assess damages for disease or illness caused by dangerous working conditions. The main factor in these cases is usually pain and suffering, and the loss of active life. In more serious cases, however, there may be permanent impairment of some bodily organ, such as the lungs, and also shortening of life.

TWO INJURIES

6.45   When two injuries are sustained, the damages cannot be assessed by adding what would be given for each of the injuries by itself: an injury to the neck, for example, has a general effect on well-being which will no doubt be increased but not doubled by an ankle injury: *Wieland v Cyril Lord Carpets Ltd* [1969] 3 All ER 1006, QBD. On the other hand, damage to both eyes or to both arms may be much worse than twice the damage to one of them.

6.46   In *Hicks v Barnes* (13 January 1988, unreported), QBD, cited in BPILS I 45.1(c), Turner J dealt with a plaintiff with a number of injuries, he stated:

'There is no satisfactorily rational way in which to evaluate a claim
such as this. It would be unrealistic to approach the individual injury
or groups of injuries and award a sum for each and arrive at a total.
What has to be done is for the judge, as best he may, to sit back from
it all and try to farm an overall impression, both of the impact of the
injuries and how as best, but imperfectly as he may, evaluate that it
terms of money. It is not just the individual judge's assessment of
money because, of course, his award has to be more or less in line
with awards in broadly comparable cases, and I lay emphasis on the
word "broadly", because no two of these cases are strictly
comparable. No two individuals respond equally to the same insult,
whether it is of a physical or non-physical kind.'

6.47   This approach was endorsed by the Court of Appeal in *Brown v
Woodall* [1995] PIQR Q36. The trial judge had arrived at a figure for pain
and suffering by adding up the various head of injuries. Sir John May
stated (at Q 39):

'I respectfully agree that the learned judge's approach of adding up
the various figures for the awards that she thought appropriate and
the various different injuries could well lead one to an award which,
compared with other awards, is in the aggregate larger than is
reasonable.

In this type of case, in which there are a number of separate injuries,
all adding up to one composite effect upon a plaintiff, it is necessary
for a learned judge, no doubt having considered the various injuries
and fixed a particular figure as reasonable compensation for each, to
stand back and have a look at what should be the aggregate figure and
ask if it is reasonable compensation for the totality of the injury to the
plaintiff or whether it would in the aggregate be larger than was
reasonable?

I think that towards the end of a very careful and detailed judgment,
the learned judge did err in failing to stand back and look at the case
as a whole. Subject to that comment, we have been shown various
guidelines from the report of the Judicial Studies Board and
comparables from Kemp on Personal Injury Damages: all of them very
valuable, but to be treated merely as signposts to what an appropriate
order for damages in a particular case should be. One case is never
precisely the same as another and one must use one's experience, together
with comparables such as I have mentioned, to enable one to arrive at
what is reasonable compensation for the plaintiff's loss.'

CHAPTER 7

Damages for shock, psychiatric injury and workplace stress

PSYCHIATRIC INJURIES AND THE LAW OF DAMAGES

7.1   In cases where a claimant is physically injured a psychiatric injury can also result. These cases are not difficult to identify: doctors reporting on the physical injury will often report on this and recommend that a psychiatric report be obtained. The most problematic cases, however, arise in cases where there are no physical injuries. In these circumstances issues of damages are interrelated with issues of liability and causation.

7.2   The law relating to damages for psychiatric injury has developed relatively recently. Much of the development has followed advances in medical diagnosis, with increased recognition of the effect that accidents can have even if the claimant is not injured. The difficulty has been not so much in accepting them as *heads of damages* as in defining the circumstances when shock, neurosis and other psychiatric injuries without any direct physical injury will give rise to *legal liability*.

SHOCK

7.3   Shock is the impact on the nervous system (and therefore on the brain, which is the centre of the nervous system) of an unexpected happening, usually unpleasant: frightening sights or sounds, or actual physical injury. Through the brain it affects the glandular system, the bloodstream, the heart, the stomach and other organs. It is therefore a physical experience and not purely mental.

Shock in itself does not give rise to a claim for damages

7.4   Nevertheless shock, without any other injury, is considered too transitory to qualify for an award of damages, even when the claimant had been in physical danger: *Nicholls v Rushton* (1992) Times, 19 June, CA. Similarly emotional reaction is not enough: *Simpson v ICI Ltd* 1983 SLT 601, Ct of Sess. Nor are grief and mental distress: *Behrens v Bertram Mills Circus Ltd* [1957] 2 QB 1, [1957] 1 All ER 583, QBD. To qualify for an award of damages, shock must be the cause of some physical, nervous or mental injury or illness.

7.5 This ruling out of simple shock, fear and grief as subjects of compensation in themselves must be regarded as a matter of policy to avoid the proliferation of trivial claims. But, of course, if there are other injuries – even if the claimant was merely knocked down and bruised – grief and shock and other feelings are taken into account under the head of pain and suffering: *Kralj v McGrath* [1986] 1 All ER 54, [1985] NLJ Rep 913, QBD. Also, in both England and Scotland damages for 'bereavement' are given by statute on the *death* of a very close relative.

Injury (mental or physical) caused by shock

7.6 Although, therefore, simple transitory shock does not qualify for damages, there is no reason in principle – once it is established that there is liability to the claimant – why damages should not be given for any kind of injury brought on by shock, whether it is physical injury, simple neurosis or more serious mental illness. Lord Macmillan said in *Hay (or Bourhill) v Young* [1943] AC 92 at 103, [1942] 2 All ER 396 at 402, HL:

'The crude view that the law should take cognisance only of physical injury resulting from actual impact has been discarded, and it is now well-recognised that an action will lie for injury by shock sustained through the medium of the eye or the ear without direct physical contact. The distinction between mental shock and bodily injury was never a scientific one.'

Physical damage arising from shock

7.7 Physical damage may result in a variety of ways. Shock may bring on a heart attack or a miscarriage, as in *Dulieu v White & Sons* [1901] 2 KB 669, 70 LJKB 837, KBD. A nauseating sight, such as the alleged decomposed snail in the lemonade bottle in *McAlister (or Donoghue) v Stevenson* [1932] AC 562 101 LJPC 109, HL, may cause gastric illness. Another possible case is a fall from a height due to being startled and losing balance.

7.8   In most cases the claim is that the shock brought on a neurotic disorder, as in *Attia v British Gas plc* [1988] QB 304, [1987] 3 All ER 455, CA where the plaintiff suffered shock and nervous breakdown on seeing her house in flames.

7.9   Neurotic disorders may, of course, be brought on by head injury or indeed by any kind of injury as well as by shock. The nature of these disorders and especially their effect on earning capacity requires separate treatment.

NEUROTIC AND MENTAL DISORDERS AS THE SUBJECT OF DAMAGES

7.10   It is better to speak of neurotic and mental disorders, rather than use the fashionable euphemism 'psychiatric' illness. This only means 'psychiatrist's illnesses' and is rather like describing other disorders as 'medical' illnesses.

7.11   All these illnesses are disorders of the central nervous system, that is to say, of the brain. They may be brought on by head injury, which in extreme cases may result in total incapacity, but, more commonly, in concussion cases, produces minor effects such as headaches, irritability and loss of memory and ability to concentrate.

Causation and the claimant with pre-existing problems

7.12   Very often in these cases the claimant had a pre-existing susceptibility to nervous disorder. Here, as in cases of exceptionally thin skulls or brittle bones, the defendant must take the claimant as he finds him, with his inherent weakness: *Page v Smith* [1996] 1 AC 155, [1995] 2 All ER 736, HL. Nevertheless all cases of neurosis have to be looked at more critically than visible injuries. So in the case of an exceptionally vulnerable person the question does arise whether continuing psychiatric symptoms are still due to the accident or whether this merely caused a temporary episode so that the claimant would be in the same state from some other cause in any event.

Legal liability for injuries caused by shock

7.13   Questions of legal liability are generally outside the scope of this book, but in the case of psychiatric injury, liability and damages have been much mixed up together, so it may be useful to give an explanation of the law on liability as it now stands.

Wilful action

7.14   In *Wilkinson v Downton* [1897] 2 QB 57, 66 LJQB 493, QBD and *Janvier v Sweeney* [1919] 2 KB 316, 88 LJKB 1231, CA it was held, as Lord Porter expressed it in *Hay (or Bourhill) v Young* [1943] AC 92, [1942] 2 All ER 396, HL (see para 7.6 above), that 'shock caused by deliberate action affords a valid ground of claim'. In both cases shock was caused by mere words: in the first by a false report that the plaintiff's husband had been involved in an accident; in the second by threats which were meant to terrify.

Negligence

7.15   Liability does not arise unless there is a duty of care to the claimant – or more accurately to persons who stand in the same relationship to the defendant as the claimant (such as other users of the road or whatever the case may be). For such a duty to arise they must be (in the words of Lord Atkin in *McAlister (or Donoghue) v Stevenson* [1932] AC 562 at 580, 101 LJPC 109, HL):

> 'persons ... so closely and directly affected by my act that I ought reasonably to have them in contemplation as being so affected ...'

How far should a defendant be expected to 'contemplate' the risk of injury to others by shock?

Those within range of physical injury

7.16   Where the claimant was actually involved in an accident and was in danger of physical injury, the House of Lords have now decided that the defendant's duty of care extends to injury by shock, so that he is liable although the claimant only sustained a shock with an aftermath of neurosis: *Page v Smith* [1996] 1 AC 155, [1995] 2 All ER 736, HL. This is so although the shock is so slight that a person of normal steady temperament would not be affected. The principle is that once a person is within range of physical injury, the duty is wide enough to cover harm of any kind, whether precisely foreseeable or not. Lord Lloyd of Berwick said (at 190, 761):

'Once it is established that the defendant is under a duty of care to avoid causing personal injury to the plaintiff, it matters not whether the injury in fact sustained is physical, psychiatric or both ...'

7.17   Those who are within the zone of immediate danger were variously described by the House of Lords as 'primary victims' or as 'participants in the incident'. This second description widens the field a little. It seems that the duty extends to participants in the incident who are not in personal danger, for instance, the crane driver who sustained shock when his crane broke and endangered those working below: *Dooley v Cammell Laird & Co Ltd* [1951] 1 Lloyd's Rep 271.

RESCUERS

7.18   It is also well established that a duty of care to a primary victim extends to a 'rescuer' who is put in danger in the aftermath of the incident: *Ward v T E Hopkins & Son Ltd* [1959] 3 All ER 225, [1969] 1 WLR 966, CA. There is liability to rescuers who sustain shock with resulting neurosis in the immediate aftermath of a disaster such as a bad railway accident: *Chadwick v British Transport Commission (or British Railways Board)* [1967] 2 All ER 945, [1967] 1 WLR 942, QBD. But this did not stretch to a man who was on a rescue ship at an oil rig disaster when he was neither assisting in the rescue operations nor in personal danger, but merely a spectator: *McFarlane v E E Caledonia Ltd* [1994] 2 All ER 1, [1994] 1 Lloyd's Rep 16, CA. Nor to men on the Forth bridge who saw a workmate blown off to his death by high winds: *Robertson and Rough v Forth Road Bridge Joint Board* [1995] IRLR 251, Ct of Sess.

PROFESSIONAL RESCUERS

7.19   It has further been held that even in the case of a rescuer, if he is a professional rescuer such as a police officer or fireman, he must be expected to have greater nervous stamina than a typical bystander so that there is no liability to him unless the incident goes beyond normal professional endurance: this seems dubious. It is inconsistent with the *Page v Smith* [1996] 1 AC 155, [1995] 2 All ER 736, HL principle that the defendant takes the claimant as he finds him, and the distinction is difficult to apply in practice. But perhaps the decision may be supported on the ground of volenti non fit injuria – voluntary acceptance of the risk.

Those outside the range of physical injury

7.20 As the *McFarlane* case[1] shows, the general rule is that there is no liability for injury caused by shock to persons who merely witnessed an accident but were not themselves endangered. This was established in *Hay (or Bourhill) v Young* [1943] AC 92, [1942] 2 All ER 396, HL where the House of Lords held that there was no liability to a woman who heard the sound of an accident and saw blood on the road, but was outside the danger zone. In this case the bystander was a stranger to the victim, and the decision went on the basis that a defendant could not be expected to foresee the risk of shock to an unconnected bystander. This remains the law.

1   *McFarlane v E E Caledonia Ltd* [1994] 2 All ER 1, [1994] 1 Lloyd's Rep 16, CA.

CLOSE RELATIONSHIPS BETWEEN THE BYSTANDER AND THE INJURED PERSON

7.21 It is otherwise if there was a close relationship between the bystander and the injured person: in *McLoughlin v O'Brian* [1983] 1 AC 410, [1982] 2 All ER 298, HL the House of Lords held that there was liability to a plaintiff who was told of an accident to her husband and children and then saw them immediately in hospital, one dead, the others injured and distressed and still covered in mud. Other cases include *Kralj v McGrath* [1986] 1 All ER 54, [1985] NLJ Rep 913, QBD (shock at death of child during birth); *Hinz v Berry* [1970] 2 QB 40, [1970] 1 All ER 1074, CA (wife saw husband killed).

POLICY ISSUES

7.22 There is obviously an element of policy in deciding how far liability of this kind can be stretched beyond those in actual danger. It is not just a question of foreseeability – shock to any bystander can be foreseen – but what are the reasonable limits which a defendant can be expected to visualise as consequences of his acts. In the case of secondary victims, as Lord Lloyd of Berwick said in *Page v Smith* [1996] 1 AC 155, [1995] 2 All ER 736, HL: 'the courts have, as a matter of policy, rightly insisted on a number of control mechanisms.'

CONTROL MECHANISMS

7.23 One of these is that there must be a very close relationship to the primary victim. Another is that the risk of injury by shock to persons of normal fortitude must be foreseeable. In *Alcock v Chief Constable of South Yorkshire Police* [1992] 1 AC 310, [1991] 3 WLR 1057, HL – a case of numerous deaths in a stampede at a football match which was not only seen by those present but also shown on television – the House of Lords have demarcated the limits of liability. The shock must be due to the sight or sound of the accident, or its immediate aftermath, as by seeing the victims' bodies at the scene, or very shortly afterwards in hospital. Viewing on television is not enough, even if relatives are known to be present.

7.24 Merely being told of an accident to a relative is not enough: *Ravenscroft v Rederiaktiebolaget Transatlantic* [1992] 2 All ER 470n, CA. Nor is identification of bodies in a mortuary, because it is not the 'immediate aftermath': *Jones v Wright* [1992] 1 AC 310, [1991] 3 All ER 88, CA (this was the *Alcock* case – *Alcock v Chief Constable of South Yorkshire Police* [1992] 1 AC 310, [1991] 3 WLR 1057, HL – in the Court of Appeal). Further, the House of Lords decided in *Alcock* that the relationship with the victim must be exceedingly close – parent and child, or husband and wife, but no other relationships or friendships unless in the particular case they are as close and affectionate as these.

Liability not dependent upon actual injury

7.25 It seems – though perhaps the decision is open to question since *Alcock v Chief Constable of South Yorkshire Police* [1992] 1 AC 310, [1991] 3 WLR 1057, HL – that shock need not necessarily be caused by fear of personal injury, either to the claimant or to others. Liability was established when the plaintiff's shock was due to seeing her home on fire: *Attia v British Gas plc* [1988] QB 304, [1987] 3 All ER 455, CA.

Questions of causation

7.26 The precise effect of shock on the claimant does not have to be foreseen. Where the plaintiff was predisposed to neurotic illness and developed severe neurosis as a result of a relatively slight shock, damages were recoverable for the neurosis: *Brice v Brown* [1984] 1 All ER 997, 134 NLJ 204, QBD.

7.27 Causation is much more open to question than it is in the case of physical injury, especially where neurotic effects arise after a long interval. The onus of proof is always on the claimant.

7.28 There may have been a pre-existing neurosis. The question then is whether the accident has caused a permanent deterioration or merely a temporary one.

7.29 Another possibility is that the claimant's nervous stamina is less than normal, so that by temperament he is susceptible to neurotic disorder which will inevitably be precipitated through one cause or another from time to time. There is then the analogous question whether this is just one episode, or whether it has thrown the claimant permanently off balance.

Air travel

7.30 In *Morris v KLM Royal Dutch Airlines, King v Bristow Helicopters Ltd* [2002] UKHL 7, [2002] 2 AC 628 it was held that mental injury or illness which lacked a physical origin could not constitute 'bodily injury' within the meaning of art 17 of the Warsaw Convention. However, the term 'bodily injury' did cover physical manifestations of mental injury and psychiatric disorders arising from injury to the brain or nervous system.

Establishing liability in psychiatric injury cases: a useful summary

7.31 The Law Commission Report *Liability for Psychiatric Injury* (Law Com no 137) contains a useful summary of the relevant principles at para 2.3:

(1) The claimant must have suffered a recognised psychiatric illness, which, at least where the claimant is a 'secondary victim', must be shock induced.

(2) It must have been reasonably foreseeable that the claimant might suffer a psychiatric illness as a result of the defendant's negligence.

(3) The claimant can recover if the foreseeable psychiatric illness arose from a reasonable fear of immediately physical injury to himself.

(4) Where the defendant has negligently injured or imperilled someone other than the claimant (but probably excluding the defendant himself) and the claimant, as a result, has foreseeably suffered a shock-induced psychiatric illness, the claimant can recover if he can establish the requisite degree of proximity in terms of:

(a) the class of persons whose claims should be recognised;

      (b) the closeness of the claimant to the accident in time and space; and

      (c) the means by which the shock is caused.

(5) Where the defendant has negligently damaged or imperilled property belonging to the claimant or a third party and the claimant has, as a result, suffered psychiatric illness in certain circumstances the claimant can recover for that illness but the necessary criteria for recovery are unclear.

(6) It is unclear whether there can be liability for the negligent communication of news to the claimant which has negligently caused him to suffer psychiatric illness.

(7) There are miscellaneous instances where a primary victim probably can recover for a psychiatric illness foreseeably caused by the defendant's negligence. For example, in *Walker v Northumberland County Council* [1995] 1 All ER 737, [1995] ICR 705, QBD where an employee claimed damages from his employer due to stress at work.

Establishing psychiatric injury

7.32 In practical terms it is often difficult to distinguish between grief arising from the scenario and the psychiatric injuries arising from the incident. In *Hinchcliffe v British Schoolboys Association & East Anglian Schoolboys Scrambling Club* (12 April 2000, unreported), QBD, Smith J (available on Lawtel) the claimants were a family who saw their eight-year-old child die in a motorcycling accident on a scrambling course. The judge recognised that the claimants had suffered considerable grief following the accident. However, it was held that this was a natural consequence of the death rather than due to witnessing the accident. Their feelings were not abnormal and did not give rise to a separate claim.

Establishing proximity

7.33 An example of the difficulties in establishing proximity is *Tranmore v T E Scudder Ltd* [1998] EWCA 1895. In that case an accident occurred at 6.00 pm when a building collapsed on a building site on which the plaintiff's son was working. The plaintiff was told of the collapse at 7.30 pm when he arrived home from work and he went to the site at about 8.00 pm. On reaching the site he was told that his son was in the building, but was not allowed to enter the site. He viewed the site from an office and, for two hours, watched knowing his son was in the building. At 10.00 pm the emergency services were able to get into the building and the plaintiff was told that his son was dead: he had been killed instantly.

7.34 The court held that it should apply the *McLoughlin v O'Brian* [1983] 1 AC 410, [1982] 2 All ER 298, HL test, ie 'a strict test of proximity by sight or hearing'. The court held that:

• In this case the plaintiff was not present at the scene of the accident.
• He did not witness the death of his son, nor the extreme danger to his son.
• Two hours passed between the collapse of the building and the plaintiff's arrival at the site.

The combination of features deprived the case of the immediacy required before the necessary proximity could be said to exist.

Cases where claims have succeeded

7.35 There are a number of cases where the claimant has recovered, examples of which are given below.

7.36 In *Marshall v Lionel Enterprises* [1971] 25 DLR (3d) 141, Ont HC a wife came upon the badly injured body of her husband shortly after he was involved in an accident.

7.37 In *McLoughlin v O'Brien* [1983] 1 AC 410, [1982] 2 All ER 298, HL Mrs McLoughlin was not present at the scene of the accident, but attended hospital two-and-a-half hours afterwards. She saw her husband and her surviving children in exactly the same blood-spattered state as if they had been at the accident scene, and in great pain and distressed. She also heard that her youngest child had been killed. The House of Lords held that she could recover. However, it has been observed that this decision was on the margin of what the process of logical progression should allow. In *Alcock v Chief Constable of South Yorkshire Police* [1992] 1 AC 310, [1991] 3 WLR 1057, HL it was observed that the striking feature of the *McLoughlin* case was that the victims were very much in the same state as they would have been if the mother had found them at the scene of the accident.

No award for survivor's guilt

7.38   In *Hunter v British Coal Corpn* [1999] QB 140, [1998] 2 All ER 97, CA the Court of Appeal considered the issue of whether an award could be made for 'survivor's guilt'. The plaintiff had damaged a hydrant at the workplace. Whilst he was away from the scene attempting to find a hose to channel the water a 'freak accident' occurred which led to the death of a colleague. The plaintiff did not witness the accident, he was not a rescuer, was not in physical danger and was not allowed back to witness the scene. However, the plaintiff did develop a nervous illness due to his involvement in the incident. The Court of Appeal refused to extend the law to cover survivor's guilt.

STRESS AT WORK: A SPECIAL CASE

Definitive Court of Appeal guidance: *Sutherland v Hatton*

7.39   In *Hatton v Sutherland Barber v Somerset County Council; Jones v Sandwell Metropolitan Borough Council; Bishop v Baker Refactories Ltd* [2002] EWCA Civ 76, [2002] 2 All ER 1 the Court of Appeal giving a combined judgment set out definitive guidelines for 'stress at work' cases. The main points of the judgment are set out here.

No special control mechanisms in stress at work cases

7.40   The court stated that whilst there were no special control mechanisms applying to claims for psychiatric injury or illness from stress at work, these claims require particular care in determination because they give rise to difficult issues of foreseeability, causation and identifying a relevant breach of duty.

Liability: the central issue

7.41   Stress at work is inevitable; indeed in many ways it could be considered good thing in that it makes jobs interesting. However, the existence of such stress does not give rise to a cause of action:

> 'Unless, however, there was a real risk of breakdown which the claimant's employers ought reasonably to have foreseen and which they ought properly to have averted, there can be no liability.'[1]

1   *Hatton v Sutherland Barber v Somerset County Council; Jones v Sandwell Metropolitan Borough Council; Bishop v Baker Refactories Ltd* [2002] EWCA Civ 76 at [22], [2002] 2 All ER 1 at 13.

Foreseeability

7.42   Usually the focus is on the individual. The Court of Appeal stressed that unless he knows of some particular problem or vulnerability, an employer is usually entitled to assume that his employee is up to the normal pressures of the job. Even if the job is stressful in itself, the employer does not have to make searching or intrusive inquiries. Generally the employer is entitled to take what he is told by or on behalf of the employee at face value. Indeed seeking further information could be an unacceptable invasion of the employee's privacy.

7.43   Further, because of the many difficulties in knowing when and why a particular person will become clinically ill as a result of workplace stress, 'the indications must be plain enough for any reasonable employer to realise that he should do something about it'.

Return to work

7.44   Many stress at work claims involve individuals who have had time off work and then return. If an employee returns to work after a period of sickness without making further disclosure or explanation to his employer, the employee is usually implying that he believes he is fit to return to the work he was doing. The employer is usually entitled to take this at face value unless they have good reasons to believe to the contrary.

The employer's duty

7.45   The employer's duty is to take reasonable care. The fact that an employee has suffered harm and that the harm was foreseeable does not mean that the employer is in breach of that duty.

7.46   In every case it is necessary to consider not only what the employer could have done, but also what they should have done.

'The employer is only in breach of duty if he has failed to take the steps which are reasonable in the circumstances, bearing in mind the magnitude of the risk of harm occurring, the gravity of the harm which may occur, the costs and practicability of preventing it, and the justifications for running the risk.'[1]

1   *Hatton v Sutherland Barber v Somerset County Council; Jones v Sandwell Metropolitan Borough Council; Bishop v Baker Refactories Ltd* [2002] EWCA Civ 76 at [43], [2002] 2 All ER 1 at 19.

7.47   The size and scope of the employer's operation is a relevant factor, including the resources it has and the interests of other employees in the workplace.

The employer can only reasonably be expected to take steps which are likely to do some good

7.48   Expert evidence will often be needed in this regard. The court was reluctant to impose a duty on an employer to sack a worker. However, if there is no alternative solution, it is for the employee to decide whether or not to carry on in the same employment.

'If the only reasonable and effective step would have been to dismiss or demote the employee, the employer will not be in breach of duty in allowing a willing employee to continue in the job.'[1]

1   *Hatton v Sutherland Barber v Somerset County Council; Jones v Sandwell Metropolitan Borough Council; Bishop v Baker Refactories Ltd* [2002] EWCA Civ 76 at [43], [2002] 2 All ER 1 at 20.

Causation

7.49   Even if a breach of duty is established, it is still necessary to show that the particular breach of duty found caused the harm. The court was categorical in its view that it is not enough to show that occupational stress caused the harm. When there are several different possible causes, as is often the case with stress-related illness of any kind, the claimant may have difficulty proving that the employer's fault was one of them. However, the employee does not have to show that the breach of duty was the whole cause of his ill-health: it is enough to show that it has made a material contribution.

Burden on the claimant to prove causation

7.50   One important point is that the employee must show that it was the *breach of duty* that caused or materially contributed to the harm suffered. It is not enough to show that occupational stress has caused the harm.

Causation and damages

7.51   If it is established that a number of symptoms suffered by the claimant arose from a number of different causes, then a sensible attempt should be made by the court to apportion liability accordingly.

No special occupations

7.52   The court was keen to stress that these tests apply no matter what the employment. There are no occupations which should be regarded as intrinsically damaging to mental health.

Confidential advice service can be enough

7.53   The court stated in clear terms that:

> 'An employer who offers a confidential advice service, with referral to appropriate counselling or treatment services, is unlikely to be found in breach of duty.'[1]

1   *Hatton v Sutherland Barber v Somerset County Council; Jones v Sandwell Metropolitan Borough Council; Bishop v Baker Refactories Ltd* [2002] EWCA Civ 76 at [43], [2002] 2 All ER 1 at 30.

SOME SPECIAL CONSIDERATIONS IN SEXUAL ABUSE CASES

7.54   Issues relating to general damages in cases of sexual abuse can raise particular questions. These were considered in detail by the Court of Appeal in *KR v Bryn Alyn Community (Holdings) Ltd (in liq)* [2003] EWCA Civ 85, [2003] QB 1441. This case was concerned with sexual abuse by adults of children in a residential home. The problem the court faced was the issue of how damages should be assessed in cases where the abused children could have had problems even if they had not been abused.

Apportionment

7.55   The court held that, in assessing damages, it had to make a comparison between how the individual actually turned out and how he would have turned out if the defendant had offered a proper standard of care. If there were other causes that led to psychiatric problems or personality, difficulties apportionment had to take place. This is a difficult exercise but one which the court must embark upon. The court stated:[1]

'... we accept that it is the duty of a judge, so far as possible, to adopt a principled and logical approach to the difficult question of apportionment ... in accordance with the practice of many judged ... [the trial judge in the current case] eschewed percentages, or at least resisted the temptation to refer to them in terms. That is not something that we criticise provided always that he had gone through the mental exercise of arriving at a global figure before assessing the percentage for which the first defendant was responsible. We have asked ourselves whether there is any objection to the "workings out" being disclosed. We can think of none and would suggest that the better practice would be for judges to show the steps by which the result, however approximate, has been achieved. To this extent we disagree with the sentiment sometimes expressed that the assessment of compensatory damages is a jury question.'

1   *KR v Bryn Alyn Community (Holdings) Ltd (in liq)* [2003] EWCA Civ 85 at [120].

Dealing with an already troubled victim

7.56   The court has to take into account that defendant must take the victim as he finds him. The abuse of an already damaged individual may have the result of pushing him over the brink. There is a possible exponential effect of abuse on children who have already suffered psychiatric damage by reason of previous experiences. The injury can compound and multiply the effect of a pre-existing condition.

Loss of earnings

7.57   If a claimant proves, on the balance of probability, that pre-trial he has earned less money than he would have earned had he not been abused, the court can award damages in a round sum. In relation to future earnings a conventional *Smith v Manchester City Council (or Manchester Corpn)* (1974) 118 Sol Jo 597, 17 KIR 1, CA approach should be adopted. (See paras 10.44–10.47 below.) The Court of Appeal observed that, although apportionment must take place in relation to loss of earnings:[1]

'... it does not follow that apportionment of loss of earnings must necessarily mirror that in relation to general damages. In this context the "push over the edge" or cumulative effect of the ... abuse may have made the difference between a claimant being able to work and not being able to work.'

1   *KR v Bryn Alyn Community (Holdings) Ltd (in liq)* [2003] EWCA Civ 85 at [134], [2003] 3 WLR 107 at 153.

Therapy

7.58   In *KR v Bryn Alyn Community (Holdings) Ltd (in liq)* [2003] EWCA Civ 85, [2003] QB 1441, the Court of Appeal was sceptical of an approach which apportioned the need for therapy to previous life experience and not to the abuse. The additional symptoms caused by the abuse could not be treated independently from those with a separate cause. Once it is established that the abuse played a significant part in the need for therapy, the whole of the anticipated cost should be recoverable from the defendant unless it can be clearly shown that the treatment is divisible.

CHAPTER 8

Assessing general damages: use of comparable cases and the Judicial Studies Board Guidelines

8.1 'Few who suffer personal injuries as the result of the negligence of others, particularly injuries with permanent effect, will feel that the general damages that they are advised to accept or that they are awarded, adequately compensates them for their pain, suffering and disability. If, despite this, victims of negligence are to feel that justice has been done, they must be treated consistently.'[1]

1   Lord Phillips MR in the Foreword to the 6th edition of the Judicial Studies Board Guideline (2002) figures.

CURRENT LEVELS OF DAMAGES AS A GUIDE TO QUANTUM

8.2   In virtually every personal injury case where general damages are not agreed the trial judge will be presented with 'comparable' cases and arguments presented as to how these relate to the claimant with the injuries in issue.

THE NEED FOR UNIFORMITY

8.3   When damages were assessed by juries there were, of course, great variations from one case to another, even where the injuries and other circumstances were similar. Likewise there have been discrepancies, sometimes quite marked, between the awards of different judges. If there is an appeal against the assessment of damages by a judge, the Court of Appeal acts upon the principle that it will not interfere unless the amount is 'so inordinately low or so inordinately high' as to be 'a wholly erroneous estimate of the damage suffered': per Viscount Simon in *Nance v British Columbia Electric Rly Co* [1951] AC 601 at 613, PC. In more modern terms, there is no precise figure of damages for any particular injury. There is a reasonable minimum and a reasonable maximum, and within these limits the decision of the trial judge is final: see *Hunt v Severs* [1994] 2 AC 350, [1994] 2 All ER 385, HL (choice of multiple by trial judge). The Scottish courts take a similar view: *McCrum v Ballantyne* 1993 SLT 788, Ct of Sess.

8.4 The fact that awards can be described as 'high' or 'low' or 'out of all proportion' presupposes a standard, although it may be a vague one. Inordinately high or inordinately low in comparison with what? Plainly the members of the Court of Appeal have always drawn upon their own combined knowledge of what was customary and reasonable for the injuries in question. Within a certain undefined range of tolerance, an assessment could not be challenged on appeal: but if it fell above or below the limits of tolerance, the assessment would be set aside and the appeal court were free to substitute their own estimate or, in the case of a jury award, to order a new trial.

Development of the 'comparable case' approach

8.5 The Court of Appeal for many years had regard to the current level of damage in comparable cases, although at first this was stated only tentatively and it took time for the practice to crystallise. For example, in *Bird v Cocking & Sons Ltd* [1951] 2 TLR 1260 at 1263, CA Birkett LJ said:

'Although there is no fixed and unalterable standard, the courts have been making these assessments for many years, and I think that they do form some guide to the kind of figure which is appropriate ... when, therefore, a particular matter comes for review, one of the questions is, how does this accord with the general run of assessments made over the years in comparable cases?'

8.6 In *Rushton v National Coal Board* [1953] 1 QB 495 at 502, [1953] 1 All ER 314 at 317, CA, Romer LJ said:

'The only way ... in which one can achieve anything approaching a uniform standard is by considering cases which have come before the courts in the past and seeing what amounts were awarded in circumstances so far as may be comparable with the case which the court has to decide.'

What is the effect of comparable cases?

8.7 These observations (as Singleton LJ said in *Waldon v War Office* [1956] 1 All ER 108 at 112, [1956] 1 WLR 51 at 56, CA) reflect 'the desire which everyone has had for years to get as near as one can towards some form of scale or regularity in assessing damages'. They do not detract from the necessity of weighing each case upon its own individual merits, since no two cases are exactly alike. But they do enable the court to seek guidance, not by referring to any particular case and treating it as a precedent, but by looking at the general level of damages in the same type of case, or cases which offer some means of comparison by analogy. The notion of a 'range' of figures is important. Thus it is sometimes said that the damages should lie within certain 'brackets' – a reasonable maximum and a reasonable minimum. In some cases, such as future epilepsy, there may be 'a more than usually wide bracket between the views of reasonable men in general, and of judges in particular as to ... the highest and lowest appropriate figures': Sachs LJ in *Jones v Griffith* [1969] 2 All ER 1015 at 1016, [1969] 1 WLR 795 at 798.

8.8   This approach has received the approval of the House of Lords and the Privy Council – it has been said that fairness between one claimant and another requires some degree of uniformity: *H West & Son Ltd v Shephard* [1964] AC 326, [1963] 2 All ER 625, HL; *Singh (infant) v Toong Fong Omnibus Co Ltd* [1964] 3 All ER 925, [1964] 1 WLR 1382, PC; *Ward v James* [1966] 1 QB 273, [1965] 1 All ER 563, CA. Diplock LJ said in *Bastow v Bagley & Co Ltd* [1961] 3 All ER 1101 at 1104, [1961] 1 WLR 1494 at 1498, CA:

> 'The choice of the right order of figure is empirical, and in practice, results from a general consensus of opinion of damage-awarding tribunals – juries, judges and appellate courts.'

and

> 'the sum awarded to one should not be out of all proportion to the sum awarded to another in respect of similar physical injuries.'

THE APPROACH OF THE TRIAL JUDGE

8.9   If the Court of Appeal may look at comparable cases in hearing appeals, then a fortiori the trial judge, who has to make the assessment, may also look at them. Singleton LJ said in *Waldon v War Office* [1956] 1 All ER 108, [1956] 1 WLR 51, CA that reference to previous cases might be a help to a judge as showing a standard by which damages should be assessed. It was made clear, however, that reference to other cases is entirely at the judge's discretion.

8.10 The latest and most authoritative pronouncement was by Lord Diplock, giving the unanimous opinion of the House of Lords in *Wright v British Railways Board* [1983] 2 AC 773 at 784, [1983] 2 All ER 698 at 705, HL (which was concerned with the related question of interest on damages):

'... it is an important function of the Court of Appeal to lay down guidelines both as to the quantum of damages appropriate to compensate for various types of commonly occurring injuries and as to the rates of interest ... such guidelines ... should be simple and easy to apply though broad enough to permit allowances to be made for special features of individual cases which make the deprivation to the particular plaintiff ... greater or less than the general run of cases involving injuries of the same kind. Guidelines laid down by an appellate court are addressed directly to judges who try personal injury actions; but confidence that trial judges will apply them means that all those who are engaged in settling out of court the many thousands of claims that never reach the stage of litigation ... or ... do not proceed as far as trial will know very broadly speaking what the claim is likely to be worth ... A guideline as to quantum of conventional damages ... is not a rule of law nor is it a rule of practice. It sets no binding precedent; it can be varied as circumstances change ... But, through guidelines should be altered if circumstances relevant ... change, too frequent alteration deprives them of their usefulness in providing a reasonable degree of predictability ... and so facilitating settlement of claims without going to trial. As regards assessment of damages for non-economic loss in personal injury cases, the Court of Appeal creates the guidelines as to the appropriate conventional figure by increasing or reducing awards ... by judges ... for various common kinds of injuries. Thus, so-called "brackets" are established, broad enough to make allowance for circumstances which make the deprivation suffered by the individual plaintiff ... greater or less than in the general run of cases, yet clear enough to reduce the unpredictability of what is likely to be the most important factor in ... settlement of claims. "Brackets" may call for alteration not only to take account of inflation, for which they ought automatically to be raised, but also, it may be, to take account of advances in medical science which may make particular ... injuries less disabling or advances in medical knowledge which may disclose hitherto unsuspected long-term effects ...'

ADJUSTMENT FOR INFLATION

8.11   The indication that standard awards should be adjusted for inflation can have a major practical effect. Such adjustment require the use of the Retail Price Index – imperfect instrument though it may be, it is the best we have. In previous editions of this book it has been suggested that it would be undesirable to make adjustments month by month and that an adjustment at the beginning of each year should be sufficient (wages, pensions and tax allowances are in general adjusted on an annual basis). However, modern computer programs mean that it is possible to give a precise updated figure for an award.

BRACKETS OR RANGES OF DAMAGES?

8.12   Lord Diplock evidently did not like the word 'bracket': perhaps the 'range' of damages for a particular injury is a better description, and it is certainly more accurate mathematically.

OTHER JURISDICTIONS

8.13   The Scottish courts have decided to take into account English awards: *Allan v Scott* 1972 SLT 45 (£14,000 for 16-year-old quadriplegic increased to £20,000). Conversely Scottish awards may help in the English courts. More generally it was said in *Singh (infant) v Toong Fong Omnibus Co Ltd* [1964] 3 All ER 925 at 927, [1964] 1 WLR 1382 at 1385, PC (an appeal from Malaya):

'... to the extent to which regard should be had to the range of awards in other cases which are comparable, such cases should as a rule be those which have been determined in the same jurisdiction or in a neighbouring locality where similar social, economic and industrial conditions exist.'

JURY AWARDS

8.14   Jury awards are extremely rare. A jury cannot be referred to awards in similar cases, but their assessment may be set aside if it is 'out of all proportion' to the current level of damages: *Ward v James* [1966] 1 QB 273, [1965] 1 All ER 563, CA.

NO 'COMPARABLE CASES' IN FINANCIAL LOSS CLAIM

8.15 Now that damages are stated separately for the personal (non-financial) loss and for the pecuniary loss, it is clear that comparable awards can be looked at only in assessing the personal loss, because the financial loss is calculated mathematically: *Lim Poh Choo v Camden and Islington Area Health Authority* [1979] 2 All ER 910 at 919a, HL.

NO DOCTRINE OF PRECEDENT IN DAMAGES

8.16 The fact that the courts can, and do, look at comparable cases should not hide the fact that there is no doctrine of precedent in fixing the quantum of damages. It would be wrong to conclude that *Rushton v National Coal Board* [1953] 1 QB 495, [1953] 1 All ER 314, CA and the other cases cited above afford any warrant for such a doctrine. In fact, they do nothing of the kind. The court does not look for precedents, but for a general guide to the current range of damages. It looks for assistance in a difficult problem, not for an inflexible pattern which would confine the courts within fixed limits. In general too it does not look at particular cases, but at the general level of recent assessments in cases which are fairly close to the case under consideration. It may happen, of course, that a certain case offers a particularly good *illustration*: for example, there have been valuable cases in the Court of Appeal on the quantum of damages on eye and leg injuries and in the House of Lords on total paralysis with a semi-conscious state.

CITATION OF CASES AS ILLUSTRATIONS

8.17 The use which the trial judge may make of awards in comparable cases was very clearly explained by Singleton LJ in *Waldon v War Office* [1956] 1 All ER 108 at 110-111, [1956] 1 WLR 51 at 54, CA:

'...this court is always most anxious not to put any additional burden on the judges of first instance.

... The decision of the Court of Appeal to which the reference was made drew attention to the desirability of approaching, as far as possible, something in the nature of a standard in certain classes of injury so as to help judges of first instances as much as possible ... One of the cases to which counsel desired to direct the attention of the learned judge was a decision of Barry J, in a case of paraplegia ... I think that reference to that case would have been of help to the judge. The circumstances were similar to those in this case, though they were not quite the same ... I do not think that a judge is bound to consider such cases. If counsel on one side or the other tenders such material, it is for the judge to say whether, in his discretion, he thinks it will be of help to him or not ... A judge in assessing damages draws on his own experience, which he acquired from knowledge of other judges' decisions as to amount, from knowledge of what is said in this court and in the House of Lords, and from his ordinary experience of life.'

THE CORRECT APPROACH: TAKING JUDICIAL NOTICE

8.18   Perhaps the most satisfactory method of stating the law (and it seems to be implied in the words of Singleton LJ) is that a *judge may take judicial notice of the current levels of damages*. For this purpose the judge is free (as he always is where judicial notice is involved) to inform himself from any reliable data.

OVER-CITATION OF AWARDS

8.19   Once it becomes clear that there is no doctrine of precedent, it is wrong to suggest that illustrations of quantum ought not to be quoted unless they are authenticated by an official law report. Certainly cases do occur from time to time whose illustrative value is so great that they ought to be included in the law reports. The *Personal Injury and Quantum Reports* report many cases.

8.20   The reporting of illustrative cases has therefore served a useful purpose, but in recent years it has been overdone. Too many cases are reported, and in unnecessary detail. Little attempt is made to assess their relative value by highlighting cases with real authority and discarding those which carry no weight. The great mass of current cases published by Halsbury's Laws Review and Current Law includes awards at every level – good, bad and indifferent – even down to agreed settlements. Sheer bulk has made it difficult to see any clear pattern.

THE DEVELOPMENT OF THE JUDICIAL STUDIES BOARD GUIDELINES

8.21   The publication in 1992 by the Judicial Studies Board of a booklet giving guidelines on damages was therefore a welcome development.

8.22 The Guidelines, issued under the authority of the Judicial Studies Board with a foreword by the Master of the Rolls, were prepared by a working group who surveyed the existing mass of illustrative cases, made an independent assessment of their relative weight and set out a fair range of values – between a reasonable maximum and a reasonable minimum – for various typical injuries. The Guide is now in its 6th edition – *Guidelines for the Assessment of General Damages in Personal Injury Cases* – and is reproduced by permission in Appendix I.

THE EFFECT OF THE GUIDELINES

8.23 The Guidelines are, without doubt, now the primary source for both the courts and litigants in estimating the range of damages for a given injury, illustrative cases being used only to supplement it. Now that most personal injury cases are decided at county court level, often by district judges, there is no other way of achieving reasonable uniformity. In their reserved judgments in *Hunt v Severs* [1993] QB 815, [1993] 4 All ER 180, CA, the Court of Appeal first looked at the Guidelines for paraplegia (at that time £75,000 to £80,000), and from that starting point decided that the quite unusually painful complications in the case justified the higher award of £90,000 by the trial judge. In *Arafa v Potter* [1995] IRLR 316, [1994] PIQR Q73 at Q79, CA Staughton LJ expressed a more reserved view. He said that the booklet, though not in itself 'law', is a slim and handy guide:

> 'But the law is to be found elsewhere in rather greater bulk and in this court – ie at Court of Appeal level – we ought to look to the sources rather than to the summary produced by the Judicial Studies Board.'

DECISIONS OF THE LOWER COURTS

8.24 The problem for practitioners is that, with the new appeal structure, it is unlikely that many cases on quantum will reach the Court of Appeal – particularly in the Fast Track. The number of cases in which the Court of Appeal considers general damages is extremely small. Although the court took great efforts to set out general principles in *Heil v Rankin* [2001] QB 272, [2000] 3 All ER 138, CA, it made it clear that such general reviews will be extremely rare. The practitioner has to rely on illustrative cases from the lower courts. The great bulk of these illustrative cases are not 'law'; they too are only indications and guidelines, and rather less reliable. There is no virtue in great bulk, especially when it is made up of good, bad and indifferent cases piled up higgledy piggledy. The Judicial Studies Board has not produced a mere 'summary'. It has performed a valuable service by reviewing this mass of uneven value and assessing its relative weight.

THE SYMBIOTIC RELATIONSHIP

8.25   The relationship is clearly a symbiotic one. At the end of the judgment in *Heil v Rankin* [2001] QB 272, [2000] 3 All ER 138, CA the Court of Appeal, giving judgment in the seminal case concerning the appropriate level of general damages, made it clear that it was 'highly desirable' that the Judicial Studies Board should produce a new edition of the Guidelines as soon as possible after their decision ([2000] PIQR Q187 at Q210).

THE GUIDELINES AND SEVERAL INJURIES

8.26   The approach of the courts when there are two or more discrete injuries is considered in detail at paras 6.45–6.47 above. In general terms it is highly misleading to seek to add two heads of injuries together to come to an overall award.

CHAPTER 9

Damages for pecuniary loss: past loss and multipliers

MEASURE OF DAMAGES: THE PROVED LOSS OR EXPENSE

9.1 Damages for personal injuries include two main components: the financial or pecuniary loss, and the personal loss.

9.2 The pecuniary loss is itself of two different types, one negative and the other positive. The first type is the deprivation of earnings or other items which would have been received but for the accident and have now been taken away; the second is the new positive burden of expenses incurred as a result of the accident.

THE PRINCIPLE – EXACT RECOMPENSATION

9.3 In principle, the measure of damages for pecuniary loss is the exact amount of money which has been lost, or has to be spent, in consequence of the injury. Lord Goddard said in *British Transport Commission v Gourley* [1956] AC 185 at 206, [1955] 3 All ER 796 at 804, HL:

'The basic principle so far as loss of earnings and out of pocket expenses are concerned is that the injured person should be placed in the same financial position, so far as can be done by an award of money, as he would have been had the accident not happened.'

PAST LOSS

9.4 It is easy enough to apply this rule in the case of earnings which have actually been lost, or expenses which have actually been incurred, up to the date of the trial. The exact or approximate amount can be proved, and, if proved, will be awarded as special damages.

FUTURE FINANCIAL LOSS – THE PROBLEM OF ASSESSMENT

9.5   In the case of future financial loss, whether it is future loss of earnings or expenses to be incurred in the future, assessment is not so easy. This prospective loss cannot be claimed as precisely calculated special damages, because it has not yet been sustained at the date of trial. It is therefore awarded as part of the general damages. No doubt the claimant is entitled, in theory, to the exact amount of his prospective loss if it can be proved, or rather to its present value at the date of trial. But in practice, since future loss cannot usually be proved, the court has to make a broad estimate, taking into account all the proved facts and the probabilities of the particular case. All this was stated very clearly (with reference to loss of future earnings) by Lord Reid in his speech in *British Transport Commission v Gourley* [1956] AC 185 at 212, [1955] 3 All ER 796 at 808, HL:

> 'If he [the plaintiff] had not been injured he would have had the prospect of earning a continuing income, it may be, for many years, but there can be no certainty as to what would have happened. In many cases the amount of that income may be doubtful, even if he had remained in good health, and there is always the possibility that he might have died or suffered from some incapacity at any time. The loss which he has suffered between the date of the accident and the date of the trial may be certain, but his prospective loss is not. Yet damages must be assessed as a lump sum once and for all, not only in respect of loss accrued before the trial but also in respect of prospective loss. Such damages can only be an estimate, often a very rough estimate, of the present value of his prospective loss.'

9.6   So too Lord Diplock said in *Mallett v McMonagle* [1969] 2 All ER 178 at 191:

> 'the court must make an estimate as to what are the chances that a particular thing will or would have happened and reflect those chances, whether they are more or less than even, in the amount of damages ¼'

CALCULATIONS IN RELATION TO FUTURE LOSS – THE MULTIPLICAND

9.7   Past editions of this book have set out in detail the various debates there have been as to the appropriate approach to multipliers. The law is now relatively settled.

(1) As stated above the court must make findings of fact as to the extent of future losses arising from the injury. Future loss of earnings, care needs and related matters must be established by evidence.
(2) If, as is common, the needs are ongoing the future loss is worked out on an annual basis – 'the multiplicand'.

THE MULTIPLIER

9.8 The court then has to arrive at a figure by which the multiplicand can properly be multiplied to give rise to a proper sum of damages. There are a number of factors here:

- The claimant receives the damages in one lump sum well ahead of the time when the loss is incurred or the expenses will occur.
- The money can be invested and produce a return over that time.

9.9 To multiply the multiplicand by the period of loss or the claimant's life expectancy would grossly over-compensate the claimant. The practice arose of taking a very rough and ready approach to the 'multiplier' with the courts taking account of 'contingencies'. There was an absence of a uniform approach. A further complication arose because there was no agreed approach to the rate of return on the capital sum (the 'discount rate'). Small differences of 0.5% could have major differences in the award made, particularly in the larger cases.

WELLS V WELLS: DEFINITIVE GUIDANCE

9.10 In *Wells v Wells* [1999] 1 AC 345, [1998] 3 All ER 481, HL guidance was given as to the proper approach to multipliers. In that case the House of Lords held that the multiplier should be calculated on the basis that a claimant would invest in index-linked government securities. These are inflation-proof, low-risk investments. A discount rate of 3% was held to be appropriate.

9.11 Although the calculations are based on the assumption that the claimant will invest in index-linked government securities, he is under no obligation to do so. The assumption is based in part on the fact that the claimant is investing through force of circumstances and not through choice. He is not in the same position as an ordinary, prudent investor, who would be able to achieve higher returns, but is (theoretically) relying on the returns from his award to maintain himself in the manner to which he has become accustomed, and is necessitated by his personal injuries. There is a risk of over-compensation if he achieves greater returns on higher-risk investments, but this is balanced by the risk of lower returns (or even losses) which he accepts in choosing those investments.

THE DAMAGES ACT 1996 RATE

9.12   The Damages Act 1996, s 1 allows the Lord Chancellor to set the discount rate used by the courts. On 25 June 2001 the discount rate was set at 2.5%. The advantages of this approach include:

- Certainty – both claimants and defendants know in advance the level of discount which will be applied.
- Simplicity – the same discount applies in all cases. There is no longer the wide variation which previously occurred.
- Suitability for use with the Ogden Tables.[1]
- Stability – the discount rate was set at a level which should be able to remain unchanged for the foreseeable future, in light of the current stability in the wider economy and, in particular, in inflation rates. The discount rate is, of course, open to review if real rates of return shift dramatically.

1   See para 9.17ff below.

AN END TO ARBITRARY DISCOUNTING FOR CONTINGENCIES OF LIFE

9.13   One consequence of *Wells v Wells* [1999] 1 AC 345, HL is that there is an end to arbitrary discounting: Lord Lloyd of Berwick stated (at 346B):

'... there is no room for any discount in the case of a whole life multiplier with an agreed expectation of life. In the case of loss of earnings the contingencies can work in only one direction – in favour of the defendant. But in the case of life expectancy, the contingency can work in either direction. The claimant may exceed the normal expectation of life, or he may fall short of it.'

9.14   The possibility of early death does not attract a discount, as this is already taken into account in the life expectancy tables used by the courts in assessing the level of awards. In any event, there is very little point in adjusting the initial prediction on the grounds that it may be wrong, as the revised figure is just as likely to be accurate (or otherwise). There is a stronger argument for allowing a further discount in relation to future loss of earnings multiplier if there is a high chance that certain contingencies will materialise to reduce the claimant's working life.

9.15   In the case of *Thomas v Brighton Health Authority* [1996] PIQR Q44, QBD, the House of Lords robustly supported the view that making further discounts for the contingency of early death was misconceived, and refused to make any discount at all in the context of the cost of care. The claimant did concede that there is some room for judicial discounting for contingencies under loss of earnings as this can only benefit the defendant. The House of Lords accepted this view as correct though it has since been queried by commentators (see, for example, *McGregor on Damages* (16th edn, 1997, 4th supplement, 2002) para 1606A).

Discount for housing costs

9.16   The House of Lords has expressly stated that the Court of Appeal's approach in *Roberts v Johnstone* [1989] QB 878, [1988] 3 WLR 1247, CA was correct. As the exercise of the Lord Chancellor's powers under the Damages Act 1996 also applies to this type of award, the current discount rate on the multiplier is 2.5%

APPROVAL OF THE 'OGDEN TABLES'

9.17   Another consequence of *Wells v Wells* [1999] 1 AC 345, [1998] 3 All ER 481, HL is that the House of Lords approved the use of the Government Actuary's Department Actuarial Tables, generally known as the 'Ogden Tables' after the Chairman of the Committee, Sir Michael Ogden QC. Lord Lloyd of Berwick stated (at 346b):

> 'I do not suggest that judges should be a slave to the tables. There may well be special factors in particular cases. But the tables should now be regarded as the starting-point, rather than a check. A judge should be slow to depart from the relevant actuarial multiplier on impressionistic grounds, or by reference to "a spread of multipliers in comparable cases" especially when the multipliers were fixed before actuarial tables were actually used.'

WHICH TABLES ARE USED?

9.18   The Tables are given at appendix II. Tables 1–18 are based on the mortality rates experienced in England and Wales in a historical three-year period (1990–92). Tables 19–36 take into account the fact that there are expected improvements of mortality rates. These Tables take into account the likely life expectancy; the actuaries on the Committee considered that these Tables provided a more accurate estimate than one based on historical longevity. There are now a number of cases where the courts have decided that Tables 19–36 are the appropriate tables to be used in practice. See *Worrall v Powergen* [1999] PIQR Q103; *Barry v Ablerex Construction (Midlands) Ltd* [2001] EWCA Civ 433, [2001] All ER (D) 251 (Mar).

USE OF THE LIFE EXPECTANCY TABLES

9.19   The Committee was anxious to clear up a misunderstanding of the use of the Tables: in para 6 of the Explanatory Notes it observes that:

> 'On the basis of some reported cases, it appears that tables for pecuniary loss of life, e.g. cost of care, may have been misunderstood ... the tables do not assume that the claimant dies after a period equating to the expectation of life, but take account of the possibilities that the claimant will live for different periods, e.g. die soon or live to be very old. The mortality assumptions relate to the general population of England and Wales. Unless there is clear evidence in an individual case to support the view that the individual is atypical and will enjoy longer or shorter expectation of life, no further increase or reduction is required for mortality alone.'

WHERE LIFE EXPECTANCY IS REDUCED

9.20   Questions arise as to the appropriate approach when life expectancy is reduced. Again valuable guidance can be found in the Guidance Notes to the Tables, at para 26:

> 'In some cases, medical evidence may be available which asserts that a claimant's health impairments are equivalent to adding a certain number of years to their current age, or to treating the individual as having a specific age different from their current age. In such cases, Tables 1, 2, 19 and 20 can be used with respect to the deemed higher

age. For the other tables the adjustment is not so straightforward, as adjusting the age will also affect the assumed retirement age, but the procedures described in paragraphs 17 to 21 may be followed [advice in the Guidance as to earlier retirement age: see appendix II], or the advice of an actuary should be sought.'

MULTIPLIERS IN OTHER CASES

9.21   Guidance on the use of multipliers in employment cases can be found in Appendix II, in particular the often overlooked (but essential) explanatory notes provided with the tables.

JUDICIAL RELUCTANCE TO WORK OUTSIDE TABLES

No factors outside the Tables to be considered

9.22   The courts have been reluctant to allow. In *Cooke v United Bristol Health Care, Sheppard v Stibbe, Page v Lee* [2003] EWCA Civ 1370, [2003] 43 LS Gaz R 32 the court of Appeal refused applications by claimants who attempted to introduce the evidence of chartered accountants. The accountancy evidence attempted to show that the cost of future care had been grossly underestimated if the conventional method of assessing damages were applied. The Court of Appeal held that this was an illegitimate attempt to subvert the Lord Chancellor's discount rate. The premise of the order was that the effects of inflation in claims for future losses were to be dealt with only by using the multiplier conditioned by the discount rate. The multiplicand was treated as based on current costs at the date of trial.

9.23   Similarly in *Prigmore v Welbourne* [2003] EWCA Civ 1687, [2003] All ER (D) 301 (Nov) Sheffield Registry District, Nelson J, the judge allowed an appeal against an order that a joint report from an actuary be obtained. Actuarial evidence was irrelevant to the issues before the court. The Ogden Tables applied to the calculation of multipliers from the date of trial. In the majority of cases the Tables alone would suffice for the purpose of the calculation.

CHAPTER 10

Claims for loss of earnings and employment prospects

10.1

'The basic principle as far as loss of earnings and out-of-pocket expenses are concerned is that the injured person should be placed in the same financial position, so far as can be done by an award of money, as he would have been had the accident not happened.'[1]

1   Lord Goddard in *British Transport Commission v Gourley* [1956] AC 185 at 206, HL.

THE BASIC POSITION

10.2   As the citation from Lord Goddard shows, the basic aim of awards for loss of earnings is to put the claimant in the position he would have been in had he not been injured. If the claimant was working before the accident and incapable of work after the accident then the calculation is based on the figure that the claimant would have earned if he had not been injured.

PARTIAL LOSS OF EARNINGS

10.3   In *Cavanagh v Ulster Weaving Co Ltd* [1960] AC 145, [1959] 2 All ER 745, HL, Lord Tucker said of a man of 20 who had lost a leg that a jury had to consider:

'what he might reasonably have been expected to earn during a working life of perhaps 45 or 50 years, taking account of the fall in the value of money, the tendency for wages to rise and the possibility of his improving his status in the labour market contrasted with his present position and future prospects in the event of an increase in the number of unemployed.'

This was a case were there was a reduction of earnings, so that as Lord Tucker says, you have to contrast the position before and after the accident, and estimate the difference.

LOSS OF EARNINGS: THE STARTING-POINT OF THE CALCULATION

10.4 The validity of any calculation depends on its starting-points, the data on which it operates.

10.5 The first essential therefore is to make an estimate of the probable average annual loss and of the period for which it will continue. This is the important thing which must be right before calculations, actuarial or otherwise, are made.

10.6 The starting-points of the calculation involve a number of factors: the probable future earnings, actual earning power after the accident and duration of incapacity. Before the loss of earning capacity can be converted into a capital sum, the judge has to consider the evidence and probabilities in the case, and arrive at firm conclusions upon three things. First, what would the claimant probably have been able to earn in the future, if he had not been injured; secondly, how long will the incapacity continue; and, thirdly, how much (if anything) is he still able to earn?

PROBABLE FUTURE EARNINGS (APART FROM THE ACCIDENT)

10.7 The starting point is naturally the rate of earnings at the time of the accident: *Phillips v London and South Western Rly Co* (1879) 4 QBD 406, 2 WR 797, CA. If the rate varied, or the work was of a casual nature, the usual practice is to take an average over a reasonable period of perhaps a year; and, as the *Phillips* case shows, if large special fees or other windfalls have accrued in the past, the probability of similar gains in the future may be allowed for.

FUTURE INCREASES OR REDUCTIONS

10.8 Allowance must be made for the probability of increase or reduction in the rate of earnings: *Fair v London and North Western Rly Co* (1869) 18 WR 66, 21 LT 326; *Johnston v Great Western Rly Co* [1904] 2 KB

250, 73 LJKB 568, CA. As was indicated in those cases, a professional who is not earning much in his present appointment may have prospects of getting better-paid posts in due course. In *Ratnasingam v Kow Ah Dek alias Kow Lian Poi* [1983] 1 WLR 1235, 127 Sol Jo 521, PC a one-third allowance was made for the chance that a teacher with a good academic record would pass a promotion examination, though he had previously failed and had only one more chance.

FUTURE INFLATION NOT TAKEN INTO ACCOUNT

10.9　No allowance must be made for any increase in the rate of earnings after the trial due to future inflation, but increases up to the date of the trial, whether due to inflation or not, *are* taken into account.

SPECIAL FACTORS IN THE TRADE

10.10　Where there is some degree of casual unemployment in the trade, this tends to decrease the average rate of earnings: see *Rouse v Port of London Authority* [1953] 2 Lloyd's Rep 179, QBD (dock worker), where the point was conceded by counsel. So, too, where a semi-skilled labourer earns high wages on a big engineering project such as the construction of a reservoir, it would not be right to take his actual weekly earnings as a fair measure of future earnings over a long period. One reason for the high wages in employment of this kind is that it is, taking a long view, casual rather than regular employment.

10.11　Where, under somewhat peculiar arrangements for extra pay to guarantee a quick finish to a job, a man was paid for periods when he was not working, this was held not to be genuine earnings and left out of account: *Fairley v John Thompson (Design and Contracting Division) Ltd* [1973] 2 Lloyd's Rep 40, CA.

SELF-EMPLOYED AND COMPANY EARNINGS

10.12　If the claimant's earnings depend on the earnings of their firm, for example, where the claimant is a director or partner, the earnings and future prospects of the firm are relevant: *Brennan v Gale* [1949] NI 178, CA. Accordingly, it is important, where the claimant is a working director or partner, to see whether his absence has reduced the profits of the firm or is likely to do so in future: the reduction of the claimant's own share of the profits due to his incapacity or absence (but not reductions in the shares of other persons) are recoverable on normal principles as loss of his own earnings: *Vaughan v Greater Glasgow Passenger Transport Executive* 1984 SC 32, 1984 SLT 44, Ct of Sess; *Lee v Sheard* [1956] 1 QB 192, [1955] 3 All ER 777, CA.

10.13 A self-employed person must produce proper accounts to show his earnings before the accident; failure to do so will leave the court to guess, and prejudice the claim: *Ashcroft v Curtin* [1971] 3 All ER 1208, [1971] 1 WLR 1731, CA. See the detailed section on loss of earnings and the self-employed at para 10.63 below.

PENSION LOSSES

10.14 Contributions out of earnings to a pension scheme are not recoverable as part of the lost *earnings* if the pension entitlement is not affected: *Dews v National Coal Board* [1988] AC 1, [1987] 2 All ER 545, HL. But if pension *rights* are lost, damages may be claimed for the value of the lost rights or alternatively for the contributions required to restore them: see para 10.32-10.34 below.

POTENTIAL FUTURE EARNINGS (AFTER THE ACCIDENT)

10.15 Where there is a total disability – either for the rest of the claimant's life or for some shorter period – it is not necessary to make any further investigation of the earnings potential after the accident. In many cases, however, after the claimant has recovered from the immediate effects of his injuries, he is still able to work, although his earning power may be reduced considerably. In these cases the defendant is liable for the difference between what the claimant could have earned but for the accident, and what he actually can earn. In this connection the rule applies that a claimant must mitigate the loss by doing whatever work he is reasonably able to do (see the detailed discussion of this in chapter 4). It frequently happens, for example, that a skilled person is no longer able to return to the pre-accident skilled work but has to do unskilled or semi-skilled work at perhaps £x a week less. He is then entitled to damages for the partial loss of earnings at £x a week.

FULL ALLOWANCE SHOULD BE MADE

10.16   The necessity for making full allowance for the residual earning capacity is shown by *Billingham v Hughes* [1949] 1 KB 643, [1949] 1 All ER 684, CA where a doctor had become incapable of carrying on as a general practitioner. He had also practised as a radiologist – which is largely sedentary work – and the Court of Appeal said that some allowance must be made for the possibility of expanding this branch of his work.

THE COURT LOOKS AT THE REALITY OF THE SITUATION

10.17   It often happens that a claimant is disabled for heavy work, that he has no talent for anything else and is unable to find light work: such a claimant has lost all the earning capacity he possesses and is compensated on the basis of total loss, as in *Ransom v Sir Robert McAlpine & Sons Ltd* (1971) 11 KIR 141, QBD and *Blair v F J C Lilley (Marine) Ltd* 1981 SLT 90, Ct of Sess.

10.18   The key point is that it is not enough to show that the claimant is able to do some work. The defendant has to show that there is work available of a type that the claimant can do and where an employer is likely to employ someone with the claimant's disability: see chapter 4, para 4.3 above on the burden of proof in relation to mitigation of loss.

THE DURATION OF THE INCAPACITY

10.19   The judge has to estimate the period during which the incapacity will continue. This may involve a finding that there will be total incapacity for a period, followed by partial incapacity for a further period. Where there is a dispute, questions of fact arise upon the medical evidence. For example, it may be said that the present disability is not due to the accident, but to some pre-existing condition such as a weak heart or osteo-arthritis which would have disabled the claimant in any event. Or, where a claimant is said to be suffering from a neurosis, it may be argued that he is merely lazy and unwilling to work. These are pure questions of fact, in which no legal principles are involved. The court can decide as a fact on what date the claimant is capable of starting work again: *Bowers v Strathclyde Regional Council* 1981 SLT 122, Ct of Sess.

THE DURATION OF THE LOSS

10.20 The court must decide on the expectation of working life; again this is primarily an issue of fact. Thus a woman teacher can retire at 60, a judge at 72; most people retire somewhere in between. Lord Goddard CJ said in *Zinovieff v British Transport Commission* (1954) Times, 1 April that it is wrong to assume that a plaintiff, at any rate a professional plaintiff, will retire at 60; many continue until 70, or, if they keep their health, considerably longer. In *Gilbertson v Harland and Wolff Ltd* [1966] 2 Lloyd's Rep 190, QBD a riveter aged 70, in good health, was held likely to continue until 75. In recent years, however, the tendency has been the other way: many people have taken early retirement, often under pressure.

10.21 Sometimes the parties are able to agree the estimated future rate of loss; if they do, they should state what contingencies have been taken into account, to avoid dispute in case of appeal: *Bennett v Chemical Construction (GB) Ltd* [1971] 3 All ER 822, [1971] 1 WLR 1571, CA.

TURNING THE ESTIMATED LOSS INTO A CAPITAL SUM: THE MULTIPLE

10.22 For details of how to apply the multiplier see chapter 9 above.

DEFINITIVE GUIDANCE FROM THE COURT OF APPEAL

10.23 Guidance relating to the appropriate approach in cases of past and future loss of earnings was given by the Court of Appeal in *Herring v Ministry of Defence* [2003] EWCA Civ 528, [2004] 1 All ER 44. In *Herring* the claimant was a seriously injured young man who was a qualified sports coach and who had planned to take up a career in the police force. The judge found that the claimant was likely to become a police officer; however, he reduced the multiplier of 15.7 taken from the Ogden Tables to 11.7 for 'uncertainty' (a discount of 25%). This uncertainty related to the question of whether the claimant would, in fact, have joined the police force and been promoted. The Court of Appeal disapproved of this approach. Potter LJ (giving a judgment with which the other two members of the court agreed) set out the process as follows.

Finding the 'career model'

10.24

'In any claim for injury to earning capacity based on long-term disability, the task of the court in assessing a fair figure for future earnings loss can only be effected by forming a view as to the most likely future working career ("the career model") of the claimant had he not been injured. Where, at the time of the accident, a claimant is in an established job or field in which he was likely to have remained but for the accident, the working assumption is that he would have continued to do so and the conventional multiplier/multiplicand method of calculation is adopted. The court takes into account any reasonable prospects of promotion and/or movement to a higher salary scale or into a better remunerated field of work by adjusting the multiplicand at an appropriate point along the scale of the multiplier. However, if a move of job or change of career at some stage is probable, it need only be allowed for so far as it is likely to increase or decrease the level of the claimant's earnings at the stage of his career at which it is regarded as likely to happen. If such a move or change is unlikely significantly to affect the future level of earnings, it may be ignored in the multiplicand/multiplier exercise, save that it will generally be appropriate to make a (moderate) discount in the multiplier in respect of the contingencies or "vicissitudes of life".'[1]

1   *Herring v Ministry of Defence* [2003] EWCA Civ 528, [2004] 1 All ER 44, per Potter LJ.

Finding an appropriate 'baseline'

10.25   The court has to find an appropriate 'baseline'. In *Herring v Ministry of Defence* [2003] EWCA Civ 528, [2004] 1 All ER 44, Potter LJ stated:

'In the situation of a young claimant who has not yet been in employment at the time of injury but is still in education or has otherwise not embarked on his career, or (as in this case) one who has taken time out from employment in order to acquire a further qualification for a desired change of direction, it may or may not be appropriate to select a specific career model in his chosen field. In this connection the court will have regard to the claimant's previous performance, expressed intentions and ambitions, the opportunities reasonably open to him and any steps he has already taken to pursue a particular path. In many cases it will not be possible to identify a specific career model and it may be necessary simply to resort to national average earnings figures for persons of the claimant's ability and qualifications in his likely field(s) of activity. In other cases, however, it may be possible with confidence to select a career model appropriate to be used as the multiplicand for calculating loss. In either case, the purpose and function of the exercise is simply to select an appropriate "baseline" for calculation of the claimant's probable future earnings whatever his future occupation may in fact turn out to be. Thus if the career model chosen is based upon a specific occupation (such as the police force in this case), the chance or possibility that the claimant will not in the event enter the occupation or, having done so, may leave it, will not be significant if the likelihood is that he will find alternative employment at a similar level of remuneration.'

No need to apply the loss of chance criteria

10.26 The assessment of future loss is, in a broad sense, the assessment of a chance or series of chances as to the likely future progress of the claimant in the employment market. However, in *Herring v Ministry of Defence* [2003] EWCA Civ 528, [2004] 1 All ER 44 the court expressly disavowed the notion that such assessment required application of the percentage assessment set out in the *Allied Maples*[1] and *Doyle v Wallace*[2] series of cases (see para 10.37ff below). Those decisions do not replace the traditional method of adjusting the multiplier and multiplicand within the career model so as to reflect (a) the likelihood of an increase in earnings at some point in the claimant's career; (b) those contingencies/vicissitudes in respect of which a discount appears to be appropriate.

1   *Allied Maples Group v Simmons & Simmons (a firm)* [1995] 4 All ER 907, [1995] 1 WLR 1602, CA.
2   *Doyle v Wallace* [1998] 30 LS Gaz R 25, [1998] PIQR Q146, CA.

Cases where loss of chance claims are appropriate

10.27 Cases where the loss of chance approach has been adopted where there was a chance that the career of the claimant will take a particular course leading to significantly higher earnings than those which it is reasonable to take as the baseline for calculation. However:

> 'In a case where the career model adopted by the judge has been chosen because it is itself the appropriate baseline and/or is one of a number or alternatives likely to give more or less similar results, then it is neither necessary not appropriate to adopt the percentage chance approach in respect of the possibility that the particular career identified will not be followed after all.'[1]

1   *Herring v Ministry of Defence* [2003] EWCA Civ 528, [2004] 1 All ER 44 at [26].

The appropriate starting point is the Ogden Tables

10.28   In *Herring v Ministry of Defence* [2003] EWCA Civ 528, [2004] 1 All ER 44 the court found that the fact that the claimant hoped to join the police force did not give rise to justification for a discount of contingencies substantially in excess of the figure to be obtained from the Notes in the Ogden Tables. Working on a broad-brush basis the court rejected a reduction of 25% but applied a discount of 10%.

BENEFITS OTHER THAN MONEY

The value of board and lodging and other perquisites

10.29   Where, before the accident, the claimant received free board and lodging as part of the terms of their employment, the monetary value of those benefits is part of their earnings and may be claimed accordingly: *Liffen v Watson* [1940] 1 KB 556, [1940] 2 All ER 213, CA (maid in hotel). Moreover, the fact (as happened in that case) that the claimant receives free board and lodging with relatives after the accident is not to be taken into account as a set-off to reduce the damages. No deduction is made for the value of free services in an institution provided by the National Health Service: *Daish v Wauton* [1972] 2 QB 262, [1972] 1 All ER 25, CA. But if expenses of institutional treatment are claimed in addition to loss of earnings, a deduction is now made of the 'maintenance' element in the cost of treatment to avoid duplication: *Lim Poh Choo v Camden and Islington Area Health Authority* [1980] AC 174, [1979] 2 All ER 910, HL. Also, by statute, any saving to the injured person through being maintained wholly or partly at public expense – that is to say, without charge or at reduced charge – in a hospital, nursing home or other institution is to be set off against loss of earnings: Administration of Justice Act 1982, s 5 (England and Wales, Northern Ireland); Administration of Justice Act 1982, s 11 (Scotland).

Benefits in kind

10.30   Other benefits in kind, such as the use of a motor car or house, must also be valued as part of the net earnings.

Wages made up by the employer

10.31   In general, if an employee continues to receive pay without having to work for it, they have sustained no loss and the full amount received is set off against the claim for loss of earnings. But there are exceptions, particularly where the amount is treated as a provisional loan by the employer and recovered on his behalf as part of the claimant's claim against a third party.

Pension rights

10.32   A pension is in principle deferred earnings. If an ultimate pension or retirement gratuity is lost or diminished because the service is shortened, the estimated loss is recoverable: *Judd v Hammersmith Hospitals* [1960] 1 All ER 607, [1960] 1 WLR 328, QBD; *Smith v Canadian Pacific Rly Co* (1963) 41 DLR (2d) 249; *Parry v Cleaver* [1970] AC 1, [1969] 1 All ER 555, HL.

10.33   The calculations employed to quantify the pension loss are lengthy and complex, and it is beyond the scope of this work to describe them in any great detail. (For a useful practitioner's guide, see Carey *Pension Loss in Personal Injuries* (CLT Professional Publishing, 1999).) The outline of the procedure is as follows: The present value of a pension has to be calculated in two stages. First, it is necessary to find the value at the date of future retirement, estimate life expectancy at that date and take the appropriate number of years' purchase to work out the capital value at that date. Secondly, that capital value has to be reduced to its present value. Future inflation should not be taken into account, any more than it is taken into account for loss of earnings, and this is so even if the pension scheme aims to keep up with the cost of living: *Auty v National Coal Board* [1985] 1 All ER 930, [1985] 1 WLR 784, CA. Where a man is forced to retire 20 years early, the basic figure for annual pension lost is taken on the basis of what he would have been earning at the date of trial, not an estimate of the rate at retirement age: *Mitchell v Glenrothes Development Corpn* 1991 SLT 284, Ct of Sess. Once the gross pension loss at retirement age has been calculated, following the conventional approach established in *Auty*, adjustments are made for tax, accelerated receipt and 'further eventualities' (this latter need not necessarily be in a downward direction, depending on the facts of the case).

10.34 If the claimant is receiving a sickness or incapacity pension prior to the date he planned to retire, this will not be deducted from the future loss of pension, as no pension loss is suffered before this date. However, credit must be given for any pension received after normal retirement age. In the case of *Longden v British Coal Corpn* [1998] AC 653, [1998] 1 All ER 289, HL, per Lord Hope, the House of Lords upheld the decision in *Parry v Cleaver* [1970] AC 1, [1969] 1 All ER 555, HL as follows:

> '[The claimant] cannot reasonably be expected to set aside the sums received as incapacity pension during this period in order to make good his loss of pension after normal retirement age. I think it would ... strike the ordinary man as unjust if the claimant's loss of pension after his normal retirement age were to be extinguished by capitalising on sums paid to him before that age as an incapacity pension to assist him during his disability.'

OTHER ISSUES RELATING TO EARNINGS AND INCOME

More work for same pay

10.35 Where after an accident claimant is able to keep their earnings to the same level (or higher) but only by working longer hours, they are entitled to damages for loss of leisure: *Kernohan v Dartmouth Auto-Castings Ltd* (17 January 1964, unreported), CA (Kemp & Kemp paras 5-128 and 13-083) (£500 in this case); *Hearnshaw v English Steel Corpn Ltd* (1971) 11 KIR 306, CA (15 hours' overtime a week to get same pay – general damages for hand injury increased from £1,000 to £2,750 for this and other reasons).

Loss of housekeeping capacity

10.36 Where the plaintiff lost her housekeeping capacity, the cost of home help was considered to be a fair measure of future loss even if she did not intend to employ anyone: *Daly v General Steam Navigation Co Ltd,*

The Dragon [1980] 3 All ER 696, [1981] 1 WLR 120, CA. But similar expenses could not be claimed for the pre-trial period unless actually incurred, though general damages could be increased for the extra effort and stress of managing without outside help. See the detailed discussion at para 11.43 below.

DISABILITY IN THE LABOUR MARKET

Restriction on future earning capacity

10.37   There are many cases where, after recovering from the immediate effects of an injury, the claimant returns to their former work at the same rate, or takes up other work with similar or better pay, so that there is no visible continuing loss. Nevertheless, there are innumerable ways in which the claimant may be worse off in future – whether they lose their present employment, which is the possibility usually envisaged, or not. They may be handicapped in getting new work at all: even appearance may tell against an injured claimant, for instance, if they have visible eye or hand injuries though they have adapted with complete success, this may lead to discrimination against them. The claimant may be a skilled person in a supervisory position, but handicapped for skilful handling or heavy work if reduced by redundancy to a lower position. They may have had plans to change to another career, for instance, to take an apprenticeship or join the armed forces, which is no longer open to them. Where pay depends on piecework or overtime, they may not be able to do so much. They may have to take time off for a painful back or a future operation.

Proper definition of such losses

10.38   These cases are sometimes described as 'loss of earning capacity', but this is inaccurate as all claims for future earnings are based on loss of capacity. What distinguishes these from other cases is that there is no immediate loss and future loss is uncertain. This does not prevent an award of damages. The court has to assess and value the chance that there will be actual loss sooner or later.

The leading cases

10.39   The leading cases on this subject are *Moeliker v A Reyrolle & Co Ltd* [1977] 1 All ER 9, [1977] 1 WLR 132, CA and *Smith v*

Manchester City Council (or Manchester Corpn) (1974) 118 Sol Jo 597, 17 KIR 1, CA where the correct approach was explained. What has to be quantified is the present value of the risk of future financial loss. If there is no significant risk of actual loss of earnings sooner or later there should be no award. If there is a significant risk, its value depends on how great the risk is and how far in the future. Where the risk lies in finding a new job if the present one is lost – the most common case – the claimant's skills and adaptability (or lack of them) should be taken into account, and the opportunities likely to be open in his area of work. The court has to apply its judgment to the relevant factors and assess a round figure. In *Cook v Consolidated Fisheries Ltd* (1977) Times, 18 January, CA, the Court of Appeal made a substantial award to a young man with an arm injury, on the basis that he was likely to have disability from osteo-arthritis late in life but this would be many years ahead. In *Smith v Manchester City Council* a woman cleaner was allowed to keep her job with the council although she was substandard on account of a disabled elbow: because she would have little chance of getting any other job, the Court of Appeal increased an award of £300 under this head to £1,000. In *Watson v Mitcham Cardboards Ltd* [1982] CLY 78, CA the Court of Appeal said that the *Moeliker* test, that there must be a 'real' or 'substantial' risk, must not be applied too narrowly: a moderate award of £200 was upheld although there was no evidence of risk that the plaintiff would lose his employment.

10.40   In *Pentney v Anglian Water Authority* [1983] ICR 464, QBD the plaintiff was unlikely to lose his employment but a moderate sum of £600 was awarded as a 'cushion' for a brief period of unemployment in the unlikely event that he did lose it.

10.41   These, of course, are only illustrations. It has been said again and again that it is a question of fact in each case what chance there was of a loss of earnings and no case is a guide to any other; there is no 'conventional' figure: *Page v Enfield and Haringey Area Health Authority* (1986) Times, 7 November, CA.

10.42   In particular, an assessment cannot be arrived at by estimating the percentage of disability and inferring a similar loss of earnings: *Chan Wai Tong v Li Ping Sum* [1985] AC 446, [1985] 2 WLR 396, PC. 'The claim is to cover the risk that, at some future date during the plaintiff's working life, he will lose his employment and will then suffer financial loss because of his disadvantage in the labour market.'

An award can be made even though the claimant has been compensated for future partial loss of earnings

10.43 In *Frost v Palmer* [1993] PIQR Q14, CA, the Court of Appeal upheld an award of £10,000 for loss of earning capacity when the trial judge had also made an award for partial loss of future earnings on the basis of a lifetime loss. The court held that it was not wrong in principle to make awards for both loss of earnings and loss of earning capacity.

A *Smith v Manchester*[1] award may be made if an assessment of future loss of earnings is not possible

10.44 In *Blamire v South Cumbria Health Authority* [1993] PIQR Q1, CA, the course that the claimant's working life would have taken had she not been injured was so uncertain as to make it impossible for the traditional multiplier/multiplicand method of calculating future loss of earnings to be used. The court held that in such circumstances, it was appropriate to take a broad approach, and make a global award covering future loss of earnings, earning capacity and pension.

1   *Smith v Manchester City Council (or Manchester Corpn)* (1974) 118 Sol Jo 597, 17 KIR 1, CA.

10.45 In *Hesp v Willemse* [2003] EWCA Civ 994, 147 Sol Jo LB 900 a talented and creative boat-builder and blacksmith suffered brain damage which damaged his creative abilities and his ability to concentrate on his work (though he could still work to a good standard with close supervision and support). The evidence relating to past loss of earnings was somewhat uncertain, as the claimant's employment history was irregular. There was doubt as to the true extent to which the claimant's earning capacity would be reduced in the future.

10.46 In light of this the Court of Appeal held that rather than attempt a multplier/multiplicand approach, a broad brush approach should have been taken as in *Blamire v South Cumbria Health Authority* [1993] PIQR Q1, CA, saying:[1]

'In all the circumstances I am firmly of the view that this was a classic case for a *Smith v Manchester*-type award,[2] rather than the selection of a multiplicand, even on an "educated guess" basis. The claimant had undoubtedly suffered reduced earning capacity and was at a disadvantage in the future labour market and the development of his future career, but the level of his actual earnings loss depended on how far he sought to decide to work full-time and/ or develop his career in a way which had not been demonstrated before the accident. These circumstances called for a broad lump sum assessment to cover the likelihood of future damage.'

1   *Willemse v Hesp* [2003] EWCA Civ 994 at [30].
2   *Smith v Manchester City Council (or Manchester Corpn)* (1974) 118 Sol Jo 597, 17 KIR 1, CA.

10.47   Potter LJ did not feel that a *Smith v Manchester*[1] award should be substituted for the award made for past loss of earnings, though he did state:[2]

'Had the judge decided that, on the general state of the evidence and his judgment of the claimant, a *Blamire*[3] (i.e. round sum) award was all that was appropriate, I cannot think that this court would have interfered.'

1   *Smith v Manchester City Council (or Manchester Corpn)* (1974) 118 Sol Jo 597, 17 KIR 1, CA.
2   *Hesp v Willemse* [2003] EWCA Civ 994 at [26].
3   *Blamire v South Cumbria Health Authority* [1993] PIQR Q1, CA.

CLAIMS FOR LOSS OF CHANCE

Loss of a 'chance' of favourable employment or prospects

10.48   This is a similar type of case where a sum may be given for the loss of a chance of good employment or other opportunities. Both this case and the case of restricted earning capacity discussed in the at para 10.37ff above are examples of loss of future earnings where the contingencies are so uncertain that the only way to make an assessment is by estimating a moderate sum in round figures. In *Herring v Ministry of Defence* [2003] EWCA Civ 528, [2004] 1 All ER 44 the Court of Appeal stated loss of chance claims do not replace the conventional means of assessing future loss of earnings but are more appropriate in cases where the chance to be assessed is where the chance is that the career of the claimant would take a particular course leading to significantly higher overall earnings than those which it is otherwise reasonable to take as the baseline for calculation: see para 10.25 above.

10.49   For example, in *Moores v Co-operative Wholesale Society Ltd* (1955) Times, 9 May, CA, the plaintiff, a police officer, had been injured in a previous accident, and as a result his prospects of continuing in the police force were very slight. The second accident rendered him unfit for police duty. The Court of Appeal held that the effect of the second accident was to deprive the plaintiff of a 'poor chance' of continuing in the police force, and they reduced the damages substantially from £3,000 to £1,000.

10.50   In *Chaplin v Hicks* [1911] 2 KB 786, 80 LJKB 1292, CA – which was not a case of personal injuries – damages were given for the loss of an opportunity to be considered (on a competitive basis) for a theatrical engagement.

10.51   The loss of an opportunity is certainly a valid head of damages, and cases may be conceived where a claimant is injured on the way to an interview where he has good prospects of being selected for an important post. Loss of an opportunity of starting or continuing an apprenticeship, or a career in the armed forces, may also be caused by an accident at the critical time; or an examination may be missed. Such opportunities may be lost if not taken promptly, and the damages might be substantial, for example, *Comer v Bolton* [1987] CLY 1159, CA where a girl lost the chance of attending a high-class secretarial course.

Two recent cases of loss of chance

Doyle v Wallace

10.52   In the 1998 case of *Doyle v Wallace* [1998] 30 LS Gaz R 25, [1998] PIQR Q146, CA the claimant was a student when injured. Her case what if she had not been injured she would have qualified as a teacher. The Court of Appeal upheld the judge's decision to base damages on the basis that she had a 50% chance of qualifying as a teacher.

Langford v Hebran

10.53   In *Langford v Hebran* [2001] PIQR Q160, the claimant was a trainee bricklayer who had also just begun a promising career as a professional kickboxer. He suffered whiplash injuries and an injury to his shoulder in a road accident, which were sufficient to put an end to his professional kickboxing career.

10.54   In his claim for loss of earnings the claimant claimed loss of earnings and also presented four alternative scenarios reflecting various degrees of success in the fighting career, each more successful than the last.

10.55   The trial judge accepted the claimant's argument that he should receive the basic claim, plus a percentage of each of the four scenarios reflecting the loss of chance of pursuing his kickboxing career to these levels. The Court of Appeal[1] rejected the defendant's argument for the defendant appellant that a *Doyle*-type[2] approach was inappropriate where there were a number of different options to choose from. The claimant was entitled to a percentage of the increased earnings he could have expected in each of the predicted scenarios, had he had the chance to progress as a professional kickboxer, with a discount to take account of the possibility that his success may have been short-lived, and that he may not have realised any of the hypothetical scenarios suggested.

1   *Langford v Hebran* [2001] PIQR Q160.
2   *Doyle v Wallace* [1998] 30 LS Gaz R 25, [1998] PIQR Q146, CA.

10.56   However, there are limits to the cases in which a 'loss of chance' will be appropriate, see the discussion in *Herring v Ministry of Defence* [2003] EWCA Civ 528, [2004] 1 All ER 44 at para 10.23ff above.

Loss of career or amenable employment

10.57   Some occupations are more attractive than others, not necessarily in money but in the interest and satisfaction they offer. Where a person is already enjoying such a career, for instance, as an actress or model, and it is cut short, for example, by disfigurement, damages may include (in addition to financial loss) something for the loss of an enjoyable career. This is really an example of loss of amenities (see chapter 5 above). The same consideration may apply in ordinary occupations, for instance, a hand injury to a craftsman: *Morris v Johnson Matthey & Co Ltd* (1967) 112 Sol Jo 32, CA; or a skilled machine operator reduced to dull unskilled work: *Hearnshaw v English Steel Corpn Ltd* (1971) 11 KIR 306, CA; or loss of a career as a fireman: *Champion v London Fire and Civil Defence Authority* (1990) Times, 5 July. In *Willbye v Gibbons* [2003] EWCA Civ 372, 147 Sol Jo LB 388, the Court of Appeal overturned an award of £15,000 for loss of amenable employment made to a young female whose injuries meant she could not work as a nursery nurse. Kennedy LJ stated (at [11]) that:

'[counsel for the defendant] tells us that that so far as he has been able to ascertain the highest award to date under this head is £10,000 and in fact awards rarely exceed £5,000. In my judgment it is important to keep this head of damages in proportion. The appellant is being compensated for being unable to pursue a career she thought she would have enjoyed. She never actually embarked on that career, although she probably had the ability to obtain the qualifications required, and in financial terms she has been fully reimbursed, so this is really an award for a particular disappointment, which may or may not be prolonged. In my judgment the award in this case should not exceed £5,000 and I would substitute that sum for the sum awarded by the Recorder.'

FRAUD AND WORKING ILLEGALLY

10.58 If the claimant has also committed fraud, he will not be able to recover his losses. This was the case in *Hunter v Butler* [1996] RTR 396, CA. The deceased husband of the claimant widow had not declared his earnings to the Inland Revenue, and claimed benefits by fraud. The widow had been party to this, and was not allowed to recover her loss of dependency. Similarly, if the loss arises entirely out of criminal activity, it will not be recoverable: *Burns v Edman* [1970] 2 QB 541, [1970] 1 All ER 886, QBD.

10.59 A slightly different question faced the Court of Appeal in *Hewison v Meridian Shipping PTE* [2002] EWCA Civ 1821, [2003] ICR 766. Here, the claimant (who had suffered injuries at work) had concealed from his employers the fact that he suffered from epilepsy. Had he not suffered the accident at work, it is likely that his condition would not have worsened and come to light, and he would probably not have lost his job. However, but for the initial deception, he would not have been in a position to suffer the accident in the first place. The Court of Appeal upheld the trial judge's ruling that public policy barred the claimant from recovering his loss of earnings. Epilepsy was a condition which specifically rendered the claimant unfit for work at sea, and continuing to do so would have constituted a significant risk to the safety of himself and others.

10.60 However this is a matter of practicality and not principle. Mr Hewison did not recover damages because, had he declared his epilepsy, he would not have earned. In *Major v Ministry of Defence* [2003] EWCA Civ 1433 the Court of Appeal allowed an appeal against a judgment that a claimant who had failed to disclose previous episodes of self-harm to employers was not entitled to damages. The claimant had been injured at the age of 13 and suffered psychological injury. She failed to disclose episodes of self-harm some five years later when applying to join the RAF. She was allowed to enter the Air Force but was discharged three-and-a-half years later when the authorities became aware of her medical history. If the claimant had disclosed the self-harm she would not have been admitted to the Air Force. The court clearly distinguished *Hewison*[1] where the claim was based on the assertion that the claimant would have continued to deceive his employers by asserting that he was not suffering from epilepsy. The doctrine of illegality prevented Mr Hewison from recovering on the basis that he would continue to commit a criminal offence.

1   *Hewison v Meridian Shipping PTE* [2002] EWCA Civ 1821, [2003] ICR 766.

10.61   In the *Major*[1] case the facts were different. The claimant could not work because of the injuries caused by the defendant. She could properly claim damages based, not on the RAF earnings, but using the RAF earnings as an indicator of her earnings and position in the labour market. The fact that she obtained RAF employment by telling a lie was not relevant to the quantification of the claim for loss of earnings.

1   *Major v Ministry of Defence* [2003] EWCA Civ 1433.

THE LIMITED NATURE OF THE ILLEGALITY DEFENCE

10.62   The limited nature of the illegality defence should be noted. It assists defendants where the claimant's claim is dependent upon his continuing in illegal employment and is not necessarily fatal just because the claimant has lied on a job application.

UNUSED EARNING CAPACITY

10.63   There are few English decisions on compensation for loss of an earning capacity which is not used, or is used in a way which does not involve the earning of money. Diplock LJ did say, obiter, in *Browning v War Office* [1963] 1 QB 750 at 766, [1962] 3 All ER 1089 at 1096, CA:

'A plaintiff is not entitled to damages for loss of capacity to earn money unless it is established that he would, but for his injuries, have exercised that capacity in order to earn money.'

10.64   This is, no doubt, right as a general rule, but it may be too sweeping in exceptional cases. Many people, of course, have a reserve earning capacity – among High Court judges have been, for example, a doctor, a pharmacist, a sea captain and a mathematician. Others work below their full capacity, because high taxation renders the extra wear and tear distasteful. Others retire early (and there is the ordinary case of retirement for age). All such cases must be taken on the basis of the choice they have exercised.

10.65 But there are other familiar cases. A member of a religious order, for example, takes a vow of poverty and does their work for nothing (often highly skilled medical or scientific work), giving their salary (if any) to the order. At one time such a person may be working in a college or hospital and receiving a salary; at another time they may be doing exactly the same work for nothing, in the order's own houses or on foreign missions. By the accident they are deprived of the power to continue this work and give it freely. There is no difference in principle between earning a salary and handing it over, and giving valuable work without payments.

10.66 As a matter of principle, the work done in such a case should be valued at the market rate and capitalised. There is real deprivation of a capacity which is fully used, and the arrangement by which it is used without remuneration is wholly collateral so far as a defendant is concerned.

10.67 In *Keating v Elvan Reinforced Concrete Co Ltd* [1967] 3 All ER 611, 65 LGR 566, CA, where an artist spent his time on unremunerative but satisfying paintings, the opinion was expressed that compensation should be assessed on the basis of what he could have earned with commercially saleable work.

LOSS OF EARNINGS AND THE SELF-EMPLOYED

Problems of the self-employed claimant

10.68 Whilst an employed claimant can point to wage slips and an employment record in support of a claim for loss of earnings, a self-employed person has more difficulty. The claimant may consider it obvious that they have lost earnings but find it difficult to show why or to quantify the loss.

Loss of profits

10.69 The loss of profits of a business are generally recoverable as damages by the injured entrepreneur. The legal basis of the way in which the loss is assessed is, in theory, relatively straightforward and is summarised by Forbes J in *Bellingham v Dhillon* [1973] QB 304, [1973] 1 All ER 20, QBD:

> 'Where a plaintiff's claim for damages was based on loss of profits of his business the damages were to be calculated in the same way whether the claim was in contract or in tort, i.e. by taking the profits which the business would have earned but for the wrong the plaintiff had suffered at the hands of the defendant and subtracting from that figure the profits which had in fact been earned after the wrong had been suffered.'

When the injured person is part of a partnership

10.70   These losses are recoverable even if the claimant is a member of a partnership. In such a situation the claim should normally be for the diminution in the claimant's share of the partnerships profits: see *Vaughan v Greater Glasgow Passenger Transport Executive* 1984 SC 32, 1984 SLT 44, Ct of Sess.

Limited companies

10.71   If the claimant carries on business through the medium of a limited company it is still possible for him to recover any loss of profits of the company even though, technically, the loss is the company's and not his own. In *Lee v Sheard* [1956] 1 QB 192, [1955] 3 All ER 777, CA the Court of Appeal gave short shrift to the argument that the separate legal personality of the company means that the injured businessman should not recover personally. The court said that in those cases where a director is effectively the proprietor of a small company the loss is not too remote and is recoverable. This is an interesting example of a case in which the courts are willing to 'lift the veil' in company law and provides an exception to the general rule in *Saloman v A Saloman & Co Ltd* [1897] AC 22, 66 LJ Ch 35, HL. However, this exception has only been held to apply to small companies where the proprietor is virtually a 'one-man band'. There are no clear principles in the cases as to the size a company will need to be before the courts refuse to consider a claim for loss of profit, but it is unlikely that the courts will consider such claims for anything more than one-man companies. Indeed the effect on insurance premiums could be dramatic if defendants had to underwrite the losses of large PLCs, and the losses in these cases would probably be held to be too remote. In any event the problem of proving that the injury was the cause of the loss would be enormous.

The black economy

10.72   If any work is being carried out 'on the side' and neither VAT nor tax is being paid the profits from this are still recoverable if the work is lost as a result of the accident. In these circumstances the court will deduct the tax and VAT that should have been paid in assessing the loss: *Duller v South East Lincs Engineers* [1981] CLY 585. In this case, the source of the earnings was legal and only the failure to declare them was illegal. This approach was followed in *Newman v Folkes* [2002] EWCA Civ 591, [2002] All ER (D) 47 (May): what Garland J referred to as 'collateral illegality' does not bar a claimant who has failed to pay income tax and National Insurance contributions from recovering loss of earnings.

Loss of a prospective business venture

10.73   If the claimant has lost the chance of participating in a business venture, the loss of this chance can be compensated. Any award under this head will undoubtedly be speculative. In *Mulvaine v Joseph* (1968) 112 Sol Jo 927 a golfer who was injured and lost the chance of completing a tournament was awarded damages as a percentage of his chances of winning the contest. The loss of opportunity, however, must not be too remote and must be proven by evidence: *Domsella v Barr (trading as AB Construction)* [1969] 3 All ER 487, [1969] 1 WLR 630, CA. (See the section on loss of chance at para 10.48ff above.)

Mitigation of loss

10.74   In *Bellingham v Dhillon* [1973] QB 304, [1973] 1 All ER 20, QBD Forbes J went on to say that in making the calculation for loss of profits '... the court has to take into account any steps which the plaintiff, as a reasonable and prudent man of business, had taken to mitigate his loss'. These issues have been considered in detail at para 4.5ff above but particular care must be taken in relation to self-employed claimants where allegations of failure to mitigate loss can be difficult to counter. The claimant should take care to ensure that the financial losses suffered as a result of the accident are minimised so far as reasonably possible. Could a locum be called in to run the business? Or could any work be done from home?

Pleading the loss

10.75   Although there is no case on the subject after the Civil Procedure Rules 1998, SI 1998/3132 it is prudent to ensure that special circumstances of the claimant's case is set out in the particulars of claim. Failure to mention circumstances such as loss of profits or loss of a business opportunity will lead to the loss not being allowed at trial: *Domsella v Barr (trading as AB Construction)* [1969] 3 All ER 487, [1969] 1WLR 630, CA; see also *Perestrello e Companhia Ltda v United Paint Co Ltd* [1969] 3 All ER 479, [1969] 1 WLR 570, CA.

Proving the loss

10.76   The need to prove the loss is emphasised in the case of *Bonham Carter v Hyde Park Hotel Ltd* [1948] WN 89, 92 Sol Jo 154, KBD:

'Plaintiffs must understand that if they bring actions for damages it is for them to prove their damage, it is not enough to write down the particulars, and, so to speak, throw themselves at the head of the court saying "This is what I have lost. I ask you to give me these damages". They have to prove it.'

10.77   This requirement to prove that a loss has occurred will present the claimant with the most problems. The onus is on the claimant to prove every item of loss claimed that is not agreed. Proving loss of profits, or potential profits, is extremely difficult in a lot of businesses. If an extra employee has been taken on to cover the absent claimant then the calculation is relatively simple; the losses caused because of absence from work, inability to supervise staff, meet business contacts etc is more problematic.

10.78   When trying to establish a loss of profits in a situation that is not straightforward the best advice that can be given is to retain an accountant who specialises in litigation support for accident victims. Many of the major accountancy practices now have specialist departments which are willing to work with lawyers and the client's usual accountants to assess the losses and give expert evidence in court. It is of great benefit to a claimant and to a defendant to have independent expertise to assist in the quantification of loss and to give evidence in court if the case is not settled. It may be desirable to consider the instruction of the accountant on a joint basis.

What the claimant has to show

10.79   The claimant has to show:
(1)   the profitability of the business did decrease, or failed to increase; and
(2)   such decrease or failure to increase was due to the claimant's impaired efficiency.

Incomplete accounts

10.80   In the case of *Ashcroft v Curtin* [1971] 3 All ER 1208 at 1213, [1971] 1 WLR 1731 at 1737, CA the Court of Appeal considered the case of a limited company whose potential profitability had decreased because of the injury of its 'proprietor'. The court was sympathetic to the plaintiff's plight, and Edmund Davies LJ said:

> 'In a one-man company of this kind, with an actively working managing director of undoubted efficiency, there is a high probability that injuries such as he sustained would not only drastically interfere with the quality of his life but would also have a damaging effect on the business which he created and still controlled.'

10.81   Unfortunately the plaintiff in *Ashcroft v Curtin* [1971] 3 All ER 1208, [1971] 1 WLR 1731, CA had not been diligent in keeping his accounts prior to the accident. Whilst there was no allegation of any wrongdoing, because of the vagueness of the accounts it was impossible for any accountant to calculate the loss suffered. As a result, even though the court conceded some loss must have occurred, no award was made for loss of profit.

10.82   If there are problems with the accounts in an accident claim it may be possible to employ an accountant to update the accounts. The costs of this will have to be borne by the claimant and therefore it is advisable to retain a separate accountant to the 'forensic' accountants used to quantify the loss since the costs of retaining the expert are likely to be recoverable.

Loss of future earning capacity in a self-employed person

10.83   In *Ashcroft v Curtin* [1971] 3 All ER 1208, [1971] 1 WLR 1731, CA the court, after deciding it could not award damages for loss of profit, did award damages for the plaintiff's 'increased vulnerability in the labour market'. The *Smith v Manchester*[1] award can be of great significance in those cases where loss of profit or loss of chance of a business opportunity cannot be proven to the satisfaction of the court. The self-employed are particularly vulnerable in the labour market and the possibility of the *Smith v Manchester* award should be thoroughly considered since in some cases, as we have seen, this could be the only amount a claimant will receive for their economic loss.

1   *Smith v Manchester City Council (or Manchester Corpn)* (1974) 118 Sol Jo 597, 17 KIR 1, CA.

There must be a loss

10.84   In *Bellingham v Dhillon* [1973] QB 304, [1973] 1 All ER 20, QBD, the plaintiff was the owner and manager of a driving school (in fact the school was a limited company in which he owned 500 out of 501 shares). He was negotiating the purchase of a driving simulator but the contract fell through because of his injuries. The price of the simulator in 1967 was to be £7,000 but the plaintiff purchased a second-hand simulator in 1971 for £2,160. He attempted to claim for loss of profit to the company of £4,816 – the loss of profit which he would have earned if the simulator had been purchased in 1967. The court held that in fact he had suffered no loss on this particular venture and the alleged 'loss of profit' could not be recovered.

CHAPTER 11

Claims for care and nursing expenses

THE GROWING IMPORTANCE OF CARE CLAIMS

11.1 Claims for future care and nursing expenses are often the major element of a claim in 'catastrophic injury' cases. In cases of severe injury, professional help is required. However, the reality of the situation in most cases is that care, particularly past care, is not provided professionally. This was recognised by the Law Commission in *Damages for Personal Injury: Medical, Nursing and Other Expenses; Collateral Benefits* (Law Com no 262) para 2.15:

> 'Our empirical research has shown that the majority of personal injury claimants rely on care provided gratuitously by family members and friends. Often simple daily tasks such as bathing, eating and dressing can no longer be performed without assistance. With a modest percentage of injured claimants receiving skilled nursing care, the burden of providing such care has fallen on unpaid individuals, usually members of the claimant's close family.'

11.2 Claims for care can form the major part of a claim in major cases. However, this head of damages has considerable relevance in more modest cases. The reality is that 'care' claims began with substantial cases of serious injury, but are now made in less serious cases, indeed in cases of relatively minor injury. In both cases the court still has to address two central issues:

(1) What is 'care'?
(2) How should the claim for 'care' be quantified?

WHAT IS 'CARE'?

11.3 'Care' is often unaddressed. However, it is a crucial issue, and it is necessary to:

(1) Distinguish care from the loss of ability to do work in the home: see *Daly v General Steam Navigation Co Ltd, The Dragon* [1980] 3 All ER 696, [1981] 1 WLR 120, CA and paras 11.45–11.49 below.
(2) Distinguish care from the help and assistance that the claimant would normally receive from family members. It is only the *additional* element of care that is recoverable.

The issue of precisely what elements of the claimant's help consists of 'care' is not dealt with in detail in the Law Commission report (Law Com no 262).

THE VAGUE DEFINITION OF CARE

11.4   The failure by the courts to identify what 'care' is and how it is to be quantified gives rise to serious practical problems. First, it is not totally clear what 'care' a seriously injured person is entitled to. Is the care to be the most basic possible so as to keep the claimant alive? Alternatively, is the claimant entitled to an expensive care regime to give him the highest quality of life possible? Secondly, when it is relatives who are providing the care there can be difficulties in drawing the line between what is 'care' of a type that should be compensated and what is not.

AN ISSUE OF FACT?

11.5   It can be said that the extent of nursing care is an issue of fact. In *Hunt v Severs* [1994] 2 AC 350, [1994] 2 All ER 385, HL Lord Bridge described the entitlement as:

'... the reasonable value of services rendered to him gratuitously by a relative or friend in the provision of nursing care or domestic assistance of the kind rendered necessary by the injuries the plaintiff has suffered.'

ISSUES THAT ASSIST IN DEFINING AND QUANTIFYING 'CARE'

11.6   The following principles are clear:
(1) The burden is on the claimant to establish the need for care and the extent of the care needed.
(2) 'A claimant is entitled to recover any medical and nursing expenses, and any other costs of care that have reasonably been incurred or will reasonably be incurred as a result of injuries arising from at tort': Law Com no 262, para 2.1.

(3) 'Recovery can be made only in respect of those expenses that are reasonable': Law Com no 262, para 2.2. If a claimant has chosen private care by a particular provider which is more expensive than is available elsewhere within the private sector, the expense may be unreasonable even though the treatment itself may be reasonable. The claimant will bear the burden of proving the more expensive treatment was reasonable.

(4) The care claim is not to be limited by subjective financial criteria. In *Rialas v Mitchell* (1984) 128 Sol Jo 704, (1984) Times, 17 July, CA (Kemp & Kemp A2-011) the Court of Appeal considered a submission that the court should introduce into care claims a 'test for the reasonableness of any proposed provisions, a requirement that they ought not to exceed what a person of average wealth would provide for himself or his child'. The court rejected this proposition and the suggestion that *Cunningham v Harrison* [1973] QB 942, [1973] 3 All ER 463, CA could be regarded as authority for such a proposition. It was held (at 705) that 'the claimant was entitled to what was reasonably necessary to alleviate his injury and diminish his disability, though not to the best possible facilities'. The Court of Appeal rejected an argument that it was unreasonable for the claimant to be cared for at home when private provision could be provided at a cheaper cost. The starting point was that a normal child would live with his parents. 'There might be cases where it would be right to conclude that it was unreasonable for a claimant to insist on being cared for at home, but the present case was not one. Once it had been concluded that it was reasonable for the claimant to remain at home, as the judge had found, his Lordship could find no acceptable ground for saying that the defendant should not paying the reasonable costs of caring for him there' (at 705).

It was held that where the cost of caring for the claimant at home was substantially greater than the cost of caring for him in an institution, the burden of proving that it was reasonable for him to be cared was on the claimant.

It is questionable whether this decision survives the Human Rights Act 1998; in particular Sch 1, art 8 – the right to respect for private and family life – means that it may be difficult to argue that someone has to be cared for in an institution.

QUANTIFYING CARE

11.7 The first stage in quantifying the care claim is to assess what care has actually been given in terms of hours spent. Similarly if there is a claim for future care, then the requirement for future care has to be quantified in terms of the extent of care required on an hourly basis. If the care was provided on a commercial basis, the cost is simple to quantify, but still has to be justified. If the care was provided on a gratuitous basis, then credit has to be given for the fact that the carer is not subject to tax or National Insurance: see para 11.15–11.25 below.

COMMERCIAL CARE

No duty to use the National Health Service

11.8   All the costs of medical treatment, travel to treatment and private care are recoverable providing they are 'reasonable'. The claimant is under no duty to use the National Health Service. The Law Reform (Personal Injuries) Act 1948, s 2(4) states:

> 'in an action for damages for personal injuries ... there shall be disregarded, in determining the reasonableness of any expenses, the possibility of avoiding those expenses or part of them by taking advantage of facilities under the National Health Service.'

11.9   The Law Commission found that only a very small percentage of claimants used private care: Law Com no 262, para 2.4.

No damages if the National Health Service is likely to be used

11.10   Damages will not, however, be awarded if it is unlikely that the costs will be incurred: *Harris v Bright's Asphalt Contractors Ltd* [1953] 1 QB 617, [1953] 1 All ER 395, QBD. The Law Reform (Personal Injuries) Act 1948, s 2(4) means that the defendant cannot argue that the claimant *should* have used the National Health Service; however, the defendant *can* argue that the claimant is unlikely to incur the expenses. In *Woodrup v Nicol* [1993] PIQR Q104 at Q114, CA Russell LJ stated:

> '... if, on the balance of probabilities, a plaintiff is going to use private medicine in the future as a matter of choice, the defendant cannot contend that the claim should be disallowed because National Health Services are available. On the other hand, if, on the balance of probabilities, private facilities are not going to be used, for whatever reason, the plaintiff is not entitled to claim for an expense which he is not going to incur. That view, in my judgment, is amply borne out by authority.'

11.11 In *Woodrup v Nicol* [1993] PIQR Q104, CA it was held, on the balance or probabilities, that one half of the physiotherapy costs would be obtained privately and the other half from the National Health Service. The plaintiff was entitled to half the physiotherapy costs claimed.

CARE PROVIDED BY FAMILY MEMBERS OR FRIENDS

The basis of the claim

11.12 The vast majority of claimants rely on care provided gratuitously by family members and friends: Law Commission no 262, para 2.15. For a period there was some confusion as to the legal basis upon which a claim was made. The position was settled by the House of Lords in *Hunt v Severs* [1994] 2 AC 350, [1994] 2 All ER 385, HL where it was held that the plaintiff is entitled to claim damages for the cost of care provided gratuitously by friends or relatives. However, the loss was the carer's and not the claimants and the sums recovered were held on trust for the carer.

No claim where the defendant is the carer

11.13 A consequence of the *Hunt v Severs* [1994] 2 AC 350, [1994] 2 All ER 385, HL decision is that where the defendant is the provider of the gratuitous care (as was the case in *Hunt*) damages for the care provided cannot be recovered. The court recognised that, in reality, an insurer was paying the damages. However, the common law ignored the existence of insurance when considering the question of liability. This approach has been criticised by the Law Commission: Law Com no 262, para 3.76. This is an issue that practitioners must consider at the outset. In cases (usually road traffic cases) where the defendant is also the carer it would be prudent to consider the position with the claimant and the carer. It may be appropriate to bring commercial care in at an early date (there is no obligation on the claimant to use the defendant or the defendant to do the work) or seek assistance from other relatives. In *McGreggor on Damages* (16th edn, 1997) p 1683 it is suggested that it would be professional negligence for a claimant's solicitor not to advise on these options and the further option of the parties entering into a formal contract in relation to the provision of the claim.

QUANTIFICATION OF THE CLAIM

11.14   The courts have tended to base awards for commercial care based on the commercial rate discounted by between one-third and one-quarter: *Housecroft v Burnett* [1986] 1 All ER 332, CA. An alternative approach is a claim based on the loss of earnings of the carer: *Woodrup v Nichol* [1993] PIQR Q104, CA. In a case where the claimant's wife was a nurse and provided the work of two full-time carers the court awarded one-and-a-half times the commercial rate: *Hogg v Doyle* (Kemp & Kemp A2-005).

THERE IS NO SET DEDUCTION: THE DECISION IN *EVANS V PONTYPRIDD ROOFING*

11.15   The Court of Appeal decision in *Evans v Pontypridd Roofing Ltd* [2001] EWCA Civ 1657, [2001] All ER (D) 13 (Nov) is a case that merits a detailed review. This case gave the Court of Appeal an opportunity to review the principles relating to the provision of care by relatives.

The facts

11.16   Mr Evans was a 34-year-old man who had been seriously injured in the course of his employment in January 1995. Liability had been agreed at 85%. The injuries were severe, and any movement caused pain. The more he moved the greater the pain. An award of £100,000 for general damages was not subject to an appeal by the defendant. However, the defendant did appeal against several items of damages: in particular, an award of £80,532.32 plus interest for past care and £378,840 for future care.

The judge's award for care

11.17   The judge awarded damages based on home-carer rates at 30 hours a week to 5 August 1995, and from 6 August 1995 to the date of trial on residential rates for full-time care. The total was £107,390.27, which the judge then reduced by 25% to take account that the claimant was looked after gratuitously by his wife.

11.18   For future care the judge carried forward the finding that the claimant would require care 24 hours a day and that the care would be provided by his wife. He built in this figure a figure for respite care for Mrs Evans, allowing her eight weeks of respite care a year: £420.00 a

week for eight weeks. For the remaining ten months he took the figure of
£60.00 per day for full-time care and applied the same discount of 25%.

The defendant's challenge to the care figures

11.19   The defendant contended that the assessment based on 24-hour
care were grossly excessive. Further it was contended that the discount of
25% was too low it should have been 33.33%. Lord Justice May considered
the history of claims for gratuitous care in detail, examining *Housecroft v
Burnett* [1986] 1 All ER 332, CA; *Donnelly v Joyce* [1974] QB 454,
[1973] 3 All ER 475, CA; and *Hunt v Severs* [1994] 2 AC 350, [1994] 2
All ER 385, HL. He summarised the court's task as an amount 'to enable
the voluntary carer to receive recompense for his or her services' (*Hunt v
Severs*), and observed at [25]:

> 'In my judgment, this court should avoid putting first instance judges
> into too restrictive a strait-jacket, such as might happen if it was
> said that the means of assessing a proper recompense for services
> provided gratuitously by a family carer had to be assessed in a
> particular way or ways. Circumstances vary enormously and what
> is appropriate and in just in one case many not be so in another. If a
> caring relation has given up remunerative employment to care for
> the claimant gratuitously, it may well be appropriate to assess the
> proper recompense for the services provided by reference to the
> carer's lost earnings. If the carer has not given up gainful
> employment, the task remains to assess proper recompense for the
> services provided. As O' Connor LJ said in *Housecroft v Burnett*,
> regard may be had to what it would cost to provide the services on
> the open market. But the services are not in fact being bought in the
> open market, so that adjustments will probably need to be made.
> Since, however, any such adjustments are not more than an element
> in a single assessment, it would not in my view by appropriate to
> bind first instance judges to a conventional formalised calculation.
> The assessment is of an amount as a whole. The means of reaching
> the assessment must depend on what is appropriate to the individual
> case. If it is appropriate, as I think it is in the present case, to have
> regard to what it would cost to buy the services which Mrs. Evans
> provides in the open market, it may well also be appropriate to scale
> them down. But I do not think that this can be done by means of a
> conventional percentage, since the appropriate extent of the scaling
> down and the reasons for it may vary from case to case.'

11.20   The defendant argued that it was wrong to take the entire estimated period of time spent with Mr Evans as care, since some time would be spent talking or visiting. May LJ observed in *Evans v Pontypridd Roofing Ltd* [2001] EWCA Civ 1657 at [23], [2002] PIQR Q5 at Q69:

> 'Any determination of the services for which the court has to assess proper recompense will obviously depend on the circumstances of each case. There will be many cases in which the care services provided will be limited to a few hours each day. The services should not exceed those which are properly determined to be care services consequent upon the claimant's injuries, but they do not, in my view, have to be limited in every case to a stop-watch calculation of actual nursing or physical assistance. Nor ... must they be limited in every case to care which is the subject of medical prescription. Persons, who need physical assistance for everything they do, do not literally receive that assistance during every minute of the day. But their condition may be so severe that the presence of a full time carer really is necessary to provide whatever assistance is necessary at whatever time unpredictably it is required. It is obviously necessary for judges to ensure that awards on this basis are properly justified on the facts, and not to be misled into findings that a gratuitous carer is undertaking full time care simply because they are for other reasons there all or most of the time.'

The 25% deduction

11.21   The court found that the 24-hour care was justified in Mr Evans' case. So far as the argument that a one-third deduction should be made from commercial rates May LJ observed that there was no 'scientific' basis for a strictly mathematical answer to the question. The assessment had to be a broad one, what was required was a single broad assessment to achieve a fair result in the particular case. Whilst a conventional discount would be convenient it could also be unfair and first instance judges must have latitude to achieve a fair result.

Factors which could affect the deduction

11.22   Tax and National Insurance inevitably play a part in assessing a discount. However, other factors could be considered. One possibility is that it could be necessary for the assessment of future care to take into account, bearing in mind the possibility that the services of the gratuitous carer may not be available for the entire period upon which the assessment is based.

11.23 The court was far from persuaded that any alteration should be made to the 25% discount on commercial figures.

Respite care

11.24 The defendant appealed the element of the award that covered respite care on the grounds that Mrs Evans was quite determined that she, and no one else, would care for her husband. The Court of Appeal concluded that the evidence supported the judge's view that Mrs Evans simply could not continue without respite during the many years which were the subject of his assessment.

No definitive guidance as to deduction from commercial approach

11.25 It can be seen that the Court of Appeal was anxious *not* to give definitive guidance on the issue of the appropriate sums for gratuitous care. However, the basis legal principles were reiterated – the court's task is to properly compensate the carer for the work done.

THE LAW COMMISSION APPROACH

11.26 In *Damages for Personal Injury: Medical, Nursing and Other Expenses; Collateral Benefits* (Law Com no 262) the Law Commission considered the issue of gratuitous care in some detail. It recommended that damages should continue to be awarded in respect of care reasonably provided, or to be provided, gratuitously to the claimant by relatives and friends. The claimant should be under a personal legal obligation to account for damages for *past* care to a relative or friend who has provided the gratuitous care, but there should be no legal duty on the claimant to pay over the damages recovered in respect of *future* gratuitous care.

The assessment of the 'deduction' from commercial costs

11.27 In the consultation paper the Law Commission described the test for quantification of gratuitous care as 'inescapably imprecise', but did not recommend statutory intervention. In the final paper, however, the Law Commission commented on the effect of *Hunt v Severs* [1994] 2 AC 350, [1994] 2 All ER 385, HL which stated that it was the carer rather than the victim that was being compensated. It cited the Pearson Commission's criticism that basing the award on the market value of the services rendered is harsh on those who give up a highly paid job to nurse an injured relative.

11.28   The discussion by the Law Commission included criticism of the reluctance of judges and lawyers to move from the one-third deduction for tax and National Insurance when, in recent years, commercial carers would have to pay a lower sum. (In *Evans v Pontypridd Roofing Ltd* [2001] EWCA Civ 1657, [2002] PIQR Q5 at Q73 at [38] this was recognised as being 25% of gross earnings.)

11.29   Further it was pointed out that while gratuitous carers were spared the expense of tax and National Insurance they did not have the benefits of paid employment, such as paid holiday or state pension contributions.

11.30   The Law Commission stated that the commercial rate provided a good starting point for the assessment of damages for commercial care but *only* where the carer was not earning wages. It stated that the discount of one-third from that rate is too high in current economic conditions. However:
(1)   Given that the purpose of compensation is to compensate the carer then, if it was reasonable for the carer to give up paid employment, the starting point should be the carer's lost earnings and the full commercial rate should not be seen as an effective ceiling to the award.
(2)   In assessing the reasonableness of a claim in such circumstances the courts should particularly consider whether care by that particular person is of special comfort and help to the claimant.
(3)   With respect to future care the award of damages should take account of the chance that the gratuitous care will cease so that the claimant will be required to pay the full commercial rate for care.
(4)   Here, however, the Law Commission did not feel that statutory intervention would assist. It should be left to the judges to work out:
'While a statutory provision might provide greater certainty, we feel it would be insufficiently flexible to deal with the variety of different situations which may arise in practice.'

11.31   The final conclusion of the Law Commission on this issue was that the law in relation to claims for gratuitous care should not be reformed by statute. It was recommended that the courts be more willing to award damages to compensate carers for their loss of earnings, even where these exceed the commercial cost of care.

There is no automatic deduction for gratuitous care

11.32 Just as there is no automatic 'set' percentage reduction for gratuitous care there is no rule of law that there *must* be a deduction at all. In *Newman v Marshall Folkes* [2002] EWCA Civ 591. [2002] All ER (D) 47 (May) the Court of Appeal refused the defendant's appeal in a case where the judge had given *no* discount from commercial rates, even though the care provided by the claimant's wife was being provided gratuitously. The claimant had become an obsessive who demanded attention day and night. Ward LJ observed that it would be difficult to provide the care required from professional carers. The decision was for the judge to make; at [38] he observed:

'It was overall an assessment to be made in the round as much as by feel as by mathematical calculation ... There is ... no conventional discount. Each case depends on its own facts. In this case there was such a broad margin of matters to take into account that the matter had to be looked at in the round. That is what the judge did, I can see no error of principle ...'

11.33 In less severe cases some judges have awarded full 'standard' rates on the basis that the claimant taking the usual workday hourly rate fails to take into account the fact that much higher rates are charged for antisocial hours. That is, work done outside normal hours, evening and weekend shifts etc.

PRACTICAL GUIDANCE ON GRATUITOUS CARE CLAIMS

11.34 Although the Law Commission report[1] was not referred to in *Evans v Pontypridd Roofing Ltd* [2001] EWCA Civ 1657, [2001] All ER (D) 131 (Nov), it does come to remarkably similar conclusions. In essence each case is up to the judge; there are no golden rules. However, there are number of practical steps that can be taken:

(1) *Advise the client on the choice of carer at the outset.*

In many cases this will not be realistic as there is, in effect, only one potential carer. However, issues such as loss of earnings and long-term ability to care have to be considered as early as possible.

(2) *Do not automatically accept a deduction of one-third.*
A deduction is not always justified. Although there are no definitive guidelines, modern practice, and the Law Commission recommendation, indicate a lower reduction of 25%.

(3) *Remember respite care.*
It is highly important, for the carer if no one else, that respite care is built into the claim. Even if this is unattractive to the carer or claimant it may, over time, become essential.

(4) *Look at the commercial rates carefully.*
Many claimants adopt a broad-brush hourly rate approach. In fact the hourly rates for evenings, weekends and bank holidays are considerably higher. If the commercial rate is the starting point then this should be taken into account.

(5) *Take care in collecting the evidence on this point.*
In extreme cases, such as *Evans*, the facts really stood for themselves. In less extreme cases it is important that the care claim is supported by evidence from the claimant, the carer and the medical evidence. Care claims are often attacked on the basis that they are exaggerated, cover matters which are not really 'care' or do not contain a sufficient deduction for the fact that the care is gratuitous.

(6) *Think of the future.*
The observation that gratuitous care may not go on forever is a salient one. For example, examine the statistics on the breakdown of marriages where one party has suffered brain damage. It may be difficult, if not impossible, to consider this with the client and carer; however, such evidence may assist in persuading the court to award a higher sum or give a reduced discount for gratuitous care.

(7) *Do not look for definitive guidance.*
It is clear that neither the Court of Appeal nor Parliament is going to give any definitive guidance on these issues. They will remain difficult issues. However, a knowledge of the *Evans* judgment, coupled with the Law Commission's views and recommendations, gives considerable assistance to those with the task of collecting and collating the evidence and preparing the case for trial.

1   *Damages for Personal Injury: Medical, Nursing and Other Expenses; Collateral Benefits* (Law Com no 262).

CLAIMS FOR FUTURE CARE: HOW FUTURE NEEDS ARE ASSESSED

11.35   It is difficult to find a definitive legal statement as to how the court should approach the quantification of future care where there is likely to be a mixture of professional and gratuitous care. In most cases the court is called upon to assess what is likely to happen in relation to future care and award damages accordingly. Although there is no duty on a gratuitous carer to continue caring, some guidance can be found in the case of *R (on the application of DB) v Criminal Injuries Compensation Appeal Panel* [2002] EWHC 698 (Admin), a case where Mr Justice Stanley Burton was considering a judicial review of a decision of the Criminal Injuries Panel. The panel had awarded £1,141.582. The claim for future care had been put at £1,500,000 but the panel awarded only £425,000. The reduction was made because the panel felt that they thought that gratuitous care would continue for some considerable time whereas the applicant's case had been put on the basis that full-time commercial care (costing £98,578 per year) would start almost immediately.

11.36   The court rejected an argument that the principles in *Daly v General Steam Navigation Co Ltd, The Dragon* [1980] 3 All ER 696, [1981] 1 WLR 120, CA (see paras 11.45-11.47 below) applied and that the common law rule was that a claimant was entitled to the cost of commercial care irrespective of whether the care package that had been costed was in fact implemented. The court considered earlier cases on the subject: the Court of Appeal's decision in *Havenhand v Jeffrey* (Kemp & Kemp 5-015/1); *Nash v Southmead Health Authority* [1994] 5 Med LR 74, QBD; and *Fairhurst v St Helens and Knowsley Health Authority* [1994] 5 Med LR 422, [1995] PIQR Q1, QBD. The court held that common law damages are assessed on the basis of whether, when and for how long the cost will in fact be incurred.

Dealing with contingencies: the decision in *Willbye v Gibbons*

11.37   In *Willbye v Gibbons* [2003] EWCA Civ 372, 147 Sol Jo LB 388 the Court of Appeal considered an award for future care in the case of a female who had suffered a serious head injury. The claim for future care included increased costs of holidays, having children and the possibility of her living alone in the future if her relationship broke down. Lord Justice Kennedy observed (at [16]) that:

'The day to day care she now receives from her partner and her family she will need for the rest of her life. Everything else, whether it be a need for extra care because she is dealing with children or living alone, or wants to go on holiday and has no one to go with her, is much more problematic, and all that can realistically be done is to increase to some extent the fund available to the appellant to satisfy her need for assistance in the future, recognising the possible ways in which demands may be made upon that fund, but not attempting to evaluate separate heads of potential demand, because if potential demands are separately evaluated it may well turn out that there is duplication, or that substantial awards have been made in respect of contingencies that have never happened.'

11.38   The court set aside awards of £45,000 for child care and £60,000 for the possibility of the claimant living alone, but increased the award for future care from £136,932 to £181,129.60.

11.39   Lord Justice Scott Baker observed at [20]:[1]

'On the question of future care, this is a compendious term that covers the various aspects of assistance that the appellant may need in the years ahead. Her future is full of uncertainties and the nature and extent of the assistance she will require depends on many factors, not least whether she continues to have a partner, whether and at what age she has children and if she does, how many. To split up the award into separate elements, as the judge did, is in my view to clothe the future with a greater degree of certainty that the circumstances warrant. There are likely to be periods in her life when, for one reason or another, she will need additional support but it is impossible to predict with any precision when these periods will occur or for how long they will last. An award under this head is very much a matter of feel with the judge keying in the various uncertainties about the appellant's future life and using her experience as to the appropriate range for a global award. In my judgment the additional help that the appellant will need if she has children and/or has to live alone are matters that ought to be taken into account, but in the award for care and assistance as a whole rather than as discrete heads of damage.'

1   *Willbye v Gibbons* [2003] EWCA Civ 372.

11.40   It can be seen, therefore, that in cases where there are potential future care needs, these are taken into account in a general rather than a specific manner.

THE CLAIMANT'S REMEDY: PUT THE CARE REGIME IN PLACE PRIOR TO TRIAL

11.41   Given that the burden is on the claimant to establish when, and if, commercial care will be put in place, there are a number of steps a claimant can take:

(1) *Use interim payments to put a commercial regime in place.*
It is difficult for a court to argue that the care regime is unlikely to be put in place.

(2) *Obtain detailed evidence in relation to the health of the carers and their future plans.*
If the carers do not plan to continue caring, or want to return to the role of relative rather than carer, this must be set out in clear and explicit terms in their evidence. If they cannot continue caring for medical reasons it would be prudent to obtain medical evidence supporting this.

CLAIMS IN MINOR AND NON-SEVERE CASES

11.42   As mentioned above, care claims have trickled down from major claims to claims of lesser severity. It is sometimes asserted that, in less serious claims, damages for care cannot be recovered. This assertion is made on the basis of the Court of Appeal in *Mills v British Rail Engineering Ltd* [1992] PIQR Q130, CA. That case related to care given by a wife to a dying husband. The Court of Appeal rejected the argument that care should only be awarded for 'full time care of a nursing nature'. Dillon LJ stated (at Q137):

'To my mind there can be no justification in principle for differentiating between full time care needing really a trained nurse and full-time care needing a carer giving love and affection to the dying patient, the dying person, to a degree far more than would be expected in any ordinary way of life. In principle it must be, in my judgment, a matter for an award only in recompense for care by the relative well beyond the ordinary call of duty for the special needs of the sufferer.'

He continued:

'So it must indeed only be in a very serious case that an award is justified – where, as here, there is no question of the carer having lost wages of her or his own to look after the patient.'

11.43 This is often held up as meaning that care awards can only be made in serious cases. This is clearly a misnomer:

(1) The decision states that the type of care of a type similar to that which would be provided by a nurse *is* recoverable.

(2) The decision is based on an old view of the legal basis on which care awards are made. In 1992, when *Mills v British Rail Engineering Ltd* [1992] PIQR Q130, CA was decided, there was no clear legal basis on which care damages were awarded. The accepted principle at that time was as set out in *Housecroft v Burnett* [1986] 1 All ER 332, CA that 'the court will make an award to enable the sufferer or his estate to make reasonable recompense to the relative who has cared so devotedly': [1992] PIQR Q130 at Q137. However, this principle of the legal enforcement of a moral obligation was rejected in *Hunt v Severs* [1994] 2 AC 350, [1994] 2 All ER 385, HL. In *Hunt* the House of Lords said that this principle diverted the court from the award's central objective of compensating the voluntary carer. If the care was provided then the plaintiff has a duty to claim the cost on behalf of the carer. There is nothing in *Hunt* that states that this principle is confined to large cases.

(3) Apart from *Mills* (which relates only to the care provided by a wife to a dying husband) there is little authority for the proposition that care claims are confined to major cases. It is not a matter, for instance, mentioned in the Law Commission report (Law Com no 262), nor does it play any part in the *Hunt* decision.

(4) In *Giambrone v Sunworld Holidays* [2004] EWCA Civ 158 the Court of Appeal roundly rejected the argument that *Mills v British Rail Engineering* [1992] 1 PIQR Q130 was authority for the proposition that gratuitous care was only available in serious cases. Brooke LJ, clearly stated that *Mills* was not binding authority on this point. This was a case involving the care costs of parents caring for children who had gastro-enteritis. The court held, at para 33, that the judge's award of £50.00 a week was reasonable balance 'between the consideration that some payment ought to be made for the unpleasant additional burden placed on the family carer and the consideration that care is being rendered in a family context and that the remuneration on this account should be relatively modest'.

11.44 There is usually a need for care in small and medium-sized cases. Sometimes immediately after the accident: sometimes for several months, possibly years, afterwards. However, it is probable that the major problem in this area comes from the failure to distinguish between 'care' and 'household' assistance. As we shall see, this distinction is an important one.

CLAIMS FOR HOUSEHOLD ASSISTANCE

11.45 Whilst claims for past *care* provided gratuitously are recoverable, claims for past *household assistance* are *not*. The position is summarised succinctly in the Law Commission report:[1]

'The loss of ability to do work in the home is a recoverable head of damages and includes "services" such as general housekeeping, gardening and maintenance. The leading case of *Daly v General Steam Navigation Co Ltd.* [1981] 1 WLR 120, while recognising that such loss can be recovered, differentiated between past and future loss. As regards future loss, once the claimant establishes that his or her ability to do work has been impaired, damages are treated as a future pecuniary loss based upon the cost of hiring commercial services, regardless of whether or not the claimant intends to engage them. The position for past loss is different. It will only be treated as a pecuniary loss if the claimant actually engaged commercial services, or if the person giving the services had to give up paid employment to provide them ... It was further held by the Court of Appeal in *Daly v General Steam Navigation Co Ltd.* that, where the past loss did not amount to a pecuniary loss, the claimant's inability to do work in the home should be considered as part of the award for non pecuniary loss. This would arise where the claimant did not engage professional services or receive the assistance of a friend, but instead chose to struggle on with the work.'

1   *Damages for Personal Injury: Medical, Nursing and Other Expenses; Collateral Benefits* (Law Com no 262) para 2.62.

11.46   In *Daly v General Steam Navigation Co Ltd, The Dragon* [1980] 3 All ER 696, [1981] 1 WLR 120, CA itself the Court of Appeal disallowed the claim for past household assistance, but added that figure to the claim for general damages for pain and suffering. It is, therefore, an important factor. It is prudent for the claimant to calculate this on an hourly/gratuitous care basis to assist the court in the quantification of general damages.

THE IMPORTANCE OF THE *DALY* PRINCIPLE

11.47   There is no doubt that the *Daly v General Steam Navigation Co Ltd, The Dragon* [1980] 3 All ER 696, [1981] 1 WLR 120, CA principles are often overlooked in practice. Many past 'care' claims are, when examined, a claim for loss of housekeeping ability – the 'carer' has been doing household tasks that the claimant would normally have done. Similarly many claims for future care are, partially at least, claims for loss of housekeeping ability. As a result they are not claimable at the full commercial rate without any discount and regardless of whether or not the services are to be hired or not.

11.48   Many practitioners can point to cases where claims for past loss of household services have been agreed by the defendant or awarded by the court. It is probable that, in all of these cases, *Daly v General Steam Navigation Co Ltd, The Dragon* [1980] 3 All ER 696, [1981] 1 WLR 120, CA was not cited to the court. In many cases it suits both parties to ignore the principles: the claimant can make a quantified claim for past assistance and the defendant is not called upon to pay future costs on a full commercial basis.

11.49   Nevertheless *Daly v General Steam Navigation Co Ltd, The Dragon* [1980] 3 All ER 696, [1981] 1 WLR 120, CA remains good law. The fact that it remains binding was confirmed by the Court of Appeal in *Lowe v Guise* [2002] EWCA Civ 197, [2002] QB 1369. Practitioners must be aware of its principles and how it can be applied to their client's benefit.

CLAIMS DO NOT EXTEND TO ASSISTANCE PROVIDED IN CLAIMANT'S BUSINESS

11.50   The claimant could be providing services to relatives or voluntary organisation. In *Hardwick v Hudson* [1999] 3 All ER 426, [1999] 1 WLR 1770 the Court of Appeal rejected a claim for damages where the claimant's wife had worked increased hours, at a nominal rate to avoid National Insurance being paid, in the claimant's business. The increased hours had been worked because of the claimant's inability to work in the business. The court was very clear in its rejection of the extension of the *Hunt v Severs* [1994] 2 AC 350, [1994] 2 All ER 385, HL principles into claims for business loss. Mr Justice Colman (at 1777) observed that:

> '... the circumstances are so different from the domestic environment that they will normally not give rise to policy considerations similar to whose which apply in that case [*Hunt v Severs*].'

(For further discussion as to loss of earnings of a business see para 10.35–10.48 above.)

A CLAIM CAN BE MADE FOR LOSS OF ABILITY TO ACT AS A CARER

11.51   In *Lowe v Guise* [2002] EWCA Civ 197, [2002] QB 1369 the Court of Appeal found that the claimant was entitled to claim for his loss of ability to look after his disabled brother. Lord Justice Rix observed ([2002] EWCA Civ 197, [2002] QB 1369 at [38]):

'... the disabled brother is part of the household and one whose care had, prior to the accident, been the appellant's prime responsibility. That care was not a mere gratuitous favour bestowed on a third party, but was a responsibility of his own, adopted by him and owed to his brother, but also to his mother with whom he shared the household. When he lost the ability to care for his brother for more than 35 hours per week, he lost something of real value to himself (as well as to his brother) which was his contribution to his family's welfare, and his loss imposed a corresponding obligation on his mother to make good by her own care what he was no longer able to provide. In my judgment the appellant is entitled to claim in respect of the loss of his ability to look after his brother. Since he will maintain his state allowance, he has suffered no loss so far as that allowance is itself concerned. But he has suffered a loss nevertheless because, even though his care was provided gratuitously, it can and ought as matter of policy to be measured in money's worth. To the extent that his mother has by her own additional care mitigated the appellant's loss, it may be that the appellant would hold that recovery in trust for his mother.'

11.52   The court also distinguished the earlier decision of *Swain v London Ambulance Service* [1999] All ER (D) 260, CA where a claim for loss of ability to clean the claimant's wife's car was refused. It was held that the car was used by the wife for her exclusive benefit and at her exclusive cost: it was not a household loss.

CHAPTER 12

Other heads of damages

THE INCREASED SOPHISTICATION OF CLAIMS FOR DAMAGES

12.1   Traditionally the two major heads of damages have been loss of earnings and care. However, the past 20 years, in particular, have seen the development of numerous other heads of damages in relation to losses, aids and appliances. A surprising aspect of these claims is that, on the whole, they have developed without a great deal of judicial comment. They have largely arisen because of the assiduity and imagination of claimant lawyers, rather than because of case law developments. In general the heads of damages developed in major injury cases tend to be taken up and adopted in less serious cases.

12.2   The development of a more sophisticated approach for general damages was recognised by the Court of Appeal in *Heil v Rankin* [2000] PIQR Q187 at Q212, CA:

'... in recent years, as a result of greater sophistication in the production of claims for pecuniary loss, many items which in the past would have been considered to be appropriately regarded as general damages are now compensated for by way of special damages. It may, for example, not be possible for a claimant to go on an ordinary holiday, but possible for the claimant to go on holiday if special arrangements are made. Quite reasonably the costs of those arrangements can be included in the schedule of pecuniary loss. The same is true with regard to the adaptation and improvement of the conditions in which the claimant lives and the help which he receives. These are now routinely made the subject of claims for pecuniary loss when that would not have happened in the past.'

12.3   It is surprisingly rare for many of these items to be disputed at trial, or the subject of reported cases. This reflects the large degree of agreement that there often is in relation to this type of claim.

12.4 In this chapter we look at the manifold heads of damages.

CLOTHING AND ITEMS DAMAGED IN THE ACCIDENT

12.5 These are routinely claimed and should not be overlooked. Given that damages are designed to put the claimant back in the position that they would have been had the accident not occurred the proper measure of damages is the value of the clothing at the time of the accident and not the replacement costs. The claimant may have to prove that the clothing was not repairable.

12.6 An exception is often made for motorcycle helmets where a motorcyclist was involved in an accident. It is accepted that, after an accident, a helmet should not be re-used; few people would buy a second-hand helmet. For these reasons the replacement value of the helmet is often awarded.

AIDS AND APPLIANCES

12.7 A large part of the sophisticated approach is due to the increased recognition of the assistance that aids and appliances can provide an injured claimant. Items such as wheelchairs, hoists, physiotherapy aids, prostheses, orthopaedic beds etc may be justifiable claims. There is, as of yet, no coherent statement from the courts as to the basis upon which damages for aids have been awarded. A useful statement of principle can be found in *Catastrophic Injuries*:[1]

'In every case the issue for determination is whether or not the plaintiff reasonably needs the piece of equipment for the purpose of rehabilitation as a result of the disability and whether the cost of the equipment is reasonable, using the standard of mitigation. When answering the two part question, the court will usually find it persuasive that the injured plaintiff intends to purchase and to use the piece of equipment once compensation funds become available.'

1   Andrews and Lee (Sweet & Maxwell, 1997) para 7.59.

EXAMPLES

12.8 An example of a carefully considered approach can be found in *Willett v North Bedfordshire Health Authority* [1993] CLY 1422, [1993]

PIQR Q166, QBD, where Hobhouse J was considering items of equipment claimed by a severely disabled child. The judge declined to award damages for an electric chair (at Q172):

> 'I do not consider that this is a reasonable expense to include in the damages. He cannot and never will on the evidence be able to make effective use of that piece of equipment, but if for some reason somebody thinks it will be agreeable for him to have it then it is essentially a luxury item and should be met out of his general damages. I do not consider it is necessary or reasonable to incur it and charge it to the defendants.'

12.9   The judge allowed a claim for a small lifting device to aid in bathing and a Parker bath.

QUANTIFICATION OF THE CLAIM FOR EQUIPMENT

12.10   The appropriate approach is to:
(1)   assess the capital cost of the equipment needed;
(2)   assess the annual cost of maintenance;
(3)   assess when the equipment will need to be replaced; and
(4)   apply the appropriate multiplier to items (2) and (3).

12.11   The total claim will comprise of the capital costs and the future costs, calculated as above.

MEDICAL AND HOSPITAL EXPENSES

12.12   The claimant is entitled to recover all expenses reasonably incurred in the treatment of their injuries. This includes fees for medical advice and for surgical operations, the cost of treatment and care in a hospital or nursing home, and the cost of surgical appliances (such as an artificial leg or eye) and of drugs and other prescriptions. Presumably the cost of a holiday for convalescence is also admissible, if the holiday is reasonably taken, on medical advice, as part of the treatment. Fresh air and good food can be curative factors just as much as medicine.

12.13   The expenses of treatment in a nursing home or of convalescence contain an element representing the cost of food. Where the claimant has been in the habit of living in hotels or other residential establishments, a deduction may be made to represent the amount which he would have had to spend on food in any event: *Shearman v Folland* [1950] 2 KB 43, [1950] 1 All ER 976, CA. The court indicated that no deduction would normally be appropriate where the claimant has a home of their own, the expenses of which continue as usual while he is in hospital.

12.14 Where the claimant takes advice in good faith from a reputable medical practitioner, the expense of taking the advice and acting upon it is admissible, notwithstanding that the diagnosis proves to have been mistaken: *Rubens v Walker* 1946 SC 215, Ct of Sess. As Lord Patrick said in that case, it is through the defendant's fault that the claimant has been reduced 'to a state in which the medical diagnosis of his condition is difficult and fraught with error'.

12.15 Provided that liability for medical expenses has been properly incurred, the expenses may be recovered although the claimant has not yet paid the accounts: *Allen v Waters & Co* [1935] 1 KB 200, 32 LGR 428, CA.

12.16 It is usual to allow the reasonable cost of transport to and from the hospital, or other place where medical treatment is given; and the expense of visits by parents or others may be allowed as part of the patient's own needs: *Donnelly v Joyce* [1974] QB 454, [1973] 3 All ER 475, CA.

ACCOMMODATION

Capital costs and alterations

12.17 An allowance may be given for the cost of specially adapting a house to the needs of an invalid, but not for its basic cost: *Moriarty v McCarthy* [1978] 2 All ER 213, [1978] 1 WLR 155, QBD. The claimant can recover all the costs of adaptations including, for example, installing ramps, stair lifts and grab rails, adapting the kitchen, bathroom and lavatories, and resiting electrical and phone sockets. The diminution in the value of the property is also recoverable.

12.18 The approach to capital costs was settled in *Roberts v Johnstone* [1989] QB 878, [1988] 3 WLR 1247, CA, when the Court of Appeal fixed the future annual cost at 2% of the difference between the cost of the new house and the proceeds of the old one, 2% being chosen because a house is resistant to inflation.

12.19 In exceptional circumstances, the court allowed the cost of temporary alterations to the parents' home as well as the adaptation of another house for the claimant, the change of plan being reasonable: *Fitzgerald v Lane* [1987] QB 781, [1987] 2 All ER 455, CA. However, in *Cunningham v Harrison* [1973] QB 942, [1973] 3 All ER 463, CA, where a tetraplegic was particularly difficult to look after and his wife died under the strain, the Court of Appeal held that a claim for a specially constructed bungalow with a housekeeper and two nurses was excessive.

Moving expenses

12.20 Where the claimant has had to move house as a result of his injuries (for example, from a house to a bungalow due to wheelchair use), he can recover the costs associate with moving, such as estate agent and conveyancing fees, stamp duty and removals expenses.

Outgoings and living expenses

12.21 The claimant can recover any additional costs which are attributable to his injuries. For example, wheelchair users may feel the cold more readily, so may incur increased heating costs. Wheelchairs and walking frames also cause more wear and tear to carpets, so the cost of more frequent redecoration is also recoverable. The cost of higher insurance premiums and increased housekeeping costs can also be claimed (see chapter 11 for detail on housekeeping).

TRANSPORT COSTS

12.22 A similar approach is taken to the claimant's need for a specially adapted car: the basic cost will not be awarded, but allowance will be made for the extra cost arising from the need for adaptations, or needing a larger car than would otherwise have been the case. The claimant can recover the cost of travel to and from medical appointments. If he is driven by a relative, friend or neighbour, a claim can also be made to recompense them for their time. Similarly, the additional cost of private transport where the claimant is unable to use public transport (due to his injuries) can be recovered.

COST OF MANAGING DISABLED PERSON'S DAMAGES

12.23 The cost of having a disabled person's damages administered by the Court of Protection will be allowed where necessary: *Rialas v Mitchell*

(1984) 128 Sol Jo 704, (1984) Times, 17 July, CA. In principle this should apply to the costs of a trust if one has to be set up. Other costs associated with managing the claimant's award can also be recovered. As the level of his award will take into account the assumption that it will be invested to provide an income, the cost of taking financial advice to achieve a suitable investment strategy can be claimed. If a receiver is appointed to manage the award (for example, where the claimant is a child), the receiver's fees may be claimed.

12.24　Although not strictly related to managing his award, if the claimant has a case manager to co-ordinate his various therapies, the fees for this service can be recovered.

'EXTRA NOURISHMENT' AND CONVALESCENCE

12.25　'Extra nourishment' is an item which, for many years, was included in the claim for special damages and allowed by the court almost as a matter of common form, but now it has become rare. Authority for the practice, if any is needed, may be found in *Shearman v Folland* [1950] 2 KB 43, [1950] 1 All ER 976, CA.

12.26　If this item is challenged, it must be substantiated by showing that money has been or will be spent on recognised invalid foods or on a special diet prescribed by medical advisers.

WRONGFUL BIRTH

The wrongful birth claim

12.27　Claims for wrongful birth typically arise when a child is born because of failed contraception or failed terminations of pregnancy. The claim is brought by the parents for the losses they sustain.

12.28　The heads of damage which have been held to be recoverable have varied somewhat over the years. It is clear that public policy has played a major part. The law is now clear.

Cost of raising and maintaining the child are generally not recoverable

12.29　This is the head of damage which has caused the most debate. Bringing up a child is expensive and there is an argument that the parents should be able to recover the expense of bringing up a child in these circumstances. For some years there were contradictory decisions, with some cases favouring the view that the parents could recover the costs of bringing up a child, including the cost of private school fees if applicable. However, it is clear that the courts have rejected the old principles. In a recent series of cases the House of Lords have vastly restricted the claims that can be made following an unwanted birth.

12.30   Generally speaking the courts have rejected the claim that giving birth to a child is an injury. The issues have been considered in *McFarlane v Tayside Health Board* [2000] 2 AC 59, [1999] 4 All ER 961, HL; *Parkinson v St James and Seacroft University Hospital NHS Trust* [2001] EWCA Civ 530, [2002] QB 266; and *Rees v Darlington Memorial Hospital NHS Trust* [2003] UKHL 52, [2003] 3 All ER 987.

McFarlane – *the healthy child*

12.31   *McFarlane v Tayside Health Board* [2000] 2 AC 59, [1999] 4 All ER 961, HL concerned the birth of a healthy child to healthy parents after they had been told that the father's sperm counts were negative. The House of Lords rejected the argument that parents could claim for the expense of bringing up a child. This was not a loss. It if was it was outweighed by the joy of having a child. They left open the issue of bringing up a disabled child.

Parkinson – *the disabled child*

12.32   The issue of giving birth to a disabled child was considered in *Parkinson v St James and Seacroft University Hospital NHS Trust* [2001] EWCA Civ 530, [2002] QB 266. The Court of Appeal had to consider many of the same issues in relation to the birth of a disabled child. Whilst the ordinary costs of bringing up the child remained the courts would to allow recovery of the additional costs associated with raising a disabled child.

Rees – *the disabled mother*

12.33   In *Rees v Darlington Memorial Hospital NHS Trust* [2003] UKHL 52, [2003] 3 All ER 987 the child was healthy, but the mother was severely visually handicapped. Indeed this was the very reason she had sought a sterilisation in the first place, as she felt that her disability would make it impossible for her to care for a child. The Court of Appeal drew a distinction between a fully able-bodied parent and a disabled parent. They allowed the claim for the extra costs involved as a result of the mother's disability.

DAMAGES THAT ARE RECOVERABLE

Costs associated with pregnancy and child birth

12.34 Some costs associated with childbirth and the immediate arrival of the baby are recoverable. This includes the cost of the layette and other baby paraphernalia (such as high chair, car seat and push chair) and any loss of earnings suffered by the mother as a result of her pregnancy. The rationale for the cost of the layette is that when a family is not expecting a new child they often get rid of baby equipment that, otherwise, would have been saved and used for the next child. However, the House of Lords overturned the Court of Appeal on this issue. It was held that the claimant was not able to recover the extra cost of raising a child due to her disability. The mother was, however, entitled to a conventional damages award of £15,000 for the negligently performed sterilisation which constituted a legal wrong and removed her freedom to limit the size of her family: *Rees v Darlington Memorial Hospital NHS Trust* [2003] UKHL 52, [2003] 3 All ER 987.

Pain and suffering

12.35 In spite of the fact that childbirth is a natural process and not an injury, damages for the pain, discomfort and inconvenience associated with pregnancy and child birth are recoverable where these are the result of negligence. Such damages have been claimed, and awarded, in nearly every reported case of wrongful birth.

CHAPTER 13

Deductions and set-offs against financial loss

DAMAGES ARE DESIGNED TO COMPENSATE

13.1   When considering whether an item should be set off it helps to go back to first principles. Damages for financial loss are assessed so as to give compensation for the actual loss in money which the claimant has sustained or will sustain. Lord Goddard said in *British Transport Commission v Gourley* [1956] AC 185 at 206, [1955] 3 All ER 796 at 804–805, HL:

> 'The basic principle so far as loss of earnings and out-of-pocket expenses are concerned is that the injured person should be placed in the same financial position, so far as can be done by an award of money, as he would have been had the accident not happened.'

SHOULD A DEDUCTION BE MADE?

13.2   The question therefore arises whether any set-off or deduction should be made for liabilities the claimant would have had. For example, as income tax on the claimant's earnings, which is no longer payable. Or for benefits he receives from an outside source such as accident insurance or a charitable fund.

The first issue: what has the claimant lost?

13.3   As Lord Reid said in *Parry v Cleaver* [1969] 1 All ER 555 at 557, HL, it is necessary to distinguish between two separate questions. The first is what the claimant actually lost. What he has lost is his *net* earnings, after payment of tax and other liabilities such as social security contributions, which are necessarily incurred by the receipt of earnings and have to be paid sooner or later, even if not deducted at source. Here, Lord Reid said, 'it is a universal rule that the plaintiff cannot recover more than he has lost ... what he really lost was what would have remained to him after payment of tax'.

13.4 So damages for loss of earnings are always calculated on the basis of net earnings – less tax and similar deductions – whether deducted at source or assessed later: *British Transport Commission v Gourley* [1956] AC 185, [1955] 3 All ER 796, HL.

The second issue: benefits received after the accident

13.5 The second question arises when, because of the accident, the claimant receives some benefit which he would not otherwise have received. (We are here talking about 'benefits' in the widest sense of the meaning and not in relation to benefits provided by the state. Social Security benefits are discussed in chapter 14 below.) There is no universal rule that all such benefits are to be set off against the financial loss. Prima facie, it has been said, such benefits should be taken into account to arrive at the total loss, but there are a number of exceptions: *Hussain v New Taplow Paper Mills Ltd* [1988] AC 514, [1988] 1 All ER 541, HL.

INSURANCE AND SIMILAR PAYMENTS DISREGARDED

13.6 Thus money received under an accident insurance, or out of a relief fund for the victims of a disaster, has always been disregarded. After the *Gourley*[1] decision had established the principle of net loss, there was much argument about whether disability pensions, payable for a period during which the claimant would otherwise have been working, should be set off against loss of earnings – not only in the English courts but in Australia, Canada and New Zealand as well. In England it was at first held that such a pension should be set off in full against loss of earnings: *Browning v War Office* [1963] 1 QB 750, [1962] 3 All ER 1089, CA.

1   *British Transport Commission v Gourley* [1956] AC 185, [1955] 3 All ER 796, HL.

Pensions

13.7 In *Parry v Cleaver* [1970] AC 1, [1969] 1 All ER 555, HL, the House of Lords held that pensions are in the same position as insurance money and are not to be set off against loss of earnings (although a *disability* pension may be set off against the loss of a *retirement* pension over the same future period). The principle is that the claimant has provided the pension either by contributions or service.

Sick pay

13.8   Sick pay which continues for a time *as of right* (for example, for policemen), in spite of being unable to work, is another matter. In such a case the earnings have not yet ceased so there is no loss (or only a partial loss) to be recovered, and in *Parry v Cleaver* [1970] AC 1, [1969] 1 All ER 555, HL this was accepted without question. See paras 13.27–13.37 below for further detail.

Accident insurance

13.9   Money received under an accident insurance policy is not deducted or taken into account in any way in assessing damages for personal injuries: *Bradburn v Great Western Rly Co* (1874) LR 10 Exch 1, 44 LJ Ex 9. It makes no difference in principle whether the payment takes the form of a lump sum or (as frequently happens) of weekly payments during disability. In either case, the reason for not taking these payments into account is that they are benefits which the claimant has provided. The accident is merely the occasion which entitles him to claim the benefits. To use the expression adopted by Lord Reid, the insurance is something 'completely collateral'. As Pigott B said in *Bradburn v Great Western Rly Co*:

> 'He [the plaintiff] does not receive that sum of money because of the accident, but because he has made a contract providing for that contingency; an accident must occur to entitle him to it, but it is not the accident, but his contract, which is the cause of his receiving it.'

When the defendant provides the insurance

13.10   In these cases the claimants had effected the insurance. But where the employers (who were the defendants) had effected a group accident insurance for the benefit of employees, although payment was made as of right under the policy, it was held that *effecting* the insurance was a voluntary charitable act and the payment was not deductible: *McCamley v*

Cammell Laird Shipbuilders Ltd [1990] 1 All ER 854, [1990] 1 WLR 963, CA. Where, on the other hand, employers agreed to keep up sick pay for a prolonged period and covered this liability by insurance, the House of Lords held that the sums received had to be set off as sick pay, and not disregarded as insurance money: *Hussain v New Taplow Paper Mills Ltd* [1988] AC 514, [1988] 1 All ER 541, HL (the employers were insuring themselves against their own liability). In *Page v Sheerness Steel Co* [1999] 1 AC 345, the House of Lords confirmed that, where the defendant had provided the insurance, any payment is treated as sick pay, and is therefore deductible.

Disability pensions

13.11   In *Parry v Cleaver* [1970] AC 1, [1969] 1 All ER 555, HL, the House of Lords decided that a disability pension is not to be set off against loss of earnings. If, however, the claimant's claim is not only for loss of earnings, but also for loss of a future retirement pension, then a disability pension may be set off against this loss for the period after retirement: for in such a case the claimant has not lost all the future pension, only part of it. It is a deduction of part pension against full pension, not pension against pay.

13.12   Previous case law, which drew distinctions between contributory and non-contributory pensions, and between pensions payable as of right and those which were discretionary, is no longer of any importance.

13.13   In *Smoker v London Fire and Civil Defence Authority* [1991] 2 AC 502, [1991] 2 All ER 449, HL the House of Lords refused to depart from the decision in *Parry v Cleaver* [1970] AC 1, [1969] 1 All ER 555, HL and reaffirmed the law as stated at para 13.11 above.

13.14   Where, under a scheme to which the employee had contributed, disability and retirement pensions were alternative, a disability pension received before retirement was not to be set off against loss of earnings; it could be set off only against pension after retirement: *Longdon v British Coal Corpn* [1995] ICR 957, [1995] IRLR 642, CA.

Charitable assistance

13.15   Charitable assistance to the victims of an accident, whether it takes the form of gifts of money or of gifts in kind, is excluded from consideration in assessing damages. Thus free board and lodging given by a relative cannot be treated as a set-off (see para 13.25ff below).

13.16   So, too, it has been held in Northern Ireland that where a voluntary fund had been raised by public contributions for the victims of a railway accident, payments out of the fund were not to go in reduction of damages: *Redpath v Belfast and County Down Rly* [1947] NI 167.

13.17   The generosity of the public, or other donor, is an independent factor which has arisen subsequently to the accident, and it would be wrong (as Andrew LCJ remarked) to allow such generosity to relieve the wrongdoer. The decision and reasoning in this case were approved by the Court of Appeal in *Peacock v Amusement Equipment Co Ltd* [1954] 2 QB 347, [1954] 2 All ER 689, CA, where a similar problem arose under the Fatal Accidents Act 1976, and by the House of Lords in *Hussain v New Taplow Paper Mills Ltd* [1988] AC 514, [1988] 1 All ER 541, HL.

13.18   The only exception to this is where the defendant himself makes a gift to the victim: *Williams v BOC Gases Ltd* [2000] PIQR Q253. In this case, the defendant made a 'gift' to the claimant, but specified that it was to be treated as an advance on any damages the claimant was entitled to recover.

Saving in living expenses

13.19   In general, a claimant who has to go into a hospital or nursing home is entitled to recover the fees, which include a component for board and lodging. Clearly there is no claim for damages under this head if no fees are charged. But board and lodging are things which the claimant would have had to pay for in any event; and he is not entitled to recover a sum in excess of his real loss.

13.20   It has therefore been held that where the claimant was living in a hotel or boarding house before the accident, and has been relieved for the time being of these living expenses, a deduction may be made from the nursing home or hospital charges to represent the cost of food, and perhaps also – if it is feasible to make any apportionment for this item – the cost of lodging: *Shearman v Folland* [1950] 2 KB 43, [1950] 1 All ER 976, CA. The Court of Appeal made it clear that this decision does not apply to the normal case of a claimant who has his own home, and continues to be responsible for all the normal expenses while he is in hospital.

13.21 In *Firth v Geo Ackroyd Junior Ltd* [2001] PIQR Q27, the local authority was paying the claimant's nursing home fees. He was not liable to reimburse the local authority, but the saving he made as a result was deductible from his damages (covering expenses such as food that he would have had to pay for in any event).

Where the claimant is in an institution

13.22 In *Mitchell v Mulholland (No 2)* [1972] 1 QB 65, [1971] 2 All ER 1205, CA, where future expenses in a psychiatric nursing home were running at £1,825 a year, £300 a year was deducted for living expenses saved; but such a deduction was available only as a set-off against a claim for charges which included maintenance, and therefore it was held that it did not arise when accommodation in an institution was free under the National Health Service: *Daish v Wauton* [1972] 2 QB 262, [1972] 1 All ER 25, CA. *Daish v Wauton* has now been overruled by the Administration of Justice Act 1982 which by s 5[1] (for England, Wales and Northern Ireland) and s 11[2] (for Scotland) directs that:

> 'any saving to the injured person which is attributable to his maintenance wholly or partly at public expense in a hospital, nursing home or other institution shall be set off against any income lost by him as a result of his injuries.'

1   Administration of Justice Act 1982, s 5.
2   Administration of Justice Act 1982, s 11.

13.23 So there is now a general rule that any saving of living expenses due to being maintained at public expense (not necessarily in a *public* institution) is set off against loss of earnings. 'Saving' in this context can mean only that the claimant must be treated as having saved the amount they would, before the injury, have spent on 'maintenance', and this amount must be deducted from the pre-accident earnings.

13.24 It is open to argument whether 'maintenance' includes expenses other than food.

Where board and lodging is provided free after the accident

13.25 Where, before the accident, the claimant received free board and lodging as part of the terms of his employment, for example, as a domestic servant, the monetary value of these benefits is a part of his earnings and must be quantified and added to the monetary earnings in order to arrive at the true net figure. If such a person receives free board and lodging with relatives after the accident, the defendant cannot claim a set-off, since the free board and lodging is a collateral benefit arising out of the kindness of the relatives: *Liffen v Watson* [1940] 1 KB 556, [1940] 2 All ER 213, CA.

Additional housing needs

13.26   Where a badly disabled claimant needs special housing, the reasonable cost of purchase or adaptation is recoverable. But this means the *extra* cost, over and above what his accommodation would have cost in any event: see *Roberts v Johnstone* [1989] QB 878, [1988] 3 WLR 1247, CA; and chapter 12, para 12.17–12.21).

Sick pay

13.27   If an injured person continues to receive his pay (in whole or in part) while unable to work, to that extent he has sustained no loss and the whole amount must be set off against his claim – or rather, not included in it. There are, however, a few exceptions, and three different types of sick pay have to be distinguished.

STATUTORY SICK PAY

13.28   The first is 'statutory sick pay', which the employer is now required by law to pay during the first few weeks of sickness or disability: Social Security Contributions and Benefits Act 1992, s 151ff. This replaced 'sickness benefit' payable by the state out of social security funds. Under the Law Reform (Personal Injuries) Act 1948 this was one of the benefits which were set off to a limited extent – one-half the amount for the first five years. But no amendment has been made to the Act to substitute statutory sick pay, which must therefore be set off in full: *Palfrey v Greater London Council* [1985] ICR 437, QBD. There is, however, one qualification. Under the 1992 Act all social security benefits are recoverable as a temporary loan out of the damages: see chapter 4 above. To a limited extent the Ministry allows the employer a credit out of sick pay, and this credit is recoverable by the Ministry out of the damages.

13.29   To avoid a double deduction, therefore, the damages must include this recoverable credit.

Contractual sick pay

13.30 The second case is where, under the terms of employment – for instance, in the police force or the civil service – the injured person is entitled *as of right* to sick pay for a period. In this case the employer's contractual liability will be satisfied by statutory sick pay, so far as it goes: Social Security Contributions and Benefits Act 1992, Sch 12, para 2.

13.31 The whole of the contractual sick pay must be deducted from the claim for loss of earnings, because so far as it goes there is no loss. The position is the same even if the right to pay continues indefinitely for the duration of the employment, and the employer has covered his liability by insurance (as part of the terms of employment): *Hussain v New Taplow Paper Mills Ltd* [1988] AC 514, [1988] 1 All ER 541, HL. The House of Lords held that the case could not be equated with one where the employee had himself insured against loss of earnings. (This man had lost an arm, his employment had not been terminated, and he was offered alternative work: if he left the employment he would apparently continue to have benefits direct from the insurers, but nothing was decided as to these – the basis of the decision was that he was still employed so the payments could not be classified as a disability pension.)

13.32 Formerly, where sick pay continued as of right, it was a common practice, especially when the injured person was in the armed forces, for the employer to sue the defendant direct in an action for 'loss of services', and recover the sick pay as the value of the services lost. However, the earlier cases were overruled, and a claim by the employer is no longer possible: *IRC v Hambrook* [1956] 2 QB 641, [1956] 3 All ER 338, CA; *Metropolitan Police District Receiver v Croydon Corpn* [1957] 2 QB 154, [1957] 1 All ER 78, CA; Administration of Justice Act 1982, s 2.

13.33 This difficulty can be overcome by adding a clause to the conditions of service to the effect that where the injury is caused by the act of a third party the payments shall be treated as a temporary loan if the third party is legally liable and shall be repayable out of damages recovered from him. The claimant then claims their full loss of earnings without regard to the advances. Such an agreement is effective though the liability to repay is contingent: *Wolland v Majorhazi* [1959] NZLR 433.

Voluntary sick pay

13.34 The third case is where the employer makes payments voluntarily without being under any liability to do so. In this case, if a third party is the defendant he will not be allowed to set off such payments, because they are due to the benevolence of the employer and fall within the same category as charitable assistance.

13.35   Where the employer is himself the defendant, the position is more complex. Prima facie, unless otherwise agreed, every payment the employer makes without obligation must be set off against their legal liability for damages, whether it is described as sick pay, or takes the form of a loan, or of a voluntary pension, or of voluntary severance payments on redundancy due to incapacity: *Fricker v Benjamin Perry & Sons Ltd* (1973) 16 KIR 356, QBD. But frequently employers who make temporary advances wish the loss to fall on their insurers if they are legally liable: if so, they should expressly stipulate that the sums in question are paid as loans, not as wages, and will be recoverable out of the damages.

13.36   In *Turner v Ministry of Defence* (1969) 113 Sol Jo 585, CA, sick pay had to be deducted though under the terms of service it was not to count against the plaintiff's other allowances if the accident was the fault of the employers.

Only the net amount is deductible

13.37   Where sick pay has been received net of PAYE and insurance contributions, only the net amount is deductible: *Franklin v British Railways Board* [1993] IRLR 441, [1994] PIQR P1, CA.

INCOME TAX, SOCIAL SECURITY CONTRIBUTIONS, AND PENSION DEDUCTIONS

Tax and similar deductions

13.38   It is now the established rule that loss of earnings will be calculated on the basis of the *net* earnings after the deduction of tax and any similar unavoidable charges. That is, both the earnings before the accident and the estimated earnings afterwards, will be taken at the net figure. For this purpose it does not matter whether tax is deducted at source or assessed later: in both cases it must be taken into account.

13.39   This follows from the decision of the House of Lords in *British Transport Commission v Gourley* [1956] AC 185, [1955] 3 All ER 796, HL. In this particular case the plaintiff was a consultant engineer with a very high income. His injuries were severe, but he returned to his work with a reduction in the rate of his earnings. Since the tax liability was high, the trial judge found that if tax were taken into account damages for loss of earnings would be reduced from £37,720 to £6,695. In a normal case, the reduction will not be anything like so great: but tax becomes important where the claimant has been earning a large income.

13.40 The main reason for taking tax into account is that a claimant is entitled to compensation only for what he has lost; and if a person who pays tax at the higher rates is compensated on the basis of their gross income, the damages will be out of proportion to the true loss.

The appropriate deduction is the effective rate of tax

13.41 The rate of tax to be taken into account is not, of course, the standard rate, but the effective rate applying to the earnings which have been lost. This was explained by Lord Goddard at some length in *British Transport Commission v Gourley* [1956] AC 185 at 207, [1955] 3 All ER 796 at 805, HL:

'Tax is imposed by law; the state exacts a certain proportion of income which varies with the amount of the taxable income. There is a standard rate of income tax, but there are allowances, and no one pays the standard rate on each pound of his income. Surtax is graded according to the amount of income. The taxpayer must pay and, in my opinion, it cannot make any difference whether he receives the gross income and pays the tax later, as he does if assessed under Schedule D, or whether it is deducted before he receives it, as is the case with tax under Schedule E or PAYE ... the rate of tax to be taken must, as it seems to me, be the effective rate of income tax and, if necessary, surtax, which would have been applicable to the sums in question if they had been earned. That rate depends on the combination of a number of factors that may vary with each case – allowances, reduced rates, surtax rates, other income of the claimant or his wife, charges or reliefs. The task of determining it may not always be an easy one, but, in complicated cases, it is to be hoped that the parties, with the help of accountants, will be able to agree figures. If not, the court must do its best to arrive at a reasonable figure, even though it cannot be said to be an exact one.'

Tax rates when there is a partial loss of earnings

13.42   It was formerly held that where there is a partial loss of earnings, this is not to be treated as the top slice or the bottom slice or any particular part of the claimant's income, so as to attract tax at the highest or lowest rates; all that can be said is that the income as a whole is diminished: *Re Houghton Main Colliery Co Ltd* [1956] 3 All ER 300, [1956] 1 WLR 1219, Ch D. The Court of Appeal has now decided that where a claimant loses the top part of his earnings, it is the top slice of tax attributable to that part which must be deducted: *Lyndale Fashion Manufacturers v Rich* [1973] 1 All ER 33, [1973] 1 WLR 73, CA.

Future possible changes in the tax regime are not generally taken into account

13.43   Obviously the extent of future tax depends on the rate of tax for the time being in force, and also on future changes in allowances. Is it right to take into account the possibility of future changes in taxation? Lord Goddard thought not. It is a general principle, however, that all contingencies must be taken into account in assessing damages, unless they are so uncertain and speculative that no reasonable forecast can be made. It must, it is suggested, be a question of fact, at any given time, whether the prospects of increase or reduction in tax are so nebulous that they must be left out of account.

Tax credits must be taken into account

13.44   If the claimant saves tax either by a rebate on their pre-accident earnings, or by a 'tax holiday' on their return to work – due in both cases to their earnings for the year as a whole being less – they must give credit for it: *Hartley v Sandholme Iron Co Ltd* [1975] QB 600, [1974] 3 All ER 475; *Brayson v Wilmot-Breedon* [1976] CLY 682.

No deduction because of improvement in working conditions

13.45   In *Arafa v Potter* [1995] IRLR 316, [1994] PIQR Q73, CA the plaintiff was employed as a restaurant manager and had been severely injured. He retrained as a teacher and at the date of trial was working as a learning resources manager. However, he was earning less than prior to the accident and the judge awarded £42,741 for loss of earnings. The defendant appealed arguing that as a restaurant manager the plaintiff had worked 70–80 hours a week for 50 weeks a year; in his new job he worked 40 hours a week for 40 weeks a year and there was a possibility of a pension in his new job. The court held that the plaintiff had acted reasonably in mitigating his loss. The courts should not reduce the multiplier or attempt to take into account 'intangible benefits'. These could not be quantified in monetary terms nor was it right in principle to do so.

Chapter 14

Statutory recoupment of DSS benefits

BENEFIT RECOVERY

14.1 Benefit recovery is governed by the Social Security (Recovery of Benefits) Act 1997 (SS(RB)A 1997). This act applies to all compensation payments made on or after 6 October 1997, regardless of when the original injury occurred or the disease was originally diagnosed. The earlier law which distinguishes between injuries and diseases occurring before and after 1 January 1989 is now largely irrelevant in practice.

14.2 The primary intention is to affect all payments of damages for personal injury by requiring the defendant to investigate, before damages are paid, whether social security benefits listed in the statute have been paid to the claimant over the same period of time as that to which the damages relate. Thus benefit recovery may take place against a damages award no matter what its size.

THE RELEVANT PERIOD

14.3 SS(RB)A 1997, s 3 defines the period during which benefits may be recovered:
- In the case of an accident, the period begins on the day after the accident.
- In the case of a disease, the period begins on the day on which the first claim for benefit because of the disease is made.

14.4 The period for recovery of benefit ends on the occurrence of one of three cut-off dates:
- the day when final compensation is paid – this is accepted by the Compensation Recovery Unit (CRU) of the DSS as being the date on which the cheque leaves the compensator's office;

- five years after the day the recovery period began; or
- the day it is agreed that an earlier compensation payment finally discharged liability. Thus the cut-off date is the date of the payment of the sum awarded (*Mitchell v Laing* 1998 SC 342, 1998 SLT 203, Ct of Sess), meaning that if the decision is appealed the recovery period will continue until the payment of the sum awarded. The *Mitchell* rule does not, however, apply where there has been a payment into court; in such cases the period for recovery of benefit ends on the day the payment was made provided that the claimant accepted it within 21 days of receiving notice of it.

THE BENEFITS EQUIVALENT TO HEADS OF DAMAGE

14.5 The basic aim of SS(RB)A 1997 is that there should be a like-for-like deduction; benefits should only be deducted if they duplicate the award of damages by being paid for purposes which are encompassed in the corresponding head of damage. The heads of damage and the corresponding benefits are listed in SS(RB)A 1997, Sch 2. Thus, for example, receipt of mobility allowance will not affect the claim for loss of earnings. SS(RB)A 1997 divides the heads of damages against which benefits can be recovered into three sections:

(1) loss of earnings;

(2) loss of mobility; and

(3) cost of care.

14.6 No benefit can be deducted from certain heads of damage, notably from compensation for pain, suffering and loss of amenity, thus in extreme cases where the benefits received outweigh the award for pecuniary losses, the injured person will still get full compensation for his non-pecuniary losses, and his overall award cannot be reduced to nothing. It should also be noted that SS(RB)A 1997 requires the compensator to reimburse the state for all recoverable benefits received even if they cannot be offset fully against the damages.

RECOVERABLE BENEFITS

14.7 Recoverable benefits, listed in SS(RB)A 1997, Sch 2, are:
- Incapacity benefit.
- Income support.
- Disability living allowance.

- Industrial injuries disablement benefit.
- Invalidity benefit.
- Severe disablement allowance.
- Sickness benefit.
- Reduced earnings allowance.
- Attendance allowance.
- Mobility allowance.
- Unemployment benefit.
- Constant attendance allowance.
- Disability working allowance.
- Jobseekers' allowance.
- Exceptionally severe disablement allowance.

NON-RECOVERABLE BENEFITS

14.8   The benefits which are not listed in SS(RB)A 1997, Sch 2 are not recoverable from any award of damages, as the benefits do not have any link with the tortious injury. Therefore the unlisted benefits which must be left out of account include:

- Child benefit.
- Family credit.
- Earnings top-up.
- Guardians' allowance.
- Housing benefit.
- Invalid care allowance.
- Maternity allowance.
- Old Cases Act benefits.
- Statutory maternity pay.
- Retirement pension.
- Retirement allowance.
- Social fund payments.
- War pensions.
- Widows' benefits.

HOW THE RECOUPMENT SYSTEM WORKS

14.9   By SS(RB)A 1997, s 23(1) when compensators receive a claim for compensation they must give the Secretary of State certain information about it within 14 days of receiving the claim, as regulated by the Social

Security (Recovery of Benefits) Regulations 1997, SI 1197/2205. This is done by completing and returning form CRU 1. Compensators are required to inform the CRU of the following:

(1) the full name and address of the injured person;
(2) the injured person's date of birth and National Insurance number;
(3) the date of the accident or injury;
(4) the nature of the accident or disease; and
(5) details of the injured person's employment (if the date of the injury or diagnosis of disease is before 6 April 1994).

14.10 The CRU will acknowledge receipt of notification of a claim by sending to the compensator a CRU 4 form. This form must be used again when the case is about to be settled, as it is the form on which application must be made for a certificate of recoverable benefit, which governs the amount of benefit required to be repaid.

14.11 Before an action is settled, a payment made into court or payment made under a judgment, the defendant obtains a certificate of recoverable benefit from the CRU. The certificate will detail the amount of the relevant benefits paid to the claimant and the defendant pays this amount direct to the DSS and the balance to the victim or into court, as the case may be.

RECOUPMENT AND THE ASSESSMENT OF DAMAGES

14.12 The underlying principle is that the benefits to be recouped do not have any effect on the way in which the court assesses damages. SS(RB)A 1997, s 17 states:

'In assessing damages in respect of any accident, injury or disease, the amount of any listed benefits paid or likely to be paid is disregarded.'

14.13 The effect was explained by Lord Hope in *Wiseley v John Fulton (Plumbers) Ltd, Wadey v Surrey Count Council* [2000] PIQR 306 at 315:

'The effect of section 17 [SS(RB)A 1997, s 17] is that damages must be assessed in a way which treats the amount which the claimant has received by way of listed benefits in exactly the same manner as any amounts which he may have received under, for example, a private insurance policy. They are to be disregarded, so that the amounts awarded under the heads described in Schedule 2 to the Act of 1997 [SS(RB)A 1997, Sch 2] as loss of wages, cost of support and loss of mobility are to be assessed without making any deduction for the relevant benefits.'

RECOUPMENT AND INTEREST

14.14   *Wiseley v John Fulton Plumbers Ltd, Wadey v Surrey Count Council* [2000] 2 All ER 545, [2000] 1 WLR 820 is also authority for the proposition that any benefits to be recouped are ignored in the calculation of interest. A claimant is entitled to interest on the full losses and expenditure, regardless of the fact that benefits have been paid and the claimant has not, in fact, suffered a full financial loss.

RECOUPMENT AND 'PART 36' OFFERS

14.15   An important issue in relation to CPR 36 and recoupment was considered in *Williams v Devon County Council* [2003] EWCA Civ 365, [2003] PIQR Q68 where the Court of Appeal considered difficult issues surrounding the interaction between the recoupment regulations and CPR 36. The issue was simple. The defendant paid £10,000 into court pursuant to CPR 36. This sum, coupled with the certificate of recoverable benefit, totalled £25,669.91. If the claimant had accepted that sum she would, after deduction of recoupable benefits, have received a balance of £10,000. At trial the judge awarded £23,05.39. However, because of the way that the recoupment provisions work, with part of the damages claim being 'ring-fenced' the claimant ended up with £15,738.19 after recoupment had taken place.

14.16   However, the trial judge held that the payment into court had not been beaten and ordered that the claimant pay the defendant's costs from the date of the Part 36 (CPR 36) payment.

14.17   So we have the anomalous result that whilst the claimant actually ended up with more in her pocket than if she had accepted the offer, she was still found not to have beaten the Part 36[1] payment into court.

1   CPR 36.

The Civil Procedure Rules

14.18   CPR 36.23 states:

'(1) This rule applies where a payment to a claimant following the acceptance of a Part 36 offer or Part 36 payment into court would be a compensation payment as defined in section 1 of the Social Security (Recovery of Benefits) Act 1997.[1]

(2) A defendant to a money claim may make an offer to settle the claim which will have the consequences set out in this Part, without making a Part 36[2] payment if,

    (a) at the time he makes the offer he has applied for, but not received a certificate of recoverable benefits; and

    (b) he makes a Part 36 payment not more than 7 days after he receives the certificate.

(3) A Part 36 Payment Notice must state:

    (a) the amount of gross compensation;

    (b) the name and amount of any benefit by which that gross amount is reduced in accordance with section 8[3] and Schedule 2[4] to the 1997 Act; and

    (c) that the sum paid in is the net amount after deduction of the amount of benefit.

(4) For the purposes of Rule 36.20, a claimant fails to better a Part 36 payment if he fails to obtain judgment for more than the gross sum specified in the Part 36 Payment Notice.'

1   SS(RB)A 1997, s 1.
2   CPR 36.
3   SS(RB)A 1997, s 8.
4   SS(RB)A 1997, Sch 2.

14.19   The CPR 36 Practice Direction provides in para 10.5 that:

'In establishing in a trial whether a claimant has bettered or obtained a judgment more advantageous than a Part 36 Payment to which this paragraph relates, the court will base its decision on the gross sum specified in the Part 36 Payment Notice.'

14.20   However, the Court of Appeal recognised that there were numerous situations in which this could cause injustice. Further it made negotiations and settlement extremely difficult.

1   *Williams v Devon County Council* [2003] EWCA Civ 365, [2003] PIQR Q68.

The problem with the trial judge's approach

14.21   The Court of Appeal recognised the problem with the approach:[1]

'If the judge's approach is correct, the compensator would be, in effect, able to transfer the burden of appealing in every case on to the claimant. If the compensator is to be entitled to bring into account for the purposes of a Part 362 payment the whole of the recoverable benefits under the certificate, it inevitably means that not only in considering whether to accept such an offer, but also when determining whether or not to accept an informal offer of settlement, the claimant may be forced to consider accepting a sum which is less than that which is appropriate for general damages. In other words the amount in the certificate will have impinged upon and reduced the amount of compensation which would otherwise be appropriate, contrary to the policy of the Act [SS(RB)A 1997].'

1   *Williams v Devon County Council* [2003] EWCA Civ 365 at [20].
2   CPR 36.

The defendant's arguments

14.22   The defendant, supported by the Secretary of State, argued that the wording of CPR 36.23 is clear. The compensator is entitled to make a payment calculated on the basis of the inclusion of the total amount of the certificate, even if that produces a payment which is less than that which the claimant would be entitled to by way of general damages. The claimant's remedy is to appeal the certificate.

The practical problems

14.23   The court rejected this argument[1] for several reasons. First, the aim of the recoupment provisions was to recover, for the tax payer, benefits which had been the compensator's fault. It was not designed to be an alternative means of compensating the claimant. The compensator remains primarily liable for the damage which has been caused to the claimant. The recoupment provisions are not designed to distort in any way the litigants' or the courts' approach to the claim. Secondly, the test for entitlement to benefit may not be the same as the test applied by the court in awarding a relevant head of damage.

1   *Williams v Devon County Council* [2003] EWCA Civ 365, [2003] PIQR Q68.

14.24   Thirdly, and most importantly, the recoupment provisions do not deal with the problem where damages are reduced by contributory negligence. There is no mechanism in the recoupment regulations for taking into account a finding of contributory negligence. The compensator has to pay the full amount on the certificate. Where, therefore, the certificate is for a sum which exceeds any realistic quantification of the relevant head of damage the amount on the certificate is inevitably going to impinge on general damages.

14.25 The Court of Appeal felt that this effect could not have been intended by Parliament.[1]

1   *Williams v Devon County Council* [2003] EWCA Civ 365, [2003] PIQR Q68.

The remedy: the defendant should read the CPR

14.26 The solution put forward by the Court of Appeal is that the defendant should read the rules and comply with them. The court stated:[1]

'Rule 36.23(3)(b) [CPR 36.23(3)(b)] requires the payment notice to state "the name and amount of any benefit by which that gross amount is reduced in accordance with section 8[2] and Schedule 2[3] to the 1997 Act". It follows that the calculations must be made in accordance with section 8; in other words, the amount by which the sum is reduced must be no more than the amount appropriate for the head of damages against which the benefits can be off-set. If that exercise is carried out properly by a compensator, resulting in the appropriate payment for general damages then the process of calculation of the Part 36[4] payment equiparates to the way in which damages would be awarded were the matter to go to trial in a way which makes sense of the primary rule as to costs contained in Rule 36.20 [CPR 36.20]. It also enables the claimant to make a properly informed decision on whether or not to accept the payment.'

1   *Williams v Devon County Council* [2003] EWCA Civ 365 at [27].
2   SS(RB)A 1997, s 8.
3   SS(RB)A 1997, Sch 2.
4   CPR 36.

The Williams case

14.27 It is illustrative to look at the facts of *Williams v Devon County Council* [2003] EWCA Civ 365, [2003] PIQR Q68 in detail.

14.28   In *Williams v Devon County Council* [2003] EWCA Civ 365, [2003] PIQR Q68 the defendant argued that the claimant had been culpable of contributory negligence and that the period that they were liable to pay loss of earnings for was less than the period of unemployment set out in the recoupment certificate. The court observed that:

'In the present case no attempt had been made by the respondents to carry out the exercise required by section 8 of the Act [SS(RB)A 1997, s 8]. They were clearly arguing that there was contributory negligence, and that the period for which they were liable for lost earnings was substantially shorter than that which the appellant was claiming. The effect of both these arguments was that the amount of the certificate was greater than the amount by which they could claim to be entitled to offset recoverable benefits against the overall damages awarded. Whilst, therefore, a literal reading of Part 36.20[1] and Part 36.23(4)[2] would suggest that the judge's approach was correct, the Part 36[3] Payment had not been calculated in accordance with the rule. The amount of recoverable benefits had clearly not been "reduced in accordance with Section 8 and Schedule 2[4] to the 1997 Act." It was not a proper and therefore effective Part 36 payment.'

1   CPR 36.20.
2   CPR 36.23(4).
3   CPR 36.
4   SS(RB)A 1997, Sch 2.

The practical results

14.29   It is for the defendant, therefore, to state precisely what benefits are being deemed to be recouped when it makes a Part 36 payment into court. This has to be clearly stated on the Part 36 payment into court. If the defendant does not do this then the CPR 36 is not proper and effective.

More difficult cases

14.30   The court recognised that there could be more difficult cases, for instance, where the compensator has overestimated the period of loss of earnings but under-estimated the amount of general damages. The Part 36[1] payment based on those calculations, would be in accordance with the rule, and could produce a gross sum which was greater than the sum awarded by the judge at trial. The court stated that:[2]

'In that situation, where the effect of the miscalculation by the compensator as to the relevant amount of recoverable benefits has impinged upon the general damages figure, it seems to us that justice requires the court to exercise its discretion under Part 36.20. The touch stone it seems to us, is that the claimant is entitled to the full value of his general damages claim. For the reasons we have given we do not consider that it is appropriate to require him or her to make up for any shortfall by appealing the certificate. It is for the compensator to make a proper assessment of the general damages figure and ensure that the Part 36 payment at least provides the claimant with that sum.'

1   CPR 36.20.
2   *Williams v Devon County Council* [2003] EWCA Civ 365, [2003] PIQR Q 68.

Should the parties wait until the certificate is appealed?

14.31   The court specifically considered the question of whether the parties should wait until after the certificate is appealed before the issue of costs is decided.[1] The court observed that this solution would involve inevitable delay and further expense and was not the preferable solution.

1   *Williams v Devon County Council* [2003] EWCA Civ 365, [2003] PIQR Q 68.

REPAYMENTS BY THE COMPENSATION RECOVERY UNIT BELONG TO THE CLAIMANT

14.32   It is important for parties to appreciate that, unless there is an agreement to the contrary, any money repaid to the CRU after an appeal have to be repaid to the claimant. The Social Security (Recovery of Benefits) Regulations 1997, SI 1997/2205, reg 11(5) provides that where the amount of compensation paid is recalculated and a fresh certificate of recoverable benefits issued, the compensatory shall pay the difference to whom the compensation payment was made.

THE JUDGMENT IN *HILTON*

14.33   Another important decision on CPR 36 can be found in the judgment of Mr Justice Pitchford in *Hilton Intl v Smith* (5 October 2000, unreported). Again close examination of the facts assists.

The facts

14.34   *Hilton Intl v Smith* (5 October 2000, unreported) was a personal injury case where there was a dispute between the parties as to the extent of the back injury. The claimant's medical evidence put the claim for loss of earnings in the £30,000–47,500 region; the defendant's medical evidence limited the claim for loss of earnings to around £15,000.

14.35   The defendant obtained a CRU certificate which showed a total of £40,124.58. The defendant then made a payment into court. The payment in was made under CCR Ord 11, r 1 on 29 March 1999. The wording of the payment in is of some significance:

> 'Take notice that the first and second defendants have today paid the sum of £6,000 into the court. This sum is in addition to the deductible C.R.U. benefits detailed below, which totals £40,124.58. The gross amount of the compensation payment is therefore £46,124.58, which sum is in satisfaction of all the causes of action in respect of which the plaintiff complains. The deductible C.R.U. benefits in accordance with s.8 of Schedule 2 to the Social Security (Recovery of Benefits) Act 1997 are calculated as follows:-
> – Incapacity benefit: £34,566.29
> – Invalidity pension and allowance: £5,407.09
> – Statutory sick pay: £152.20
> If you accept the payment made in satisfaction of your claim, you must give written notice of acceptance to the court and every other party within 21 days after you receive this notice.'

14.36   The offer was accepted on 13 April 1999 in a notice that stated:

> 'Take notice that the plaintiff hereby accepts the sum of £46,124.58 paid into court by the defendants on the 9th of April 1999 in full and final settlement of the claim herein.'

14.37   The defendants discharged the sum of £40,124.58 to the Secretary of State. *Both* parties appealed to the Secretary of State for a reconsideration of the certified sum. As a result a fresh certificate was issued on 16 September 1999, in which the sum certified was nil.

14.38   The defendants were reimbursed and the claimant, upon discovering this, asked the defendant for the additional sum of £40,124.58. The defendant refused.

14.39   As a result both parties made cross-applications to the County Court. The claimant sought the lifting of the stay on the proceedings in order that he could recover the new balance with interest. The defendants also sought an order that the stay be lifted in order that the notice of payment in could be amended to delete any reference to the certified sum.

14.40 The circuit judge acceded to the claimant's application and ordered the payment of the balance due, together with interest.

14.41 The arguments centred around whether the issue of whether the claimant must have known that the defendants were labouring under a misapprehension and took unconscionable advantage of it. The judge held that:
(1) The notice of payment in was unequivocal in its terms.
(2) The claimant accepted it.
(3) There was no evidence that the claimant either did know or should have known that the defendants had made a mistake.
(4) There was no evidence that the claimant took unconscionable advantage of the defendants.
(5) The defendants placed themselves in the position that they did as a result of their own foolhardiness.

How can defendants protect themselves?

14.42 Pitchford J observed that there were two means by which the defendants could have achieved the object they were pursuing:
(1) Either they could have identified the gross compensation payment in their notice as nil, or such lesser sum than £40,124.58 as they assessed.
(2) They could have served a Calderbank letter making their intention clear.

14.43 However, as it was they told the claimant that the gross compensation payment was £46,124.58 without reservation of any kind.

Exercise of the judge's discretion

14.44 The circuit judge held that he should acceded to the defendant's application only if the circumstances were exceptional. This meant a finding that the claimant had taken unfair advantage of the defendants. He could not find any such circumstances in the current case. This decision was upheld by Pitchford J, who observed:

'I have reviewed the decision made in the light of submissions made to me that the County Court and I should apply the overriding principle that the court should deal with cases justly. It is trine, perhaps, to mention that the principle underlying the exercise of discretion in the cases cited to me, and to His Honour Judge Reid, is identical. The court must deal with cases justly to both parties, not just the party who makes a mistake. It does not follow that, because one party makes an error of judgment in the course of litigation, it is just to permit that party to escape its consequences.'

ANOTHER EXAMPLE

14.45   A similar decision was reached by McKinnon J in *Bruce v Genesis Fast Food Ltd* [2003] EWHC 788. The claimant was held to be entitled to sums received after a recoupment appeal. The judge rejected arguments of unjust enrichment or that the defendant was entitled to rectification.

PRACTICAL CONSEQUENCES

14.46   The practical consequences for defendants are profound. It may be important, indeed is *very important*, for claimant lawyers to check the precise wording of cases where payments into court have been made and there is a significant amount of CRU. The wording of Part 36[1] notices must be drafted carefully.

1   CPR 36.

CHAPTER 15

Damages on death: basic principles

RIGHTS OF ACTION ON DEATH

15.1 Damages for death raise different questions from damages for a living claimant. Unless the injured person lived long enough to recover judgment or reach a settlement on his own account, the damages will not be received by the deceased or by his dependants or personal representatives. The assessment of the damages therefore depends on the nature of the right of action which the law gives to those persons.

HISTORICAL BACKGROUND

15.2 The key point to understanding the law relating to fatal accidents is that common law principles have been grafted onto statutory rights. Historically, the common law did not allow any claim for wrongful death or any claims by the dependants – the right of action was held to have died with the victim.

15.3 The right of dependants to bring an action was first brought into being by the Fatal Accidents Act 1846. However, this was, in essence, a statute that gave a right of action to certain dependants. It permitted a jury to award 'such damages as they may think proportioned to the injury resulting from such death parties to the injury resulting from such death to the parties respectively for whom and for whose benefit such action shall be brought': s 2.

15.4 There were a number of amendments in the twentieth century, primarily designed to ensure that insurance policies, widow's pensions and the like were *not* deducted from damages awarded to the dependants. The Fatal Accidents Act 1976 was, essentially, a consolidating statute. That Act was amended substantially by the Administration of Justice Act 1982.

THE TWO ELEMENTS OF THE CLAIM

15.5   There are two different elements to a fatal accident claim, although they can overlap:
(1) The Law Reform (Miscellaneous Provisions) Act 1934.

   This allows an action to be brought on behalf of the *estate*. These claims relate to:

   (a)   pain and suffering prior of the deceased prior to death;
   (b)   any financial losses incurred by the deceased prior to death; and
   (c)   funeral expenses.

(2) The Fatal Accidents Act 1976, as amended.

   This allows an action to be brought on behalf of the *dependants* of the deceased. In essence it attempts to put the dependants in the same position as they would have in had the death not occurred.

THE TYPE OF INCIDENT THAT CAN GIVE RISE TO A FATAL ACCIDENT ACT CLAIM

15.6   The Fatal Accidents Act 1976, s 1(1) states:

'If death is caused by any wrongful act, neglect or default which is such as would (if death had not ensued) have entitled the person injured to maintain an action and recover damages in respect thereof, the person who would have been liable if death had not ensued shall be liable to an action for damages, notwithstanding the death of the person injured.'

STANDING IN THE SHOES OF THE DECEASED

15.7   In *Gray v Barr* [1971] 2 QB 554, [1971] 2 All ER 949, CA Lord Denning MR summarised the effect of the Fatal Accidents Act 1976, s 1(1) (at 569D):

'If [the deceased] had lived, ie, only been injured and not died, and living would have been entitled to maintain an action and recover damages – then his widow and children can do so. They stand in his shoes in regard to *liability*, but not as to damages' (emphasis in original).

CLAIMANTS UNDER THE FATAL ACCIDENTS ACT MUST BE DEPENDANTS

15.8 There are two points here:
(1) The claimants must be dependants as defined by statute.
(2) The claimants must have had a reasonable expectation of financial benefit from the deceased.

THE STATUTORY DEFINITION

15.9 These important definitions are dealt with in the Fatal Accident Act 1976, s 1:

'1—(1) If death is caused by any wrongful act, neglect or default which is such as would (if death had not ensued) have entitled the person injured to maintain an action and recover damages in respect thereof, the person who would have been liable if death had not ensued shall be liable to an action for damages, notwithstanding the death of the person injured.

(2) Subject to section 1A(2) below, every such action shall be for the benefit of the dependants of the person ("the deceased") whose death has been so caused.

(3) In this Act "dependant" means—
(a) the wife or husband or former wife or husband of the deceased;
(b) any person who—
  (i) was living with the deceased in the same household immediately before the date of the death; and
  (ii) had been living with the deceased in the same household for at least two years before that date; and
  (iii) was living during the whole of that period as the husband or wife of the deceased;
(c) any parent or other ascendant of the deceased;
(d) any person who was treated by the deceased as his parent;
(e) any child or other descendant of the deceased;
(f) any person (not being a child or the deceased) who, in the case of any marriage to which the deceased was at any time a party, was treated by the deceased as a child of the family in relation to that marriage;
(g) any person who is, or is the issue of, a brother, sister, uncle or aunt of the deceased.

(4) The reference to the former wife or husband of the deceased in subsection (3)(a) above includes a reference to a person whose marriage to the deceased has been annulled or declared void as well as a person whose marriage to the deceased has been dissolved.

(5) In deducing any relationship for the purpose of subsection (3) above—
(a) any relationship by affinity shall be treated as a relationship of consanguinity, any relationship of the half blood as a relationship of the whole blood, and the stepchild of any person as his child, and
(b) an illegitimate person shall be treated as the legitimate child of his mother and reputed father.'

THE DEPENDANT HAS TO SHOW A LOSS OF A BENEFIT

15.10   In every case a dependant has to show a loss. In *Yelland v Powell Duffryn Associated Collieries Ltd (No 2)* [1941] 1 KB 519 at 533, CA Du Parcq LJ stated:

'Any dependants who have suffered no such loss acquire no rights at all under the Act. If they bring an action and prove no loss, actual or prospective, the defendant is entitled to the verdict.'

THE TYPE OF LOSS THAT MUST BE SHOWN: THE 'REASONABLE EXPECTATION' TEST

15.11   The courts set about defining the type of damages that could be recovered. In *Franklin v South Eastern Railway Co* (1858) 3 H & N 211 at 214, (1843–60) All ER Rep 849 at 850 Pollock CB stated:

'Now it is clear that damage must be shown ... [these] should be calculated in reference to a reasonable expectation of benefit, as of right or otherwise, from the continuance of life ... a jury ought to be satisfied that there has been a loss of sensible and appreciable pecuniary benefit, which might have been reasonably expected from the continuance of life.'

WHAT KIND OF LOSS SUPPORTS A CLAIM

15.12   It follows, therefore, that loss of support, or the reasonable expectation of support, to some degree, is an essential element of the cause of action. None of the dependants can succeed unless they can prove actual dependence on the deceased at or before his death, or a probability that they would have received some support from him in the future if he had lived.

15.13   The position was summarised by the Law Commission:[1]

'... damages awarded under the Fatal Accidents Act 1976 generally compensate the loss of any non-business benefit that the claimant reasonably expected to receive from the deceased had the deceased continued to live (often referred to as "loss of dependency"). Thus, damages under the Act may provide compensation for the loss of money brought into the household by the deceased, for the loss of gratuitous services performed by the deceased, (including domestic work) and for the loss of fringe benefits, such as a company car.'

1   *Claims for Wrongful Death* (Law Com no 263) para 2.9.

THE BURDEN OF PROOF

15.14   In most cases the fact of dependency is clear and presents no practical difficulties. However, in less obvious cases the crucial point for claimant advisers to bear in mind is that a claimant is not called upon to prove definitively that there is a loss. Rather the claimant has to establish a loss of chance. The question of the burden of proof was considered in detail by the House of Lords in *Davies v Taylor* [1974] AC 207, [1972] 3 All ER 836, HL. The widow had left the deceased husband five weeks before he was killed. Her dependency claim was initially dismissed because the trial judge held that she had not shown that a reconciliation with her husband, had he lived, was more probable than not. The matter proceeded to the House of Lords where it was held that a claimant in these circumstances had to show a substantial chance of financial benefit. Lord Reid stated (at 212):

'The peculiarity in the present case is the appellant had left her husband some five weeks before his death and there was no immediate prospect of her returning to him. He wanted her to come back but she was unwilling to come. But she says that there was a prospect or chance or probability that she might have returned to him later and it is only in the event that she would have benefited from his survival. To my mind the issue and the sole issue is whether that chance or probability was substantial. If it was it must be evaluated. If it was a mere possibility it must be ignored. Many different words could be and have been used to indicate the dividing line. I can think of none better than "substantial" on one hand, or "speculative" on the other. It must be left to the good sense of the tribunal to decide on broad lines, without regard to legal niceties, but on a consideration of all the facts in proper prospective.'

The House of Lords expressly rejected the balance of probability test. Lord Reid considered this issue at length at 213:

'But here we are not and could not be seeking a decision either that the wife would or that she would not have returned to her husband. You can prove that a past event happened, but you cannot prove that a future event will happen and I do not think that the law is so foolish as to suppose that you can. All that you can do is to evaluate the chance. Sometimes it is virtually 100 per cent: sometimes virtually nil. But often it is somewhere in between. And if it is somewhere in between I do not see much difference between a probability of 51 per cent and a probability of 49 per cent.

"Injury" in the Fatal Accidents Act does not and could not possibly mean loss of a certainty. It must and can only mean loss of a chance. The chance may be a probability of over 99 per cent but it still only a chance. So I can see no merit in adopting here the test used for proving whether a fact did or did not happen. There it must be all or nothing.

If the balance of probability were the proper test what is to happen in the two cases which I have supposed of a 60 per cent and a 40 per cent probability. The 40 per cent case would get nothing but what about the 60 per cent case. Is it to get a full award on the basis that it has been proved that the wife would have returned to her husband? That would be the logical result. I can see no ground at all for saying that the 40 per cent case fails altogether but the 60 per cent case gets 100 per cent. But it would be almost absurd to say that the 40 per cent case gets nothing while the 60 per cent case is scaled down to that proportion of what the award would have been if the spouses had been living together. That would be applying the two different rules to the two cases. So I reject the balance of probability test ...'

15.15   This test can have important ramifications in difficult dependency cases such as the loss of an adult or minor child.

15.16   The case of *Davis v Bonner* (6 April 1995, unreported), CA (Kemp & Kemp M5-017/2 and M5-103) is very much to point. The deceased was

29 when he died. He had special educational needs. He was in full-time employment and lived in a flat provided by a college that provided for his needs. The dependency claim was brought by the parents, who argued that the deceased's father planned to retire in 1995 and the deceased would have then lived with them and have been a wage earner who contributed to their household.

15.17   The trial judge rejected the dependency claim. He found that the parents were not dependent upon the deceased at the time of his death. The Court of Appeal, applying *Davies v Taylor* [1974] AC 207, [1972] 3 All ER 836, HL, held that the test was *not* whether a dependency claim was established on the balance of probabilities, but to consider whether the chance of such being established was substantial, that is, beyond a mere possibility or speculation.

15.18   The court rejected a strictly arithmetical approach to the issue of dependency and awarded £5,000 by way of damages.

15.19   This 'overview' approach, rather than a strictly mathematical approach, is supported in several other cases. In *Doleman v Deakin* (1990) Times, 30 January, CA, the Court of Appeal upheld an award of £1,500 by Potts J to the parents of an 18-year-old man.

A 'JURY ISSUE'

15.20   Historically, it was left to the jury to determine the appropriate compensation for the dependants. This has led to observations that these issues of damages are similar to general damages and a matter of impression. Claimants are often met with arguments that damages should be 'rounded down' to reflect a jury's approach. However, there are signs that this approach is finding less favour with the courts.

15.21   In *Bordin v St Mary's NHS Trust* [2000] LL R 287 Mr Justice Crane considered arguments in relation to the assessment being a jury award. He observed:

'First of all, in my judgment the words of the Act are important. The reference to juries, as I have noted, no longer appears, although in *Spittle v Bunney*[1] and indeed in *Stanley v Saddique*[2] the Court of Appeal indicated that the judge should direct himself on the principles which a jury would properly adopt. But, unlike a jury, a judge must deliver a reasoned judgment and it seems to me that it would be inappropriate for a judge to shelter behind the proposition that he should act like a jury and decline a reasoned approach, if one is available on the evidence.'

The judge was suspicious of the 'broad brush' approach:

'In so far as there is a reasoned basis which can be found for the assessment, it seems to me to be appropriate for the judge to use that basis, checking at each stage the reasonableness of the claim and standing back at the end of the calculation to check that there has been no over-compensation. It would be inappropriate to use a "broad brush" artificially to the total, or to do so artificially ...'

After carrying out the analysis the judge considered the issue of whether the figures should be revised since the award was a jury award, he stated:

'It does not seem to me that, having made those calculations and made those reductions where, in my view, appropriate, that I should simply produce some round figures because a jury might, if a jury was still to hear such a case, be likely to produce a round figure in the end. If one looks at Kemp & Kemp, there are some examples of judges making calculations. I accept the submissions of counsel for the second claimant that I should not simply reduce the final figure arbitrarily to make it look, as it were, more like a jury award. Provided there has been careful attention to the need to avoid overcompensation along the way, I see no reason not to award the final figure at which I have arrived by this process. There is in the end some difficulty in seeing why one has to be more arbitrary in a Fatal Accidents Act case, bearing in mind the terms of s. 3 of the Act, that one does in other kinds of tortious recovery. That seems to me to some extent to be a matter of convention.'

1   [1988] 3 All ER 1031, [1988] 1 WLR 847, CA.
2   [1992] QB 1, [1991] 1 All ER 529, CA.

THE FATAL ACCIDENTS ACT 1976, S 4

15.22   The Fatal Accidents Act 1976, s 4 states:

'In assessing damages in respect of a person's death in an action under this Act, benefits which have accrued or will accrue to any person from his estate or otherwise as a result of his death shall be disregarded.'

15.23 This amendment was introduced because of recommendations by the Law Commission[1] and the Pearson Commission. It replaced the 'list' of items to be disregarded that was in the previous fatal accident legislation and gave rise to some anomalies.

1   *Claims for Wrongful Death* (Law Com no 263).

Construing the Fatal Accidents Act 1976, s 4

15.24 The width of the Fatal Accidents Act, s 4 has been criticised by the Law Commission. However, even the Law Commission observe that:[1]

'Nevertheless, a natural reading of the section suggests that all benefits accruing as a result of death should be disregarded.'

1   *Claims for Wrongful Death* (Law Com no 263) para 2.39.

15.25 The word 'benefits' has been given a wide construction, as demonstrated by the examples below. It goes beyond financial benefits and covers care, services and, possibly, even remarriage.

15.26 In *Auty v National Coal Board* [1985] 1 All ER 930, [1985] 1 WLR 784, CA a widow received a pension after the death of her husband. She claimed that she should recover damages for the post-retirement widow's pension that she would have received, that the Fatal Accidents Act 1976, s 4 should be applied and that the widow's pension that she had received since her husband's death should be ignored. The court held that:

(1)   As against her claim for the loss of her husband's (pre-retirement) support, the pension she received was ignored.

(2)   As against that part of her loss, she had suffered no loss as she was in receipt of a widow's pension.

15.27 In *Stanley v Siddique* [1992] QB 1, [1991] 1 All ER 529, CA a child claimed damages under the Fatal Accidents Act 1976 following the death of his mother. After the accident his father met and married another woman. It was found that the child was receiving better care from his father's wife than he would have expected from his mother. The court held that this was a benefit resulting from the death within the Fatal Accidents Act 1976, s 4 and so should not be taken into account in assessing the child's damages.

15.28 In *Hayden v Hayden* [1992] 4 All ER 681, [1992] 1 WLR 986, CA a child lost her mother in a driving accident caused by her father's negligence. The father gave up work to look after his daughter. The Court of Appeal decided that the plaintiff's damages should be reduced to the extent that her father remedied the loss of her mother's services.

The prospect of remarriage of a widower

15.29   In *Topp v London Country Bus (South West) Ltd* [1993] 3 All ER 448, [1993] 1 WLR 976, CA, both parties had agreed that the court was bound to ignore the prospects of remarriage as a result of the decision in *Stanley v Siddique* [1992] QB 1, [1991] 1 All ER 529, CA. However, the defendant reserved the right to argue a different position in a different court (although the Law Commission does not appear to agree with this[1]).

1   *Claims for Wrongful Death* (Law Com no 263).

Insurance policies, life insurance etc

15.30   The Fatal Accidents Act 1976, s 4 was designed to ensure that matters such as insurance policies, life insurance and similar types of policy were not deducted.

Adoption replaces loss of dependency

15.31   As a result of the wide interpretation of the Fatal Accidents Act 1976, s 4 it is unlikely that the decision in *Watson (Administrators of) v Willmott* [1991] 1 QB 140, [1991] 1 All ER 473 is sustainable. In *Watson* a young child's parents were both killed because of the defendant's negligence. The child was subsequently adopted by his uncle and aunt. It was held that the adoption replaced the loss of dependency.

CHAPTER 16

Valuing a dependency claim

NOT JUST MATHEMATICS

16.1 Whilst the parties will consider the multiplier and multiplicand issues in considerable detail, the calculation can go beyond a consideration of mathematics. In *Daniels v Jones* [1961] 3 All ER 24, [1961] 1 WLR 1103, CA Holroyd Pearce LJ observed (at 1104) that:

> 'If ... arithmetically the conclusion must be that there is no loss in the case, arithmetic has failed to provide the answer which common sense demands. It must be remembered that this is a question of fact expressly left to the jury ... Since the question is one of actual material loss, some arithmetical calculations are necessary. But they do not provide a substitute for commonsense. Much of the calculation must be in the realms of hypothesis, and in that region arithmetic is a good servant, but a bad master.'

See, for example, *O'Loughlin v Cape Distribution Ltd* [2001] EWCA Civ 178, [2001] All ER (D) 887 (Feb).

THE DECEASED'S INCOME

16.2 One of the first matters that needs to be ascertained is the loss of income. This is the starting point in most claims. However:
(1) The investigation should not only be based on the deceased's income at the date of death. Care should be taken to ensure that the court is presented with evidence to show the earnings that the deceased would have earned up to the date of trial.
(2) The deceased's future income and prospects must be taken into account. For instance, a trainee solicitor may have been earning a

relatively modest income at the date of death; however, it is clear that the income would increase upon the trainee qualifying.

See eg *Young v Percival* [1974] 3 All ER 677, [1975] 1 WLR 17, CA; *Malone v Rowan* [1984] 3 All ER 402, QBD.

LOSSES ARE NOT CONFINED TO PURE INCOME

16.3   The losses are not confined to pure income. So, for example:

Loss of fringe benefits

16.4   The loss of fringe benefits, such as a company car, can be recovered: *Clay v Pooler* [1982] 3 All ER 570, CA.

Loss of reasonable expectation of benefit

16.5   In *Betney v Rowland and Mallard* [1992] CLY 1786, HC a daughter claimed for the loss of the contribution her parents would have made to her wedding.

Payment of estate duty on gifts

16.6   In *Davies v Whiteways Cyder Co Ltd* [1975] QB 262, [1974] 3 All ER 168, QBD the dependants claimed damages for the estate duty they had to pay on gifts from the deceased as a result of the death occurring less than seven years after the gifts were made.

Loss of gifts which were anticipated

16.7   An example of this is cited at para 16.5 above in *Betney v Rowland and Mallard* [1992] CLY 1786, HC: the loss of the contribution expected from the parents to their daughter's wedding.

Loss of a right of action

16.8   In *Singh v Aitken* [1998] PIQR Q37 the deceased died from a heart attack, the defendants having misdiagnosed his condition. He would have survived if a correct diagnosis had been made. He had previously been seriously injured in a road traffic accident and had an unanswerable claim against the Motor Insurers Bureau (MIB) which had a value of £120,497.

16.9 After the death, the action against the MIB was settled for £20,000. The dependants, therefore, claimed 75% of the difference between that value and the sum paid under the compromise as damages under the Fatal Accidents Act 1976. The defendants contended that loss of the capital sum was not reasonably foreseeable and that damages for that loss were irrecoverable.

16.10 The judge gave judgment for the claimants. The injury resulting from the death to Mr Singh's dependants was the loss of the capital sum which would otherwise have been received by them from Mr Singh's personal injury damages had he survived. It was entirely foreseeable that the misdiagnosis of the heart condition would lead to Mr Singh's death. The defendants were required to take Mr Singh as they found him, a man with an unanswerable claim to a large sum which was forfeited by their negligence.

16.11 The dependants were also entitled to interest from the date which they would have received the capital sum of which they had been deprived.

Loss of unpaid services

16.12 This includes, for example, the 'DIY' claim which often prevails in personal injury cases. In *Crabtree v Wilson* [1993] PIQR Q24, CA it was said that the deceased's work around the home had an annual value of £1,500, this figure being used by the trial judge in calculating the award.

16.13 In *W v H* (11 February 2000, unreported), QBD Judge Rodgers QC (summary available on Lawtel), a 44-year old man was awarded £446,084 for loss of dependency suffered as a result of his wife's death. The claimant suffered from multiple sclerosis. His wife had provided care for him at their home, but after the accident the claimant was forced to move into a nursing home. At trial the cost of the claimant's nursing care was found to be recoverable from the defendant.

THE DEPENDENCY CALCULATION

The 'conventional' approach

16.14 There is some debate as to whether the approach in *Harris v Empress Motors Ltd* [1983] 3 All ER 561, [1984] 1 WLR 212, CA is always the appropriate approach. This provides a rough and ready approach to a dependency claim in circumstances where partners were married or living as husband and wife. To take account of the money the deceased would have spent on themselves:

- 33.33% is deducted if the deceased left only a dependent spouse.
- 25% is deducted if there are dependent children as well as a spouse.

The multiplier will often have to be approached carefully because part of the multiplier will be attributed to the period when the children are dependent and the balance when they cease to be dependent.

16.15   The conventional approach is not always applicable. For example, in *Coward v Comex Houlder Diving Ltd* (1988) Independent, 25 July (Kemp & Kemp 23-003.11-13), an increased percentage dependency was allowed by the Court of Appeal because the husband worked as a diver in the North Sea for long periods and was considered to have been likely to have spent less money on himself as a result.

If a spouse is earning

16.16   If a spouse is earning before the death and continues earning after death then the calculation is slightly more complex.

16.17   The dependency is assessed by calculating two-thirds of the *joint* income and deducting from that figure the amount of the survivor's earnings.

16.18   So, for example, if both husband and wife with no children are earning £25,000 a year net each.

- The joint income is £50,000.
- Two-thirds of the joint income is £33,300.
- Deduct the surviving partner's earnings of £25,000.
- The annual loss is £8,300.

16.19   This can give rise to some disappointing and surprising results; however, it is not open to the court to ignore the surviving spouse's income: see *Crabtree v Wilson* [1993] PIQR Q24, CA.

The multiplier

The multiplier runs from the date of death

16.20   In *Cookson v Knowles* [1979] AC 556, [1978] 2 All ER 604, HL the House of Lords held that the multiplier should be calculated from the date of death. The court then divides the multiplier between the pre-trial period and post-trial period. That part of the multiplier which remains after trial is applied to assess the post-trial losses.

16.21 In cases where there has been some delay between the death and trial, the multiplier could, therefore, be 'used up'. In these circumstances the Court of Appeal has held that the calculation can be more flexible to reflect the fact that the length of time has reduced the element of uncertainty: *Corbett v Barking, Havering and Brentwood Health Authority* [1991] 2 QB 408, [1991] 1 All ER 498, CA.

16.22 This approach was criticised by the Law Commission in its report *Claims for Wrongful Death* (Law Com no 263), where it was advocated that the multiplier should be calculated from the date of trial. It has been suggested that this proposal can be put in place without legislation.

Factors affecting the multiplier

16.23
(1) Expectation of life of deceased and dependants.
(2) Expectation of dependency of child dependants.
    This will effect how the 'dependency percentage' is apportioned.
(3) Expectation of divorce or separation of deceased and dependant.
    In *Owen v Martin* [1992] PIQR Q151, CA, the marriage was regarded as fragile and the multiplier reduced from 15 to 11 by the Court of Appeal. The Law Commission was critical of this approach.

Other factors influencing the multiplier

16.24
(1) *The prospects of remarriage of a widow (and her actual remarriage) is ignored: Fatal Accidents Act 1976, s 3(3).*
    The prospects of remarriage of a widow is ignored as is her actual remarriage. (As we have seen at para 15.29 above, it is arguable that this also applies to remarriage of a widower.) The prospects of marriage of a widow or the actual remarriage cannot, therefore, be used to reduce the multiplier.
(2) *The fact that a couple are not married is taken into account: Fatal Accidents Act 1976, s 3(4).*
    In practice this usually leads to a reduced multiplier.

SOME DIFFICULT ISSUES IN DEPENDENCY CLAIMS

Illegal means of support

16.25   There is some controversy surrounding less legitimate, or totally illegitimate, means of earning an income.

16.26   In *Burns v Edman* [1970] 2 QB 541, [1970] 1 All ER 886, QBD the deceased's life had been 'devoted to crime' and it was highly unlikely that he would have reformed. His dependants were held not to be entitled to damages for their loss of dependency because the support came directly from the proceeds of criminal offences.

16.27   In *Hunter v Butler* [1996] RTR 396, CA, an argument that there was a dependency based on the deceased working 'on the side' whilst still claiming social security benefits was rejected on the basis that this amounted to fraud. However, the Court of Appeal did, on the facts, find that the deceased would have found legitimate work and awarded damages on that basis.

16.28   Note that these decisions are heavily criticised in *Kemp on Personal Injury Damages*, vol 1, paras 25-006–25-008. The issue may be different if legal work is being done but the proceeds not declared to the Revenue: see *Duller v South East Lincs Engineers* [1981] CLY 585 (Kemp & Kemp 25-008/1).

Social security is the main source of income

16.29   In *Hunter v Butler* [1996] RTR 396, CA the court considered an argument that a loss of social security was a recoverable loss. The widow had received Widow's Allowance and Widowed Mother's Allowance which were higher than Supplementary Benefit would be. Lord Justice Waite observed (at 402(J)):

'The argument that the appellant in these circumstances suffered "injury" within the terms of s 3 as a result of the deceased's death appears to me to be wholly untenable. In respect of Supplementary Benefit, she no less than he, was dependent in that regard upon the state.'

16.30   In *Cox v Hockenhull* [1999] 3 All ER 577, [2000] 1 WLR 750, CA a husband was denied recovery for the loss of the invalid care allowance which he had been paid as carer of his severely disabled wife. This was not a benefit derived from the relationship of husband and wife. The husband had been employed by the state to care for a severely disabled person.

16.31 *However*, the husband's loss of financial dependency *was* measured by a proportion of the state benefits received, in the form of disability living allowance, disablement allowance and – to an extent – income support. It was held to be immaterial that the source of income both before and after the death was the state and it made no difference at all that the benefits had been non-contributory. *Hunter v Butler* [1996] RTR 396, CA was distinguished because the state benefits there to the wife were to continue after the husband's death. For this reason there was no recovery in respect of housing benefit and council tax benefit.

16.32 The husband also recovered for his loss of his wife's services, although her disability and deteriorating health meant that the Court of Appeal reduced the award substantially.

Where a dependant is also the tortfeasor

16.33 There has been considerable discussion as to what the results should be if the tortfeasor is also a dependant: see the Law Commission report *Claims for Wrongful Death* (Law Com no 263) para 5.54. It is far from clear how the House of Lords decision in *Hunt v Severs* [1994] 2 AC 350, [1994] 2 All ER 385, HC affects fatal accident claims. However, it is clear that:

(1) The negligent dependent cannot claim against himself for his own losses.

(2) It is unlikely that any expenditure, including care, provided by the negligent party will be recoverable, even as another dependant's loss or damage. In *Hayden v Hayden* [1992] 4 All ER 681, [1992] 1 WLR 986, CA a child lost her mother in a driving accident caused by her father's negligence. The father gave up work to look after his daughter. The Court of Appeal decided that the plaintiff's damages should be reduced to the extent that her father remedied the loss of her mother's services.

NON-PECUNIARY LOSSES

Damages for death of a mother or carer

16.34   The Law Commission report, *Claims for Wrongful Death* (Law Com no 263) observes at that:

> '.... a mother obviously does more for her children than mere housekeeping and childminding, and she provides her services with more commitment than would a hired help. The deceased mother will usually have unique qualities that no hired replacement can offer.'

Addressing the issue of 'loss of a mother' is increasingly a misnomer. What we are concerned with here is the issue of loss of a person who provides services rather than income.

The judicial approach

16.35   The courts have never approached the issue of valuation of loss of a mother's services on a strict mathematical basis. There are a number of variables. In particular, the benefit received by a child from its mother varies with the age of a child. In *Regan v Williamson* [1976] 1 WLR 305, 120 Sol Jo 217, Watkins J considered a strictly arithmetical approach to the issue of loss of a mother based on the hiring of a housekeeper. He observed (at 308) that:

> 'The simplicity of such an exercise would, in my opinion, work an injustice upon the deceased's dependants which I think the average member of the public would describe as quite monstrous.'

He continued (at 309):

> '... the word "services" has been too narrowly construed. It should, at least, include an acknowledgment that a wife and mother does not work to set hours and, still less, to rule. She is in constant attendance, save for those hours when she is, if that is the fact, at work. During some of those hours she may well give the children instruction on essential matters to do with their upbringing and, possibly, with such things as their homework. This sort of attention seems to be as much of a service, and probably more valuable to them, than the other kinds of service conventionally so described.'

General principles

16.36 Some general principles can be ascertained:
(1) The courts tend to look kindly on the hiring of relatives even if these are more expensive than other alternatives.

In *Morris v H Rigby (Road Haulage) Ltd* (1966) 110 Sol Jo 834, CA the widower employed his wife's sister to care for his children. The Court of Appeal held this to be entirely reasonable even though this was more costly than market rates. Similarly in *Regan v Williamson* [1976] 1 WLR 305, 120 Sol Jo 217 it was held entirely reasonable for the plaintiff to bring into his home someone who he knew, who knew the children and who had an attachment to them.
(2) The courts will make a separate, distinct, award for the financial value of the loss of a mother's services: *Regan v Williamson* [1976] 1 WLR 305, 120 Sol Jo 217; *Mehmet v Perry* [1977] 2 All ER 529, QBD.

Separate award for 'intangible loss' of mother's services

16.37 There is now a well-recognised head of damages dealing with the 'intangible' loss of a mother's services. These cannot be quantified, but are real losses. The sums are relatively modest. In *Corbett v Barking, Havering and Brentwood Health Authority* [1991] 2 QB 408, [1991] 1 All ER 498, CA, £3,000 was awarded. In *Johnson v British Midland Airways Ltd* [1996] PIQR Q8, a 13-year-old son was awarded £3,500. In *ATH v MS* [2002] EWCA Civ 792, [2003] QB 965, the Court of Appeal reduced awards of £5,000 and £7,000, to children aged 11 and 8 at their mother's death, to £3,500 and £4,500.

Dependency claims following the death of a child

Parents claim following the death of a child

16.38 The primary issue here is establishing a loss of a reasonable expectation of benefit. There is long-established case law where damages have been awarded to parents following the death of an adult child. However, the old cases rely on previous social mores; it may be less common today for parents to expect to be dependent upon their children.

16.39 In the case of a very young child it may well be that the loss is now regarded as too speculative. The claim for the loss of a 13-year-old child succeeded in *Buckland v Guildford Gas Light and Coke Co* [1949] 1 KB 410, [1948] 2 All ER 1086, KBD. However, in *Barnett v Cohen* [1921] 2 KB 461, 19 LGR 623, KBD, a claim for a very young child, aged four, was rejected because it was not possible to show a reasonable probability of reasonable financial support to the parents.

16.40   In these cases the kindest, and usually the most accurate, advice is that the bereavement payment plus the funeral expenses is the only feasible claim.

16.41   In the case of older children, some care should be taken. In these circumstances there is no bereavement payment if the child died after the age of 18. If a reasonable expectation of benefit can be shown then a claim could succeed, albeit contained within modest limits.

Examples of claims succeeding in relation to the death of a minor child

16.42   In *Wathen v Vernon* [1970] RTR 471, CA, the deceased was 17½ years of age and an apprentice. The sum of £500 was awarded under the Fatal Accidents Act 1976. The court held that the deceased would have helped his parents, particularly if their position worsened; however, he would also have had his own life to lead and the prospect of his marrying and having to look after a family of his own had to be taken into account when calculating a multiplier. It is important to note that the court was clear on the point that it was entitled to give damages for loss of *potential* support in cases where no support has yet been forthcoming and the possibility of support being necessary in the future or being provided was rather remote.

16.43   However, it has to be emphasised that claims for loss of dependency following the death of a minor child are extremely problematic. Unless there are specific cultural of family features which demonstrate a likelihood of dependence, these cases will rarely succeed and the awards made are likely to be minimal.

Examples of claims succeeding following the death of an adult child

16.44   The case of *Davis v Bonner* (6 April 1995, unreported), CA (Kemp & Kemp M5-017/2 and M5-103) is of some interest. The deceased was 29 when he died. He had special educational needs. He was in full time employment and lived in a flat provided by a college that provided for his needs. The dependency claim was brought by the parents who argued that the deceased's father planned to retire in 1995 and the deceased would have then lived with them and have been a wage earner who contributed to their household.

16.45 The trial judge rejected the dependency claim. He found that the parents were not dependent upon the deceased at the time of his death. The Court of Appeal, applying *Davies v Taylor* [1974] AC 207, [1972] 3 All ER 836, HL, held that the test was *not* whether a dependency claim was established on the balance of probabilities but to consider whether the chance of such being established was substantial, that is beyond a mere possibility or speculation. (See the detailed discussion at para 15.14 above.)

16.46 The court rejected a strictly arithmetical approach to the issue of dependency and awarded £5,000 by way of damages. Neill LJ observed:[1]

'Counsel for both parties accepted that the test to be applied was that explained in the speeches in the House of Lords in *Davies v Taylor* [1974] AC 207, particularly in the speech of Lord Reid. The dividing line is between a substantial prospect and a speculative prospect. It is not a test on the balance of probabilities.

One should be very careful not to examine a judgment as though it were a statute. But for my part, I am not convinced that the learned judge asked himself the right question in this case: was there a substantial prospect that the deceased would have contributed to the support of his parents if he had survived? If that question is posed on the facts of this case ... the answer is "yes", though the uncertainties to which the judge drew attention in his very careful judgment, must mean that the prospect is certainly not near the top of the scale. The Court must look at the matter broadly and consider all the facts. I agree with Mr. Justice Cazalet's assessment that £5,000 fairly represents the injury suffered by the two dependants jointly.'

1 *Davis v Bonner* (6 April 1995, unreported), CA (Kemp & Kemp M5-017/2 and M5-103 at 64160).

The overview approach

16.47 This 'overview' approach, rather than a strictly mathematical approach, is supported in several other cases. In *Doleman v Deakin* (1990)

Times, 30 January, CA the Court of Appeal upheld an award of £1,500 by Potts J to the parents of an 18-year-old man. Potts J stated:

> 'This is not a case for a multiplicand or a multiplier ... This is a case which the court must on the evidence do its best to decide what a reasonable figure is in all the circumstances, giving full weight to the many uncertainties of life to which counsel referred me, and not overlooking the fact that any award is an award in respect of items of dependency that would not necessarily arise for some years to come.'

CHAPTER 17

Non-dependency damages in fatal cases

FUNERAL EXPENSES

17.1 It is well established that funeral expenses are recoverable. However, for all the expenses to be recoverable they must be reasonable in all the circumstances, including the deceased's station in life, creed and racial origin: *Gammell v Wilson* [1982] AC 27, [1981] 1 All ER 578, CA.

17.2
(1) Claims for a tombstone have succeeded: *Goldstein v Salvation Army Assurance Society* [1917] 2 KB 291, 86 LJKB 793, KBD.
(2) Claims for embalming have succeeded: *Hart v Griffiths-Jones* [1948] 2 All ER 729.
(3) Friends who helped a widow after her husband was killed in France and arranged for the return of the body recovered their expenses: *Schneider v Eisovitch* [1960] 2 QB 430, [1960] 1 All ER 169, QBD.

17.3 The cost of a wake and a memorial or monument to the deceased failed in *Gammell v Wilson* [1982] AC 27, [1981] 1 All ER 578, CA, but succeeded in *Kegworth v British Midland Airways* (Kemp & Kemp 20-022). It can be difficult to distinguish between a tombstone and a memorial. In *Gammell v Wilson* Mr B A Hytner QC (sitting as a deputy judge of the High Court) stated (at 43):

'that there is a distinction between a headstone finishing off, describing and marking the grave, which is part of the funeral service, and a memorial which is not.'

17.4 In *Quainoo and Brent & Harrow Health Authority* (1982) 132 NLJ 1000 the deceased was a member of the Ghanaian royal family.
(1) Items recovered included three air fares from London to Accra; air freight of the coffin; the charges of a London funeral director; and the

cost of hiring cars for the funeral procession of 80 miles from Accra
to Kumasi.

(2) Items disallowed included printing and stationery for the funeral
announcements; wreaths and other decorations; photographer's fees;
telephone calls before and after the funeral; hire of a hall in London
for a reception before the funeral for 500 people; and funeral clothes.

A CLAIM IN RESPECT OF A LIVING CLAIMANT WHO IS SHORTLY TO DIE

17.5   In *Bateman v Hydro Agri (UK) Ltd* (Kemp & Kemp 20-24) the
plaintiff was suffering from mesothelioma and was likely to die within
three months of the date of the trial. Mr Anthony Temple QC allowed the
cost of the future funeral expenses. The editors of Kemp observe that this
was a bold decision, but that they believe it to be right in principle (Kemp
& Kemp 20-24).

BEREAVEMENT DAMAGES

17.6   The Administration of Justice Act 1982, s 3 inserted the Fatal
Accidents Act 1976, s 1A and introduced a statutory claim for damages
for bereavement in respect of the death of a limited class of close relatives.
The sum currently stands at £10,000.

A very limited class of claimants

17.7   There is a very limited class of relatives entitled to the bereavement
payment. The Fatal Accidents Act 1976, s 1A(2) states:

'(2) A claim for damages for bereavement shall only be for the
benefit—
(a) of the wife or husband, or the deceased; and
(b) where the deceased was a minor who was never married—
(i) of his parents, if he was legitimate, and
(ii) of his mother, if he was illegitimate.'

The excluded categories

17.8   Note that:

(1) The former husband or wife is excluded from recovery. However, this section tends to be construed strictly. If, at the date of death, the decree nisi has been made but not the decree absolute, then the spouse is entitled to recover.
(2) Cohabitees cannot recover.
(3) The father of an illegitimate child cannot claim under the section.
(4) Where both parents claim bereavement damages the damages are divided equally between them: Fatal Accidents Act 1976, s 1A(4). There is some dispute as to what should happen if one of the parents is responsible for the death and unable to recover. Judicial authority suggests that the parent not at fault recovers half of the payment: *Navaei v Navaei* (6 January 1995, unreported) (reported in Kemp & Kemp 4-007/2).
(5) The crucial date is the date of the death. In *Doleman v Deakin* (1990) Times, 30 January, CA (Kemp & Kemp M5-018) the Court of Appeal upheld a decision not to award bereavement damages to parents when their son was injured shortly before his eighteenth birthday, in a coma for six weeks and died shortly after his eighteenth birthday.

17.9 Interest runs at the full rate from the date of death: *Prior v Hastie* [1987] CLY 1219.

INJURIES AND LOSSES OF THE DECEASED PRIOR TO DEATH

Action brought by the estate

17.10 An important practical point is that a claim for injuries and losses prior to the death can only be made by the deceased's estate and not by his dependants. In these circumstances it is necessary for a grant of probate to be taken out.

Pain and suffering prior to death

17.11 The law here is that:
(1) If the death was instantaneous, or almost instantaneous, then there is no award. In *Hicks v Chief Constable of the South Yorkshire Police* [1992] 2 All ER 65, 8 BMLR 70, HL, CA the Court of Appeal held that where unconsciousness and death occur in such a short period after the injury which causes death no damages are payable. The last few moments of mental agony and pain are in reality part of the death itself.

(2) If there is pain and suffering prior to death then an award can be made to the *estate*. In theory general damages in these cases are assessed in a similar way to general damages in other cases.

17.12   There are relatively few cases on this issue. A selection can be found in Kemp & Kemp L7-023. The approach that is adopted is that the court isolates the 'pain and suffering' element of the claim for personal injury and awards damages for that element. In *Fallon v Beaumont* (1994) CLY 1749, for instance, it was common ground that if the deceased had lived he would have received damages in the £70,000–75,000 region.

Losses and expenses prior to the death

17.13   The estate can also claim losses and expenses incurred by the deceased prior to his death. In cases where there is a considerable gap between the event which caused the death and the death itself, this can be a matter of considerable practical importance:

(1) A claim for loss of income will be on the basis of the *full* loss of earnings rather than on *Owen v Martin* [1992] PIQR Q151, CA principles.

(2) There could be a considerable claim for nursing expenses, including the cost of hospital visits and gratuitous care provided.

CHAPTER 18

Damages and procedure

18.1 There is remarkably little guidance on the preparation of claims for damages in personal injury cases.[1] In particular the drafting of the Schedule. In this chapter we look at the most important aspect of procedure and damages.

1 The one exception being Longstaff, Buchan and Mortimer *Personal Injury Schedules*.

THE PRE-ACTION PROTOCOL

18.2 The Pre-Action Protocol sets out some requirements in relation to damages.

The letter of claim

18.3 The claimant is enjoined:
- To send *two* copies of the letter of claim, immediately sufficient information is available to substantiate a realistic claim and before issues of quantum are addressed in detail.
- The letter must contain *a clear summary of the facts* on which the claim is based together with the *nature of any injuries* suffered and of *any financial loss incurred*.
- *Sufficient information* must be given in order to enable the defendant to commence investigations and, at least, to put a broad valuation on the 'risk'.

Special damages

18.4 A Schedule of Special Damages, with supporting documents, must be submitted as soon as possible: see para 18.15 below.

Instructing experts: a massive change in culture

18.5   The Protocol sets out requirements in relation to the instruction of experts, including medical experts.

- Before any prospective party to the action instructs an expert he should give the other party a list of the names of one or more experts in the relevant speciality which he considers are suitable to instruct.
- Within 14 days the other party may indicate an objection to one or more of the experts. The first party should then instruct a mutually acceptable expert.
- If all the experts are objected to then the parties may instruct experts of their own. It would be for the court to decide subsequently, if proceedings are issued, whether either party had acted unreasonably.
- If the second party does not object to a nominated expert then he shall not be entitled to rely on his own expert within that particular speciality unless:
  (a) the first party agrees;
  (b) the court directs; or
  (c) the first party's report has been amended and the first party is not prepared to disclose the original report.
- *Either party* may send to the expert written questions on the report, relevant to the issues, via the first party's solicitors. The expert should send answers to the questions separately and directly to each party.

Particular provisions in relation to medical experts

18.6   As noted above, all of these provisions apply to medical experts. Further:

- When a medical expert is instructed then the claimant's solicitor should organise access to the relevant medical records.
- A recommended letter of instructions to a medical expert is annexed to the Protocol.

ISSUING PROCEEDINGS – HIGH COURT OR COUNTY COURT? RULES GOVERNING THE CHOICE OF COURT

18.7   The Civil Procedure Rules restrict the choice of court of issue.

(1) You cannot issue in the High Court (in any action) unless the value of the claim is £15,000 or more.
(2) In a personal injury action the value of the action must be £50,000 or more.

THE CONTENTS OF THE CLAIM FORM

18.8 The claim form must:
- Contain a concise statement of the nature of the claim.
- Specify the remedy which the claimant seeks.
- Contain a statement of value.

The statement of value

18.9 The claim form must state whether the claimant expects to recover:
- more than £5,000;
- between £5,000 and £15,000; or
- more than £15,000,

or that the claimant cannot say how much the claim is worth.

The High Court

18.10 If issuing in the High Court it must be stated that:
- In non-personal injury actions that the claim exceeds £15,000.
- In personal injury cases that the claim exceeds £50,000.

CALCULATING VALUE FOR THE PURPOSE OF THE STATEMENT OF VALUE

18.11 In calculating the value the following matters are *disregarded*:
- interest;
- costs;
- the possibility of a finding of contributory negligence;
- any diminution of the claim due to a counterclaim or set off; and
- any sums due to be recouped by the DSS.

THE CONTENTS OF THE PARTICULARS OF CLAIM

Matters the Particulars of Claim must contain

18.12   The Particulars of Claim:
- Must contain a concise statement of the facts upon which the claimant relies.
- If interest is sought then the contractual or statutory basis for the interest calculation must be set out.

Personal injury cases

18.13   In personal injury cases the Particulars of Claim must contain:
- The claimant's date of birth.
- Brief details of the claimant's personal injuries.
- A Schedule of *past and future* losses must be served with the Particulars of Claim.
- A medical report must be served with the Particulars of Claim if medical evidence is relied upon.
- A provisional damages claim must set out the statutory basis for the claim and the nature of the deterioration. (For detail see chapter 19.)
- Fatal Accidents Act 1976 claims.

DRAFTING SCHEDULES: GUIDANCE FROM THE RULES

18.14   As we have seen both the Pre-Action Protocol and the Civil Procedure Rules require the claimant to serve a Schedule of Damages. However, the rules give no assistance at all as to what is required. CPR 16 PD 4.2 states:

'The Claimant must attach to his particulars of claim a schedule of details of any part and future expenses and losses which he claims.'

Guidance as to the Schedule

18.15   There is no guidance in the rules as to form or format of the Schedule. The best guidance can be found in *Personal Injury Schedules.*[1] The authors suggest seven general principles:
(1) 'If you don't ask you don't get.'
(2) 'If in doubt, include.'

(3) 'Only claim the arguably recoverable.'
(4) 'Be realistic.'
(5) 'Don't overstate your case.'
(6) 'Double check your figures.'
(7) 'Presentation, presentation, presentation.'

1   Langstaff, Buchan and Latimer-Sayer *Personal Injury Schedules* (Butterworths, 2002) pp 7–9.

The importance of the Schedule

18.16   The authors also suggest that the Schedule is an immediate 'giveaway'. They suggest that:[1]

'Any schedule, whether simple or complex, will tell the defendants the experience of the claimant's lawyers. A poorly-drafted schedule will not impress defendants and provides them with an opportunity to make lower offers from the start than they otherwise would. Equally a well drafted schedule will tell experienced defendants' lawyers that the claimant's lawyers are on top of the case and will give them a good run for their money.'

1   Langstaff, Buchan and Latimer-Sayer *Personal Injury Schedules* (Butterworths, 2002), p 3.

Judicial guidance

18.17   In relation to the overall strategy in preparing the Schedule there is, again, little definitive guidance.

18.18   In *Moser v Enfield and Haringey Health Authority* (1982) 133 NLJ 105, QBD (Kemp vol 2, section A4) Michael Davies J observed:

'Thorough preparation of a case is admirable. Catering for every possible contingency may be desirable or at least excusable. It may even be legitimate tactics to pitch one's case very high, although it is dangerous with some tribunals. But there are limits ..., the preparation of production of vast, detailed and, I would add, exaggerated costings, often on principles not recognised by the courts ... is very expensive. I would advise parties to this sort of litigation to be moderate and practical in their approach, both as to the volume and nature of the evidence which they call, and as to the amount claimed. They may be surprised how effective this approach is.'

THE DANGERS OF EXAGGERATION

18.19   There are dangers for claimants in exaggerating the claim.

The Civil Procedure Rules

18.20   CPR 44.3(4) states:

'In deciding what order (if any) to make about costs, the court must have regard to all the circumstances, including –
   (a) the conduct of all the parties;
   (b) whether a party has succeeded on part of his case, even if he has not been wholly successful; and
   (c) any payment into court or admissible offer to settle made by a party which is drawn to the court's attention (whether or not made in accordance with Part 36).'

18.21   CPR 44.3(5) states:

'The conduct of the parties includes –
   (a) conduct before, as well as during, the proceedings, and in particular the extent to which the parties followed any relevant pre-action protocol;
   (b) whether it was reasonable for a party to raise, pursue or contest a particular allegation or issue;
   (c) the manner in which a party has pursued or defended his case or a particular allegation or issue;
   (d) whether a claimant who has succeeded in his claim in whole or in part exaggerated his claim.'

Case law on exaggeration

18.22   It is clear that the over-inflation of a claim can lead to the claimant being penalised. In *Molloy v Shell UK Ltd* [2001] EWCA Civ 1272, [2002] PIQR P7 at P60 the claimant had filed a Schedule of Loss claiming over £300,000, which included a claim that he would never be able to return to his previous employment as an oil-platform worker. Days before the trial the defendant discovered that the claimant had, in fact, returned to work on the oil platform and had worked offshore regularly for a prolonged period. The judge awarded the claimant £18,897 which was less than the payment into court. The trial judge ordered the claimant to pay 75% of the defendant's costs after the day of the payment into court. The Court of Appeal allowed an appeal and ordered the claimant to pay *all* the defendant's costs. Laws LJ observed (at [18]):

'For my part I entertain considerable qualms as to whether, faced with manipulation of the civil justice system on so grand a scale, the court should once it knows the facts entertain the case at all save to make the dishonest claimant pay the defendant's costs.'

18.23 In *Devine v Franklin* [2002] EWHC 1846 (Gray J) a claimant was found to have exaggerated his claim for damages and his injuries. As a result his award for costs was limited to that the fixed costs permitted under the Small Claims Track.

STATEMENT OF TRUTH

18.24 A Schedule of Damages must contain a Statement of Truth.

THE DEFENDANT'S RESPONSE TO THE CLAIM FOR DAMAGES

The defence and damages

18.25 The rules relating to the contents of the defence are set out in CPR 16.

End of the general denial

18.26 One of the central changes to the drafting of a defence is the end of the general 'denial'. CPR 16.5 deals with the drafting of the defence:

'(1) In his defence, the defendant must state—
  (a) which of the allegations in the particulars of claim he denies;
  (b) which allegations he is unable to admit or deny, but which he requires the claimant to prove;
  (c) which allegations he admits.
(2) Where the defendant denies an allegation—
  (a) he must state his reasons for doing so; and
  (b) if he intends to put forward a different version of events from that given by the claimant, he must state his own version.
(3) A defendant who—

(a) fails to deal with an allegation; but

(b) has set out in his defence the nature of his case in relation to the issue to which that allegation is relevant, shall be taken to require that allegation to be proved.

(4) Where the claim includes a money claim, a defendant shall be to taken to require that any allegation relating to the amount of money claimed be pressed unless he expressly admits the allegation.

(5) Subject to paragraphs (3) and (4), a defendant who fails to deal with an allegation shall be taken to admit that allegation.'

Particular rules for the defence personal injury cases

18.27   The Practice Direction to CPR 16 imposes additional obligations upon a defence in a personal injury claim.

When the Particulars of Claim are accompanied by a medical report

18.28   When a medical report is attached to the Particulars of Claim (ie in most cases) the defendant *must* state in the defence whether he:

12.1(1)   agrees;

(2)   disputes; or

(3)   neither agrees nor disputes but has no knowledge of,

the matters contained in the medical report.

18.29   When the defendant disputes any part of the medical report he must set out in the defence the reasons for doing so. Further if the defendant has obtained its own medical report upon which it intends to rely this must be attached to the defence.

Responding to the Schedule of Loss

18.30   Further when the Particulars of Claim are accompanied by a Schedule of Loss (in most cases) the defendant should include in the defence, or attach to the defence a counter-Schedule stating:

12.2.(1)   which of those items he—

(a)   agrees,

(b)   disputes, or

(c)   neither agrees or disputes but has no knowledge of, and

(2) where any items are disputed, supplying alternative figures where appropriate.

Other obligations on the defendant

18.31 The rules put forward other obligations in relation to the drafting of the defence.

18.32 We have seen in previous chapters that there is an obligation on the claimant to give a statement of value. If the defendant disputes that statement then the defence must state why it is disputed and give its own statement of the value of the claim. The law as to mitigation of loss is contained, in detail, in chapter 4. There is an interesting issue as to who should plead issues relating to mitigation of loss. Interestingly the rules state that the Particulars of Claim should deal with 'any facts relating to mitigation of loss or damage' (CPR 16 PD 5.2(8)).

Pleading mitigation of loss

18.33 This last aspect of the requirement on the claimant (which is set out in the Practice Direction and not the Rules) appears ridiculous in the extreme. In the interim report Lord Woolf considered imposing a specific obligation on *the defendant* to plead matters such as mitigation of loss. This is clearly the correct approach since the burden of proof in establishing mitigation of loss is on the defendant (see chapter 4).

Who has the burden to plead mitigation of loss?

18.34 As we have seen CPR 16 PD 8.2(8) imposes an obligation upon a claimant specifically to set out:

'any facts relating to mitigation of loss or damage.'

18.35 There is no obligation on the defendant in the rules to plead mitigation of loss. This contrasts with judicial views on the duty on the defendant. That the burden of proof is on the defendant is set out in chapter 4. In the Privy Council decision in *Geest plc v Lansiquot* [2002] UKPC 48, [2003] 1 All ER 383 the council observed:

'Had there been pleadings, however, it would have been the clear duty of the company to plead in its defence that the plaintiff had failed to mitigate her damage and to give appropriate particulars sufficient to alert the plaintiff to the nature of the company's case, enable the plaintiff to direct her evidence to the real areas of dispute and avoid surprise (see Bullen & Leake & Jacob's Precedents of Pleadings, 14th ed (2001), vol 2 1103, paragraph 71-13; Rules of the Supreme Court Order 18 rule 12(1)(c); Order 18 rule 8(1)(b) ... It should however be clearly understood that if a defendant intends to content that plaintiff has failed to act reasonably to mitigate his or her damage, notice of such contention should be clearly given to the plaintiff long enough before the hearing to enable the plaintiff to prepare to meet it. If there are no pleadings, notice should be given by letter.'

A DISTINCT DIFFERENCE OF VIEWS

18.36   We have a distinct difference therefore between the CPR – which imposes a duty to plead mitigation of loss only on the claimant and no such duty on the defendant – and the Privy Council (in views that would presumably be echoed in the House of Lords) that firmly places the obligation to plead failure to mitigate on the defendant. It is interesting to speculate what the Council would have had to say if it was considering the Civil Procedure Rules rather than the old rules of the Supreme Court.

WITNESS STATEMENTS AND DAMAGES

The importance of witness statements and damages

18.37   The importance of using the witness statement to prove a claim for damages is often overlooked. Apart from the medical evidence the witness statements are often the *only* way in which a party can prove their case as to damages.

18.38   The Practice Direction for the Fast Track contains provision for the exchange of witness statements and that:

'The evidence in chief for each party will be contained in witness statements and reports ...'

18.39   This makes it clear that, on the fast track, evidence in chief will normally be by way of witness statements. In practice some judges allow some supplementary questions. However, this is not guaranteed and is usually aimed at clarifying matters already set out in the witness statement;

it will be very rare for a party to be allowed to introduce totally new elements at this stage

The rules

18.40 The rules relating to witness statements are at CPR 32 and supplemented by a very important draft Practice Direction. The salient part of the rule (from a drafting viewpoint) is that:

'32.8 A witness statement must comply with the requirements set out in the relevant practice direction. (Part 22 requires that a witness statement be verified by a statement of truth).'

The form of a witness statement

18.41 CPR 32 PD 17 states that:
1 The witness statement should be headed with the title of the proceedings. Where the proceedings are between several parties with the same status it is possible to truncate the heading.
2 At the top right hand corner of the first page there should be clearly written:
  (1) the party on whose behalf it is made;
  (2) the initials and surname of the witness;
  (3) the number of the statement in relation to that witness;
  (4) the identifying initials and number of each exhibit referred to; and
  (5) the date the statement was made.

The body of the witness statement

18.42 CPR 32 PD 18 states:

'18.1 The witness statement must, if practicable, be in the intended witness's own words. The statement should be expressed in the first person and should also state:
1. the full name of the witness,
2. his place of residence or, if he is making the statement in his professional, business or other occupational capacity, the address at which he works, the position he holds and the name of his firm or employer,

3.   his occupation, or if he has none, his description,
4.   the fact that he is a party to the proceedings or is the employee of such a party if it be the case.

18.2 A witness statement must indicate:
1.   which of the statements in it are made from the witness's own knowledge and which are matters of information or belief,
2.   the source for any matters of information or belief.

18.3 An exhibit used in conjunction with a witness statement should be verified and identified by the witness and remain separate from the witness statement.

18.4 Where a witness refers to an exhibit or exhibits he should state 'I refer to the (description of exhibit) marked "...".

18.5 The provisions of paragraphs 11.3 to 15.3 (Exhibits) apply similarly to witness statements as they do to affidavits.

18.6 Where a witness makes more than one witness statement to which there are exhibits, in the same action, the numbering of the exhibits should run consecutively throughout and not start again with each witness statement.'

The format of witness statements

18.43   It is important that litigators are aware of the precise format required of witness statements (a failure to comply with the requirements can lead to the evidence not being admitted or the costs of preparation being disallowed. CPR 32 PD 19–20 states:

'19.1 A witness statement must:
1.   be produced on durable quality A4 paper with a 3.5cm margin,
2.   be fully legible and should normally be typed on one side of the paper only,
3.   where possible, be bound securely in a manner which would not hamper filing, or otherwise each page should be indorsed with the case number and should bear the initials of the witness,
4.   have the pages numbered consecutively as a separate statement (or one of several statements contained in a file),
5.   be divided into numbered paragraphs,
6.   have all numbers, including dates, expressed in figures,

7.   give in the margin the reference to any document or documents mentioned.

19.2 It is usually convenient for a witness statement to follow the chronological sequence of the events or matters dealt with. Each paragraph of a witness statement should as far as possible be confined to a distinct portion of the subject.

20.1 A witness statement is the equivalent of the oral evidence which the witness would, if called, give in his evidence in chief at the trial; it must include a statement by the intended witness that he believes the facts in it are true.

20.2 To verify a witness statement the statement of truth is as follows:

"I believe that the facts stated in this witness statement are true".

20.3 Attention is drawn to rule 32.14 which sets out the consequences of verifying a witness statement containing a false statement without an honest belief in its truth (it is a contempt of court).'

Witness statement and damages an example of the dangers involved in poor preparation

18.44   The case of *McRae v Chase Intl Express Ltd* [2003] EWCA Civ 505 provides an object lesson in the difficulties that can be caused by inadequate evidence when attempting to prove a claim for damages.

McRae[1] – THE FACTS

18.45   Mr McRae was injured in a motorcycle accident. Liability was not in dispute. As a result of his injuries he had to give up work as a motorcycle courier. Damages for pain suffering and loss of amenity were agreed at £20,000. The balance of the claim was disputed.

1   *McRae v Chase Intl Express Ltd* [2003] EWCA Civ 505, [2003] All ER (D) 219 (Mar).

THE ABSENCE OF EVIDENCE

18.46   The defendant appealed aspects of the awards made to the claimant because of the absence or paucity of evidence. The Court of Appeal upheld many of the defendant's contentions.

FUTURE LOSS OF EARNINGS

18.47   Kennedy LJ observed that, on the question of loss of earnings: 'The judge had before him in relation to this issue practically no evidence.'[1] The claimant had answered some questions posed by the defendant; however, no indication was given as to whether the sums mentioned in replies were net or gross or whether there were gaps between employment. The gaps in the evidence were telling:

(1)   'There was no evidence at all before the district judge as to whether this claimant could now, with his damaged wrist, undertake, for example, any of the jobs he did before joining [the motorcycle courier firm].'

(2)   The trial judge concluded that had the claimant been able to go out post-accident and acquire a better-paid job he would have do so. Kennedy LJ observed:

> '... there was simply no evidence before the judge to substantiate that finding. There was no assertion in the pleadings. There was no assertion in the pleadings; there was nothing in the statement filed on behalf of the claimant. When the claimant came to give oral evidence he was not asked about that matter at all.'

(3)   Kennedy LJ observed that in order to calculate the multiplier/ multiplicand basis 'it was necessary for the judge to have before him reliable evidence as to the claimant's pre-accident earning capacity and as to his post accident earning capacity'. The evidence in relation to past earnings was inadequate. There was no evidence as to whether, or when, the claimant would be able to obtain better paid employment.

(4)   The judge awarded damages for future loss of earnings on a multiplier/multiplicand basis. Kennedy LJ observed:

> 'The claimant here simply had not laid before the court the materials which might well, had they been laid before the court, have enabled the judge to adopt the approach that he did. But the materials were not there. In the absence of those materials it was not appropriate to attempt to use figures which were patently, for the reasons I have endeavoured to explain, unreliable.'

As a result an award of loss of earnings of £41,871.43 was reduced to £12,500.

1   *McRae v Chase Intl Express Ltd* [2003] EWCA Civ 505, [2003] All ER (D) 219 (Mar).

LOSS OF CONGENIAL EMPLOYMENT

18.48   A similar observation was made in relation to an award for loss of congenial employment. Again the evidence was sparse. There was an assertion in the Particulars of Claim that the claimant found his work as a motorcycle courier satisfying. However, nothing was said in the witness statement or when the claimant was in the witness box. An award of £2,000 under this head was set aside.

18.49 The kernel of the guidance given by this case is in the short judgment of Mr Justice Newman. He too was concerned about the way in which the evidence was presented:[1]

'If the method and presentation adopted in this case reflects a common circumstances in connection with personal injury cases in the district court it has, in my judgment, departed too far from the basic principle that a claimant must prove his case by evidence capable of supporting the conclusions to which the court is invited to come. It may be that the days of a formal advice on evidence are long gone but the need which such advice fulfil remains. Someone on each side in litigation such as this, with sufficient skill to do so, must, at some timely stage before trial, draw up a lost of the issues which remain contentious and then consider whether or not there is evidence available to meet those issues ... There is a need for evidence and there is a need for an analysis of such evidence; then the judge can make findings of fact by drawing inferences and doing the best he can, but on the evidence which is available.'

1   *McRae v Chase Intl Express Ltd* [2003] EWCA Civ 505, [2003] All ER (D) 219 (Mar).

PROVING THE LOSS

18.50 What is interesting is that the observations made in *McCrae*[1] are similar to those made over 50 years ago in the case of *Bonham Carter v Hyde Park Hotel Ltd* [1948] WN 89, 92 Sol Jo 154, KBD:

'Plaintiffs must understand that if they bring actions for damages it is for them to prove their damage, it is not enough to write down the particulars, and, so to speak, throw themselves at the head of the court saying "This is what I have lost. I ask you to give me these damages." They have to prove it.'

1   *McRae v Chase Intl Express Ltd* [2003] EWCA Civ 505, [2003] All ER (D) 219 (Mar). See para 18.44ff above.

The need to consider the evidence for proving damages with extreme care

18.51   There are a number of issues that have to be addressed:
- Proving the damages themselves – ie that losses have, or will be, sustained.
- Proving that the damages flow from the breach.
- Proving the amount of the damages.
- If the claim is not one that can be quantified, for instance, a claim for loss of congenial employment or disability in the labour market, then make sure the statement sets out the facts which would allow the court to make an award.

Particular matters to watch

18.52   There are a number of evidential matters that require special care.

Damages for pain and suffering in personal injury cases

18.53   Much of the basic commentary on the injuries is left to the medical reports. It is probably unwise to repeat the report in the witness statement; the client cannot give evidence of many technical matters in any event. However, it is important that the claimant be given an opportunity to explain the *effect* of the injuries. If, for instance, the whole of the claimant's social life centred around the golf-course and he can no longer play golf, then this is something that should be set out. The detail of the statement is clearly an issue of judgment and skill for the lawyer. It has to be said that the drafting of witness statements is a vastly underrated and overlooked skill.

Employment issues in personal injury cases

18.54   The *McRae*[1] case provides an object lesson in the dangers posed by a failure to give, or obtain, full details in relation to employment history and employment prospects. The claimant should set out his employment history and state what jobs he cannot now do. Employment experts are a rarity nowadays and it is the claimant who may have to comment on issues of employability and prospects in his line of work. As long as these matters are done briefly, and are confined to issues of fact, they should lay the foundation upon which the court can make an award.

1   *McRae v Chase Intl Express Ltd* [2003] EWCA Civ 505, [2003] All ER (D) 219
     (Mar). See para 18.44ff above.

18.55   Similar principles apply in relation to claims for loss of congenial
employment. The witness statement must deal this issue, not by asserting
a loss but by explaining it.

18.56   All of this, of course, has to be underwritten by the caveat that the
witness statement is a vehicle for facts and not arguments of law.

Issues of dependency in fatal accident cases

18.57   This may sound like to obvious a point to make. However, in *L (a
child) v Barry May Haulage* [2002] PIQR Q35 at Q36:

> 'At the outset of the hearing ... I expressed surprise that no witness
> statements had been served by the claimant. I was effectively being
> asked ... to perform a "conventional" assessment on the basis that
> the deceased had been the sole source of support both and financial
> and other (the provision of "services" support for the claimant.'

18.58   Fortunately the judge allowed oral evidence to be given at trial. If
not, following the logic of *McRae*,[1] it is doubtful whether the court would
have been in a position to award damages (except perhaps the bereavement
award and any admitted special damages).

1   *McRae v Chase Intl Express Ltd* [2003] EWCA Civ 505, [2003] All ER (D) 219
     (Mar). See para 18.44ff above.

18.59   Not filing evidence is an extremely dangerous step.

Special damages

18.60   In relation to issues of special damages the person taking the witness
statement has to walk a difficult line between going into excruciating detail
or being accused of missing important elements of the claim out.

18.61   There are a number of points that can assist:
*   If you are going to have to go into detail then make the reader's life
    easy (that is make the judge's life easier) by:
    (1) using short paragraphs;
    (2) using headings and sub-headings; and
    (3) ensuring that the statement is logically laid out.

- If detailed figures, charts or graphs are needed then refer to these and annex them to the statement rather than repeat them. A judge rarely wants to read things twice.
- Avoid the jargon or technical phraseology of the trade unless absolutely necessary. If technical terms are inevitable then explain these or provide a glossary.

APPEALS AND DAMAGES

18.62   A distinction has to be made between an appeal from the verdict of a jury and an appeal from a judge sitting alone, although both go to the Court of Appeal.

18.63   At common law the verdict of a jury was final, provided that there was no misdirection and that all proper factors had been taken into account. But a new trial could be ordered if there was a misdirection on the law, or if the damages were so grossly excessive or so grossly inadequate as to show that the jury had been influenced by prejudice or had failed to take some element of damages into account: see, for example, *Phillips v London and South Western Rly Co* (1879) 5 QBD 78, 43 JP 749, CA.

18.64   If the verdict was set aside on these grounds, the proper remedy was to order a new trial: *Lambkin v South Eastern Rly Co* (1880) 5 App Cas 352, 28 WR 837, PC. The court had no power to assess the damages and substitute its own figure for the verdict unless all parties gave their consent: *Watt v Watt* [1905] AC 115, 69 JP 249, HL. Under the present Rules (RSC Ord 59, r 11(4), made under the Courts and Legal Services Act 1990, s 8), the Court of Appeal has power to reassess the damages whenever they are excessive or inadequate.

18.65   Appeals from a judge alone do not give rise to these problems, as the Court of Appeal has power to make whatever order the judge ought to have made.

18.66   However, as the quantum of damages is very much a question of fact and degree, the Court of Appeal is reluctant to interfere with the assessment of either a judge or a jury unless there has been a misdirection in law, or the amount is manifestly too much or too little. In general, it has been said that an appeal against the decision of a judge upon the quantum of damages will not be allowed unless either (i) the judge has applied a wrong principle of law or (ii) 'the amount awarded is either so inordinately low or so inordinately high that it must be a wholly erroneous estimate of the damage': per Viscount Simon LC in *Nance v British Columbia Electric Rly Co Ltd* [1951] AC 601, [1951] 2 All ER 448, PC.

18.67 'Inordinately' high or low is perhaps rhetorical: in modern practice the Court of Appeal recognises that within a fairly wide range the amount is a question of degree for the trial judge, but if the amount is outside that reasonable range they do not hesitate to alter it.

18.68 When a case has been tried by jury, the test is even stricter, and the court will not set aside the verdict unless it is wholly out of proportion to the facts and such as no reasonable man could reach: *Bocock v Enfield Rolling Mills Ltd* [1954] 3 All ER 94, [1954] 1 WLR 1303, CA; *Scott v Musial* [1959] 2 QB 429, [1959] 3 All ER 193, CA; *Mallett v McMonagle* [1970] AC 166, [1969] NI 91, HL.

18.69 In a series of cases in the Court of Appeal it has been held that the court, in deciding whether damages are too high or too low, may have regard to the general level of awards made in comparable cases: see *Bird v Cocking & Sons Ltd* [1951] 2 TLR 1260, CA; *Rushton v National Coal Board* [1953] 1 QB 495, [1953] 1 All ER 314, CA; and *Waldon v War Office* [1956] 1 All ER 108, [1956] 1 WLR 51, CA. The practice has been approved by the House of Lords and the Privy Council. This question of using comparable awards as a guide to the assessment to damages is considered at length in chapter 19. On an appeal from a jury, the Court of Appeal cannot leave out of account the general level of awards in considering what is 'wholly out of proportion'; Lord Denning MR said in *Ward v James* [1966] 1 QB 273, [1965] 1 All ER 563, CA:

'In future this court will not feel the same hesitation in upsetting an award of damages by a jury. If it is "out of all proportion to the circumstances of the case" (that is, if it is far too high or far too low) this court will set it aside.'

And he expressed the opinion that a new trial could be ordered before a judge alone.

18.70 The House of Lords has said that it is peculiarly within the province of the Court of Appeal to establish guidelines which indicate the standard range of damages for particular injuries: see *Wright v British Railways Board* [1983] 2 AC 773, [1983] 2 All ER 698, HL.

18.71 An appeal ought not to be restricted to one head of damages only; the damages must be considered as a whole, and deficiency under one head may be balanced by excess under another: *Povey v W E and E Jackson* *(a firm)* [1970] 2 All ER 495, [1970] 1 WLR 969, CA. However, if defendants say that the whole is adequate though one head may be deficient, they should file a counter-notice to the appeal: *George v Pinnock* [1973] 1 All ER 926, [1973] 1 WLR 118, CA. Where there is an agreed figure for future rate of earning loss, the court should be told what factors and contingencies have been allowed for: *Bennett v Chemical Construction (GB) Ltd* [1971] 3 All ER 822, [1971] 1 WLR 1571, CA.

18.72   It is not the practice of the Court of Appeal to inspect a claimant's injuries, except obvious things like scars: *Stevens v William Nash Ltd* [1966] 3 All ER 156, [1966] 1 WLR 1550, CA. In a remarkable and unusual case which had been conducted by both sides on the basis that the defendants would continue to employ the plaintiff, the assessment was re-opened on appeal when the defendants (although acting in good faith) almost immediately dismissed him: *Murphy v Stone-Wallwork (Charlton) Ltd* [1969] 2 All ER 949, [1969] 1 WLR 1023, HL. In an earlier case fresh evidence had similarly been admitted after the trial when the plaintiff proved unable to do the alternative work offered: *Jenkins v Richard Thomas & Baldwins Ltd* [1966] 2 All ER 15, [1966] 1 WLR 476, CA; but in the *Murphy* case the House of Lords felt that this was going too far and that events after the trial should be admitted only where the court has been misled by the conduct of a party.

18.73   This comment must be understood in the context of loss of employment, and not as limiting the court's discretion where some other change transforms the picture. In *Mulholland v Mitchell* [1971] AC 666, [1971] 1 All ER 307, HL the House of Lords approved the admission of further evidence and consequent re-opening of the case where the whole basis of assessment of damages had been undermined, because the plaintiff, instead of being nursed at home as expected, had to go to a psychiatric nursing home at much greater cost. In another extreme and unusual case, the Court of Appeal re-opened the assessment of damages and greatly reduced them where the assessment at the trial was made on the basis that the plaintiff would live for many years, but he died unexpectedly before the appeal was heard: *McCann v Sheppard* [1973] 2 All ER 881, [1973] 1 WLR 540, CA.

18.74   The *amount* of any payment into court should not be disclosed to the Court of Appeal or appear in any transcript put before them: *Thornton v Swan Hunter (Shipbuilders) Ltd* [1971] 3 All ER 1248n, [1971] 1 WLR 1759, CA.

CHAPTER 19

Provisional damages

19.1 The courts have had power to award provisional damages since 1 July 1985. Provisional damages were introduced to cater for those cases where there is a chance that the claimant's condition will deteriorate in the future. The initial award is made on the assumption that the claimant's condition will remain stable, but a provisional damages award leaves open the possibility of returning to court for further compensation in the event of such deterioration. The aim is to avoid the potential injustice to both the claimant and the defendant of a single conventional award. The advantages of this approach were outlined by Simon Brown J in *Patterson v Ministry of Defence* [1987] CLY 1194:

'Of course, one great advantage ... is that it is unnecessary to resolve differences such as arise here between specialists, as to the precise risks to which the plaintiff is now exposed. Justice can be done whichever view is correct ...'

NO OBLIGATION TO CLAIM PROVISIONAL DAMAGES

19.2 It is important to note that there is no obligation on a claimant to make a claim for provisional damages where his future condition is uncertain. A claimant is perfectly entitled to seek a final award and will not be penalised for making this election. This was firmly established in *Cowan v Kitson Instruments Ltd* [1992] PIQR Q19 where the defendants were critical of the claimant's failure to claim provisional damages, and went as far as to suggest that his award should be smaller as a result. Crowley QC rejected this, saying (at Q23):

'In my view, the plaintiff is not to be disadvantaged in any way by seeking a final assessment now. The court should not be astute to

207

assist the defendants, who are after all at fault ... What I have to do is make the best judgment I can as to what is a fair level of award.'

WHEN IS A CLAIM FOR PROVISIONAL DAMAGES APPROPRIATE?

19.3   For a claim for provisional damages to succeed there must be a chance that the claimant's condition, either physical or mental, will deteriorate seriously at some point in the future (see the practice direction accompanying CPR 16, quoted in chapter 18 at para 18.32–18.25 above). Simon Brown J said in *Patterson v Ministry of Defence* [1987] CLY 1194:

'... it appears to me desirable to limit the employment of this valuable new statutory power to cases where the adverse prospect is relatively clear-cut and where there would be little room for later dispute whether or not the contemplated deterioration had actually occurred.'[1]

1   Cited in BPILS XV/4006.

WHAT IS MEANT BY A 'CHANCE'

19.4   In *Willson v Ministry of Defence* [1991] 1 All ER 638, [1991] ICR 595, it was held that the likelihood of deterioration had to be measurable rather than merely fanciful to qualify as a 'chance', a point reiterated in *Iane Brandenbugo Curi v Louis Ignacia Colina* (29 July 1998, unreported), CA. However, it must not be so likely as to be probable. This was the principal reason in the latter case that an award of provisional damages was not made. The likelihood of deterioration was sufficiently certain to enable it to be properly taken into account in a conventional award of damages. Taken together, these cases give the result that, provided the chance, though small, is quantifiable, it can be the basis for a provisional damages:

'However so slim those chances may be, I think they are measurable within the meaning of this section [Supreme Court Act 1981, s 32A].'[1]

1   Scott Baker J in *Willson v Ministry of Defence* [1991] 1 All ER 638 at 642.

SERIOUS DETERIORATION

19.5   The meaning of 'serious deterioration' was also considered in *Willson v Ministry of Defence* [1991] 1 All ER 638, [1991] ICR 595 and

Iane Brandenbugo Curi v Louis Ignacia Colina (29 July 1998, unreported), CA. This is, of course, rather harder to quantify precisely, as it could encompass a range of circumstances. Scott Baker J held in *Willson* (at 642) that what was envisaged was:

'something beyond ordinary deterioration. Whether deterioration is serious in any particular case seems to me to be a question of fact depending on the circumstances of that case, including the effect of the deterioration upon the plaintiff.'

19.6   Relevant effects on the claimant include any reduction in his activities and capabilities, or indeed his life expectancy, or adverse effects on his financial position as a result of the deterioration (perhaps due to increased care needs, or a further reduction in his earning capacity). If a conventional award including a sum for the chance would be insufficient compensation in the event of the chance materialising, the discretion conferred by the Supreme Court Act 1981, s 32A and the County Courts Act 1984, s 51 to make a provisional award may then be exercised.

19.7   In respect of both the chance of deterioration and the seriousness of it, the natural likely progression of the claimant's condition must be distinguished from the slight risk that he will suffer to a greater degree than people with similar injuries/diseases. Only the latter will give grounds for a provisional award; the former can be fully accounted for in a conventional award of damages.

SPECIFIC CONDITIONS

Osteo-arthritis

19.8   The possibility that the claimant will develop osteo-arthritis in the future has not been accepted as a valid basis for making an award of provisional damages. This is the condition which was under consideration in *Willson v Ministry of Defence* [1991] 1 All ER 638, [1991] ICR 595. It was held that osteo-arthritis was a degenerative condition; it was an aspect of the progression of a disease and not deterioration. Provisional damages were not applicable.

Small but definite risk of post-traumatic epilepsy

19.9   In *O'Kennedy v Harris* (9 July 1990, unreported), cited in BPILS XV/4008, the plaintiff was at a very slight (0.25%) risk of developing epilepsy in the future as a result of her accident. The judge rejected the defendant's argument that the risk was too small to merit a provisional award, holding instead that this was the very type of situation the Supreme Court Act, s 32A was designed to cover.

CONSEQUENCES OF A PROVISIONAL AWARD

If the claimant subsequently dies

19.10   Where the claimant dies after the award of provisional damages, but prior to bringing a further claim, what is the position if his dependants wish to bring a claim under the Fatal Accidents Act 1976? A problem arose in *Middleton v Elliot Turbomachinery Ltd* (1990) Times, 29 October, CA where a declaration that the dependants could bring a further claim under the Fatal Accidents Act 1976 was held to be unlawful.

19.11   The problem was resolved by the introduction of the Damages Act 1996. The Damages Act 1996, s 3 states that a previous award of provisional damages does not constitute a bar to bringing a claim under the Fatal Accidents Act 1976, but that it will be taken into account in assessing the level of any award under the 1976 Act.

Only one further award may be made

19.12   The claimant may only claim further damages once in respect of each specified deterioration. If his condition worsens after a second claim has been made, no further claim can be made. Nor can he claim in respect of illnesses or disabilities which arise from the original injury which were not specified in the initial award.

MAKING A CLAIM FOR PROVISIONAL DAMAGES

The pre-action protocol

19.13   The personal injury pre-action protocol does not mention provisional damages specifically. It would assist with the 'spirit' of the protocol for the claimant to inform the defendant that provisional damages are being considered.

The Civil Procedure Rules 1998

19.14 CPR 41 deals with provisional damages. CPR 41.2(1) states:

'(1) The court may make an order for an award of provisional damages if –
(a) the particulars of claim include a claim for provisional damages and;
(b) the court is satisfied that SCA s.32A [Supreme Court Act 1981, s 32A] or CCA s.51 [County Courts Act 1984, s 51] applies.'

19.15 The wording of CPR 41.2(1) leaves open the court's discretion as to whether or not to make a provisional damages award. For example, in *Ivory v Martens* (21 October 1988, unreported), cited in BPLIS XV/4009, French J was unconvinced that the requirements were met, so declined to make a provisional award and made a conventional lump sum award instead.

The particulars of claim

19.16 It is important to note that it is a mandatory requirement that the claim for provisional damages *must* be included in the particulars of claim.

19.17 CPR 16.4(1)(d) states that:

'if the claimant is seeking provisional damages, [the claimant must include] a statement to that effect and his grounds for claiming them.'

What you need to plead

19.18 The Practice Direction that accompanies CPR 16 states that the claimant must state in his particulars of claim:

'4.4(1) that he is seeking an award of provisional damages under either section 32A of the Supreme Court Act 1981 or section 51 of the County Courts Act 1984,
(2) that there is a chance that at some future time the claimant will develop some serious disease or suffer some serious deterioration in his physical or mental condition, and
(3) specify the disease or type of deterioration in respect of which an application may be made at a future date.'

Default judgment in a provisional damages case

19.19   Under the old Rules it was never a simple matter to enter a judgment in default when provisional damages were being claimed; leave of the court was always needed. This practice has been continued in the CPR. Paragraph 5.1 of the Practice Direction that accompanies CPR 41 states that where a defendant fails to file an acknowledgment of service or a defence within the specified time then the claimant may not enter judgment in default, unless he abandons his claim for provisional damages. The proper course of action is for the claimant to make an application for directions.

19.20   Thereafter the Master or district judge will order the following issues to be decided:
*   whether the claim is an appropriate one for an award of provisional damages and, if so, on what terms, and
*   the amount of immediate damages.

Payments into court and offers to settle in a provisional damages case

19.21   CPR 36.7 deals with the position of the defendant making an offer to settle or payment into court when a claimant is seeking provisional damages.
*   It is made clear that a defendant can make a Part 36 (CPR 36) payment (a payment into court) in respect of a claim which includes a claim for provisional damages.
*   Where a defendant makes a Part 36 payment into court in such a case, the payment notice must specify whether or not the defendant is offering to agree to the making of an award of provisional damages.
*   If the defendant is offering to agree to the making of an award of provisional damages the payment notice must state:
    (a) that the sum paid into court is in satisfaction of the claim for damages on the assumption that the injured person will not develop the disease or suffer the type of deterioration specified in the notice;
    (b) that the offer is subject to the condition that the claimant must make any claim for further damages within a limited period; and
    (c) what the period is.
*   If the claimant accepts the Part 36 payment he must, within seven days of doing so, apply to the court for an award of provisional damages under CPR 41.2.

Claimant's offer to settle

19.22 The CPR do not deal expressly with a claimant's offer to settle in a provisional damages claim. Presumably the procedure here is precisely the same as in any other claimant's offer to settle. The claimant must set out:

- the sum he seeks immediately;
- the nature of the deterioration in respect of which provisional damages is sought; and
- the period of time over which an application can be made.

19.23 There will be scope here for considerable argument as to whether an offer or payment has been 'beaten'. What happens, for instance, where the sum offered immediately is not beaten but the claimant obtains a greater period of time in which to make the application

19.24 Similarly a claimant may obtain a higher immediate award than that for which he offered to settle but a shorter period of time to make a further application.

An order for provisional damages

19.25 CPR 41.2(2) states that an order for an award of provisional damages:

- must specify the disease or type of deterioration in respect of which an application may be made at a future date;
- must specify the period within which such an application may be made; and
- may be made in respect of more than one disease or type of disease or type of deterioration and may, in respect of each disease or type of disease, specify a different period within which a subsequent application may be made.

CAUSATION AT A LATER DATE

19.26 This final point raises questions of causation. It may be that there is not sufficient evidence, at the time of the initial award, of a link between the defendant's wrongdoing and the future situation in which the claimant wishes to be able to bring a further claim. The point was considered in *Mann v Merton and Sutton Health Authority* (15 November 1988, unreported), cited in BPILS XV/4011. In that case, the plaintiff could only demonstrate a higher incidence of the particular disease in people who had been exposed to asbestos, but no causal link. It was held that there was no need to establish the link at that stage; if the disease materialised, the question of fact of whether or not it was as a result of the defendant's negligence could be decided, in the light of any advances in medical knowledge, when the future claim was brought.

NO UPPER LIMIT ON TIME FOR SUBSEQUENT APPLICATION

19.27   The Practice Direction to CPR 41 makes it clear that the court can specify the period for a subsequent application as being the duration of the life of the claimant.

19.28   The Practice Direction to CPR 41 states that the documents to be preserved should be set out in a schedule to the judgment. The issue of causation of any further damages and whether they are within the scope of the order should be determined when any further application is made.

Applications to extend time

19.29   CPR 41.2(3) makes it clear that a claimant can make more than one application to extend the time to apply for a further award under provisional damages.

Consent orders

19.30   Paragraph 4.1 of the Practice Direction to CPR 41 deals with consent orders. It makes it clear that:
* An application for a consent order should be made in accordance with CPR 23.
* If the claimant is a child or patient the approval of the court must be sought and the application for approval will normally be dealt with at the hearing.
* The order should be in the form of a consent judgment and should contain:
    (1) The details as to disease, deterioration and time set out above.
    (2) A direction as to the documents to be preserved (see para 19.32 below).

- The claimant, or his legal representative, must lodge the case file documents in court office in order that they can be preserved.

Practical considerations: preservation of the case file

19.31 The Practice Direction to CPR 41 makes it clear that the case file documents must be preserved until the expiry of the period or periods specified and for any extension of the periods.

19.32 The case file documents will normally include:
- the judgment as entered;
- the statements of case;
- the transcript of the judge's oral judgment;
- all medical reports relied on; and
- a transcript of any parts of the claimant's own evidence which the judge considers necessary.

19.33 There is a duty on the associate/court clerk to ensure that the case file documents are provided by the parties where necessary and placed on the court file. Thereafter the associate/court clerk should endorse the file to the effect that it contains the case file documents and with the period during which the case file documents must be preserved. The case file documents should be preserved in the court office where the proceedings took place.

Subsequent orders

19.34 Any subsequent order extending the period for which further damages may be claimed, or of the Court of Appeal discharging or varying the provisions of the original judgment, will become one of the case file documents and must be preserved. Further, any variation of the period within which an application for further damages may be made should be endorsed on the court file containing the case file documents.

Subsequent applications to extend the period

19.35 Paragraph 3.5 of the Practice Direction to CPR 41 states that an application to extend the period for applying for provisional damages should be supported by a current medical report.

Duty of legal representatives to preserve own case file

19.36   Paragraph 3.6 of the Practice Direction to CPR 41 contains a succinct prompt:

> 'Legal representatives are reminded that it is their duty to preserve their own case file.'

CHAPTER 20

Interest on damages

THE STATUTORY BASIS OF THE AWARD

20.1 The power to award interest is dependent upon a power given by statute. There is no common law power for interest to be awarded. The Supreme Court Act 1981, s 35A (which was introduced by the Administration of Justice Act 1982, s 15 and replaces earlier legislation with amendments) gives the court a discretionary power to award interest on any debt or damages from the date when the cause of action arose to the date of judgment – or for any shorter part of that period. The new section (unlike its predecessors) also allows interest to be given up to the date of payment, if all or any part of the claim is paid before judgment. The court may give only simple interest, not compound interest, and may give different rates for different periods.

THE OBLIGATORY NATURE OF THE POWER

20.2 The Supreme Court Act 1981, s 35A(2) makes the exercise of this power obligatory if judgment is given for damages for personal injuries or death and the amount exceeds £200, unless there are 'special reasons to the contrary'. But this does not necessarily mean interest on the whole of the damages, because the power relates to 'all or any part'.

THE COUNTY COURT

20.3 The County Courts Act 1984, s 69 confers a similar power, with a similar obligatory direction for damages exceeding £200 for personal injuries or death.

EXPLANATION OF THE POWER

20.4   For some time there was considerable debate as to how the court's power to award interest should be exercised. Definitive guidance was given in *Jefford v Gee* [1970] 2 QB 130, [1970] 1 All ER 1202, CA where the court explained the reason for this power and offered guidelines for the normal practice in exercising it: these guidelines have since been approved with variations by the House of Lords in *Cookson v Knowles* [1979] AC 556, [1978] 2 All ER 604, HL and *Wright v British Railways Board* [1983] 2 AC 773, [1983] 2 All ER 698, HL. The purpose of giving interest is to compensate the claimant for receiving his money later than he should have done. Accordingly:

No interest on future loss

20.5   No interest at all should be given on damages for future losses, because they are not yet due and the assessment is based on their present value at the date of the judgment.

Damages for the personal injury

20.6   Other general damages – that is, for the injury itself and the personal loss as distinct from the financial loss – should carry interest from the date when the claim form was served to the date of judgment.

20.7   In *Pickett v British Rail Engineering Ltd* [1980] AC 136, [1979] 1 All ER 774, HL the House of Lords held that the plaintiff is entitled to interest for the personal loss as compensation for being kept out of his money, irrespective of the fact that the award will be increased in line with inflation. In *Wright v British Railways Board* [1983] 2 AC 773, [1983] 2 All ER 698, HL, approving *Birkett v Hayes* [1982] 2 All ER 710, [1982] 1 WLR 816, CA, the House of Lords held that the adjustment of the award for inflation is indeed relevant to the *rate* of interest allowed: this should be limited to 2%.

Interest on financial losses

20.8   The rate of interest on short-term funds is used as a basis for the special damages for financial loss up to the date of trial.

Ongoing losses

20.9 When there are ongoing losses from the date of injury up to the date of trial. It was thought that rough justice would be done by allowing *half* the short-term interest rate on the full amount: *Dexter v Courtaulds Ltd* [1984] 1 All ER 70, [1984] 1 WLR 372, CA. Interest is calculated from the date of injury to the date of trial.

Losses crystallised some time before trial

20.10 In the case of *Prokop v Department of Health and Social Security* [1985] CLY 1037, CA the court discussed the issue of how interest should be calculated where all the losses are incurred within a short time of the accident. It was decided that the appropriate approach was to award the claimant interest at the *full rate* from half-way through the period of loss.

INTEREST CAN BE VARIED TO SUIT THE JUSTICE OF THE CASE

20.11 It is important to remember that the above cases are only guidelines as to interest calculations. They apply in many cases. However, it may be appropriate for some heads of damage (for example, car-hire costs) to be calculated at the full rate, whereas loss of earnings can be approached at the full rate. Further, there may be cases where a totally different approach is justified. A good example of this is found in *Hobin v Douglas* (1998) 143 Sol Jo LB 21, CA. In that case the plaintiff had suffered loss of earnings due to decreased trading in a business which eventually closed down. Roch LD observed that the judge approached the award of interest on an actuarial basis as compared with the rough and ready approach normally adopted by the courts following *Jefford v Gee* [1970] 2 QB 130, [1970] 1 All ER 1202, CA. In *Hobin v Douglas* (at 21), it was observed that:

'There can be no doubt that it is open to the Judge to depart from the *Jefford v Gee* approach in an appropriate case. See for example *Prokop v DHSS* [1985] CLY 1037.

In this case ..., the annual losses sustained by the Plaintiff were substantially greater in the years immediately prior to trial than they had been in the years following the accident. Accordingly, if the *Jefford v Gee* approach had been taken in this case the Plaintiff would have been over compensated.

The method adopted by the judge was to award interest for each separate year up to the end of that year at one half rate and thereafter at the full rate. The Judge commented that that was a fair approach, recognising that the Plaintiff had lost money progressively during any given year and that thereafter she had lost the whole of a year's income. No possible exception could be taken, in this case, to that approach. It produced a more accurate and fairer figure in this case than adopting the *Jefford v Gee* approach. Furthermore, on the question of interest, the Judge was exercising a discretion as to the manner of his approach and it is quite impossible to say that he exercised that discretion on any erroneous principle. The Judge commented in the course of discussion with counsel: "That seems to me to be a very fair way of doing it. I would be surprised if the Court of Appeal took the view that there was a fairer way of doing it." We agree.'

INTEREST WHEN THERE ARE COMPENSATION RECOVERY UNIT PAYMENTS OR WHERE MONEY IS TO BE REPAID TO EMPLOYERS

20.12   The fact that benefits are paid to the claimant and that the defendant will have to pay a sum to the Compensation Recovery Unit does not affect interest. Interest has to be paid on the total special damages claim. The fact that benefits have been paid or are subject to recoupment is irrelevant to the interest calculation: *Wisely v John Fulton (Plumbers) Ltd, Wadley v Surrey County Council* [2000] 2 All ER 545, [2000] 1 WLR 820, CA. Similarly the fact that earnings are paid to an *employer by an employee* on the basis that those wages will be repaid if compensation is recovered is irrelevant to the interest calculation. Interest is paid on the loss and held on trust for the employer: *Davies v Inman* [1999] PIQR Q26.

DELAY AND ADJOURNMENTS

20.13   There are some cases relating to delay which could be important. Some caution must be exercised because these decisions were made prior to the introduction of the Civil Procedure Rules in 1998.

Unjustified delay

20.14   Where there is unjustifiable delay in taking a case for trial, interest may be disallowed for the period of delay: *Spittle v Bunney* [1988] 3 All ER 1031, [1988] 1 WLR 847, CA.

Adjournments

20.15   Entitlement is not cut down by adjournment of the hearing at the claimant's request, because the defendant has the interim use of the money: *May v A G Bassett & Sons Ltd* (1970) 114 Sol Jo 269, QBD.

WHEN A PARTY IS BROUGHT INTO AN ACTION AFTER THE ISSUE OF PROCEEDINGS

20.16   Where a defendant is first brought into an action as a Part 20 defendant and later added as defendant by the original claimant, interest on the general damages runs from the Part 20 Notice which brought him into the proceedings: *Slater v Hughes* [1971] 3 All ER 1287, [1971] 1 WLR 1438, CA.

INTEREST WHEN THERE IS AN INTERIM PAYMENT

20.17   In cases where interim payments are made, helpful guidance was given by the Court of Appeal in *Bristow v Judd* [1993] PIQR Q117, CA. In essence:

(1)   Until an interim payment reduces the amount due for special damages a claimant is entitled to interest based on normal calculations (see paras 20.4–20.8 above).

(2)   Where an interim payment is made it should be taken as compensation first of all for the financial losses incurred up to the date of the interim payment.

(3)   If the interim payment exceeds the amount of special damages due at that date the balance should be taken to have been paid in diminution of the compensation payable as general damages.

(4)   Thereafter the claimant is entitled to interest at the normal rate on special damages accruing between the date of payment of the interim payment and the date of trial and 2% on the outstanding amount of damages.

20.18   The courts have rejected the notion that a claimant should set off interest earned on interim payments against the final damages award: *Edward Maxim Parry v North West Area Health Authority* (2000) Times, 5 January.

NO TAX ON INTEREST

20.19   By the Income and Corporation Taxes Act 1988, s 329, interest given under these statutes – in England and Wales, Northern Ireland or Scotland – is exempt from income tax. This was passed to relieve claimants from liability, and should not reduce the amount payable by the defendant: *Mason v Harman* [1972] RTR 1, 115 Sol Jo 931, QBD.

Appendix I

Guidelines for the assessment of general damages in personal injury cases (sixth edition)

Compiled for the Judicial Studies Board

Foreword to the First Edition by Lord Donaldson of Lymington

Paradoxical as it may seem, one of the commonest tasks of a judge sitting in a civil court is also one of the most difficult. This is the assessment of general damages for pain, suffering or loss of the amenities of life. Since no monetary award can compensate in any real sense, these damages cannot be assessed by a process of calculation. Yet whilst no two cases are ever precisely the same, justice requires the there be consistency between awards.

The soluton to this dilemma has lain in using the amount of damages awarded in reported cases as guidelines or markers and seeking to slot the particular case into the framework thus provided. This is easier stated than done, because reports of the framework cases are scattered over a variety of publications and not all the awards appear, from the sometimes brief reports, to be consistent with one another. Furthermore some of the older cases are positively misleading unless account is taken of changes in the value of money and the process of revaluation is far from being an exact science.

It was against this background that the Judicial Studies Board set up a working party under the chairmanship of Judge Roger Cox to prepare 'Guidelines for Assessment of General Damages in Personal Injury Cases'. It was not indended to represent, and does not prepresent, a new or different approach to the problem. Nor is it intended to be a 'ready reckoner' or in any way to fetter the individual judgment which must be brought to bear upon the unique features of each paticular case. What it is intended to do, and what it does quite admirably, is to distil the conventional wisdom contained in the reported cases, to supplement it from the collective experience of the working party and to present the result in a convenient, logical and coherent form.

There can be do doubt about the practical value of this report and it has been agreed by the four Heads of Division that it shall be circulated to all judges, recorders and district judges who may be concerned with the assessment of general damanges in personal injury cases. We also consider that it shoudl be made available to the two branches of the practising professiona dnt o any others who would be assisted by it.

224

Judges and practitioners will, as always, remain free to take full account of the amount of damages awarded in earlier cases, but it is hoped that with teh publication of this report this will less often be necessary. They will also need to take account of the cases reported after the effective date of the working party's report since that report, while to some extent providig a new baseline is not intended to, and could not, freeze the scale of damages either absolutely or in relative terms as between different categories of loss.

May I convey my sincere congratulations to the authors upon the excellent way in which they have performed their tak.

Lord Donaldson of Lymington

25 March 1992

INTRODUCTION

The figures in the sixth edition of this book have been revised in the light of decisions and inflation since the last edition which took particular note of *Heil v Rankin* so far as awards over £10,000 are concerned.

The members of the Working Party are always grateful for comments, contributions and criticisms from colleagues in all sections of the profession. We are very conscious that guidelines such as these can become self-fulfilling prophesies, and we particularly welcome information about awards where there has been express comment on, or criticism of, the guidelines, or the judge has simply made an award which is outside the bracket which we have chosen. It is particularly important that we get to know of such cases. We do our best to scour the formal and informal reports of awards, but by the sheer nature of things many awards are bound to go unreported. No award is too small to be of interest.

Two related criticisms which we have received, in various forms since the last edition, are that some of the brackets are unduly wide, and the descriptive text insufficiently detailed. Whilst the existing format, size and length of the book seem to meet with general approval, and introducing a greater number of more detailed categories would stage by stage turn the book into a larger and more cumbersome animal than it is intended to be, we have made some additions at the bottom end of some categories.

The section on internal organs has been revised and enlarged, particularly in relation to awards for respiratory disability and injury to the digestive system. A section has been added on dermatitis. We have added some comments on sexual abuse and physical abuse in breach of trust, in the section on psychiatric damage, although such cases are difficult to categorise because of the wide differences in types and duration of abuse and the identifiable consequences.

We have kept some of the brackets or the bottom or top figures the same in some instances, despite inflation, where the original brackets were large enough to cope with the modest inflationary increase since the fifth edition. We have followed our usual practice of keeping to round figures rather than adhering to the exact figure after inflation. We have steered clear of awards of general damages by consent (settlements), because the parties may have a variety of reasons for compromise of this head of claim, particularly if there are significant consequential losses.

As always, we stress that the guidelines hope to reflect the general level of current awards; they do not reflect the views of the Working Party on what the levels should be. They are designed to provide the starting point for the assessment of damages in any particular case.

Ron Sutcliffe has decided to retire from the Working Party. He made a very considerable contribution to all of the previous editions, and he leaves with our thanks and best wishes, and those of the Judicial Studies Board. His place has been taken by Martin S. Bruffell whose experience of personal injury litigation is second to none.

All comments and contributions should be sent to Andrea Dowsett, the Board's publications coordinator, at 9th Floor, Millbank Tower, Millbank, London SW1 4QU, or andrea.dowsettijsb.gsi.gov.uk. Andrea's commitment and unceasing help have been vital to the production of this new edition.

The figures in this edition are dated to July 2002.

I Injuries involving paralysis

(a) Quadriplegia **£165,000 to £205,000**

The level of the award within the bracket will be affected by the following considerations:
(i) the extent of any residual movement;
(ii) the presence and extent of pain;
(iii) depression;
(iv) age and life expectancy.

The top of the bracket will be appropriate only where there is significant effect on senses or ability to communicate. It will also often involve significant brain damage: see 2(A)(a).

(b) Paraplegia **£115,000 to £145,000**

The level of the award within the bracket will be affected by the following considerations:
(i) the presence and extent of pain;
(ii) the degree of independence;
(iii) depression;
(iv) age and life expectancy.

The presence of increasing paralysis or the degree of risk that this will occur, for example, from syringomyelia, might take the case above this bracket. The latter might be the subject of a provisional damages order.

2 Head injuries

A Brain damage

(a) Very severe brain damage **£145,000 to £205,000**

In cases at the top of this bracket the injured person will have a degree of insight. There may be some ability to follow basic commands, recovery of eye opening and return of sleep and waking patterns and postural reflex movement. There will be little, if any, evidence of meaningful response to environment, little or no language function, double incontinence and the need for full-time nursing care.

The level of the award within the bracket will be affected by:
(i)   the degree of insight;
(ii) life expectancy;
(iii) the extent of physical limitations.

The top of the bracket will be appropriate only where there is significant effect on the senses and severe physical limitation.

Where there is a persistent vegetative state and/or death occurs very soon after the injuries were suffered and there has been no awareness by the injured person of his or her condition the award will be solely for loss of amenity and will fall substantially below the above bracket.

(b) Moderately severe brain injury **£115,000 to £145,000**

The injured person will be very seriously disabled. There will be substantial dependence on others and a need for constant professional and other care. Disabilities may be physical, for example, limb paralysis, or cognitive, with marked impairment of intellect and personality. Cases otherwise within (a) above may fall into this bracket if life expectancy has been greatly reduced.

The level of the award within the bracket will be affected by the following considerations:
(i)   the degree of insight;
(ii)   life expectancy;
(iii) the extent of physical limitations;
(iv)   the degree of dependence on others;
(v)   ability to communicate;
(vi)   behavioural abnormality;
(vii) epilepsy or a significant risk of epilepsy (unless a provisional damages order provides for this risk).

(c) Moderate brain damage

This category is distinguished from (b) by the fact that the degree of dependence is markedly lower.
(i)   Cases in which there is moderate to severe intellectual deficit, a personality change, an effect on sight, speech and senses with a significant risk of epilepsy and no prospect of employment. **£77,500 to £115,000**
(ii) Cases in which there is a moderate to modest intellectual deficit, the ability to work is greatly reduced if not removed and there is some risk of epilepsy (unless a provisional damages order provides for this risk). **£46,500 to £77,500**

(iii) Cases in which concentration and memory are affected, the ability to work is reduced, where there is a small risk of epilepsy and any dependence on others is very limited. **£22,250 to £46,500**

(d) Minor Brain Damage **£8,000 to £22,250**

In these cases the injured person will have made a good recovery and will be able to take part in normal social life and return to work. There may not have been a restoration of all normal functions so there may still be persistent problems such as poor concentration and memory or disinhibition of mood, which may interfere with lifestyle, leisure activities and future work prospects. At the top of this bracket there may be a small risk of epilepsy.

The level of the award within the bracket will be affected by:
(i)   the extent and severity of the initial injury;
(ii)   the extent of any continuing, and possibly permanent, disability;
(iii) the extent of any personality change.

B Minor head injury

£1,000 to £6,500

In these cases brain damage, if any, will have been minimal.

The level of the award will be affected by the following considerations:
(i)   the severity of the initial injury;
(ii)   the period taken to recover from any symptoms;
(iii) the extent of continuing symptoms;
(iv)   the presence or absence of headaches.

The bottom of the bracket will reflect full recovery within a few weeks.

C Epilepsy

(a) Established Grand Mal **£52,000 to £77,500**

(b) Established Petit Mal **£28,500 to £67,500**

The level of the award within these brackets will be affected by the following factors:
(i)   whether attacks are successfully controlled by medication and the extent to which the need for medication is likely to persist;
(ii)   the extent to which the appreciation of life is blunted by such medication;
(iii) the effect on working and/or social life;
(iv)   the existence of associated behavioural problems;
(v)   the prognosis.

(c) Other Epileptic Conditions **£5,500 to £13,500**

Cases where there are one or two discrete epileptic episodes, or a temporary resurgence of epilepsy, but there is no risk of further recurrence beyond that applicable to the population at large. The level of the award within the bracket will be affected by the extent of any consequences of the attacks on, for example, education, sporting activities, working and social life, and their duration.

3   Psychiatric damage

In part (A) of this chapter some of the brackets contain an element of compensation for post-traumatic stress disorder. This is of course not a universal feature of cases of psychiatric injury and hence a number of the awards upon which the brackets are based did not reflect it. Where it does figure any award will tend towards the upper end of the bracket. Cases where post-traumatic stress disorder is the sole psychiatric condition are dealt with in part (B) of this chapter. Where cases arise out of sexual and/or physical abuse in breach of parental, family or other trust, involving victims who are young and/or vulnerable, awards will tend to be at the upper end of the relevant bracket to take into account (A)(vii) below.

(A) Psychiatric Damage General

The factors to be taken into account in valuing claims of this nature are as follows:
(i)   the injured person's ability to cope with life and work;
(ii)   the effect on the injured person's relationships with family, friends and those with whom he or she comes into contact;
(iii) the extent to which treatment would be successful;
(iv)   future vulnerability;
(v)   prognosis;
(vi)   whether medical help has been sought;
(vii) (a) whether the injury results from sexual and/or physical abuse and/or breach of trust;
       (b) if so, the nature of the relationship between victim and abuser, the nature of the abuse, its duration and the symptoms caused by it.

(a) Severe **£28,500 to £60,000**

In these cases the injured person will have marked problems with respect to factors (i) to (iv) above and the prognosis will be very poor.

(b) Moderately Severe **£10,000 to £28,500**

In these cases there will be significant problems associated with factors (i) to (iv) above but the prognosis will be much more optimistic than in (a) above. While there are awards which support both extremes of this bracket, the majority were between £15,000 and £20,000. Cases of work-related stress resulting in a permanent or long-standing disability preventing a return to comparable employment would appear to come within this category.

(c) Moderate **£3,000 to £10,000**

While there may have been the sort of problems associated with factors (i) to (iv) above there will have been marked improvement by trial and the prognosis will be good.

(d) Minor **£750 to £3,000**

The level of the award will take into consideration the length of the period of disability and the extent to which daily activities and sleep were affected. Awards have been made below this bracket in cases of temporary 'anxiety'.

(B) Post-traumatic stress disorder

Cases within this category are exclusively those where there is a specific diagnosis of a reactive psychiatric disorder in which characteristic symptoms are displayed following a psychologically distressing event which was outside the range of normal human experience and which would be markedly distressing to almost anyone. The guidelines below have been compiled by reference to cases which variously reflect the criteria established in the 4th edition of *Diagnostic and Statistical Manual of Mental Disorders* (DSM-IV-TR). The symptoms affect basic functions such as breathing, pulse rate and bowel and/or bladder control. They also involve persistent re-experience of the relevant event, difficulty in controlling temper, in concentrating and sleeping, and exaggerated startle response.

(a) Severe **£32,500 to £52,000**

Such cases will involve permanent effects which prevent the injured person from working at all or at least from functioning at anything approaching the pre-trauma level. All aspects of the life of the injured person will be badly affected.

(b) Moderately Severe **£12,000 to £30,000**

This category is distinct from (a) above because of the better prognosis which will be for some recovery with professional help. However, the effects are still likely to cause significant disability for the foreseeable future. While there are awards which support both extremes of this bracket, the majority are between £20,000 and £25,000.

(c) Moderate **£4,250 to £12,000**

In these cases the injured person will have largely recovered and any continuing effects will not be grossly disabling.

(d) Minor **£2,000 to £4,250**

In these cases a virtually full recovery will have been made within one to two years and only minor symptoms will persist over any longer period.

4   Injuries affecting the senses

(A)   Injuries affecting sight

(a) Total Blindness and Deafness **In the region of £205,000**

Such cases must be considered as ranking with the most devastating injuries.

(b) Total Blindness **In the region of £140,000**

(c) Loss of Sight in One Eye with Reduced Vision in the Remaining Eye
(i)   Where there is serious risk of further deterioration in the remaining eye, going beyond some risk of sympathetic ophthalmia. **£50,000 to £92,500**
(ii) Where there is reduced vision in the remaining eye and/or additional problems such as double vision. **£33,000 to £55,000**

(d) Total Loss of One Eye **£28,750 to £34,000**

The level of the award within the bracket will depend on age and cosmetic effect.

(e) Complete Loss of Sight in One Eye **£25,750 to £28,750**

This award takes account of some risk of sympathetic ophthalmia. The upper end of the bracket is appropriate where there is scarring in the region of the eye which is not sufficiently serious to merit a separate award.

(f) Cases of serious but incomplete loss of vision in one eye without significant risk of loss or reduction of vision in the remaining eye, or where there is constant double vision. **£12,500 to £20,000**

(g) Minor but permanent impairment of vision in one eye, including cases where there is some double vision, which may not be constant. **£6,500 to £10,750**

(h) Minor Eye Injuries **£2,000 to £4,500**

In this bracket fall cases of minor injuries, such as being struck in the eye, exposure to fumes including smoke, or being splashed by liquids, causing initial pain and some temporary interference with vision.

(i) Transient Eye Injuries **£1,000 to £2,000**

In these cases the injured person will have recovered completely within a few weeks.

(B) Deafness

The word 'deafness' is used to embrace total and partial hearing loss. In assessing awards for hearing loss regard must be had to the following:

(i)   whether the injury is one that has an immediate effect, allowing no opportunity to adapt, or whether it occurred over a period of time, as in noise exposure cases;

(ii) whether the injury or disability is one which the injured person suffered at an early age so that it has had or will have an effect on his or her speech, or is one that is suffered in later life;

(iii) whether the injury or disability affects balance;

(iv) in cases of noise-induced hearing loss (NIHL) age is of particular relevance as noted in paragraph (d) below.

(a) Total Deafness and Loss of Speech **£57,500 to £72,500**

Such cases arise, for example, where deafness has occurred at an early age (for example, rubella infection) so as to prevent or seriously to affect the development of normal speech.

(b) Total Deafness **£46,500 to £57,500**

The lower end of the bracket is appropriate for cases where there is no speech deficit or tinnitus. The higher end is appropriate for cases involving both of these.

(c) Total Loss of Hearing in One Ear **£16,500 to £23,750**

Cases will tend towards the higher end of the bracket where there are associated problems, such as tinnitus, dizziness or headaches.

(d) Partial Hearing Loss/Tinnitus

This category covers the bulk of deafness cases which usually result from exposure to noise over a prolonged period. The disability is not to be judged simply by the degree of hearing loss; there is often a degree of tinnitus present. Age is particularly relevant because impairment of hearing affects most people in the fullness of time and impacts both upon causation and upon valuation.

(i)   Severe tinnitus/hearing loss. **£15,500 to £23,750**

(ii) Moderate tinnitus/hearing loss. **£7,750 to £15,500**

(iii) Mild tinnitus with some hearing loss. **£6,500 to £7,750**

(iv) Slight or occasional tinnitus with slight hearing loss. **£4,000 to £6,500**

(C) Impairment of taste and smell

(a) Total Loss of Taste and Smell **In the region of £20,000**

(b) Total Loss of Smell and Significant Loss of Taste **£17,000 to £20,000**

It must be remembered that in nearly all cases of loss of smell there is some impairment of taste. Such cases fall into the next bracket.

(c) Loss of Smell **£13,000 to £17,000**

(d) Loss of Taste **£10,000 to £13,000**

5   Injuries to internal organs

(A)   Chest injuries

This is a specially difficult area because the majority of awards relate to industrial *disease* (see (B) below) as distinct from traumatic *injury*. Cases of traumatic damage to, or loss of, a lung are comparatively rare: the range is as wide as £1,000 to £77,500.

The levels of awards within the brackets set out below will be affected by:
(i)   age and gender;
(ii)   scarring;
(iii)   the effect on the capacity to work and enjoy life;
(iv)   the effect on life expectancy.
(a)   The worst type of case will be of total removal of one lung and/or serious heart damage with serious and prolonged pain and suffering and permanent significant scarring. **£52,000 to £77,500**
(b)   Traumatic injury to chest, lung(s) and/or heart causing permanent damage, impairment of function, physical disability and reduction of life expectancy. **£34,000 to £52,000**
(c)   Damage to chest and lung(s) causing some continuing disability. **£16,500 to £28,500**
(d)   A relatively simple injury (such as a single penetrating wound) causing some permanent damage to tissue but with no significant long-term effect on lung function.   **£6,500 to £9,250**
(e)   Toxic fume/smoke inhalation, leaving some residual damage, not serious enough to interfere permanently with lung function. **£2,750 to £6,500**
(f)   Injuries leading to collapsed lungs from which a full and uncomplicated recovery is made. **£1,000 to £2,750**
(g)   Fractures of ribs, causing serious pain and disability over a period of weeks only. **Up to £2,000**

(B)   Lung Disease

The level of the appropriate award for lung disease necessarily, and often principally, reflects the prognosis for what is frequently a worsening condition and/or the risk of the development of secondary sequelae.

Most of the reported cases are of asbestos-related disease (as to which see (C) below) but, save for asthma (which is also dealt with separately in (D) below), the brackets set out are intended to encompass all other lung disease cases irrespective of causation. In many cases falling under this head provisional awards will be appropriate. At the upper end of the range where serious disabling consequences will already be present and the prognosis is likely to be relatively clear such an award may not be appropriate. Furthermore, in some cases awards may be enhanced where classifiable psychiatric illness is present.

(a) For a young person with serious disability where there is a probability of progressive worsening leading to premature death. **£52,000 to £70,000**

(b) Lung cancer (typically in an older person) causing severe pain and impairment both of function and of quality of life. The duration of pain and suffering accounts for variations within this bracket. **£41,250 to £52,000**

(c) Disease, e.g., emphysema, causing significant and worsening lung function and impairment of breathing, prolonged and frequent coughing, sleep disturbance and restriction of physical activity and employment. **£28,500 to £41,250**

(d) Breathing difficulties (short of disabling breathlessness) requiring fairly frequent use of an inhaler; where there is inability to tolerate a smoky environment and an uncertain prognosis but already significant effect on social and working life. **£16,500 to £28,500**

(e) Bronchitis and wheezing not causing serious symptoms; little or no serious or permanent effect on working or social life; varying levels of anxiety about the future. **£10,750 to £16,500**

(f) Some slight breathlessness with no effect on working life and the likelihood of substantial and permanent recovery within a few years of the exposure to the cause or the aggravation of an existing condition. **£5,500 to £10,750**

(g) Provisional awards for cases otherwise falling within (f), or the least serious cases within (e) where the provisional award excludes any risk of malignancy. **£2,750 to £5,500**

(h) Temporary aggravation of bronchitis or other chest problems resolving within a very few months. **£1,000 to £2,750**

(C) Asbestos-related Disease

Mesothelioma, lung cancer and asbestosis are the most serious of these. The first is typically of shorter duration than either of the other two and almost always proves fatal within a period of between six and 18 months from first diagnosis. The second and third, again, are likely to have a fatal outcome but often endure for several years.

(a) Mesothelioma causing severe pain and impairment of both function and quality of life. This may be of the pleura (the lung lining) or of the peritoneum (the lining of the abdominal cavity); the latter being typically more painful.

The duration of pain and suffering accounts for variations within this bracket, three to four years justifying an award at the top end and between six and nine months towards the bottom end of the bracket. **£40,000 to £60,000**

(b)   Lung cancer, again a disease proving fatal in most cases, the symptoms of which may not be as painful as those of mesothelioma, but more protracted. **£40,000 to £50,000**

(c)   Asbestosis, causing impairment of the extremities of the lungs so that oxygen uptake to the blood stream is reduced. In the early stages the disease may be symptomless but progresses to cause severe breathlessness. Mobility is likely to become seriously impaired and quality of life reduced. Respiratory disability of between 10 and 20 per cent will probably attract an award in the region of £40,000. **£25,000 to £55,000**

(d)   Pleural thickening, typically causing progressive symptoms of breathlessness by inhibiting expansion of the lungs (the so-called *cuirasse* restriction). Disease may gradually progress to cause more serious respiratory disability. **£20,000 to £40,000**

(e)   Pleural plaques involving some, but limited, disability and often putting continued employment in jeopardy because of the diagnosis of the disease. **£15,000 to £20,000**

(f)   Provisional awards for cases otherwise falling within (e) or the least serious cases within (d) where the provisional award excludes any risk of the development of mesothelioma, lung or other cancer or asbestosis. **£5,000 to £25,000**

(D) Asthma

(a)   Severe and permanent disabling asthma, causing prolonged and regular coughing, disturbance of sleep, severe impairment of physical activity and enjoyment of life and where employment prospects, if any, are grossly restricted. **£22,250 to £34,000**

(b)   Chronic asthma causing breathing difficulties, the need to use an inhaler from time to time and restriction of employment prospects, with uncertain prognosis. **£13,500 to £22,250**

(c)   Bronchitis and wheezing, affecting working or social life, with the likelihood of substantial recovery within a few years of the exposure to the cause. **£10,000 to £13,500**

(d)   Relatively mild asthma-like symptoms often resulting, for instance, from exposure to harmful irritating vapour. **£5,500 to £10,000**

(e)   Mild asthma, bronchitis, colds and chest problems (usually resulting from unfit housing or similar exposure, particularly in cases of young children) treated by a general practitioner and resolving within a few months. **Up to £2,500**

(E) Reproductive System: Male

(a) **Impotence**
(i) Total impotence and loss of sexual function and sterility in the case of a young man. **In the region of £77,500**

The level of the award will depend on:
(1) age;
(2) psychological reaction and the effect on social and domestic life.
(ii) Impotence which is likely to be permanent, in the case of a middle-aged man with children. **£22,250 to £41,250**

(b) Cases of sterility usually fall into one of two categories: surgical, chemical and disease cases (which involve no traumatic injury or scarring) and traumatic injuries (frequently caused by assaults) which are often aggravated by scarring.
(i) The most serious cases merit awards approaching **£72,500**
(ii) The bottom of the range is the case of the much older man and merits an award of about **£10,000**

(c) An uncomplicated case of sterility without impotence and without any aggravating features for a young man without children. **£29,500 to £37,000**

(d) A similar case but involving a family man who might have intended to have more children. **£12,500 to £16,000**

(e) Cases where the sterility amounts to little more than an 'insult'. **In the region of £3,500**

(F) Reproductive System: Female

The level of awards in this area will typically depend on:
(i) whether or not the affected woman already has children and/or whether the intended family was complete;
(ii) scarring;
(iii) depression or psychological scarring;
(iv) whether a foetus was aborted.

(a) Infertility whether by reason of injury or disease, with severe depression and anxiety, pain and scarring. **£60,000 to £87,500**

(b) Infertility without any medical complication and where the injured person already has children. The upper end of the bracket is appropriate in cases where there is significant psychological damage. **£9,250 to £19,000**

(c) Infertility where the injured person would not have had children in any event (for example, because of age). **£3,350 to £6,500**

(d) Failed sterilisation leading to unwanted pregnancy where there is no serious psychological impact or depression. **In the region of £5,000**

(G) Digestive System

The risk of associated damage to the reproductive organs is frequently encountered in cases of this nature and requires separate consideration.

(a) Damage Resulting from Traumatic Injury
(i) Severe damage with continuing pain and discomfort. **£22,250 to £32,000**
(ii) Serious non-penetrating injury causing long-standing or permanent complications, for example, severe indigestion, aggravated by physical strain. **£8,750 to £14,500**
(iii) Penetrating stab wounds or industrial laceration or serious seat-belt pressure cases. **£3,350 to £6,500**

(b) Illness/damage Resulting from Non-traumatic Injury, e.g., food poisoning

There will be a marked distinction between those, comparatively rare, cases having a long-standing or even permanent effect on quality of life and those in which the only continuing symptoms may be allergy to specific foods and the attendant risk of short-term illness.
(i) Severe toxicosis causing serious acute pain, vomiting, diarrhoea and fever, requiring hospital admission for some days or weeks and some continuing incontinence, haemorrhoids and irritable bowel syndrome, having a significant impact on ability to work and enjoyment of life. **£20,000 to £30,000**
(ii) Serious but short-lived food poisoning, diarrhoea and vomiting diminishing over two to four weeks with some remaining discomfort and disturbance of bowel function and impact on sex life and enjoyment of food over a few years. **£5,000 to £10,000**
(iii) Food poisoning causing significant discomfort, stomach cramps, alteration of bowel function and fatigue. Hospital admission for some days with symptoms lasting for a few weeks but complete recovery within a year or two. **£2,000 to £5,000**
(iv) Varying degrees of disabling pain, cramps and diarrhoea continuing for some days or weeks. **£500 to £2,000**

(H) Kidney
(a) Serious and permanent damage to or loss of both kidneys. **£87,500 to £110,000**
(b) Where there is a significant risk of future urinary tract infection or other total loss of natural kidney function. **Up to £33,000**

Such cases will invariably carry with them substantial future medical expenses, which in this field are particularly high.
(c) Loss of one kidney with no damage to the other. **£16,000 to £22,250**

(I) Bowels
(a) Total loss of natural function and dependence on colostomy, depending on age. **Up to £77,500**
(b) Severe abdominal injury causing impairment of function and often necessitating temporary colostomy (leaving disfiguring scars) and/or restriction on employment and on diet. **£23,250 to £36,000**
(c) Penetrating injuries causing some permanent damage but with an eventual return to natural function and control. **£6,500 to £12,500**

(J) Bladder

It is perhaps surprising that awards in cases of loss of bladder function have often been higher than awards for injury to the bowels. This is probably because bladder injuries frequently result from carcinogenic exposure. The reported decisions are seriously out of date and merely increasing them to reflect inflation may be misleading.
(a) Complete loss of function and control. **Up to £72,500**
(b) Serious impairment of control with some pain and incontinence. **£33,000 to £41,250**
(c) Where there has been almost a complete recovery but some fairly long-term interference with natural function. **£12,000 to £15,500**

The cancer risk cases still occupy a special category and can properly attract awards at the top of the ranges even where natural function continues for the time being. However, these cases will now more appropriately be dealt with by provisional awards at a low level (£5,250) unless the foreseeable outcome is clear. Once the prognosis is firm and reliable the award will reflect any loss of life expectancy, the level of continuing pain and suffering and most significantly the extent to which the injured person has to live with the knowledge of the consequences which his or her death will have for others. The appropriate award for the middle-aged family man or woman whose life expectancy is reduced by 15 or 20 years is £28,500 to £41,250.

(K) Spleen
(a) Loss of spleen where there is continuing risk of internal infection and disorders due to the damage to the immune system. **£10,750 to £13,750**
(b) Where the above risks are not present or are minimal. **£2,250 to £4,500**

(L) Hernia

(a) Continuing pain and/or limitation on physical activities, sport or employment, after repair. **£7,750 to £12,500**

(b) Direct (where there was no pre-existing weakness) inguinal hernia, with some risk of recurrence, after repair. **£3,750 to £4,750**

(c) Uncomplicated indirect inguinal hernia, possibly repaired, and with no other associated abdominal injury or damage. **£1,600 to £3,750**

6   Orthopaedic injuries

(A) Neck injuries

There is a very wide range of neck injuries. Many are found in conjunction with back and shoulder problems.

At the highest level are injuries which shatter life and leave claimants very severely disabled. These may have a value of up to £77,500.

At the lowest level, claimants may suffer a minor strain, may not have time off work, and may suffer symptoms for two or three weeks, justifying as little as £500.

(a) Severe

(i)   Neck injury associated with incomplete paraplegia or resulting in permanent spastic quadriparesis or where the injured person, despite wearing a collar 24 hours a day for a period of years, still has little or no movement in the neck and suffers severe headaches which have proved intractable. **£77,500**

(ii)   Injuries which give rise to disabilities which fall short of those in (a)(i) above but which are of considerable severity; for example, permanent damage to the brachial plexus. **£34,000 to £67,500**

(iii) Injuries causing severe damage to soft tissues and/or ruptured tendons. They result in significant disability of a permanent nature. The precise award depends on the length of time during which the most serious symptoms are ameliorated, and on the prognosis. **In the region of £27,500**

(iv) Injuries such as fractures or dislocations which cause severe immediate symptoms and which may necessitate spinal fusion. They leave markedly impaired function or vulnerability to further trauma, and some limitation of activities. **£13,000 to £17,000**

(b) Moderate

(i)   Cases involving whiplash or wrenching-type injury and disc lesion of the more severe type resulting in cervical spondylosis, serious limitation of movement, permanent or recurring pain, stiffness or discomfort and the possible need for further surgery or increased vulnerability to further trauma. **£7,250 to £13,000**

(ii) Injuries which may have exacerbated or accelerated some pre-existing unrelated condition. There will have been a complete recovery or recovery to 'nuisance' level from the effects of the accident within a few years. This bracket will also apply to moderate whiplash injuries where the period of recovery has been fairly protracted and where there remains an increased vulnerability to further trauma. **£4,000 to £7,250**

(c) Minor

Minor soft tissue and whiplash injuries and the like where symptoms are moderate:
(i)   and a full recovery takes place within about two years; **£2,000 to £4,000**
(ii) and a full recovery takes place within a year. **£500 to £2,000**

(B) Back Injuries

Relatively few back injuries which do not give rise to paralysis command awards above about £25,000. In those that do there are special features.

(a) Severe
(i)   Cases of the most severe injury which do not involve paralysis but where there may be very serious consequences not normally found in cases of back injury, such as impotence or double incontinence. **£52,000 to £87,500**
(ii) Cases which have special features taking them outside any lower bracket applicable to orthopaedic injury to the back. Such features include impaired bladder and bowel function, severe sexual difficulties and unsightly scarring and the possibility of future surgery. **In the region of £42,500**
(iii) Cases of disc lesions or fractures of discs or of vertebral bodies where, despite treatment, there remain disabilities such as continuing severe pain and discomfort, impaired agility, impaired sexual function, depression, personality change, alcoholism, unemployability and the risk of arthritis. **£20,000 to £36,000**

(b) Moderate
(i)   Cases where any residual disability is of less severity than that in (a)(iii) above. The bracket contains a wide variety of injuries. Examples are a case of a crush fracture of the lumbar vertebrae where there is a substantial risk of osteoarthritis and constant pain and discomfort with impairment of sexual function; that of a traumatic spondylolisthesis with continuous pain and a probability that spinal fusion will be necessary; or that of a prolapsed intervertebral disc with substantial acceleration of back degeneration. **£14,500 to £20,000**
(ii) Many frequently encountered injuries to the back such as disturbance of ligaments and muscles giving rise to backache, soft tissue injuries resulting in exacerbation of an existing back condition or prolapsed discs necessitating laminectomy or resulting in repeated relapses. The precise figure depends

upon the severity of the original injury and/or whether there is some permanent or chronic disability. **£6,500 to £14,500**

(c) Minor

Strains, sprains, disc prolapses and soft tissue injuries from which a full recovery or recovery to 'nuisance' level has been made without surgery:
(i)   within about five years; **£4,000 to £7,000**
(ii)   within about two years. **Up to £4,000**

(C)   Shoulder Injuries

(a) Severe **£10,000 to £25,000**

Often associated with neck injuries and involving damage to the brachial plexus (see (A)(a)(ii)) resulting in significant disability.

(b) Serious **£6,500 to £10,000**

Dislocation of the shoulder and damage to the lower part of the brachial plexus causing pain in shoulder and neck, aching in elbow, sensory symptoms in the forearm and hand, and weakness of grip.

(c) Moderate **£4,250 to £6,500**

Frozen shoulder with limitation of movement and discomfort with symptoms persisting for about two years.

(d) Minor

Soft tissue injury to shoulder with considerable pain but almost complete recovery:
(i)   in less than two years; **£2,000 to £4,250**
(ii)   within a year. **Up to £2,000**

(e) Fracture of Clavicle **£2,500 to £6,250**

The level of the award will depend on extent of fracture, level of disability, residual symptoms, and whether temporary or permanent, and whether union is anatomically displaced.

(D)   Injuries to the pelvis and hips

The most serious of injuries to the pelvis and hip can be as devastating as a leg amputation and accordingly will attract a similar award of damages. Such cases apart, the upper limit for these injuries will generally be in the region of £35,000. Cases where there are specific sequelae of exceptional severity would call for a higher award.

(a) Severe

(i) Extensive fractures of the pelvis involving, for example, dislocation of a low back joint and a ruptured bladder, or a hip injury resulting in spondylolisthesis of a low back joint with intolerable pain and necessitating spinal fusion. Inevitably there will be substantial residual disabilities such as a complicated arthrodesis with resulting lack of bladder and bowel control, sexual dysfunction or hip deformity making the use of a calliper essential. Or may present difficulties for natural delivery. **£41,250 to £67,500**

(ii) Injuries only a little less severe than in (a)(i) above but with particular distinguishing features lifting them above any lower bracket. Examples are: (a) fracture dislocation of the pelvis involving both ischial and pubic rami and resulting in impotence; or (b) traumatic myositis ossificans with formation of ectopic bone around the hip. **£32,000 to £41,250**

(iii) Many injuries fall within this bracket: a fracture of the acetabulum leading to degenerative changes and leg instability requiring an osteotomy and the likelihood of hip replacement surgery in the future; the fracture of an arthritic femur or hip necessitating hip replacement; or a fracture resulting in a hip replacement which is only partially successful so that there is a clear risk of the need for revision surgery. **£20,000 to £27,000**

(b) Moderate **£14,000 to £20,000**

Significant injury to the pelvis or hip but any permanent disability is not major and any future risk not great.

(c) Injuries of Limited Severity **£6,500 to £14,000**

These cases may involve hip replacement. Where it has been carried out wholly successfully the award will tend to the top of the bracket, but the bracket also includes cases where hip replacement may be necessary in the foreseeable future.

(d) Lesser Injuries

(i) Cases where despite significant injury there is little or no residual disability. **£2,000 to £6,500**

(ii) Minor injuries with complete recovery. **Up to £2,000**

(E) Amputation of arms

(a) Loss of Both Arms **£125,000 to £155,000**

There is no recent case to offer guidance but the effect of such an injury is to reduce a person with full awareness to a state of considerable helplessness.

(b) Loss of One Arm

(i) Arm Amputated at the Shoulder **Not less than £72,500**

(ii) Above-elbow Amputation **£57,500 to £67,500**

A shorter stump may create difficulties in the use of a prosthesis. This will make the level of the award towards the top end of the bracket. Amputation through the elbow will normally produce an award at the bottom end of the bracket.

(iii) Below-elbow Amputation **£50,000 to £57,500**

Amputation through the forearm with residual severe organic and phantom pains would attract an award at the top end of the bracket.

The value of such an injury depends upon:
(i)   whether the amputation is above or below the elbow. The loss of the additional joint adds greatly to the disability;
(ii)   whether or not the amputation was of the dominant arm;
(iii)   the intensity of any phantom pains.

(F)   Other arm injuries

(a) Severe Injuries £50,000 to £67,500

Injuries which fall short of amputation but which are extremely serious and leave the injured person little better off than if the arm had been lost; for example, a serious brachial plexus injury.

(b) Injuries resulting in Permanent and Substantial Disablement **£20,000 to £31,000**

Serious fractures of one or both forearms where there is significant permanent residual disability whether functional or cosmetic.

(c) Less Severe Injury **£10,000 to £20,000**

While there will have been significant disabilities, a substantial degree of recovery will have taken place or will be expected.

(d) Simple Fractures of the Forearm **£3,500 to £10,000**

Uncomplicated fractures of the radius and/or ulna with a complete recovery within a short time would justify an award of £3,500. Injuries resulting in modest residual disability or deformity would merit an award towards the upper end of this bracket.

(G)   Injuries to the elbow

(a) A Severely Disabling Injury **£20,000 to £28,500**

(b) Less Severe Injuries **£8,250 to £16,500**

Injuries causing impairment of function but not involving major surgery or significant disability.

(c) Moderate or Minor Injury **Up to £6,750**

Most elbow injuries fall into this category. They comprise simple fractures, tennis elbow syndrome and lacerations; i.e. those injuries which cause no permanent damage and do not result in any permanent impairment of function.

(H) Wrist injuries
(a)   Injuries resulting in complete loss of function in the wrist, for example, where an arthrodesis has been performed. **£24,750 to £31,000**
(b)   Injury resulting in significant permanent disability, but where some useful movement remains. **£12,750 to £20,000**
(c)   Less severe injuries where these still result in some permanent disability as, for example, a degree of persisting pain and stiffness. **£6,500 to £12,750**
(d)   Where recovery is complete the award will rarely exceed **£5,000**
(e)   An uncomplicated Colles' fracture. **£4,000**

(I)   Hand injuries
The hands are cosmetically and functionally the most important component parts of the upper limbs. The loss of a hand is valued not far short of the amount which would be awarded for the loss of the arm itself. The upper end of any bracket will generally be appropriate where the injury is to the dominant hand.

(a) Total or Effective Loss of Both Hands **£72,500 to £105,000**

Serious injury resulting in extensive damage to both hands such as to render them little more than useless will justify an award of £72,500 or more. The top of the bracket is applicable where no effective prosthesis can be used.

(b) Serious Damage to Both Hands **£28,500 to £43,750**

Such injuries will have given rise to permanent cosmetic disability and significant loss of function.

(c) Total or Effective Loss of One Hand **£50,000 to £57,500**

This bracket will apply to a hand which was crushed and thereafter surgically amputated or where all fingers and most of the palm have been traumatically amputated. The upper end of the bracket is indicated where the hand so damaged was the dominant one.

(d) Amputation of Index and Middle and/or Ring Fingers **£32,000 to £46,500**

The hand will have been rendered of very little use and such grip as remains will be exceedingly weak.

(e) Serious Hand Injuries **£15,000 to £32,000**

Such injuries will, for example, have reduced the hand to about 50 per cent capacity. Included would be cases where several fingers have been amputated but rejoined to the hand leaving it clawed, clumsy and unsightly, or amputation of some fingers together with part of the palm resulting in gross diminution of grip and dexterity and gross cosmetic disfigurement.

(f) Less Serious Hand Injury **£7,500 to £15,000**

Such as a severe crush injury resulting in significantly impaired function without future surgery or despite operative treatment undergone.

(g) Moderate Hand Injury **£3,250 to £7,000**

Crush injuries, penetrating wounds, soft tissue type and deep lacerations. The top of the bracket would be appropriate where surgery has failed and permanent disability remains.

(h) Severe Fractures to Fingers **Up to £19,000**

These may lead to partial amputations and result in deformity, impairment of grip, reduced mechanical function and disturbed sensation.

(i) Total Loss of Index Finger **In the region of £10,000**

(j) Partial Loss of Index Finger **£6,250 to £9,250**

This bracket also covers cases of injury to the index finger giving rise to disfigurement and impairment of grip or dexterity.

(k) Fracture of Index Finger **£4,750 to £6,250**

This level is appropriate where a fracture has mended quickly but grip has remained impaired, there is pain on heavy use and osteoarthritis is likely in due course.

(l) Total Loss of Middle Finger **In the region of £8,000**

(m) Serious Injury to Ring or Middle Fingers **£7,750 to £8,500**

Fractures or serious injury to tendons causing stiffness, deformity and permanent loss of grip or dexterity will fall within this bracket.

(n) Loss of the Terminal Phalanx of the Ring or Middle Fingers **£2,000 to £4,000**

(o) Amputation of Little Finger **£4,500 to £6,250**

(p) Loss of Part of the Little Finger **£2,000 to £3,000**

This is appropriate where the remaining tip is sensitive.

(q) Amputation of Ring and Little Fingers **In the region of £11,000**

(r) Amputation of the Terminal Phalanges of the Index and Middle Fingers **In the region of £13,000**

Such injury will involve scarring, restriction of movement and impairment of grip and fine handling.

(s) Fracture of One Finger **£1,500 to £2,500**

Depending upon recovery time.

(t) Loss of Thumb **£18,500 to £28,750**

(u) Very Serious Injury to Thumb **£10,000 to £18,500**

This bracket is appropriate where the thumb has been severed at the base and grafted back leaving a virtually useless and deformed digit, or where the thumb has been amputated through the metacarpophalangeal joint.

(v) Serious Injury to the Thumb **£6,500 to £8,750**

Such injuries may involve amputation of the tip, nerve damage or fracture necessitating the insertion of wires as a result of which the thumb is cold and ultra-sensitive and there is impaired grip and loss of manual dexterity.

(w) Moderate Injuries to the Thumb **£5,000 to £6,500**

These are injuries such as those necessitating arthrodesis of the interphalangeal joint or causing damage to tendons or nerves. Such injuries result in impairment of sensation and function and cosmetic deformity.

(x) Severe Dislocation of the Thumb **£2,000 to £3,500**

(y) Minor Injuries to the Thumb **In the region of £2,000**

Such an injury would be a fracture which has recovered in six months except for residual stiffness and some discomfort.

(z) Trivial Thumb Injuries **In the region of £1,000**

These may have caused severe pain for a very short time but will have resolved within a few months.

(J) Vibration white finger

This particular disability is similar to the constitutional condition of Raynaud's Phenomenon, and is caused by prolonged exposure to vibration. Degrees of severity are measured both on the Taylor–Pelmear Scale and on the Stockholm Workshop Scale (for the sensorineural aspects). From the Taylor–Pelmear Scale the relevant categories are:

(i)   extensive blanching of most fingers with episodes in summer and winter of such severity as to necessitate changing occupation to avoid exposure to vibration;
(ii) extensive blanching with episodes in summer and winter resulting in interference at work, at home and with hobbies and social activities;
(iii) blanching of one or more fingers with numbness, usually occurring only in winter and causing slight interference with home and social activities;
(iv) blanching of one or more fingertips with or without tingling or numbness.

The top of the bracket would normally represent the most disabled stage 3/4 case on the Taylor-Pelmear Scale ((i) to (ii) above). The position within the bracket depends upon:
(i)   length and severity of attacks and symptoms;
(ii) extent and/or severity and/or rapidity of deterioration;
(iii) age and prognosis.

In some cases these factors are more important than the stage the disease has reached.

The brackets can best be defined and valued as follows:
(i)   Most Serious **£16,500 to £20,000**
(ii) Serious **£8,750 to £16,500**
(iii) Moderate **£4,500 to £8,750**
(iv) Minor **£1,500 to £4,500**

(K) Work-related upper limb disorders

This section covers a range of upper limb injury in the form of the following pathological conditions:
(a)   Tenosynovitis: inflammation of synovial sheaths of tendons usually resolving with rest over a short period. Sometimes this condition leads to continuing symptoms of loss of grip and dexterity.
(b)   De Quervain's tenosynovitis: a form of tenosynovitis, rarely bilateral, involving inflammation of the tendons of the thumb.
(c)   Stenosing tenosynovitis: otherwise, trigger finger/thumb: thickening tendons.
(d)   Carpal tunnel syndrome: constriction of the median nerve of the wrist or thickening of surrounding tissue. It is often relieved by a decompression operation.
(e)   Epicondylitis: inflammation in the elbow joint: medial golfer's elbow; lateral tennis elbow.

The brackets below apply to all these conditions but the level of the award is affected by the following considerations regardless of the precise condition:
(i)   are the effects bilateral or one sided?

(ii)   the level of symptoms, i.e., pain, swelling, tenderness, crepitus;

(iii) the ability to work;

(iv)   the capacity to avoid the recurrence of symptoms;

(v)   surgery.

(a)   Continuing bilateral disability with surgery and loss of employment **£11,250 to £11,750**

(b)   Continuing, but fluctuating and unilateral symptoms **£7,750 to £8,500**

(c)   Symptoms resolving in the course of two years **£4,500 to £5,000**

(d)   Complete recovery within a short period **£1,000 to £1,800**

(L) Leg injuries

(a)Amputations

(i)   Total Loss of Both Legs **£125,000 to £145,000**

This is the appropriate award where both legs are lost above the knee and particularly if near to the hip leaving one or both stumps less than adequate to accommodate a useful prosthesis.

(ii)   Below-knee Amputation of Both Legs **£105,000 to £140,000**

The top of the bracket is appropriate where both legs are amputated just below the knee. Amputations lower down result in a lower award.

(iii) Above-knee Amputation of One Leg **£50,000 to £72,500**

The area within the bracket within which the award should fall will depend upon such factors as the level of the amputation; the severity of phantom pains; whether or not there have been any problems with a prosthesis and any side effects such as depression or backache.

(iv)   Below-knee Amputation of One Leg **£47,500 to £67,500**

The straightforward case of a below-knee amputation with no complications would justify an award at the bottom of this bracket. At or towards the top of the range would come the traumatic amputation which occurs in a devastating accident, where the injured person remained fully conscious, or cases where attempts to save the leg led to numerous unsuccessful operations so that amputation occurred years after the event.

(b)   Severe Leg Injuries

(i)   The Most Serious Injuries short of Amputation **£50,000 to £70,000**

Some injuries, although not involving amputation, are so severe that the courts have awarded damages at a comparable level. Such injuries would include extensive degloving of the leg, where there is gross shortening of the leg or where fractures have not united and extensive bone grafting has been undertaken.

(ii)   Very Serious **£28,500 to £43,750**

Injuries leading to permanent problems with mobility, the need for crutches for the remainder of the injured person's life; injuries where multiple fractures have taken years to heal and have led to serious deformity and limitation of movement, or where arthritis has developed in a joint so that further surgical treatment is likely.

(iii)   Serious **£20,000 to £28,500**

Serious injuries to joints or ligaments resulting in instability, prolonged treatment, a lengthy period of non-weight-bearing, the near certainty that arthritis will ensue; injuries involving the hip, requiring arthrodesis or hip replacement, extensive scarring. To justify an award within this bracket a combination of such features will generally be necessary.

(iv)   Moderate **£14,500 to £20,000**

This bracket includes severe, complicated or multiple fractures. The level of an award within the bracket will be influenced by the period off work; the presence or risk of degenerative changes; imperfect union of fractures, muscle wasting; limited joint movements; instability in the knee; unsightly scarring or permanently increased vulnerability to future damage.

(c) Less Serious Leg Injuries
(i)   Fractures from which an Incomplete Recovery is Made **£9,250 to £14,500**

The injured person will be left with a metal implant and/or defective gait, a limp, impaired mobility, sensory loss, discomfort or an exacerbation of a pre-existing disability.

(ii)   Simple Fracture of a Femur with no Damage to Articular Surfaces **Up to £7,250**
(iii)   Simple Fractures and Soft Tissue Injuries **Up to £4,750**

At the top of the bracket will come simple fractures of the tibia or fibula from which a complete recovery has been made. Below this level fall a wide variety of soft-tissue injuries, lacerations, cuts, bruising or contusions, all of which have recovered completely or almost so and any residual disability is cosmetic or of a minor nature.

(M) Knee injuries

Knee injuries fall within a bracket extending from a few hundred pounds for a simple twisting injury up to £45,000 or more where there have been considerable problems leading to an arthrodesis or arthroplasty.

(a) Severe

(i)   Serious knee injury where there has been disruption of the joint, gross ligamentous damage, lengthy treatment, considerable pain and loss of function and an arthrodesis or arthroplasty has taken place or is inevitable. **£36,000 to £50,000**

(ii)   Leg fracture extending into the knee joint causing pain which is constant, permanent, limiting movement or impairing agility and rendering the injured person prone to osteoarthritis and the risk of arthroplasty. **£27,000 to £36,000**

(iii) Less severe injuries than those in (a)(ii) above and/or injuries which result in less severe disability. There may be continuing symptoms by way of pain and discomfort and limitation of movement or instability or deformity with the risk that degenerative changes may occur in the long term as a result of damage to the kneecap, ligamentous or meniscal injury or muscular wasting. **£14,000 to £22,250**

(b) Moderate

(i)   Injuries involving dislocation, torn cartilage or meniscus or which accelerate symptoms from a pre-existing condition but which additionally result in minor instability, wasting, weakness or other mild future disability. **£7,750 to £14,000**

(ii)   This bracket includes injuries similar to those in (b)(i) above, but less serious, and also lacerations, twisting or bruising injuries. Where recovery has been complete the award is unlikely to exceed £3,000. Where there is continuous aching or discomfort, or occasional pain the award will be towards the upper end of the bracket. **Up to £7,000**

(N) Ankle injuries

The vast majority of ankle injuries are worth significantly less than £10,000. The ceiling, however, is in the region of £35,000. This will be appropriate where the degree of disablement is very severe.

(a) Very Severe **£26,000 to £36,000**

Examples of injuries falling within this bracket are limited and unusual. They include cases of a transmalleolar fracture of the ankle with extensive soft-tissue damage resulting in deformity and the risk that any future injury to the leg might necessitate a below-knee amputation, or cases of bilateral ankle fractures causing degeneration of the joints at a young age so that arthrodesis is necessary.

(b) Severe **£16,500 to £26,000**

Injuries necessitating an extensive period of treatment and/or a lengthy period in plaster or where pins and plates have been inserted and there is significant residual disability in the form of ankle instability, severely limited ability to walk. The level of the award within the bracket will be determined in part by such features as a failed arthrodesis, regular sleep disturbance, unsightly scarring and any need to wear special footwear.

(c) Moderate **£7,000 to £14,000**

Fractures, ligamentous tears and the like which give rise to less serious disabilities such as difficulty in walking on uneven ground, awkwardness on stairs, irritation from metal plates and residual scarring.

(d) Modest Injuries **Up to £7,000**

The less serious, minor or undisplaced fractures, sprains and ligamentous injuries. The level of the award within the bracket will be determined by whether or not a complete recovery has been made and, if recovery is incomplete, whether there is any tendency for the ankle to give way, and whether there is scarring, aching or discomfort or the possibility of later osteoarthritis.

Where recovery is within a year, the award is unlikely to exceed £3,000.

(O) Achilles tendon

(a) Most Serious **In the region of £20,000**

Severance of the tendon and the peroneus longus muscle giving rise to cramp, swelling and restricted ankle movement necessitating the cessation of active sports.

(b) Serious **£12,750 to £15,500**

Where complete division of the tendon has been successfully repaired but there is residual weakness, a limitation of ankle movements, a limp and residual scarring and where further improvement is unlikely.

(c) Moderate **£7,750 to £9,250**

Complete division of the tendon but where its repair has left no significant functional disability.

(d) Minor **£4,000 to £5,250**

A turning of the ankle resulting in some damage to the tendon and a feeling of being unsure of ankle support.

(P) Foot injuries

(a) Amputation of Both Feet **£87,500 to £105,000**

This injury is treated similarly to below-knee amputation of both legs because the common feature is loss of a useful ankle joint.

(b) Amputation of One Foot **£43,250 to £57,500**

This injury is also treated as similar to a below-knee amputation because of the loss of the ankle joint.

(c) Very Severe **£43,250 to £57,500**

To fall within this bracket the injury must produce permanent and severe pain or really serious permanent disability. Examples would include the traumatic amputation of the forefoot where there was a significant risk of the need for a full amputation and serious exacerbation of an existing back problem, or cases of the loss of a substantial portion of the heel so that mobility was grossly restricted.

(d) Severe **£23,750 to £35,000**

Fractures of *both* heels or feet with a substantial restriction on mobility or considerable or permanent pain. The bracket will also include unusually severe injury to a single foot resulting, for example, in heel fusion, osteoporosis, ulceration or other disability preventing the wearing of ordinary shoes. It will also apply in the case of a drop foot deformity corrected by a brace.

(e) Serious **£13,000 to £20,000**

Towards the top end of the bracket fall cases such as those of grievous burns to both feet requiring multiple operations and leaving disfiguring scars and persistent irritation. At the lower end of the bracket would be those injuries less severe than in (d) above but leading to fusion of foot joints, continuing pain from traumatic arthritis, prolonged treatment and the future risk of osteoarthritis.

(f) Moderate **£7,000 to £13,000**

Displaced metatarsal fractures resulting in permanent deformity and continuing symptoms.

(g) Modest **Up to £7,000**

Simple metatarsal fractures, ruptured ligaments, puncture wounds and the like. Where there are continuing symptoms, such as a permanent limp, pain or aching, awards between £3,500 and £7,000 would be appropriate. Straightforward foot injuries such as fractures, lacerations, contusions etc. from which complete or near complete recovery is made would justify awards of £3,500 or less.

(Q) Toe injuries

(a) Amputation of All Toes **£18,750 to £29,000**

The position within the bracket will be determined by, for example, whether or not the amputation was traumatic or surgical and the extent of the loss of the forefoot together with the residual effects on mobility.

(b) Amputation of the Great Toe **In the region of £15,000**

(c) Severe Toe Injuries **£7,000 to £10,000**

This is the appropriate bracket for severe crush injuries, falling short of the need for amputation or necessitating only partial amputation. It also includes bursting wounds and injuries resulting in severe damage and in any event producing significant continuing symptoms.

(d) Serious Toe Injuries **£5,000 to £7,000**

Such injuries will be serious injuries to the great toe or crush and multiple fractures of two or more toes. There will be some permanent disability by way of discomfort, pain or sensitive scarring to justify an award within this bracket. Where there have been a number of unsuccessful operations or persisting stabbing pains, impaired gait or the like the award will tend towards the top end of the bracket.

(e) Moderate Toe Injuries **Up to £5,000**

These injuries include relatively straightforward fractures or the exacerbation of a pre-existing degenerative condition. Only £3,000 or less would be awarded for straightforward fractures of one or more toes with complete resolution within a short period of time and less still for minor injuries involving lacerations, cuts, contusions and bruises, in respect of all of which there would have been a complete or near complete recovery.

7 Facial injuries

The assessment of general damages for facial injuries is an extremely difficult task, there being three elements which complicate the award.

First, while in most of the cases dealt with below the injuries described are skeletal, many of them will involve an element of disfigurement or at least some cosmetic effect.

Second, in cases where there is a cosmetic element the courts have invariably drawn a distinction between the awards of damages to males and females, the latter attracting the higher awards.

Third, in cases of disfigurement there may also be severe psychological reactions which put the total award at the top of the bracket, or above it altogether.

The subject of burns is not dealt with separately. Burns of any degree of severity are particularly painful and disfiguring, and awards are invariably at the upper ends of the brackets, or above them altogether.

(A) Skeletal Injuries

(a) Le Fort Fractures of Frontal Facial Bones **£12,500 to £19,000**

(b) Multiple Fractures of Facial Bones **£7,750 to £12,500**

Involving some facial deformity of a permanent nature.

(c) Fractures of Nose or Nasal Complex
(i)   Serious or multiple fractures requiring a number of operations and/or resulting in permanent damage to airways and/or nerves or tear ducts and/or facial deformity. **£5,500 to £12,000**
(ii) Displaced fracture where recovery complete but only after surgery. **£2,000 to £2,500**
(iii) Displaced fracture requiring no more than manipulation. **£1,300 to £1,600**
(iv) Simple undisplaced fracture with full recovery. **£750 to £1,250**

(d) Fractures of Cheekbones
(i)   Serious fractures requiring surgery but with lasting consequences such as paraesthesia in the cheeks or the lips or some element of disfigurement. **£5,250 to £8,250**
(ii) Simple fracture of cheekbones for which some reconstructive surgery is necessary but from which there is a complete recovery with no or only minimal cosmetic effects. **£2,200 to £3,300**
(iii) Simple fracture of cheekbone for which no surgery is required and where a complete recovery is effected. **£1,250 to £1,500**

(e) Fractures of Jaws
(i)   Very serious multiple fractures followed by prolonged treatment and permanent consequences, including severe pain, restriction in eating, paraesthesia and/or the risk of arthritis in the joints. **£16,000 to £23,750**
(ii) Serious fracture with permanent consequences such as difficulty in opening the mouth or with eating or where there is paraesthesia in the area of the jaw. **£9,250 to £16,000**
(iii) Simple fracture requiring immobilisation but from which recovery is complete. **£3,350 to £4,500**

(f) Damage to Teeth

In these cases there will generally have been a course of treatment as a result of the initial injury. The amounts awarded will vary according to the extent and/or the degree of discomfort of such treatment. Any difficulty with eating increases the award. These cases may overlap with fractures of the jaw, meriting awards in the brackets for such fractures. Awards may be greater where the damage itself is the result of protracted dentistry.

(i)   Loss of or serious damage to several front teeth. **£4,500 to £6,000**
(ii) Loss of or serious damage to two front teeth. **£2,200 to £4,000**
(iii) Loss of or serious damage to one front tooth. **£1,000 to £2,000**
(iv) Loss of or damage to back teeth: per tooth: **£550 to £900**

(B)   Facial Disfigurement

In this class of case the distinction between male and female and the subjective approach are of particular significance. Larger awards than those indicated may be justified if there have been many operations.

(a) Females
(i)   Very Severe Scarring **£25,000 to £50,000**

In a relatively young woman (teens to early 30s) where the cosmetic effect is very disfiguring and the psychological reaction severe.

(ii)   Less Severe Scarring **£15,500 to £25,000**

Where the disfigurement is still substantial and where there is a significant psychological reaction.

(iii)   Significant Scarring **£9,250 to £15,500**

Where the worst effects have been or will be reduced by plastic surgery leaving some cosmetic disability and where the psychological reaction is not great or, having been considerable at the outset, has diminished to relatively minor proportions.

(iv)   Less Significant Scarring **£2,000 to £7,250**

In these cases there may be but one scar which can be camouflaged or, though there is a number of very small scars the overall effect is to mar but not markedly to affect the appearance and the reaction is no more than that of an ordinarily sensitive young woman.

(v)   Trivial Scarring **£900 to £1,800**

In these cases the effect is minor only.

(b) Males
(i) Very Severe Scarring **£15,500 to £34,000**

These are to be found especially in males under 30, where there is permanent disfigurement even after plastic surgery and a considerable element of psychological reaction.

(ii)   Less Severe Scarring **£9,250 to £15,500**

This will have left moderate to severe permanent disfigurement.

(iii) Significant Scarring **£4,750 to £9,250**

Such scars will remain visible at conversational distances.

(iv) Less Significant Scarring **£2,000 to £4,750**

Such scarring is not particularly prominent except on close inspection.

(v) Trivial Scarring **£900 to £1,800**

In these cases the effect is minor only.

8   Scarring to other parts of the body

This is an area in which it is not possible to offer much useful guidance. The principles are the same as those applied to cases of facial disfigurement. It must be remembered that many of the physical injuries already described involve some element of disfigurement and that element is of course taken into account in suggesting the appropriate bracket. There remain some cases where the element of disfigurement is the predominant one in the assessment of damages. Where the scarring is not to the face or is not usually visible then the awards will tend to be lower than those for facial or readily visible disfigurement.

A large proportion of awards for a number of noticeable laceration scars, or a single disfiguring scar, of leg(s) or arm(s) or hand(s) or back or chest (male), fall in the bracket of **£4,000 to £7,000**.

In cases where an exploratory laparotomy has been performed but no significant internal injury has been found, the award for the operation and the inevitable scar is in the region of **£4,500**.

A single noticeable scar, or several superficial scars, of leg(s) or arm(s) or hand(s), with some minor cosmetic deficit justifies **£1,250 to £2,000**.

The effects of burns will normally be regarded as more serious since they tend to cause a greater degree of pain and to lead to greater disfigurement.

9   Damage to hair
(a) Damage to hair in consequence of defective permanent waving, tinting or the like, where the effects are dermatitis or tingling or 'burning' of the scalp causing dry, brittle hair, which breaks off and/or falls out, leading to distress, depression, embarrassment and loss of confidence, and inhibiting social life. In the more serious cases thinning continues and the prospects of regrowth are poor or there has been total loss of areas of hair and regrowth is slow. **£3,750 to £5,750**

There may be a larger award in cases of psychological disability.

(b)   Less serious versions of the above where symptoms are fewer or only of a minor character; also, cases where hair has been pulled out leaving bald patches. The level of the award will depend on the length of time taken before regrowth occurs. **£2,000 to £3,750**

10   Dermatitis

Apart from dermatitis of the scalp (see Section 9), most of the reported cases relate to dermatitis of the hands.

(a)   Dermatitis of both hands, with cracking and soreness, affecting employment and domestic capability, possibly with some psychological consequences, lasting for some years, perhaps indefinitely. **£7,000 to £10,000**

(b)   Dermatitis of both hands, continuing for a significant period, but settling with treatment and/or use of gloves for specific tasks. **£4,500 to £6,000**

(c)   Itching, irritation of and/or rashes on one or both hands, but resolving within a few months with treatment. **£1,000 to £1,500**

Appendix II

Government Actuary's Department

ACTUARIAL TABLES

With explanatory notes for use in

PERSONAL INJURY AND FATAL ACCIDENT CASES

(the 'Ogden' Tables)

Prepared by an Inter-disciplinary Working Party of Actuaries, Lawyers, Accountants and other interested parties

Fourth edition

INTRODUCTION TO THE FOURTH EDITION

Recommendation 7.14 in The Law Commission's Report No 263 (Claims for Wrongful Death) recommended that the Working Party should be reconvened to "consider, and explain more fully," how the Tables should be used, or amended, to produce accurate assessments of damages in Fatal Accident Act cases (as opposed to personal injury cases). This recommendation was under the general heading "Should the multiplier be calculated from death or from trial?" This is the reason for the publication of this edition at this time.

When we examined the problem, it became plain that it was more difficult than had been appreciated when earlier editions were published. We have concluded that the Law Commission's basic criticism of the present system is valid and the new Section D in this edition contains guidance on what ought to be done when calculating damages in such cases.

In *Wells v Wells*, when deciding that the rate should be 3% until it was set by the Lord Chancellor, Lord Lloyd said that 3% "sounds about right", adding that it was less precise than could be achieved but that it was important to keep the calculations simple as well as accurate.

Of course, if the rate is to be rounded to the nearest 0.5% and altered infrequently, rather than using the precise current figure as published in the Financial Times, it is inevitable that the resultant figures will be less precise than would otherwise be the case. (We do not, of course, know what the Lord Chancellor is going to determine on this when he sets the rate.) Furthermore, since almost everybody will live either longer or shorter than their life expectancy, any figure decided upon will not prove to be precisely accurate for that particular individual, whatever method is used.

The three cases which were considered by the House of Lords and which resulted in the principles in question were personal injury cases. In fatal accident cases the problem is greater because more than one life has to be the subject of consideration. It would be possible to achieve more precise figures than would be obtained by following the approach which we have recommended. However, this would involve production of a very large number of further tables. Bearing in mind the need for simplicity, we are confident that our recommended procedure will produce figures which are "about right" and fair to all parties.

We considered whether courts would be precluded from adopting our recommended procedure because of earlier judicial decisions. The cases of *Cookson v Knowles* [1979] 2 A.C. 556, *Graham v Dodds* [1983] 1 W.L.R. 808 and *Corbett v Barking* [1991] 2 Q.B. 426 determined that multipliers must be selected at the date of death which, of course, is not what is done in our recommended procedure, requiring as it does calculations to be made from different dates. However, it is plain from the speeches in *Wells v Wells* that the House of Lords was stating that courts were to use the Government Actuary's tables and, as Lord Lloyd put it, it was "a new approach". It seems obvious to us that, when directing courts to use the tables, the House of Lords would have regarded it as absurd that the tables should be used in such a way as to produce an inaccurate answer through using them in a fashion which was appropriate to the old approach.

Consequently, we do not consider that any of the cases decided before *Wells v Wells* precludes courts from using our recommended procedure.

As well as changes to the text, the tables themselves have been expanded to include retirement ages of 55 and 70. The figures in those tables which are based on projected mortality rates have also been updated and are now calculated using the projected mortality rates for England & Wales assumed in the latest 1998-based population projections.

In the Consultation Paper about Damages issued by the Lord Chancellor's Department in March, it is said that the Government intends to bring into force Section 10 of the Civil Evidence Act 1995. This long overdue step will result in my ceasing to have responsibility for the tables, which will be the Government Actuary's responsibility, being something which I had rashly assumed would have happened long ago when I wrote the introduction to the Third Edition in 1998.

The Working Party is extremely grateful to the Bar Council for providing us with the invaluable services of Mr John Horne, BCL as Secretary and the not inconsiderable back-up required and to Lincoln's Inn for allowing us to hold our meetings there and for the assistance of its staff. As before, the greatest burden has been undertaken by the Government Actuary and members of his Department, without which our task would have been immeasurably greater.

Sir Michael Ogden QC, Hon FIA

August 2000

EXPLANATORY NOTES

SECTION A: GENERAL

Purpose of tables

1. The tables have been prepared by the Government Actuary's Department. They provide an aid for those assessing the lump sum appropriate as compensation for a continuing future pecuniary loss or consequential expense or cost of care in personal injury and fatal accident cases.

Application of tables

2. The tables set out multipliers. These multipliers enable the user to assess the present capital value of future annual loss (net of tax) or annual expense calculated on the basis of various assumptions which are explained below. Accordingly, to find the present capital value of a given annual loss or expense, it is necessary to select the appropriate table, find the appropriate multiplier and then multiply the amount of the annual loss or expense by that figure.

3. Tables 1 to 36 deal with annual loss or annual expense extending over three different periods of time. In each case there are separate tables for men and women.

- In Tables 1, 2, 19 and 20 the loss or expense is assumed to begin immediately and to continue for the whole of the rest of the claimant's life, allowing for different potential lifespans, including the possibility of early death or prolonged life. The tables apply to both the deceased and the dependants' lives in fatal accident cases.
- In Tables 3 to 10 and 21 to 28 the loss or expense is assumed to begin immediately but to continue only until the claimant's retirement or earlier death. The age of retirement is assumed to be 55 in Tables 3, 4, 21 and 22, 60 in Tables 5, 6, 23 and 24, 65 in Tables 7, 8, 25 and 26 and 70 in Tables 9, 10, 27 and 28.
- In Tables 11 to 18 and 29 to 36 it is assumed that the annual loss or annual expense will not begin until the claimant reaches retirement but will then continue for the whole of the rest of his or her life.

4. In Tables 13 and 31 (males) and Tables 14 and 32 (females) the age of retirement is assumed to be 60. In Tables 15 and 33 (males) and Tables 16 and 34 (females) the age of retirement is assumed to be 65 (and similarly for retirement ages 55 and 70). These tables all make due allowance for the chance that the claimant may not live to reach the age of retirement.

Mortality assumptions for Tables 1 to 18

5. As in previous editions of these tables, Tables 1 to 18 are based on the mortality rates experienced in England & Wales in a historical three-year period, in this case the years 1990 to 1992, and published by the Government Actuary's Department as English Life Table No. 15 (ELT15). Given this assumption about mortality, the accuracy of these tables, which were prepared by the Government Actuary's Department, has been accepted by all the actuaries on the Working Party, which included actuaries nominated by the Institute and the Faculty of Actuaries, and the Association of British Insurers (ABI). Consequently, the courts can have confidence in the accuracy of these tables. Members of the Working Party nominated by the ABI have reservations about the application of the tables and other matters and these are set out in Appendix C.

6. On the basis of some reported cases, it appears that tables for pecuniary loss for life, e.g. cost of care, may have been misunderstood. As stated hereafter in Paragraph 25, the tables do not assume that the claimant dies after a period equating to the expectation of life, but take account of the possibilities that the claimant will live for different periods, e.g. die soon or live to be very old. The mortality assumptions relate to the general population of England & Wales. Unless there is clear evidence in an individual case to support the view that the individual is atypical and will enjoy longer or shorter expectation of life, no further increase or reduction is required for mortality alone.

Tables adjusted to take account of projected mortality (Tables 19 to 36)

7. The actuaries on the Working Party consider that failure to have regard to current and reasonable projected future improvements in mortality rates will result in awards of damages which are lower than they should be. At Appendix A is an extract from ELT15 which shows graphs indicating rates of mortality expressed in percentages of 1911 rates on a logarithmic scale. They demonstrate in a stark fashion the improvement in longevity which has taken place since 1911 and which, according to all the available evidence, is continuing. The sole exception to this trend is a small increase recently in the mortality of males in their late twenties and early thirties due to AIDS and increasing numbers of suicides. The same effect is present, albeit to a lesser degree, for females. Even if this slight worsening of mortality at these ages were to continue, the effect on the tables of multipliers would not be significant. (For comments by the ABI see Appendix C.)

8. The graphs, and the figures on which they are based, point to the conclusion that, on the balance of probabilities, the mortality rates which will actually be experienced in future by those who are alive today will be significantly lower than in ELT15, which is already nearly a decade out of date, and will be increasingly so

the further into the future one goes. This implies the need for higher multipliers. For the purposes of preparing the official national population projections, the Government Actuary makes a prudent estimate of the extent of future improvements in mortality. Tables 19 to 36 show the multipliers which result from the application of these projected mortality rates (derived from the mid- 1998 based population projections for England & Wales). The actuaries on the Working Party (save for the dissenting views expressed at Appendix C) consider that these alternative tables provide a more appropriate estimate of the value of future income streams than Tables 1 to 18, which are based on historic mortality and almost certainly underestimate future longevity. The Working Party therefore recommends the Courts to use Tables 19 to 36 rather than Tables 1 to 18.

9. Paragraphs 5 to 8 appeared in the Third Edition. So far as the Working Party is aware, all Judges are now using the tables based on projected mortality rates (Tables 19 to 36). Consequently, the majority of the Working Party would have omitted the tables which are based on historic mortality (Tables 1 to 18). However, they have been retained at the request of the ABI in case any of its members wishes to test the point on appeal.

Use of tables

10. To find the appropriate figure for the present value of a particular loss or expense, the user must first choose that table which relates to the period of loss or expense for which the individual claimant is to be compensated and to the sex of the claimant, or, where appropriate, the claimant's dependants.

11. If, for some reason, the facts in a particular case do not correspond with the assumptions on which one of the tables is based (e.g. it is known that the claimant will have a different retiring age from that assumed in the tables), then the tables can only be used if an appropriate allowance is made for this difference; for this purpose the assistance of an actuary should be sought, except for situations where specific guidance is given in these explanatory notes.

Rate of return

12. The basis of the multipliers set out in the tables is that the lump sum will be invested and yield income (but that over the period in question the claimant will gradually reduce the capital sum, so that at the end of the period it is exhausted). Accordingly, an essential factor in arriving at the right figure is to choose the appropriate rate of return. The tables set out 7 multipliers based on annual rates of return ranging from 1.2% to 5% (previous editions gave multipliers based on annual rates of return between 11.2% and 5%). In addition, a 0% column has been included to show the multiplier without any discount for interest (i.e. expectations

of life, or the equivalent for different periods). These are supplied to assist in the calculation of multipliers in Fatal Accident Act cases (see Section D).

13. Currently, the annual rate of return to be applied is 3% (net of tax), based on the judgment of the House of Lords in *Wells v Wells*. After a Commencement Order has been made in respect of the Damages Act 1996 Section 1, the rate or rates of return are expected to be specified by the Lord Chancellor, after receiving advice from the Government Actuary and the Treasury. Should it become necessary, further tables will be issued.

14. Previous editions of these tables explained how the current yields on index-linked government bonds could be used as an indicator of the appropriate real rate of return for valuing future income streams. Such considerations were endorsed by the House of Lords in *Wells v Wells* and it is expected that this will continue to be the case when the Lord Chancellor sets the rate on commencement of Section 1 of the Damages Act 1996. A description of how to use market rates of return on index-linked gilts to determine the appropriate rate of return is given in Appendix B. In cases outwith the scope of these tables, the advice of an actuary should be sought.

Tax

15. In order to arrive at a true present capital value of the claimant's future loss or expense it is necessary to consider whether he or she will have to pay a significant amount of tax on the investment return arising from his compensation. If he or she will pay little or no tax, no adjustment of the rate of return will be required. If he or she will have to pay a significant percentage of that income in tax, then the rate of return chosen to determine the present capital value of the loss or expense should be reduced accordingly. Attention is drawn to the decision of the House of Lords in *Hodgson v Trapp* [1989] AC 807 concerning the treatment of the incidence of higher rate tax on the income arising from a compensatory fund. This position was confirmed by Lord Steyn in the House of Lords judgment in *Wells v Wells*, namely that:

> "the position regarding higher tax rates should remain as Lord Oliver of Aylmerton in *Hodgson v Trapp* [1989] 1 AC 807 at 835B described it, viz. that in such exceptional cases plaintiffs would be free to place their arguments for a lower rate before the court."

16. In cases where the impact of personal Income Tax and Capital Gains Tax is likely to be significant, more accurate calculation of the value net of tax of payments to the individual may be desirable. Such calculations may be able to be carried out by using software of the type referred to in paragraph 73 but the advice of an accountant and an actuary should be sought.

Different retirement ages

17. In paragraph 11 above, reference was made to the problem that will arise when the claimant's retiring age is different from that assumed in the tables. Such a problem may arise in valuing a loss or expense beginning immediately but ending at retirement; or in valuing a loss or expense which will not begin until the claimant reaches retirement but will then continue until death. Tables are provided for retirement ages of 55, 60, 65 and 70. Where the claimant's actual retiring age would have been between two of these retirement ages for which tables are provided, the correct multiplier can be obtained by consideration of the tables for retirement age immediately above and below the actual retirement age, keeping the period to retirement age the same. Thus a woman of 42 who would have retired at 58 can be considered as being in between the cases of a woman of 39 with a retirement age of 55 and a woman of 44 with a retirement age of 60. The steps to take are as follows:

(1)   Determine between which retirement ages, for which tables are provided, the claimant's actual retirement age R lies. Let the lower of these ages be A and the higher be B.

(2)   Determine how many years must be subtracted from the claimant's actual retirement age to get to A and subtract that period from the claimant's age. If the claimant's age is x, the result of this calculation is $(x+A-R)$.

(3)   Look up this new reduced age in the Table corresponding to retirement age A at the appropriate rate of return. Let the resulting multiplier be M.

(4)   Determine how many years must be added to the claimant's actual retirement age to get to B and add that period to the claimant's age. The result of this calculation is $(x+B-R)$.

(5)   Look up this new increased age in the Table corresponding to retirement age B at the appropriate rate of return. Let the resulting multiplier be N.

(6)   Interpolate between M and N. In other words, calculate:
$(B-R) \times M + (R-A) \times N$
and divide the result by 5.

18. In the example given in paragraph 17, the steps would be as follows:

(1) A is 55 and B is 60

(2)   Subtracting 3 years from the claimant's age gives 39.

(3)   Looking up age 39 in Table 22 (for retirement age 55) gives 12.61 at a rate of return of 3%.

(4)   Adding 2 years to the claimant's age gives 44.

(5)   Looking up age 44 in Table 24 (for retirement age 60) gives 12.54 at a rate of return of 3%.

(6)   Calculating 2 x 12.61 + 3 x 12.54 and dividing by 5 gives 12.57 as the multiplier.

19. If the claimant's actual retiring age would have been earlier than 55 (but not less than 50), he or she may be treated as correspondingly older than his or her true age,

but keeping the same period to retirement age. Thus a woman of 42 who would have retired at 52 is treated as though she were 45 and retiring at 55. The appropriate multiplier is then obtained from Table 4 or 22. A further correction should then in principle be made, because the claimant's chances of survival for ten years are slightly greater at 42 than if she were in fact 45. However, the effect of this would be small for retirement ages down to 50.

20. When the claimant would have expected to retire later than the highest retirement age for which tables are available (age 70), say up to 75, the procedure is reversed. Thus a man of 42 who would have retired at 75 is treated as though he were 37 and retiring at 70. The appropriate multiplier is then obtained from the table (in this case Table 9 or 27) and the further correction required is made by reducing the multiplier for a male by three-quarters of one per cent for each year by which the retiring age of the claimant exceeds the retiring age assumed in the table. So, in this example, the multiplier from Table 27 at 3% rate of return would be 20.21 at age 37. Reducing the multiplier by three-quarters of one per cent for each of 5 years' later retirement means taking off 33.4% (or multiplying by 0.9625), which brings the multiplier to 19.45 (= 20.21 x (1 – 5 x 0.0075)). In the case of a woman the reduction would be by one half of one per cent for each year. So, for a woman of 49 who would have retired at 73, the multiplier from Table 28 for a woman aged 46 (three years younger to correspond to the difference between a retirement age of 73 and one of 70) would be 16.57. Reducing the multiplier by one half of one per cent for each year of early retirement means subtracting 11.2% for three years' early retirement (or multiplying by 0.985), bringing the multiplier to 16.32 (= 16.57 x (1 – 3 x 0.005)).

21. When the loss or expense to be valued is that from the date of retirement to death, and the claimant's date of retirement differs from that assumed in the tables, a different approach is necessary, involving the following three steps.
(1)   Assume that there is a present loss which will continue for the rest of the claimant's life and from Table 1 or 2 (or 19 or 20) establish the value of that loss or expense over the whole period from the date of assessment until the claimant's death.
(2)   Establish the value of such loss or expense over the period from the date of assessment until the claimant's expected date of retirement following the procedure explained in paragraphs 17 to 20 above.
(3)   Subtract the second figure from the first. The balance remaining represents the present value of the claimant's loss or expense between retirement and death.

22. The adjustments described in paragraphs 19 and 20 for retirement ages below 55 and above 70 cannot reliably be applied for retirement ages of less than 50 or more than 75. In such rare cases the advice of an actuary should be sought.

Younger ages

23. Tables 1, 2, 19 and 20, which concern pecuniary loss for life, and Tables 11 to 18 and 29 to 36, which concern loss of pension from retirement age, have been extended

down to age 0. In some circumstances the multiplier at age 0 is slightly lower than that at age 1; this arises because of the relatively high incidence of deaths immediately after birth.

24. Tables for multipliers for loss of earnings (Tables 3 to 10 and 21 to 28) have not been extended below age 16. In order to determine the multiplier for loss of earnings for someone who has not yet started work, it is first necessary to determine an assumed age at which the claimant would have commenced work and to find the appropriate multiplier for that age from Tables 3 to 10 or 21 to 28, according to the assumed retirement age. This multiplier should then be multiplied by the deferment factor from Table 37 which corresponds to the appropriate rate of return and the period from the date of the trial to the date on which it is assumed that the claimant would have started work. A similar approach can be used for determining a multiplier for pecuniary loss for life where the loss is assumed to commence a fixed period of years from the date of the trial. For simplicity the factors in Table 37 relate purely to the impact of compound interest and ignore mortality. At ages below 30 this is a reasonable approximation (for example, allowance for male mortality in accordance with ELT15 from age 5 to 25 would only reduce the multiplier by a further 1 per cent, i.e. apply a factor of 0.99 to the multiplier) but at higher ages it would normally be appropriate to allow explicitly for mortality and the advice of an actuary should be sought.

Contingencies

25. Tables 1 to 18 have been calculated to take into account the chances that the claimant will live for different periods, including the possibility that they will die young or live to be very old, based on historical levels of population mortality. Tables 19 to 36 make reasonable provision for the levels of mortality which members of the population of England & Wales alive today may expect to experience in future. The tables do not take account of the other risks and vicissitudes of life, such as the possibility that the claimant would for periods have ceased to earn due to ill-health or loss of employment. Nor do they take account of the fact that many people cease work for substantial periods to care for children or other dependants. Section B suggests ways in which allowance may be made to the multipliers for loss of earnings, to allow for certain risks other than mortality.

Impaired lives

26. In some cases, medical evidence may be available which asserts that a claimant's health impairments are equivalent to adding a certain number of years to their current age, or to treating the individual as having a specific age different from their actual age. In such cases, Tables 1, 2, 19 and 20 can be used with respect to the deemed higher age. For the other tables the adjustment is not so straightforward, as

adjusting the age will also affect the assumed retirement age, but the procedures described in paragraphs 17 to 21 may be followed, or the advice of an actuary should be sought.

Fixed periods

27. In cases where pecuniary loss is to be valued for a fixed period, the multipliers in Table 38 may be used. These make no allowance for mortality or any other contingency but assume that regular frequent payments (e.g. weekly or monthly) will continue throughout the period. These figures should in principle be adjusted if the periodicity of payment is less frequent, especially if the payments in question are annually in advance or in arrears.

Variable loss or expense

28. The tables do not provide an immediate answer when the annual loss or expense to be valued is not assumed to be stable; where, for instance, the claimant's lost earnings were on a sliding scale or promotion was likely to be achieved. It may be possible to use the tables to deal with such situations by increasing the basic figure of annual loss or expenses; or by choosing a lower rate of interest and so a higher multiplier than would otherwise have been chosen. In some cases it may be appropriate to split the overall multiplier into two or more parts and apply different multiplicands to each. More complicated cases may be suited to the use of the software referred to in paragraph 73. In addition to contingent widows' pensions, cases such as *Singapore Bus v Lim Soon Yong* [1985] 1 WLR 1075 at 1079D – 1080A, *Taylor v O'Connor* [1971] AC 115 at 127, 130, *Davies and others v Whiteways Cyder Co Ltd and another* [1974] 3 All ER 168 etc may necessitate actuarial advice with regard to other losses.

29. If doubt exists whether the tables are appropriate to a particular case which appears to present significant difficulties of substance, it would be prudent to take actuarial advice. This might be appropriate in relation to the level of spouses' benefits, if these are to be assessed, since these are not readily valued using Tables 1 to 36. The value of these would generally be very small for a female claimant (i.e. benefits to the male spouse) but could add 10 to 20% to the pension loss for a male claimant.

SECTION B: CONTINGENCIES OTHER THAN MORTALITY

30. As stated in paragraph 25, the tables for loss of earnings (Tables 3 to 10 and 21 to 28) take no account of risks other than mortality. This section shows how the multipliers in these tables may be reduced to take account of risks other than

mortality. This is based on work commissioned by the Institute of Actuaries and carried out by Professor S Haberman and Mrs D S F Bloomfield (*Work time lost to sickness, unemployment and stoppages: measurement and application* (1990), Journal of the Institute of Actuaries 117, 533-595). Although there was some debate within the actuarial profession about the details of this work, and in particular about the scope for developing it further, the findings were broadly accepted and were adopted by the Government Actuary and the other actuaries who were members of the Working Party when the Second Edition of the Tables was published.

31. Since the risk of mortality (including the risks of dying early or living longer) has already been taken into account in the tables, the principal contingencies in respect of which a further reduction is to be made, particularly for earnings loss up to retirement age, are illness and unemployment. Even with the effective disappearance of the "job for life" there appears to be no scientific justification in the generality of cases for assuming significantly larger deductions than those given in this section. It should be noted that the authors of the 1990 paper (Professor Haberman and Mrs Bloomfield) wrote "All the results discussed in this paper should be further qualified by the caveat that the underlying models ... assume that economic activity rates and labour force separation and accession rated do not vary in the future from the bases chosen. As mentioned already in the text, it is unlikely to be true that the future would be free from marked secular trends." The paper relied on Labour Force Surveys for 1973, 1977, 1981 and 1985 and English Life Tables No. 14 (1980- 82). However, although it is now somewhat out of date, it is the best study presently available. It is hoped that further research into the impact of contingencies other than mortality will be carried out in due course.

32. Specific factors in individual cases may necessitate larger reductions. By contrast, there will also be cases where the standard multipliers should be increased, to take into account positive factors of lifestyle, employment prospects and life expectancy.

33. The extent to which the multiplier needs to be reduced will reflect individual circumstances such as occupation and geographical region. In the short term, levels of economic activity and unemployment, including time lost through industrial action, are relevant. Reductions may be expected to be smaller for clerical workers than for manual workers, for those living in the South rather than the North, and for those in "secure" jobs and in occupations less affected by redundancy or industrial action.

34. The factors described in subsequent paragraphs are for use in calculating loss of earnings up to retirement age. The research work did not investigate the impact of contingencies other than mortality on the value of future pension rights. Some reduction to the multiplier for loss of pension would often be appropriate when a reduction is being applied for loss of earnings. This may be less of a reduction than in the case of loss of earnings because of the ill-health contingency (as opposed to the unemployment contingency), particularly in cases where there are significant

ill-health retirement pension rights. A bigger reduction may be necessary in cases where there is significant doubt whether pension rights would have continued to accrue (to the extent not already allowed for in the post-retirement multiplier) or in cases where there may 11 be doubt over the ability of the pension fund to pay promised benefits. In the case of a defined contribution pension scheme, loss of pension rights may be able to be allowed for simply by increasing the future earnings loss (adjusted for contingencies other than mortality) by the percentage which the employer pays to the scheme in contributions.

35. The suggestions which follow are intended only to provide a "ready reckoner", as opposed to precise figures.

The basic deduction for contingencies other than mortality

36. Subject to the adjustments which may be made as described below, the multiplier which has been selected from the tables, i.e. in respect of risks of mortality only, should be reduced by *multiplying* it by a figure selected from the table below, under the heading "Medium".

Table A
Loss of Earnings to Pension Age 65 (Males)

Age at date of trial	High	Medium	Low
20	0.99	0.98	0.97
25	0.99	0.98	0.96
30	0.99	0.97	0.95
35	0.98	0.96	0.93
40	0.98	0.96	0.92
45	0.97	0.95	0.90
50	0.96	0.93	0.87
55	0.95	0.90	0.82
60	0.95	0.90	0.81

Levels of economic activity and employment

37. The medium set of reductions is appropriate if it is anticipated that economic activity is likely to correspond to that in the 1970s and 1980s (ignoring periods of high and low unemployment). The high set is appropriate if higher economic activity and lower unemployment rates are anticipated. The low set is appropriate if lower economic activity and higher unemployment rates are anticipated.

Lower pension ages (Males)

38. The figures will be higher for a lower pension age. For example, if pension age is 60, the figures should be as shown in Table B.

Table B
Loss of Earnings to Pension Age 60 (Males)

Age at date of trial	High	Medium	Low
20	0.99	0.99	0.98
25	0.99	0.99	0.97
30	0.99	0.98	0.97
35	0.99	0.98	0.96
40	0.98	0.97	0.94
45	0.98	0.96	0.93
50	0.97	0.94	0.92
55	0.96	0.93	0.88

Female lives

39. As a rough guide, for female lives between ages 35 and 55 with a pension age of 60, the figures should be as shown in Table C. As for males, the factors will be lower if the pension age is higher (e.g. 65) and higher if the pension age is lower (e.g. 55).

Table C
Loss of Earnings to Pension Age 60 (Females)

Age at date of trial	High	Medium	Low
35	0.95	0.95	0.94
40	0.93	0.93	0.92
45	0.90	0.90	0.88
50	0.91	0.90	0.88
55	0.95	0.94	0.93

Variations by occupation

40. The risks of illness, injury and disability are less for persons in clerical or similar jobs, e.g. civil servants, the professions and financial services industries,

and greater for those in manual jobs, e.g. construction, mining, quarrying and ship-building. However, what matters is the precise nature of the work undertaken by the person in question, rather than the industry as such; for example, a secretary in the headquarters office of a large construction company may be at no greater risk than a secretary in a solicitor's office.

41. In less risky occupations the figures in Tables A to C should be *increased* by a maximum of the order of 0.01 up to age 40, rising to 0.03 at age 55.

42. In more risky occupations the figures in Tables A to C should be *reduced* by a maximum of the order of 0.01 at age 25, 0.02 at age 40 and 0.05 at age 55.

Variations by geographical region

43. For persons resident in the South East, East Anglia, South West and East Midlands, the figures in Tables A to C should be *increased* by a maximum of the order of 0.01 up to age 40, rising to 0.03 at age 55.

44. For persons resident in the North, North West, Wales and Scotland, the figures in Tables A to C should be *reduced* by a maximum of the order of 0.01 at age 25, 0.02 at age 40 and 0.05 at age 55.

SECTION C: SUMMARY OF PERSONAL INJURY APPLICATIONS

45. To use the tables take the following steps:

(1) Choose the tables relating to the appropriate period of loss or expense.
(2) Choose the table, relating to that period, appropriate to the sex of the claimant and according to whether historical mortality is to be used (Tables 1 to 18) or a realistic estimate of actual mortality (Tables 19 to 36).
(3) Choose the appropriate rate of return, before allowing for the effect of tax on the income to be obtained from the lump sum.
(4) Allow for a reduction in the rate of return to reflect the effect of tax on the income from the lump sum.
(5) Find the figure under the column in the table chosen given against the age at trial of the claimant.
(6) Adjust the figure to take account of contingencies other than mortality, as specified in Section B above.
(7) Multiply the annual loss (net of tax) or expense by that figure.

46. In principle an allowance for an expected increase in the annual loss or expense (not due to inflation) can be made by choosing a lower rate of return or by increasing the figure of annual loss or expense. In cases where the claimant's expected age of retirement differs from that assumed in the tables, the more complicated procedure explained in paragraphs 17 to 21 should be followed.

Example 1

47. The following is an example of the use of the tables in a personal injury case: The claimant is female, aged 35 at the date of the trial. She lives in London and is an established civil servant who was working in an office at a salary of £25,000 net of tax. As a result of her injuries, she has lost her job. Her loss of earnings to retirement age of 60 is assessed as follows:

(1) Look up Table 24 for loss of earnings to pension age 60 for females.
(2) The appropriate rate of return is decided to be 3% (based on the decision of the House of Lords in *Wells v Wells*).
(3) Table 24 shows that, on the basis of a 3% rate of return, the multiplier for a female aged 35 is 17.41.
(4) Now take account of risks other than mortality. On the assumption of high economic activity for the next few years, Table C would require 17.41 to be multiplied by 0.95.
(5) Based on Section B, further adjustment is necessary because the claimant (a) is in a secure non-manual job, and (b) lives in the South East.
(6) The adjustments should be made as follows:

Basic adjustment to allow for short-term high economic activity (Table C)	0.95
Adjustment to allow for occupation, say	+0.01
	0.96
Adjustment for geographical region, say	+0.01
	0.97

(7) The original multiplier taken from Table 24, namely 17.41, must therefore be multiplied by 0.97, resulting in a revised multiplier of 16.89.
(8) The damages for loss of earnings are assessed as £422,250 (16.89 x 25,000).

This example takes no account of the incidence of tax on investment return (see paragraph 15) above. It is assumed that this was taken into account when determining the 3% rate of return.

Example 2

48. The following is a second example of the use of the tables in a personal injury case: The claimant is male, aged 48 at the date of the trial. He lives in Manchester and was working in a factory. His retirement age was 65 and his pre-retirement multiplicand has been determined as £20,000 a year net of tax. The multiplicand for costs of care is deemed to be £50,000 a year. As a result of his injuries, he has lost his job. His loss of earnings to retirement age of 65 is assessed as follows:

(1) Look up Table 25 for loss of earnings to pension age 65 for males.
(2) The appropriate rate of return is decided to be 3% (based on the decision of the House of Lords in *Wells v Wells*).

(3) Table 25 shows that, on the basis of a 3% rate of return, the multiplier for a male aged 48 is 12.88.

(4) Now take account of risks other than mortality. On the assumption of medium economic activity for the next few years, Table A would require 12.88 to be multiplied by 0.93.

(5) Based on Section B, further adjustment is necessary because the Plaintiff (a) is in a risky manual job, and (b) lives in the North West.

(6) The adjustments should be made as follows:

Basic adjustment to allow for short-term medium economic activity (Table A)	0.93
Adjustment to allow for occupation, say	–0.02
	0.91
Adjustment for geographical region, say	–0.03
	0.88

(7) The original multiplier taken from Table 25, namely 12.88, must therefore be multiplied by 0.88, resulting in a revised multiplier of 11.33.

(8) The damages for loss of earnings are assessed as £226,600 (11.33 x 20,000).

49. The damages for cost of care are assessed as follows:

(1) Look up Table 19 for the multiplier at age 48.

(2) The appropriate rate of return is 3%.

(3) Table 19 shows that, on the basis of a 3% rate of return, the multiplier at age 48 is 20.22.

(4) No further adjustment is made for risks other than mortality.

(5) The damages for cost of care are assessed at £1,011,000 (20.22 x 50,000).

SECTION D: APPLICATION OF TABLES TO FATAL ACCIDENT CASES

50. Whereas in personal injury cases the problem to be solved is that of setting a value on an income stream during the potential life of one person (the claimant), the situation is generally more complicated in fatal accident cases. Here the compensation is intended to reflect the value of an income stream during the lifetime of one or more dependants of the deceased (or the expected period for which the dependants would have expected to receive the dependency, if shorter) but limited according to the expectation of how long the deceased would have been able to provide the financial support, had he or she not been involved in the fatal accident.

51. In principle, therefore, the compensation for post-trial dependency should be based on the present value at the date of the trial of the dependency during the expected future joint lifetime of the deceased and the dependant or claimant (had

the deceased survived naturally to the date of the trial), subject to any limitations on the period of dependency and any expected future changes in the level of dependency, for example, on attaining retirement age. In addition there should be compensation for the period between the date of accident and the date of trial.

52. A set of actuarial tables to make such calculations accurately would require tables similar to Tables 1 to 36 but for each combination of ages as at the date of the trial of the deceased and the dependant to whom compensation is to be paid. The Working Party concluded that this would not meet the criterion of simplicity of application which was a central objective of these tables and recommends that, in complex cases, or cases where the accuracy of the multiplier is thought by the parties to be of critical importance and material to the resulting amount of compensation (for example in cases potentially involving very large claims where the level of the multiplicand is unambiguously established), the advice of a professionally qualified actuary should be sought. However, for the majority of cases, a certain amount of approximation will be appropriate, bearing in mind the need for a simple and streamlined process, and taking into consideration the other uncertainties in the determination of an appropriate level of compensation. The following paragraphs describe a methodology using Tables 1 to 36 which can be expected to yield satisfactory answers.

Damages for the period from the fatal accident to the date of trial

53. The period of pre-trial dependency will normally be equal to the period between the date of the fatal accident and the date of the trial, substituting where appropriate the lower figure of the expected period for which the deceased would have provided the dependency, had he or she not been killed in the accident, or if the period of dependency would have been limited in some way, for example if the dependant is a child.

54. A deduction may be made for the risk that the deceased might have died anyway, in the period between the date of the fatal accident and the date at which the trial takes place. In many cases this deduction will be small and could usually be regarded as de minimis. The need for a deduction becomes more necessary the longer the period from the date of accident to the date of trial and the older the deceased at the date of death. As an illustration of the order of magnitude of the deduction, Table D shows some examples of factors by which the multiplier should be multiplied for different ages of the deceased and for different periods from the date of accident to the date of the trial.

TABLE D

Factor by which pre-trial damages should be multiplied to allow for the likelihood that the deceased would not in any case have survived to provide the dependency for the full period to the date of trial

Age of deceased at date of accident	Period from date of accident to date of trial or date of cessation of dependency, if earlier (years)					
	Male deceased			Female deceased		
	3	6	9	3	6	9
10	1.00	1.00	1.00	1.00	1.00	1.00
20	1.00	1.00	1.00	1.00	1.00	1.00
30	1.00	1.00	1.00	1.00	1.00	1.00
40	1.00	0.99	0.99	1.00	1.00	0.99
50	0.99	0.99	0.98	1.00	0.99	0.99
60	0.98	0.96	0.94	0.99	0.98	0.96
70	0.95	0.90	0.85	0.97	0.94	0.90
80	0.88	0.76	0.65	0.92	0.83	0.73

Note: The factor is clearly one for a period of zero years. Factors for other ages and periods not shown in the table may be obtained approximately by interpolation.

55. The resultant multiplier, after application of any discount for the possibility of early death of the deceased before the date of trial, even had the accident not taken place, is to be applied to the multiplicand, which is determined in the usual way. Interest will then be added up to the date of trial on the basis of special damages.

Damages from the date of trial to retirement age

56. The assessment of the multiplier involves the following steps:

(1) Determine the expected period for which the deceased would have been able to provide the dependency (see paragraph 57).
(2) Determine the expected period for which the dependant would have been able to receive the dependency (see paragraph 57).
(3) Take the lesser of the two periods.
(4) Treat the resulting period as a term certain for which the multiplier is to be determined and look up the figure in Table 38 for this period at the appropriate rate of interest.

(5)   Apply any adjustment for contingencies other than mortality in accordance with Section B.

(6)   If necessary, make an allowance for the risk that the deceased might have died anyway before the date of the trial (see paragraph 59).

57. The expected periods at (1) and (2) of paragraph 56 may be obtained from the 0% column of the appropriate table at the back of this booklet. For (1), if historical mortality is to be used, Tables 3 to 10 will be relevant, according to the sex of the deceased and the expected age of retirement, or Tables 21 to 28 if the Court agrees with the recommendation of the Working Party that projected mortality is more appropriate. The age at which the table should be entered is the age which the deceased would have been at the date of the trial. For (2) Tables 1 and 2 or 19 and 20 can be used, according to the sex of the dependant and looking up the table at the age of the dependant at the date of the trial.

58. If the period for which the dependency would have continued is a short fixed period, as in the case of a child, the figure at (2) would be the outstanding period at the date of the trial.

59. A deduction may be made for the risk that the deceased might have died anyway before the date of trial. The need for such a deduction becomes more necessary the longer the period from the date of accident to the date of trial and the older the deceased at the date of death. As an illustration of the order of magnitude of the deduction, Table E shows some examples of the factor by which the multiplier, determined as above, should be multiplied for different ages of the deceased and for different periods from the date of accident to the date of the trial.

60. The resulting multiplier, after application of any discount for the possibility of early death of the deceased before the date of trial, even had the accident not taken place, is to be applied to the appropriate multiplicand, determined in relation to dependency as assessed for the period up to retirement age.

61. If there are several dependants, to whom damages are to be paid in respect of their own particular lifetime (or for a fixed period of dependency), separate multipliers should be determined for each and multiplied by the appropriate multiplicand using the procedure in paragraphs 56 to 60. The total amount of damages is then obtained by adding the separate components. If a single multiplicand is determined, but the damages are to be shared among two or more dependants so long as they are each alive, or during a period of common dependency, then the multiplier will be calculated using the procedure in paragraphs 56 to 60. However, at step (2) of paragraph 56 the expected period will be the longest of the expected periods for which the dependency might last.

TABLE E

Factor by which post-trial damages should be multiplied to allow for the likelihood that the deceased would not in any case have survived to the date of trial in order to provide any post-trial dependency

Age of deceased at date of accident	Period from date of accident to date of trial (years)					
	Male deceased			Female deceased		
	3	6	9	3	6	9
10	1.00	1.00	1.00	1.00	1.00	1.00
20	1.00	0.99	0.99	1.00	1.00	1.00
30	1.00	0.99	0.99	1.00	1.00	0.99
40	0.99	0.99	0.98	1.00	0.99	0.99
50	0.99	0.97	0.95	0.99	0.98	0.97
60	0.97	0.92	0.87	0.98	0.95	0.92
70	0.90	0.80	0.68	0.94	0.87	0.78
80	0.75	0.53	0.33	0.83	0.64	0.45

Note: The factor is clearly one for a period of zero years. Factors for other ages and periods not shown in the table may be obtained approximately by interpolation.

Damages for the period of dependency after retirement age

62. The method described in paragraphs 56 to 61 for pre-retirement age dependency cannot satisfactorily be applied directly to post-retirement age dependency with a sufficient degree of accuracy. We therefore propose a method which involves determining the multiplier by looking at dependency for the rest of life from the date of trial and then subtracting the multiplier for dependency up to retirement age.

63. The assessment of the multiplier for whole of life dependency involves the following steps:

(1) Determine the expectation of life which the deceased would have had as at the date of trial, or such lesser period for which the deceased would have been able to provide the dependency (see paragraph 64).
(2) Determine the expected period for which the dependant would have been able to receive the dependency (see paragraph 64).
(3) Take the lesser of the two periods.

(4) Treat the resulting period as a term certain for which the multiplier is to be determined and look up the figure in Table 38 for this period at the appropriate rate of interest.

64. The expected periods at (1) and (2) of paragraph 63 may be obtained from the 0% column of the appropriate table at the back of this booklet. For (1), if historical mortality is to be used, Tables 1 or 2 will be relevant, according to the sex of the deceased, or Tables 19 or 20 if the Court agrees with the recommendation of the Working Party that projected mortality is more appropriate. The age at which the table should be entered is the age which the deceased would have attained at the date of the trial. For (2) Tables 1 and 2 or 19 and 20 can be used, according to the sex of the dependant and looking up the table at the age of the dependant at the date of the trial.

65. Deduct the corresponding multiplier for post-trial pre-retirement dependency, as determined in paragraphs 56 to 61, but without any adjustment for contingencies other than mortality, or that the deceased may have died anyway before the date of trial. The result is the multiplier for post-retirement dependency, which must then be applied to the appropriate multiplicand, assessed in relation to dependency after retirement age. The adjustment for contingencies other than mortality in respect of the damages for the period of dependency after retirement age will often be less than that required for pre-retirement age damages (see paragraph 34).

66. A deduction may finally be made for the risk that the deceased might have died anyway before the date of trial. The need for such a deduction becomes more necessary the longer the period from the date of accident to the date of trial and the older the deceased at the date of death. As an illustration of the order of magnitude of the deduction, Table E shows some examples of the factor by which the multiplier, determined as above, should be multiplied for different ages of the deceased and for different periods from the date of accident to the date of the trial. The factors for this purpose are exactly the same deductions as used in the calculation at paragraphs 56 to 61.

Cases where dependency is not related to employment

67. The layout of paragraphs 56 to 66 is based on the assumption that the dependency provided by the deceased would have changed at retirement age. This may not be appropriate in some cases, particularly in the important case of the deceased wife and mother whose contribution has been solely in the home or in the case of an adult child caring for an elderly parent or parents. In cases like this, where the deceased might have provided the dependency throughout their lifetime, paragraphs 62 to 66 should be ignored and paragraphs 56 to 61 used, with the difference that the expected period required at step (1) of paragraph 56 should be

a whole of life expectancy, taken from Tables 1 and 2 or 19 and 20. This is also the approach to use when the deceased was already a pensioner.

Example 3

68. The dependant is female, aged 38 at the date of the trial, which is taking place 6 years after the date of the fatal accident which killed the male deceased, at that time aged 37, on whom the dependant was financially dependent. The Court has determined a multiplicand, up to the deceased's normal retirement age of 65, of £30,000 and has decided that no post-retirement damages are payable. The damages are to be calculated as follows:

Pre-trial damages:

(1) Period between fatal accident and trial: 6 years.
(2) Factor for possible early death
     (Table D for male aged 37 and 6 years):   0.99
(3) Therefore pre-trial damages = 6 x 0.99 x £30,000
                                  = £178,200 (plus interest as special damages)

Post-trial damages:

(1) Expected period for which the deceased would have provided the dependency (Table 25 at 0% for male aged 43, the age as at the date of trial): 21.14 18
(2) Expected period for which the dependant would have been able to receive the dependency (Table 20 at 0% for female aged 38): 46.36
(3) Lesser of two periods at (1) and (2) = 21.14
(4) Multiplier for term certain of 21.14 years at 3% rate of return (interpolating between the values for 21 and 22 years in Table 38)
     = (22 – 21.14) x 15.65 + (21.14 – 21) x 16.17
     = 15.72
(5) Adjustment factor for contingencies other than mortality (in accordance with Section B). Assume medium economic activity. Factor from Table A: 0.96
(6) Adjustment factor for the risk that the deceased might have died anyway before the date of trial (Table E for male aged 37 and 6 years): 0.99
(7) Post-trial damages = 15.72 x 0.96 x 0.99 x £30,000
                         = £448,209
                         or £450,000 say.

Example 4

69. The dependant is female, aged 50 at the date of the trial, which is taking place 4 years after the date of the fatal accident which killed the man, at that time aged 47, on whom she was financially dependent. The Court has determined a

multiplicand, up to the deceased's normal retirement age of 60, of £50,000 and has decided that post-retirement damages should be payable based on a multiplicand of £30,000. The damages are to be calculated as follows:

Pre-trial damages:

(1) Period between fatal accident and trial: 4 years
(2) Factor for possible early death (Table D for male aged 47 and 4 years): 0.99
(3) Therefore pre-trial damages = 4 x 0.99 x £50,000
                                = £198,000 (plus interest as special damages)

Post-trial pre-retirement damages:

(1) Expected period for which the deceased would have provided the dependency (Table 23 at 0% for male aged 51, the age as at the date of trial): 8.80
(2) Expected period for which the dependant would have been able to receive the dependency (Table 20 at 0% for female aged 50): 34.49
(3) Lesser of two periods at (1) and (2) = 8.80
(4) Multiplier for term certain of 8.80 years at 3% rate of return (interpolating between the values for 8 and 9 in Table 38)
     = (9-8.80) x 7.12 + (8.80 – 8) x 7.90
     = 7.74
(5) Adjustment factor for contingencies other than mortality (in accordance with Section B). Assume medium economic activity. Factor from Table B: 0.94
(6) Adjustment factor for the risk that the deceased might have died anyway before the date of trial (Table E for male aged 47 and 4 years): 0.98
(7) Post-trial pre-retirement damages = 7.74 x 0.94 x 0.98 x £50,000 = £356,504

Post-retirement damages:

(1) Expectation of life of deceased at date of trial (Table 19 at 0% for male aged 51): 29.91 19
(2) Expected period for which the dependant would have been able to receive the dependency (Table 20 at 0% for female aged 50): 34.49
(3) Lesser of two periods at (1) and (2) = 29.91
(4) Multiplier for time certain of 29.91 years at 3% rate of return (interpolating between the values for 29 and 30 in Table 38)
     = (30-29.91) x 19.47 + (29.91 – 29) x 19.89 = 19.85
(5) Deduct multiplier for post-trial pre-retirement damages before application of adjustment factors for contingencies other than mortality and for the risk that the deceased might have died anyway before the date of trial: 19.85 – 7.74 = 12.11
(6) Adjustment factor for the risk that the deceased might have died anyway before the date of trial (Table E for male aged 47 and 4 years): 0.98
(7) Post-retirement damages = 12.11 x 0.98 x £30,000
                            = £356,034

Example 5

70. There are two dependants, respectively a child aged 10 and a male aged 41 at the date of the trial, which is taking place 3 years after the date of the fatal accident which killed the woman, at that time aged 35, on whom both were financially dependent. She worked in London for a computer company and future economic activity is deemed by the Court to be high. The Court has determined a multiplicand, up to the deceased's normal retirement age of 62, of £50,000 for the male dependant and £10,000 for the child, up to the age of 21, and has decided that post-retirement damages should be payable based on a multiplicand of £20,000. The damages are to be calculated as follows:

Pre-trial damages:

(1) Period between fatal accident and trial: 3 years
(2) Factor for possible early death (Table D for female aged 35 and 3 years): 1.00
(3) Therefore, pre-trial damages = 3 x 1.00 x (£50,000 + £10,000)
$$= £180,000 \text{ (plus interest as special damages)}$$

Post-trial pre-retirement damages:

(1) Expected period for which the deceased would have provided the dependency should be based on female aged 38 at the date of trial with retirement age of 62. First calculate as though deceased were aged 36 and had retirement age of 60 (Table 24 at 0% for female aged 36): 23.57
Then calculate as though deceased were aged 41 and had retirement age of 65 (Table 26 at 0% for female aged 41): 23.34
Interpolate for age 38 with retirement age of 62
$$= (3 \times 23.57 + 2 \times 23.34)/5 = 23.48$$
(2) Expected period for which the male dependant would have been able to receive the dependency (Table 19 at 0% for male aged 41): 39.71 Expected period for which child would have been able to receive the dependency = 11.00
(3) Lesser of two periods at (1) and (2) = 11.00 (in case of child)
$$= 23.48 \text{ (in case of man).}$$
(4) Multiplier for term certain of 11 years at 3% (Table 38): 9.39 Multiplier for term certain of 23.48 years at 3% rate of return (interpolating between the values for 23 and 24 in Table 38)
$$= (24 - 23.48) \times 16.69 + (23.48 - 23) \times 17.19$$
$$= 16.93$$
(5) Adjustment factor for contingencies other than mortality (in accordance with Section B). Factor from Table C, allowing for occupation and geographical area: 0.96 (does not apply to child) 20
(6) Adjustment factor for the risk that the deceased might have died anyway before the date of trial (Table E for female aged 35 and 3 years): 1.00

(7) Pre-retirement damages = 9.39 x 1.00 x £10,000 + 16.93 x 0.96 x 1.00 x
£50,000

$$= £93,900 + £812,640$$
$$= £906,540$$

Post-retirement damages:

(1) Expectation of life of deceased at date of trial (Table 20 at 0% for female aged
38): 46.36
(2) Expected period for which the dependant would have been able to receive the
dependency (Table 19 at 0% for male aged 41): 39.71 (no post retirement
dependency for child)
(3) Lesser of two periods at (1) and (2) = 39.71
(4) Multiplier for time certain of 39.71 years at 3% rate of return (interpolating
between the values for 39 and 40 in Table 38)
= (40 – 39.71) x 23.15 + (39.71 – 39) x 23.46 = 23.37
(5) Deduct multiplier for post-trial pre-retirement damages before application of
adjustment factors for contingencies other than mortality and for the risk that
the deceased might have died anyway before the date of trial: 23.37 – 16.93
= 6.44
(6) Adjustment factor for the risk that the deceased might have died anyway
before the date of trial (Table E for female aged 35 and 3 years) = 1.00
(7) Post-retirement damages = 6.44 x 1.00 x £20,000
$$= £128,800$$

SECTION E: CONCLUDING REMARKS

71. These tables are designed to assist the courts to arrive at suitable multipliers in
a range of possible situations. However, they do not cover all possibilities and in
more complex situations advice should be sought from a Fellow of the Institute of
Actuaries or a Fellow of the Faculty of Actuaries.

72. In cases in which the award will be large, say, about £2 million or more at
current prices, or where there are significant pension rights to be taken into
consideration, more accurate calculations may be necessary. In such cases advice
from an actuary will be desirable.

73. In the Family Division a software program (the Duxbury Method) is used for
making similar calculations in complex cases. A similar facility would be useful for
more complex personal injury and fatal accident cases and it is hoped that such a
programme can be made available.

Christopher Daykin CB, MA, FIA   London
Government Actuary   August 2000

APPENDIX A

Rates of mortality expressed as percentages of 1911 rates (logarithmic scale)

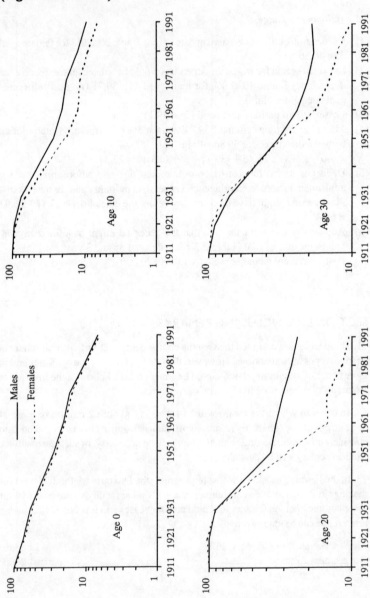

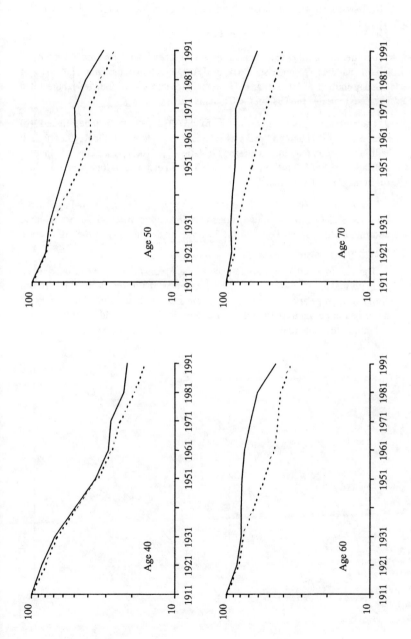

APPENDIX B

How to select the rate of return

1. In order to identify the real rate of return on index linked government stocks on a particular date, reference should be made to the section of the *Financial Times* for that day entitled "FTSE Actuaries Government Securities UK Indices" (abbreviated to "Fixed interest indices" in the Contents list).

2. The most appropriate figures will be found (a) in the section "Index-linked" (b) within the sub-section on "real yields" under the column for the day in question within the group of columns headed "Inflation 5%" (or a figure closer to that for "Inflation 0%" if 5% is thought to be too high an estimate of long term inflation) (c) in the line "Over 5 Years"

3. This figure is also published at quarterly intervals within the "Data Page" in the *Law Society's Gazette*; real returns on index-linked securities are generally stable and major fluctuations between the intervals of publication in the Gazette are unusual.

4. The rate thus obtained by reference to the *Financial Times* or *Law Society's Gazette* makes no allowance for the incidence of tax on the income from a compensation award. Accordingly, the rate should be adjusted if necessary, as described in paragraphs 15 and 16 of Section A, in order to identify the correct column of the table to be used.

APPENDIX C

Reservations and comments of the Association of British Insurers (ABI)

Introduction

1. The Association of British Insurers (ABI) represents insurance companies transacting 95 per cent of insurance company business in the United Kingdom. The ABI is pleased once again to have participated in the discussions of the Working Party responsible for this 4th edition of the tables and explanatory notes.

2. The addition of new tables dealing with a range of retirement ages and the broadening of the range of ages included in the tables can only further assist those involved in dealing with personal injury and fatal accident cases in reaching timely and accurate assessments of the probable damages involved.

3. During the Working Party's preparatory work on this edition, the Lord Chancellor published, on 17 March 2000, a consultation paper on damages entitled "The Discount Rate and Alternatives to Lump Sums". This sought views on the exercise of the Lord Chancellor's power to prescribe a rate of return under Section 1 of the Damages Act 1996. At the time of writing, the results of this consultation are not yet known. We return to this below.

Multipliers in Fatal Accident Act cases

4. The Working Party was reconvened following a recommendation made by the Law Commission in its report entitled "Claims for Wrongful Death" (Law Com No 263) published in November 1999. At paragraph 4.23, the Commission states: *"We therefore recommend that, in the first instance, the Ogden Working Party (which includes the Government Actuary) should consider, and explain more fully, how the existing actuarial Ogden Tables should be used, or amended, to produce accurate assessments of damages in Fatal Accident Act cases (as opposed to personal injury cases). We would point out to that Working Party our preferred approach ..."*

5. The Commission's *"preferred approach"* is that multipliers in Fatal Accident Act cases should be calculated from the date of trial, as opposed to from the date of death. This conflicts with the decision in House of Lords *Cookson v Knowles* [1979] 2 AC 556, in which it was held that the multiplier is to be calculated from the date of death.

6. The Chairman of the Working Party argues in the introduction to this edition that after *Wells v Wells* [1999] 1 AC 345, courts are not precluded from using a new method of calculating Fatal Accident Act damages. Hence the body of the text of the explanatory notes to this 4th edition, at Section D, adopts the Commission's preferred approach and sets out a multi-stage methodology for the computation damages in Fatal Accident Act cases. We believe it is necessary to question this assertion.

7. In cases of future loss, whether fatal or non-fatal, the principle is that damages are calculated from when the uncertainty as to the future begins. This is clear from the speech of Lord Fraser, in *Cookson v Knowles* [1979] AC 556 at 576C-D: *"In a personal injury case, if the injured person has survived until the date of trial, that is a known fact and the multiplier appropriate to the length of his future working life has to be ascertained as at the date of trial. But in a fatal accident case the multiplier has to be selected once and for all as at the date of death, because everything that might have happened after that date remains uncertain."*

8. It is therefore consistent to calculate the multiplier from these different dates in fatal and non-fatal cases. We contend that until *Cookson v Knowles* is expressly overruled either by the House of Lords or by legislation, it is highly questionable whether a lower court has the freedom to depart from the principle that the starting point for assessing the multiplier in fatal accident cases should be the date of death.

9. This is not to say that we take issue with the actuarial calculations set in Section D – we recognise the expertise involved in its preparation. However, as a matter of legal principle, we do not accept that this Working Party can effect a change in the law as set out in Section D and are therefore unable to support it.

10. We have previously noted that there is perhaps a danger that the use of overly scientific approaches in this area may bring a spurious accuracy to a calculation which, almost by definition, will prove wrong in the future.

Rate of return

11. In the 3rd edition of these tables, we noted (at paragraph 16, page 36) that: *"It is not for this Working Party to advocate the use of any particular rate of return. Under the Damages Act 1996, this is a matter for the Lord Chancellor (if he is so minded) who is likely to make his decision after the House of Lords has given its judgment in Wells v Wells. Until Wells is decided and until the Lord Chancellor has considered exercising his power under the Damages Act, we would therefore caution against adoption of the argument in support of Index-Linked Government Stock".*

12. However, Appendix B of this 4th edition offers guidance as to selecting a rate of return to use with the tables. It recommends selecting a rate based on the return on Index-Linked Government Stock. This text previously appeared in earlier editions of these tables which were published before *Wells v Wells* was decided and before a net real rate of 3 per cent was adopted.

13. Since *Wells*, both the Court of Appeal in *Warren v Northern General Hospital Trust (No2)* [2000] 1 WLR 1404 and the Court of Session in *Macey-Lillie v Lanarkshire Health Board* [Times Law Report, 28 June 2000] have held that the net real rate of return of 3 per cent adopted in *Wells* should apply until the Lord Chancellor (or Secretary of State for Scotland) decides whether to exercise the power in Section 1 of the Damages Act 1996.

14. In light of these decisions we are unable to support the recommendation in Appendix B of this edition and maintain our view that it is appropriate for the Working Party to give its views from time to time as to the appropriate rate of return, which is now solely a matter for the Lord Chancellor.

Association of British Insurers

July 2000

Table 1   Multipliers for pecuniary loss for life (males)

Age at date of trial	Multiplier calculated with allowance for population mortality and rate of return of											Age at date of trial
	0.0%	0.5%	1.0%	1.5%	2.0%	2.5%	3.0%	3.5%	4.0%	4.5%	5.0%	
0	73.42	61.05	51.47	43.97	38.02	33.25	29.38	26.22	23.60	21.41	19.57	0
1	73.02	60.86	51.41	43.98	38.08	33.34	29.49	26.34	23.72	21.53	19.68	1
2	72.06	60.20	50.95	43.66	37.86	33.18	29.38	26.26	23.67	21.49	19.66	2
3	71.09	59.52	50.47	43.32	37.62	33.01	29.26	26.17	23.60	21.45	19.62	3
4	70.11	58.83	49.99	42.98	37.37	32.84	29.13	26.08	23.53	21.40	19.58	4
5	69.13	58.14	49.49	42.63	37.12	32.65	29.00	25.98	23.46	21.34	19.54	5
6	68.14	57.44	48.99	42.27	36.86	32.47	28.86	25.88	23.39	21.28	19.50	6
7	67.16	56.73	48.49	41.90	36.59	32.27	28.72	25.77	23.31	21.22	19.45	7
8	66.17	56.02	47.98	41.53	36.32	32.07	28.57	25.66	23.22	21.16	19.41	8
9	65.18	55.31	47.46	41.16	36.05	31.87	28.42	25.55	23.14	21.10	19.35	9
10	64.19	54.60	46.94	40.77	35.76	31.66	28.26	25.43	23.05	21.03	19.30	10
11	63.21	53.88	46.41	40.38	35.48	31.44	28.10	25.31	22.95	20.95	19.24	11
12	62.22	53.15	45.88	39.99	35.18	31.22	27.93	25.18	22.85	20.88	19.19	12
13	61.23	52.43	45.34	39.59	34.88	30.99	27.76	25.05	22.75	20.80	19.12	13
14	60.24	51.70	44.80	39.19	34.58	30.76	27.58	24.91	22.65	20.72	19.06	14
15	59.26	50.97	44.26	38.78	34.27	30.53	27.41	24.77	22.54	20.63	18.99	15
16	58.28	50.24	43.71	38.37	33.96	30.29	27.22	24.63	22.43	20.55	18.93	16
17	57.31	49.52	43.17	37.96	33.65	30.05	27.04	24.49	22.32	20.46	18.86	17
18	56.36	48.80	42.63	37.55	33.33	29.82	26.86	24.35	22.21	20.38	18.79	18
19	55.41	48.08	42.08	37.13	33.02	29.57	26.67	24.21	22.10	20.29	18.72	19
20	54.45	47.36	41.54	36.71	32.70	29.33	26.48	24.06	21.98	20.20	18.65	20
21	53.50	46.63	40.98	36.29	32.37	29.07	26.28	23.90	21.86	20.10	18.57	21
22	52.54	45.91	40.42	35.86	32.03	28.81	26.08	23.74	21.74	20.00	18.49	22
23	51.59	45.17	39.86	35.42	31.69	28.55	25.87	23.58	21.60	19.90	18.41	23
24	50.63	44.44	39.28	34.97	31.35	28.27	25.65	23.41	21.47	19.79	18.32	24
25	49.68	43.70	38.71	34.52	30.99	27.99	25.43	23.23	21.33	19.67	18.23	25

26	48.72	42.95	38.12	34.06	30.63	27.70	25.20	23.04	21.18	19.55	18.13	26
27	47.76	42.20	37.53	33.59	30.26	27.41	24.96	22.85	21.02	19.43	18.03	27
28	46.80	41.44	36.93	33.12	29.88	27.10	24.72	22.66	20.86	19.30	17.92	28
29	45.84	40.68	36.33	32.64	29.49	26.79	24.47	22.45	20.70	19.16	17.81	29
30	44.88	39.92	35.72	32.15	29.10	26.47	24.21	22.24	20.52	19.02	17.69	30
31	43.92	39.15	35.10	31.65	28.70	26.15	23.94	22.02	20.34	18.87	17.57	31
32	42.96	38.38	34.48	31.15	28.29	25.81	23.67	21.80	20.16	18.71	17.44	32
33	42.01	37.61	33.86	30.64	27.87	25.47	23.38	21.56	19.96	18.55	17.30	33
34	41.05	36.83	33.22	30.12	27.44	25.12	23.09	21.32	19.76	18.38	17.16	34
35	40.09	36.05	32.59	29.60	27.01	24.76	22.80	21.07	19.55	18.21	17.01	35
36	39.14	35.27	31.94	29.07	26.57	24.40	22.49	20.82	19.34	18.03	16.86	36
37	38.18	34.49	31.30	28.54	26.13	24.03	22.18	20.56	19.12	17.84	16.70	37
38	37.24	33.71	30.65	28.00	25.68	23.65	21.86	20.29	18.89	17.64	16.53	38
39	36.29	32.92	30.00	27.45	25.22	23.26	21.54	20.01	18.65	17.44	16.36	39
40	35.35	32.14	29.34	26.90	24.76	22.87	21.20	19.73	18.41	17.23	16.18	40
41	34.41	31.35	28.68	26.34	24.28	22.47	20.86	19.43	18.16	17.02	15.99	41
42	33.47	30.56	28.01	25.78	23.80	22.06	20.51	19.13	17.90	16.79	15.80	42
43	32.54	29.77	27.34	25.21	23.32	21.64	20.15	18.82	17.63	16.56	15.60	43
44	31.61	28.98	26.67	24.63	22.83	21.22	19.79	18.51	17.36	16.32	15.39	44
45	30.68	28.19	26.00	24.05	22.33	20.79	19.41	18.18	17.07	16.07	15.17	45
46	29.76	27.41	25.32	23.47	21.82	20.35	19.03	17.85	16.78	15.82	14.94	46
47	28.85	26.62	24.64	22.89	21.31	19.91	18.65	17.51	16.48	15.55	14.71	47
48	27.95	25.84	23.97	22.30	20.80	19.46	18.25	17.16	16.18	15.28	14.47	48
49	27.05	25.06	23.29	21.71	20.28	19.01	17.85	16.81	15.87	15.01	14.22	49
50	26.16	24.29	22.61	21.11	19.76	18.55	17.45	16.45	15.55	14.72	13.97	50
51	25.28	23.52	21.94	20.52	19.24	18.09	17.04	16.09	15.22	14.43	13.71	51
52	24.41	22.75	21.27	19.93	18.72	17.62	16.62	15.72	14.89	14.14	13.44	52
53	23.55	21.99	20.60	19.33	18.19	17.15	16.20	15.34	14.55	13.83	13.17	53
54	22.70	21.24	19.93	18.74	17.66	16.68	15.78	14.96	14.21	13.52	12.89	54
55	21.86	20.50	19.26	18.15	17.13	16.20	15.35	14.57	13.86	13.21	12.60	55

Table 1   Multipliers for pecuniary loss for life (males)

Age at date of trial	Multiplier calculated with allowance for population mortality and rate of return of											Age at date of trial
	0.0%	0.5%	1.0%	1.5%	2.0%	2.5%	3.0%	3.5%	4.0%	4.5%	5.0%	
56	21.03	19.76	18.60	17.55	16.60	15.72	14.92	14.18	13.51	12.88	12.31	56
57	20.21	19.03	17.95	16.97	16.07	15.24	14.49	13.79	13.15	12.56	12.01	57
58	19.41	18.31	17.30	16.38	15.54	14.76	14.05	13.39	12.79	12.23	11.71	58
59	18.62	17.60	16.66	15.80	15.01	14.28	13.61	13.00	12.42	11.89	11.40	59
60	17.85	16.90	16.03	15.22	14.49	13.81	13.18	12.60	12.06	11.56	11.09	60
61	17.09	16.21	15.40	14.66	13.97	13.33	12.74	12.20	11.69	11.22	10.78	61
62	16.36	15.54	14.79	14.10	13.45	12.86	12.31	11.80	11.32	10.88	10.46	62
63	15.64	14.89	14.19	13.55	12.95	12.40	11.88	11.40	10.95	10.54	10.15	63
64	14.94	14.25	13.60	13.01	12.45	11.94	11.46	11.01	10.59	10.20	9.83	64
65	14.27	13.63	13.03	12.48	11.97	11.49	11.04	10.62	10.23	9.86	9.52	65
66	13.61	13.02	12.47	11.96	11.49	11.04	10.63	10.24	9.87	9.53	9.21	66
67	12.98	12.44	11.93	11.46	11.02	10.61	10.22	9.86	9.52	9.20	8.90	67
68	12.36	11.87	11.40	10.97	10.56	10.18	9.82	9.49	9.17	8.87	8.59	68
69	11.77	11.31	10.89	10.49	10.11	9.76	9.43	9.12	8.82	8.55	8.28	69
70	11.19	10.77	10.38	10.02	9.67	9.35	9.04	8.75	8.48	8.22	7.98	70
71	10.62	10.25	9.89	9.55	9.24	8.94	8.66	8.39	8.14	7.90	7.68	71
72	10.08	9.73	9.41	9.10	8.81	8.54	8.28	8.04	7.80	7.58	7.37	72
73	9.56	9.24	8.95	8.67	8.40	8.15	7.91	7.69	7.47	7.27	7.08	73
74	9.06	8.77	8.50	8.25	8.00	7.77	7.56	7.35	7.15	6.97	6.79	74
75	8.57	8.31	8.07	7.84	7.62	7.41	7.21	7.02	6.84	6.67	6.50	75
76	8.11	7.87	7.65	7.44	7.24	7.05	6.87	6.69	6.53	6.37	6.22	76
77	7.66	7.45	7.25	7.05	6.87	6.70	6.53	6.37	6.22	6.08	5.94	77
78	7.23	7.04	6.86	6.69	6.52	6.36	6.21	6.07	5.93	5.80	5.67	78
79	6.83	6.65	6.49	6.33	6.18	6.04	5.90	5.77	5.65	5.53	5.41	79
80	6.44	6.28	6.14	5.99	5.86	5.73	5.61	5.49	5.37	5.26	5.16	80

Age												Age
81	6.07	5.93	5.80	5.67	5.55	5.43	5.32	5.21	5.11	5.01	4.91	81
82	5.72	5.59	5.47	5.36	5.25	5.14	5.04	4.94	4.85	4.76	4.67	82
83	5.38	5.27	5.16	5.06	4.96	4.86	4.77	4.68	4.60	4.52	4.44	83
84	5.06	4.96	4.87	4.77	4.68	4.60	4.52	4.44	4.36	4.28	4.21	84
85	4.76	4.67	4.59	4.50	4.42	4.35	4.27	4.20	4.13	4.06	4.00	85
86	4.48	4.40	4.32	4.25	4.17	4.10	4.04	3.97	3.91	3.85	3.79	86
87	4.21	4.14	4.07	4.01	3.94	3.88	3.82	3.76	3.70	3.65	3.59	87
88	3.97	3.90	3.84	3.78	3.72	3.67	3.61	3.56	3.51	3.46	3.41	88
89	3.73	3.68	3.62	3.57	3.52	3.47	3.42	3.37	3.32	3.28	3.24	89
90	3.51	3.46	3.41	3.36	3.31	3.27	3.23	3.18	3.14	3.10	3.06	90
91	3.29	3.24	3.20	3.15	3.11	3.07	3.03	3.00	2.96	2.92	2.89	91
92	3.07	3.03	2.99	2.95	2.92	2.88	2.85	2.81	2.78	2.75	2.72	92
93	2.87	2.84	2.80	2.77	2.74	2.70	2.67	2.64	2.61	2.59	2.56	93
94	2.69	2.66	2.63	2.60	2.57	2.54	2.52	2.49	2.46	2.44	2.41	94
95	2.53	2.50	2.48	2.45	2.42	2.40	2.37	2.35	2.33	2.30	2.28	95
96	2.38	2.36	2.33	2.31	2.29	2.26	2.24	2.22	2.20	2.18	2.16	96
97	2.24	2.22	2.20	2.18	2.16	2.14	2.12	2.10	2.08	2.06	2.04	97
98	2.11	2.09	2.07	2.06	2.04	2.02	2.00	1.98	1.97	1.95	1.93	98
99	1.99	1.97	1.96	1.94	1.92	1.91	1.89	1.87	1.86	1.84	1.83	99
100	1.87	1.86	1.84	1.83	1.81	1.80	1.78	1.77	1.76	1.74	1.73	100

Table 2   Multipliers for pecuniary loss for life (females)

Age at date of trial	Multiplier calculated with allowance for population mortality and rate of return of											Age at date of trial
	0.0%	0.5%	1.0%	1.5%	2.0%	2.5%	3.0%	3.5%	4.0%	4.5%	5.0%	
0	78.96	64.89	54.15	45.85	39.35	34.21	30.08	26.73	23.99	21.70	19.79	0
1	78.46	64.62	54.03	45.82	39.38	34.27	30.16	26.83	24.08	21.80	19.88	1
2	77.50	63.98	53.59	45.52	39.18	34.13	30.07	26.76	24.04	21.77	19.86	2
3	76.53	63.31	53.14	45.21	38.97	33.99	29.97	26.69	23.99	21.73	19.84	3
4	75.55	62.64	52.68	44.89	38.75	33.83	29.86	26.61	23.93	21.69	19.81	4
5	74.56	61.96	52.21	44.57	38.52	33.67	29.74	26.53	23.87	21.65	19.78	5
6	73.57	61.28	51.73	44.24	38.28	33.51	29.63	26.45	23.81	21.61	19.75	6
7	72.58	60.59	51.25	43.90	38.05	33.34	29.51	26.36	23.75	21.56	19.71	7
8	71.59	59.90	50.77	43.56	37.80	33.16	29.38	26.27	23.68	21.51	19.68	8
9	70.60	59.21	50.28	43.21	37.55	32.98	29.25	26.17	23.61	21.46	19.64	9
10	69.61	58.51	49.78	42.86	37.30	32.80	29.12	26.08	23.54	21.41	19.60	10
11	68.62	57.81	49.28	42.50	37.04	32.61	28.98	25.97	23.47	21.35	19.56	11
12	67.63	57.10	48.78	42.13	36.78	32.42	28.84	25.87	23.39	21.29	19.51	12
13	66.64	56.39	48.27	41.76	36.51	32.22	28.69	25.76	23.31	21.23	19.46	13
14	65.65	55.68	47.75	41.39	36.23	32.02	28.54	25.65	23.22	21.17	19.42	14
15	64.66	54.97	47.23	41.01	35.95	31.81	28.39	25.54	23.14	21.10	19.37	15
16	63.67	54.25	46.71	40.63	35.67	31.60	28.23	25.42	23.05	21.03	19.31	16
17	62.69	53.53	46.18	40.24	35.38	31.39	28.07	25.30	22.95	20.96	19.26	17
18	61.71	52.81	45.66	39.85	35.09	31.17	27.91	25.17	22.86	20.89	19.20	18
19	60.73	52.09	45.12	39.45	34.80	30.95	27.74	25.04	22.76	20.82	19.15	19
20	59.75	51.37	44.58	39.05	34.49	30.72	27.57	24.91	22.66	20.74	19.08	20
21	58.77	50.64	44.04	38.64	34.18	30.48	27.39	24.77	22.55	20.65	19.02	21
22	57.79	49.90	43.49	38.22	33.87	30.24	27.20	24.63	22.44	20.57	18.95	22
23	56.80	49.17	42.93	37.80	33.55	30.00	27.01	24.48	22.33	20.48	18.88	23
24	55.82	48.43	42.37	37.37	33.22	29.74	26.82	24.33	22.21	20.38	18.81	24
25	54.84	47.68	41.80	36.94	32.88	29.49	26.61	24.17	22.09	20.29	18.73	25

Age												Age
26	18.65	20.18	21.96	24.01	26.41	29.22	32.54	36.50	41.23	46.93	53.86	26
27	18.56	20.08	21.82	23.84	26.19	28.95	32.20	36.05	40.65	46.18	52.88	27
28	18.47	19.97	21.68	23.67	25.97	28.67	31.84	35.59	40.07	45.43	51.90	28
29	18.38	19.85	21.54	23.49	25.75	28.39	31.48	35.13	39.48	44.67	50.92	29
30	18.28	19.73	21.39	23.30	25.52	28.09	31.11	34.67	38.88	43.91	49.94	30
31	18.18	19.60	21.23	23.11	25.28	27.80	30.74	34.20	38.28	43.14	48.96	31
32	18.07	19.47	21.07	22.91	25.03	27.49	30.36	33.72	37.68	42.38	47.98	32
33	17.96	19.34	20.91	22.71	24.78	27.18	29.97	33.23	37.07	41.61	47.01	33
34	17.84	19.20	20.74	22.50	24.53	26.86	29.58	32.74	36.46	40.84	46.03	34
35	17.72	19.05	20.56	22.28	24.26	26.54	29.18	32.25	35.84	40.06	45.06	35
36	17.59	18.90	20.38	22.06	23.99	26.21	28.77	31.75	35.22	39.29	44.09	36
37	17.46	18.74	20.19	21.83	23.71	25.87	28.36	31.24	34.59	38.51	43.12	37
38	17.32	18.58	19.99	21.60	23.43	25.53	27.94	30.73	33.96	37.73	42.16	38
39	17.18	18.41	19.79	21.36	23.14	25.18	27.51	30.21	33.33	36.95	41.20	39
40	17.03	18.23	19.58	21.11	22.84	24.82	27.08	29.68	32.69	36.17	40.24	40
41	16.88	18.05	19.37	20.85	22.54	24.45	26.64	29.15	32.04	35.39	39.28	41
42	16.72	17.86	19.14	20.59	22.22	24.08	26.19	28.61	31.40	34.60	38.32	42
43	16.55	17.67	18.92	20.32	21.91	23.70	25.74	28.07	30.74	33.82	37.37	43
44	16.38	17.46	18.68	20.04	21.58	23.31	25.28	27.53	30.09	33.03	36.43	44
45	16.20	17.25	18.44	19.76	21.25	22.92	24.82	26.98	29.43	32.25	35.48	45
46	16.01	17.04	18.19	19.47	20.91	22.52	24.35	26.42	28.77	31.46	34.54	46
47	15.82	16.82	17.93	19.17	20.56	22.12	23.88	25.86	28.11	30.68	33.61	47
48	15.62	16.59	17.67	18.87	20.21	21.71	23.40	25.30	27.45	29.90	32.68	48
49	15.41	16.36	17.40	18.56	19.85	21.29	22.91	24.73	26.79	29.12	31.76	49
50	15.20	16.11	17.12	18.24	19.48	20.87	22.42	24.16	26.12	28.34	30.85	50
51	14.98	15.86	16.84	17.91	19.11	20.44	21.92	23.59	25.45	27.56	29.94	51
52	14.76	15.61	16.55	17.58	18.73	20.00	21.42	23.01	24.79	26.78	29.03	52
53	14.52	15.35	16.25	17.24	18.34	19.56	20.92	22.43	24.12	26.01	28.13	53
54	14.28	15.07	15.94	16.90	17.95	19.12	20.41	21.84	23.45	25.24	27.24	54
55	14.03	14.80	15.63	16.54	17.55	18.66	19.89	21.26	22.77	24.47	26.36	55

Table 2 Multipliers for pecuniary loss for life (females)

Multiplier calculated with allowance for population mortality and rate of return of

Age at date of trial	0.0%	0.5%	1.0%	1.5%	2.0%	2.5%	3.0%	3.5%	4.0%	4.5%	5.0%	Age at date of trial
56	25.48	23.70	22.10	20.67	19.38	18.21	17.15	16.19	15.31	14.51	13.78	56
57	24.61	22.94	21.44	20.08	18.86	17.75	16.74	15.82	14.98	14.22	13.52	57
58	23.76	22.19	20.77	19.49	18.33	17.28	16.33	15.45	14.65	13.92	13.25	58
59	22.91	21.44	20.11	18.91	17.81	16.82	15.91	15.08	14.32	13.62	12.98	59
60	22.08	20.70	19.45	18.32	17.29	16.35	15.49	14.70	13.98	13.31	12.70	60
61	21.26	19.97	18.80	17.74	16.77	15.88	15.07	14.32	13.63	13.00	12.42	61
62	20.45	19.25	18.16	17.16	16.25	15.41	14.64	13.94	13.29	12.69	12.13	62
63	19.66	18.54	17.52	16.58	15.73	14.94	14.22	13.55	12.93	12.36	11.84	63
64	18.88	17.84	16.89	16.01	15.21	14.47	13.79	13.16	12.58	12.04	11.54	64
65	18.11	17.15	16.26	15.45	14.70	14.01	13.37	12.77	12.22	11.71	11.24	65
66	17.36	16.47	15.64	14.89	14.19	13.54	12.94	12.38	11.87	11.38	10.94	66
67	16.62	15.79	15.03	14.33	13.68	13.07	12.51	11.99	11.50	11.05	10.63	67
68	15.90	15.13	14.43	13.77	13.17	12.61	12.08	11.59	11.14	10.71	10.32	68
69	15.19	14.48	13.83	13.23	12.66	12.14	11.65	11.20	10.77	10.37	10.00	69
70	14.49	13.84	13.24	12.68	12.16	11.68	11.22	10.80	10.40	10.03	9.68	70
71	13.80	13.21	12.66	12.14	11.66	11.21	10.79	10.40	10.03	9.68	9.36	71
72	13.13	12.59	12.08	11.61	11.17	10.75	10.36	10.00	9.66	9.33	9.03	72
73	12.48	11.98	11.52	11.09	10.68	10.30	9.94	9.60	9.29	8.99	8.70	73
74	11.85	11.40	10.98	10.58	10.21	9.86	9.53	9.21	8.92	8.64	8.38	74
75	11.23	10.82	10.44	10.08	9.74	9.42	9.11	8.83	8.55	8.30	8.06	75
76	10.63	10.26	9.91	9.58	9.27	8.98	8.70	8.44	8.19	7.95	7.73	76
77	10.04	9.71	9.39	9.09	8.81	8.54	8.29	8.05	7.82	7.60	7.40	77
78	9.48	9.18	8.89	8.62	8.36	8.12	7.89	7.67	7.46	7.26	7.07	78
79	8.93	8.66	8.40	8.16	7.93	7.71	7.50	7.30	7.11	6.93	6.75	79
80	8.41	8.17	7.94	7.72	7.51	7.31	7.12	6.94	6.76	6.60	6.44	80

81	7.91	7.70	7.49	7.29	7.10	6.92	6.75	6.58	6.43	6.28	6.13	81
82	7.43	7.24	7.05	6.87	6.70	6.54	6.39	6.24	6.10	5.96	5.83	82
83	6.97	6.80	6.63	6.47	6.32	6.18	6.04	5.90	5.77	5.65	5.53	83
84	6.53	6.38	6.23	6.09	5.95	5.82	5.69	5.57	5.46	5.35	5.24	84
85	6.11	5.97	5.84	5.71	5.59	5.48	5.36	5.26	5.15	5.05	4.96	85
86	5.72	5.59	5.48	5.36	5.25	5.15	5.05	4.95	4.86	4.77	4.68	86
87	5.35	5.24	5.14	5.04	4.94	4.85	4.76	4.67	4.59	4.51	4.43	87
88	5.00	4.91	4.81	4.72	4.64	4.55	4.47	4.40	4.32	4.25	4.18	88
89	4.67	4.58	4.50	4.42	4.34	4.27	4.20	4.13	4.06	4.00	3.94	89
90	4.35	4.28	4.21	4.14	4.07	4.00	3.94	3.88	3.82	3.76	3.71	90
91	4.06	4.00	3.93	3.87	3.81	3.75	3.70	3.64	3.59	3.54	3.49	91
92	3.80	3.74	3.68	3.63	3.57	3.52	3.47	3.42	3.37	3.33	3.28	92
93	3.55	3.50	3.45	3.40	3.35	3.31	3.26	3.22	3.18	3.13	3.09	93
94	3.32	3.28	3.23	3.19	3.15	3.11	3.07	3.03	2.99	2.95	2.92	94
95	3.11	3.07	3.03	2.99	2.96	2.92	2.88	2.85	2.81	2.78	2.75	95
96	2.92	2.89	2.35	2.82	2.78	2.75	2.72	2.69	2.66	2.63	2.60	96
97	2.75	2.72	2.69	2.66	2.63	2.60	2.57	2.54	2.52	2.49	2.46	97
98	2.59	2.56	2.53	2.50	2.48	2.45	2.42	2.40	2.38	2.35	2.33	98
99	2.42	2.40	2.37	2.35	2.32	2.30	2.28	2.26	2.23	2.21	2.19	99
100	2.27	2.25	2.22	2.20	2.18	2.16	2.14	2.12	2.10	2.08	2.06	100

Table 3   Multipliers for loss of earnings to pension age 55 (males)

Age at date of trial	Multiplier calculated with allowance for population mortality and rate of return of											Age at date of trial
	0.0%	0.5%	1.0%	1.5%	2.0%	2.5%	3.0%	3.5%	4.0%	4.5%	5.0%	
16	38.10	34.66	31.65	28.99	26.65	24.58	22.75	21.12	19.66	18.36	17.19	16
17	37.12	33.85	30.97	28.44	26.19	24.20	22.43	20.85	19.44	18.17	17.04	17
18	36.15	33.04	30.30	27.88	25.72	23.81	22.10	20.58	19.21	17.98	16.88	18
19	35.18	32.24	29.63	27.31	25.25	23.41	21.77	20.30	18.98	17.78	16.71	19
20	34.21	31.42	28.94	26.73	24.77	23.00	21.43	20.01	18.73	17.58	16.53	20
21	33.24	30.60	28.25	26.15	24.27	22.59	21.07	19.71	18.48	17.36	16.35	21
22	32.27	29.78	27.55	25.56	23.77	22.16	20.71	19.40	18.21	17.13	16.16	22
23	31.30	28.95	26.85	24.96	23.25	21.72	20.33	19.08	17.94	16.90	15.95	23
24	30.32	28.12	26.13	24.35	22.73	21.27	19.95	18.74	17.65	16.65	15.74	24
25	29.35	27.28	25.41	23.72	22.20	20.81	19.55	18.40	17.35	16.39	15.52	25
26	28.37	26.44	24.68	23.09	21.65	20.33	19.14	18.04	17.04	16.12	15.28	26
27	27.40	25.59	23.95	22.45	21.09	19.85	18.71	17.67	16.72	15.84	15.04	27
28	26.42	24.74	23.20	21.80	20.52	19.35	18.27	17.29	16.38	15.55	14.78	28
29	25.44	23.88	22.45	21.14	19.94	18.84	17.82	16.89	16.03	15.24	14.50	29
30	24.47	23.02	21.69	20.47	19.34	18.31	17.36	16.48	15.67	14.91	14.22	30
31	23.49	22.15	20.92	19.78	18.74	17.77	16.88	16.05	15.29	14.58	13.92	31
32	22.51	21.28	20.14	19.09	18.12	17.22	16.39	15.61	14.89	14.22	13.60	32
33	21.53	20.40	19.36	18.39	17.49	16.66	15.88	15.16	14.48	13.85	13.27	33
34	20.55	19.52	18.57	17.68	16.85	16.08	15.36	14.68	14.06	13.47	12.92	34
35	19.57	18.64	17.77	16.95	16.19	15.48	14.82	14.20	13.61	13.07	12.55	35
36	18.60	17.75	16.96	16.22	15.52	14.87	14.27	13.69	13.15	12.65	12.17	36
37	17.62	16.86	16.14	15.47	14.84	14.25	13.70	13.17	12.68	12.21	11.77	37
38	16.64	15.96	15.32	14.72	14.15	13.62	13.11	12.63	12.18	11.76	11.35	38
39	15.67	15.06	14.49	13.95	13.45	12.96	12.51	12.08	11.67	11.28	10.91	39
40	14.69	14.16	13.66	13.18	12.73	12.30	11.89	11.50	11.13	10.78	10.45	40

Age												Age
41	9.97	10.27	10.58	10.91	11.25	11.61	11.99	12.39	12.81	13.25	13.71	41
42	9.46	9.72	10.00	10.29	10.59	10.91	11.24	11.59	11.96	12.34	12.74	42
43	8.93	9.16	9.40	9.65	9.92	10.19	10.48	10.78	11.09	11.42	11.76	43
44	8.37	8.57	8.78	9.00	9.22	9.46	9.70	9.96	10.22	10.50	10.79	44
45	7.78	7.95	8.13	8.31	8.51	8.70	8.91	9.12	9.34	9.57	9.81	45
46	7.16	7.31	7.46	7.61	7.77	7.93	8.10	8.28	8.46	8.64	8.84	46
47	6.52	6.64	6.76	6.88	7.01	7.14	7.28	7.42	7.56	7.71	7.86	47
48	5.84	5.93	6.03	6.13	6.23	6.33	6.43	6.54	6.65	6.77	6.89	48
49	5.13	5.20	5.27	5.34	5.42	5.50	5.58	5.66	5.74	5.82	5.91	49
50	4.38	4.43	4.48	4.53	4.59	4.64	4.70	4.76	4.81	4.87	4.93	50
51	3.59	3.63	3.66	3.70	3.73	3.77	3.80	3.84	3.88	3.92	3.95	51
52	2.77	2.79	2.80	2.82	2.85	2.87	2.89	2.91	2.93	2.95	2.97	52
53	1.89	1.90	1.91	1.92	1.93	1.94	1.95	1.96	1.97	1.98	1.99	53
54	0.97	0.97	0.98	0.98	0.98	0.98	0.99	0.99	0.99	0.99	1.00	54

Table 4   Multipliers for loss of earnings to pension age 55 (females)

Multiplier calculated with allowance for population mortality and rate of return of

Age at date of trial	0.0%	0.5%	1.0%	1.5%	2.0%	2.5%	3.0%	3.5%	4.0%	4.5%	5.0%	Age at date of trial
16	38.53	35.03	31.97	29.28	26.90	24.80	22.94	21.29	19.82	18.50	17.32	16
17	37.54	34.21	31.29	28.72	26.44	24.42	22.62	21.02	19.59	18.31	17.16	17
18	36.55	33.39	30.61	28.15	25.97	24.02	22.29	20.75	19.36	18.12	17.00	18
19	35.56	32.57	29.92	27.57	25.48	23.62	21.96	20.46	19.12	17.92	16.83	19
20	34.57	31.74	29.22	26.99	24.99	23.21	21.61	20.17	18.88	17.71	16.65	20
21	33.58	30.90	28.52	26.39	24.49	22.78	21.25	19.86	18.62	17.49	16.47	21
22	32.59	30.07	27.81	25.79	23.98	22.35	20.88	19.55	18.35	17.26	16.27	22
23	31.60	29.22	27.09	25.18	23.45	21.90	20.49	19.22	18.07	17.02	16.06	23
24	30.61	28.38	26.37	24.56	22.92	21.44	20.10	18.88	17.78	16.77	15.85	24
25	29.62	27.53	25.63	23.92	22.38	20.97	19.70	18.53	17.47	16.51	15.62	25
26	28.63	26.67	24.89	23.28	21.82	20.49	19.28	18.17	17.16	16.23	15.38	26
27	27.64	25.81	24.15	22.63	21.26	20.00	18.85	17.80	16.83	15.95	15.13	27
28	26.65	24.95	23.39	21.97	20.68	19.49	18.41	17.41	16.49	15.65	14.87	28
29	25.66	24.08	22.63	21.30	20.09	18.97	17.95	17.01	16.14	15.34	14.59	29
30	24.67	23.20	21.86	20.62	19.49	18.44	17.48	16.59	15.77	15.01	14.31	30
31	23.68	22.33	21.08	19.94	18.88	17.90	17.00	16.16	15.39	14.67	14.00	31
32	22.69	21.45	20.30	19.24	18.25	17.34	16.50	15.72	14.99	14.31	13.68	32
33	21.70	20.56	19.51	18.53	17.62	16.77	15.99	15.26	14.58	13.94	13.35	33
34	20.72	19.67	18.71	17.81	16.97	16.19	15.46	14.78	14.15	13.56	13.00	34
35	19.73	18.78	17.90	17.08	16.31	15.59	14.92	14.29	13.70	13.15	12.63	35
36	18.74	17.89	17.09	16.34	15.64	14.98	14.36	13.79	13.24	12.73	12.25	36
37	17.76	16.99	16.27	15.59	14.95	14.35	13.79	13.26	12.76	12.29	11.85	37
38	16.77	16.08	15.44	14.83	14.25	13.71	13.20	12.72	12.26	11.83	11.42	38
39	15.78	15.18	14.60	14.06	13.54	13.05	12.59	12.16	11.75	11.35	10.98	39
40	14.80	14.26	13.75	13.27	12.82	12.38	11.97	11.58	11.21	10.85	10.52	40

Age											
41	10.03	10.33	10.65	10.98	11.33	11.69	12.07	12.48	12.90	13.35	13.82
42	9.52	9.79	10.07	10.36	10.66	10.98	11.32	11.67	12.04	12.43	12.83
43	8.98	9.22	9.46	9.72	9.98	10.26	10.55	10.85	11.17	11.50	11.85
44	8.42	8.62	8.83	9.05	9.28	9.52	9.77	10.02	10.29	10.57	10.86
45	7.83	8.00	8.18	8.37	8.56	8.76	8.97	9.18	9.41	9.64	9.88
46	7.21	7.35	7.50	7.66	7.82	7.98	8.15	8.33	8.51	8.70	8.90
47	6.56	6.67	6.80	6.92	7.05	7.18	7.32	7.46	7.61	7.76	7.91
48	5.87	5.97	6.06	6.16	6.26	6.37	6.47	6.58	6.69	6.81	6.93
49	5.16	5.23	5.30	5.37	5.45	5.53	5.61	5.69	5.77	5.86	5.94
50	4.40	4.45	4.50	4.56	4.61	4.67	4.72	4.78	4.84	4.90	4.96
51	3.61	3.64	3.68	3.71	3.75	3.78	3.82	3.86	3.89	3.93	3.97
52	2.78	2.79	2.81	2.83	2.86	2.88	2.90	2.92	2.94	2.96	2.98
53	1.90	1.91	1.92	1.93	1.93	1.94	1.95	1.96	1.97	1.98	1.99
54	0.97	0.98	0.98	0.98	0.98	0.99	0.99	0.99	0.99	1.00	1.00

Table 5   Multipliers for loss of earnings to pension age 60 (males)

Age at date of trial	\ 0.0%	0.5%	1.0%	1.5%	2.0%	2.5%	3.0%	3.5%	4.0%	4.5%	5.0%	Age at date of trial
	Multiplier calculated with allowance for population mortality and rate of return of											
16	42.62	38.33	34.63	31.43	28.64	26.20	24.07	22.20	20.55	19.09	17.79	16
17	41.64	37.54	33.99	30.91	28.22	25.86	23.79	21.97	20.36	18.93	17.66	17
18	40.67	36.76	33.35	30.39	27.79	25.51	23.51	21.74	20.17	18.78	17.54	18
19	39.70	35.97	32.71	29.86	27.36	25.16	23.22	21.50	19.98	18.62	17.40	19
20	38.74	35.17	32.06	29.33	26.92	24.80	22.92	21.26	19.77	18.45	17.26	20
21	37.77	34.38	31.40	28.78	26.47	24.43	22.61	21.00	19.56	18.27	17.12	21
22	36.80	33.58	30.74	28.23	26.01	24.05	22.30	20.74	19.34	18.09	16.96	22
23	35.83	32.77	30.07	27.67	25.55	23.66	21.97	20.46	19.11	17.90	16.80	23
24	34.87	31.96	29.39	27.11	25.07	23.26	21.64	20.18	18.87	17.69	16.63	24
25	33.90	31.15	28.70	26.53	24.59	22.85	21.29	19.89	18.62	17.48	16.45	25
26	32.92	30.33	28.01	25.94	24.09	22.43	20.93	19.58	18.37	17.26	16.26	26
27	31.95	29.50	27.31	25.34	23.58	21.99	20.56	19.27	18.10	17.03	16.07	27
28	30.98	28.67	26.60	24.74	23.06	21.55	20.18	18.94	17.82	16.79	15.86	28
29	30.00	27.84	25.88	24.12	22.53	21.09	19.79	18.60	17.52	16.54	15.64	29
30	29.03	27.00	25.16	23.50	21.99	20.63	19.39	18.25	17.22	16.28	15.41	30
31	28.06	26.15	24.43	22.87	21.44	20.15	18.97	17.89	16.91	16.00	15.17	31
32	27.08	25.31	23.69	22.22	20.88	19.66	18.54	17.52	16.58	15.72	14.92	32
33	26.11	24.45	22.95	21.57	20.31	19.16	18.10	17.13	16.24	15.42	14.66	33
34	25.13	23.60	22.19	20.91	19.73	18.64	17.65	16.73	15.88	15.10	14.38	34
35	24.16	22.74	21.43	20.24	19.13	18.12	17.18	16.32	15.52	14.78	14.09	35
36	23.19	21.88	20.67	19.55	18.53	17.58	16.70	15.89	15.14	14.44	13.79	36
37	22.22	21.01	19.90	18.87	17.91	17.03	16.21	15.45	14.74	14.08	13.47	37
38	21.25	20.14	19.12	18.17	17.28	16.47	15.70	14.99	14.33	13.71	13.14	38
39	20.28	19.27	18.33	17.46	16.65	15.89	15.18	14.52	13.91	13.33	12.79	39
40	19.31	18.39	17.54	16.74	16.00	15.30	14.65	14.04	13.46	12.93	12.42	40

Age												Age
41	18.34	17.51	16.74	16.01	15.33	14.70	14.10	13.53	13.01	12.51	12.04	41
42	17.38	16.63	15.93	15.27	14.66	14.08	13.53	13.02	12.53	12.07	11.64	42
43	16.41	15.74	15.12	14.53	13.97	13.44	12.95	12.48	12.04	11.62	11.22	43
44	15.44	14.85	14.30	13.77	13.27	12.80	12.35	11.93	11.53	11.15	10.78	44
45	14.48	13.96	13.47	13.00	12.56	12.14	11.74	11.36	10.99	10.65	10.32	45
46	13.52	13.06	12.63	12.22	11.83	11.46	11.10	10.77	10.44	10.14	9.84	46
47	12.56	12.16	11.79	11.43	11.09	10.77	10.45	10.16	9.87	9.60	9.34	47
48	11.60	11.26	10.94	10.63	10.34	10.06	9.79	9.53	9.28	9.04	8.81	48
49	10.64	10.36	10.08	9.82	9.57	9.33	9.10	8.88	8.67	8.46	8.26	49
50	9.68	9.45	9.22	9.00	8.79	8.59	8.40	8.21	8.03	7.85	7.68	50
51	8.72	8.53	8.35	8.17	8.00	7.83	7.67	7.52	7.37	7.22	7.08	51
52	7.77	7.61	7.47	7.33	7.19	7.05	6.93	6.80	6.68	6.56	6.44	52
53	6.81	6.69	6.58	6.47	6.36	6.26	6.16	6.06	5.96	5.87	5.78	53
54	5.85	5.76	5.68	5.60	5.52	5.44	5.36	5.29	5.22	5.15	5.08	54
55	4.89	4.83	4.77	4.71	4.65	4.60	4.55	4.49	4.44	4.39	4.34	55
56	3.92	3.88	3.85	3.81	3.77	3.74	3.70	3.67	3.63	3.60	3.57	56
57	2.95	2.93	2.91	2.89	2.87	2.85	2.83	2.81	2.79	2.77	2.75	57
58	1.98	1.97	1.96	1.95	1.94	1.93	1.92	1.91	1.90	1.89	1.88	58
59	0.99	0.99	0.99	0.99	0.98	0.98	0.98	0.98	0.97	0.97	0.97	59

Table 6   Multipliers for loss of earnings to pension age 60 (females)

Multiplier calculated with allowance for population mortality and rate of return of

Age at date of trial	0.0%	0.5%	1.0%	1.5%	2.0%	2.5%	3.0%	3.5%	4.0%	4.5%	5.0%	Age at date of trial
16	43.23	38.86	35.08	31.81	28.97	26.50	24.33	22.42	20.74	19.26	17.94	16
17	42.24	38.06	34.44	31.29	28.55	26.15	24.05	22.19	20.56	19.11	17.82	17
18	41.26	37.26	33.79	30.76	28.12	25.80	23.76	21.96	20.37	18.95	17.69	18
19	40.27	36.46	33.13	30.23	27.68	25.44	23.47	21.72	20.17	18.79	17.55	19
20	39.28	35.65	32.47	29.68	27.23	25.07	23.16	21.47	19.96	18.62	17.41	20
21	38.29	34.83	31.80	29.13	26.78	24.70	22.85	21.21	19.75	18.44	17.26	21
22	37.31	34.02	31.12	28.57	26.31	24.31	22.53	20.94	19.52	18.25	17.11	22
23	36.32	33.19	30.44	28.00	25.84	23.91	22.20	20.66	19.29	18.06	16.94	23
24	35.33	32.37	29.75	27.42	25.35	23.51	21.86	20.38	19.05	17.85	16.77	24
25	34.34	31.54	29.05	26.83	24.86	23.09	21.50	20.08	18.80	17.64	16.59	25
26	33.35	30.70	28.35	26.24	24.35	22.66	21.14	19.77	18.53	17.42	16.40	26
27	32.36	29.87	27.63	25.63	23.84	22.22	20.77	19.45	18.26	17.18	16.20	27
28	31.38	29.02	26.91	25.02	23.31	21.77	20.38	19.12	17.98	16.94	15.99	28
29	30.39	28.18	26.19	24.40	22.78	21.31	19.99	18.78	17.69	16.69	15.77	29
30	29.40	27.33	25.46	23.77	22.23	20.84	19.58	18.43	17.38	16.42	15.55	30
31	28.41	26.47	24.72	23.12	21.68	20.36	19.16	18.07	17.06	16.15	15.30	31
32	27.43	25.61	23.97	22.47	21.11	19.87	18.73	17.69	16.73	15.86	15.05	32
33	26.44	24.75	23.22	21.82	20.53	19.36	18.29	17.30	16.39	15.56	14.79	33
34	25.45	23.89	22.46	21.15	19.95	18.84	17.83	16.90	16.04	15.24	14.51	34
35	24.47	23.02	21.69	20.47	19.35	18.32	17.36	16.48	15.67	14.92	14.22	35
36	23.49	22.15	20.92	19.78	18.74	17.77	16.88	16.05	15.29	14.58	13.92	36
37	22.50	21.27	20.14	19.09	18.12	17.22	16.38	15.61	14.89	14.22	13.60	37
38	21.52	20.39	19.35	18.38	17.48	16.65	15.87	15.15	14.48	13.85	13.27	38
39	20.54	19.51	18.56	17.67	16.84	16.07	15.35	14.68	14.05	13.47	12.92	39
40	19.56	18.63	17.75	16.94	16.18	15.47	14.81	14.19	13.61	13.06	12.55	40

Age												Age
41	18.58	17.74	16.95	16.21	15.51	14.86	14.26	13.68	13.15	12.64	12.17	41
42	17.60	16.84	16.13	15.46	14.83	14.24	13.69	13.16	12.67	12.20	11.76	42
43	16.62	15.95	15.31	14.70	14.14	13.60	13.10	12.62	12.17	11.75	11.34	43
44	15.65	15.04	14.48	13.94	13.43	12.95	12.49	12.06	11.66	11.27	10.90	44
45	14.67	14.14	13.64	13.16	12.71	12.28	11.87	11.49	11.12	10.77	10.44	45
46	13.70	13.23	12.79	12.37	11.98	11.60	11.24	10.89	10.56	10.25	9.95	46
47	12.72	12.32	11.94	11.58	11.23	10.90	10.58	10.28	9.99	9.71	9.45	47
48	11.75	11.41	11.08	10.77	10.47	10.18	9.91	9.64	9.39	9.15	8.91	48
49	10.78	10.49	10.21	9.95	9.69	9.45	9.21	8.99	8.77	8.56	8.36	49
50	9.80	9.56	9.33	9.11	8.90	8.69	8.50	8.31	8.12	7.94	7.77	50
51	8.83	8.64	8.45	8.27	8.09	7.92	7.76	7.60	7.45	7.30	7.16	51
52	7.86	7.70	7.56	7.41	7.27	7.14	7.00	6.88	6.75	6.63	6.51	52
53	6.88	6.77	6.65	6.54	6.43	6.33	6.22	6.12	6.03	5.93	5.84	53
54	5.91	5.82	5.74	5.65	5.57	5.49	5.42	5.34	5.27	5.20	5.13	54
55	4.93	4.87	4.81	4.75	4.70	4.64	4.59	4.53	4.48	4.43	4.38	55
56	3.95	3.91	3.88	3.84	3.80	3.77	3.73	3.69	3.66	3.63	3.59	56
57	2.97	2.95	2.93	2.91	2.89	2.86	2.84	2.82	2.80	2.78	2.77	57
58	1.99	1.98	1.97	1.96	1.95	1.94	1.93	1.92	1.91	1.90	1.89	58
59	1.00	0.99	0.99	0.99	0.99	0.98	0.98	0.98	0.98	0.97	0.97	59

Table 7   Multipliers for loss of earnings to pension age 65 (males)

Multiplier calculated with allowance for population mortality and rate of return of

Age at date of trial	0.0%	0.5%	1.0%	1.5%	2.0%	2.5%	3.0%	3.5%	4.0%	4.5%	5.0%	Age at date of trial
16	46.83	41.68	37.29	33.54	30.32	27.54	25.14	23.05	21.23	19.63	18.23	16
17	45.86	40.90	36.68	33.05	29.93	27.23	24.89	22.86	21.07	19.51	18.12	17
18	44.89	40.14	36.07	32.56	29.54	26.92	24.65	22.66	20.91	19.38	18.02	18
19	43.93	39.37	35.45	32.07	29.15	26.61	24.39	22.45	20.75	19.24	17.91	19
20	42.97	38.60	34.83	31.57	28.75	26.28	24.13	22.24	20.57	19.10	17.80	20
21	42.00	37.82	34.20	31.07	28.34	25.95	23.86	22.02	20.39	18.96	17.68	21
22	41.04	37.04	33.57	30.55	27.92	25.61	23.58	21.79	20.21	18.80	17.55	22
23	40.07	36.25	32.93	30.03	27.49	25.26	23.29	21.56	20.01	18.64	17.42	23
24	39.11	35.46	32.28	29.50	27.05	24.90	23.00	21.31	19.81	18.48	17.28	24
25	38.14	34.67	31.63	28.96	26.61	24.53	22.69	21.06	19.60	18.30	17.14	25
26	37.18	33.87	30.97	28.41	26.15	24.15	22.38	20.80	19.39	18.12	16.98	26
27	36.21	33.07	30.30	27.85	25.69	23.77	22.05	20.53	19.16	17.93	16.82	27
28	35.24	32.26	29.62	27.29	25.22	23.37	21.72	20.24	18.92	17.73	16.65	28
29	34.27	31.44	28.94	26.71	24.73	22.96	21.38	19.95	18.67	17.52	16.48	29
30	33.30	30.63	28.25	26.13	24.24	22.54	21.02	19.65	18.42	17.30	16.29	30
31	32.33	29.80	27.55	25.54	23.73	22.11	20.66	19.34	18.15	17.07	16.10	31
32	31.36	28.98	26.85	24.94	23.22	21.68	20.28	19.02	17.87	16.84	15.89	32
33	30.39	28.15	26.14	24.33	22.70	21.23	19.89	18.69	17.59	16.59	15.68	33
34	29.42	27.31	25.42	23.71	22.17	20.77	19.50	18.34	17.29	16.33	15.45	34
35	28.45	26.48	24.70	23.08	21.62	20.29	19.09	17.98	16.98	16.06	15.22	35
36	27.48	25.64	23.97	22.45	21.07	19.81	18.67	17.62	16.66	15.78	14.97	36
37	26.51	24.79	23.23	21.81	20.51	19.32	18.24	17.24	16.33	15.49	14.71	37
38	25.55	23.95	22.49	21.16	19.94	18.82	17.79	16.85	15.98	15.18	14.44	38
39	24.59	23.10	21.74	20.50	19.35	18.30	17.34	16.45	15.63	14.87	14.16	39
40	23.63	22.25	20.99	19.83	18.76	17.78	16.87	16.03	15.26	14.54	13.87	40

Age												Age
41	22.67	21.40	20.23	19.15	18.16	17.24	16.39	15.60	14.87	14.19	13.56	41
42	21.71	20.54	19.47	18.47	17.55	16.69	15.90	15.16	14.48	13.84	13.24	42
43	20.75	19.68	18.69	17.78	16.92	16.13	15.39	14.71	14.06	13.47	12.91	43
44	19.79	18.82	17.92	17.07	16.29	15.56	14.87	14.24	13.64	13.08	12.56	44
45	18.84	17.96	17.13	16.36	15.64	14.97	14.34	13.75	13.20	12.68	12.19	45
46	17.89	17.09	16.34	15.64	14.99	14.37	13.79	13.25	12.74	12.26	11.81	46
47	16.94	16.22	15.55	14.92	14.32	13.76	13.23	12.74	12.27	11.83	11.41	47
48	16.00	15.35	14.75	14.18	13.64	13.14	12.66	12.21	11.78	11.37	10.99	48
49	15.05	14.48	13.95	13.44	12.96	12.50	12.07	11.66	11.27	10.91	10.56	49
50	14.11	13.61	13.14	12.69	12.26	11.85	11.47	11.10	10.75	10.42	10.10	50
51	13.18	12.74	12.32	11.93	11.55	11.19	10.85	10.52	10.21	9.92	9.63	51
52	12.24	11.87	11.50	11.16	10.83	10.52	10.22	9.93	9.65	9.39	9.14	52
53	11.31	10.99	10.68	10.38	10.10	9.83	9.56	9.31	9.07	8.84	8.62	53
54	10.38	10.11	9.85	9.60	9.35	9.12	8.90	8.68	8.48	8.28	8.08	54
55	9.45	9.23	9.01	8.80	8.60	8.40	8.21	8.03	7.85	7.68	7.52	55
56	8.53	8.34	8.16	7.99	7.82	7.66	7.51	7.36	7.21	7.07	6.93	56
57	7.60	7.45	7.31	7.17	7.04	6.91	6.78	6.66	6.54	6.43	6.31	57
58	6.67	6.56	6.45	6.34	6.23	6.13	6.04	5.94	5.85	5.76	5.67	58
59	5.74	5.65	5.57	5.49	5.42	5.34	5.27	5.19	5.12	5.05	4.99	59
60	4.80	4.74	4.69	4.63	4.58	4.52	4.47	4.42	4.37	4.32	4.27	60
61	3.86	3.83	3.79	3.75	3.72	3.68	3.65	3.61	3.58	3.55	3.51	61
62	2.92	2.90	2.37	2.85	2.83	2.81	2.79	2.77	2.75	2.73	2.72	62
63	1.96	1.95	1.94	1.93	1.92	1.91	1.90	1.89	1.89	1.88	1.87	63
64	0.99	0.99	0.98	0.98	0.98	0.98	0.97	0.97	0.97	0.97	0.97	64

Table 8 Multipliers for loss of earnings to pension age 65 (females)

Age at date of trial	Multiplier calculated with allowance for population mortality and rate of return of											Age at date of trial
	0.0%	0.5%	1.0%	1.5%	2.0%	2.5%	3.0%	3.5%	4.0%	4.5%	5.0%	
16	47.75	42.44	37.93	34.08	30.78	27.93	25.47	23.34	21.47	19.84	18.41	16
17	46.77	41.67	37.32	33.59	30.39	27.62	25.23	23.14	21.32	19.72	18.31	17
18	45.78	40.88	36.70	33.10	30.00	27.31	24.98	22.94	21.16	19.59	18.21	18
19	44.79	40.10	36.07	32.60	29.60	26.99	24.72	22.73	20.99	19.46	18.10	19
20	43.81	39.31	35.44	32.09	29.19	26.66	24.45	22.52	20.82	19.31	17.98	20
21	42.82	38.52	34.80	31.57	28.77	26.32	24.18	22.30	20.64	19.17	17.86	21
22	41.84	37.72	34.15	31.05	28.34	25.98	23.90	22.07	20.45	19.01	17.74	22
23	40.85	36.92	33.50	30.52	27.91	25.62	23.61	21.83	20.25	18.85	17.61	23
24	39.86	36.11	32.84	29.98	27.47	25.26	23.31	21.58	20.05	18.69	17.47	24
25	38.88	35.30	32.17	29.43	27.02	24.89	23.00	21.33	19.84	18.51	17.32	25
26	37.89	34.49	31.50	28.87	26.56	24.51	22.69	21.07	19.62	18.33	17.17	26
27	36.90	33.67	30.82	28.31	26.09	24.11	22.36	20.79	19.39	18.14	17.01	27
28	35.91	32.85	30.14	27.74	25.61	23.71	22.02	20.51	19.16	17.94	16.84	28
29	34.93	32.02	29.44	27.16	25.12	23.30	21.68	20.22	18.91	17.73	16.66	29
30	33.94	31.19	28.74	26.57	24.62	22.88	21.32	19.92	18.65	17.51	16.48	30
31	32.96	30.36	28.04	25.97	24.12	22.45	20.96	19.61	18.39	17.29	16.29	31
32	31.97	29.52	27.33	25.36	23.60	22.01	20.58	19.28	18.11	17.05	16.08	32
33	30.99	28.68	26.61	24.75	23.07	21.56	20.19	18.95	17.83	16.80	15.87	33
34	30.01	27.84	25.89	24.13	22.54	21.10	19.79	18.61	17.53	16.55	15.65	34
35	29.02	26.99	25.16	23.50	21.99	20.63	19.39	18.26	17.22	16.28	15.42	35
36	28.04	26.14	24.42	22.86	21.44	20.14	18.97	17.89	16.90	16.00	15.17	36
37	27.06	25.29	23.68	22.21	20.87	19.65	18.53	17.51	16.57	15.71	14.92	37
38	26.09	24.43	22.93	21.55	20.30	19.15	18.09	17.12	16.23	15.41	14.65	38
39	25.11	23.58	22.17	20.89	19.71	18.63	17.63	16.72	15.87	15.09	14.37	39
40	24.13	22.71	21.41	20.22	19.11	18.10	17.17	16.30	15.50	14.77	14.08	40

Age												Age
41	23.16	21.85	20.64	19.53	18.51	17.56	16.68	15.87	15.12	14.42	13.78	41
42	22.19	20.98	19.87	18.84	17.89	17.01	16.19	15.43	14.72	14.07	13.46	42
43	21.21	20.11	19.09	18.14	17.26	16.44	15.68	14.97	14.31	13.70	13.12	43
44	20.24	19.24	18.30	17.43	16.62	15.86	15.16	14.50	13.89	13.31	12.77	44
45	19.27	18.36	17.51	16.71	15.97	15.27	14.62	14.01	13.44	12.91	12.41	45
46	18.31	17.48	16.71	15.98	15.31	14.67	14.07	13.51	12.99	12.49	12.02	46
47	17.34	16.60	15.90	15.25	14.63	14.05	13.51	12.99	12.51	12.05	11.62	47
48	16.38	15.72	15.09	14.50	13.95	13.42	12.93	12.46	12.02	11.60	11.21	48
49	15.42	14.83	14.27	13.75	13.25	12.78	12.33	11.91	11.51	11.13	10.77	49
50	14.46	13.94	13.45	12.98	12.54	12.12	11.72	11.34	10.98	10.64	10.31	50
51	13.50	13.05	12.61	12.20	11.81	11.44	11.09	10.75	10.43	10.12	9.83	51
52	12.54	12.15	11.78	11.42	11.08	10.75	10.44	10.15	9.86	9.59	9.33	52
53	11.58	11.25	10.93	10.62	10.33	10.05	9.78	9.52	9.27	9.03	8.81	53
54	10.63	10.35	10.07	9.81	9.56	9.32	9.09	8.87	8.66	8.45	8.25	54
55	9.67	9.44	9.21	8.99	8.79	8.58	8.39	8.20	8.02	7.85	7.68	55
56	8.72	8.52	8.34	8.16	7.99	7.83	7.66	7.51	7.36	7.21	7.07	56
57	7.76	7.61	7.46	7.32	7.18	7.05	6.92	6.79	6.67	6.55	6.44	57
58	6.80	6.69	6.57	6.46	6.36	6.25	6.15	6.05	5.96	5.86	5.77	58
59	5.84	5.76	5.67	5.59	5.51	5.44	5.36	5.29	5.21	5.14	5.07	59
60	4.88	4.82	4.77	4.71	4.65	4.60	4.54	4.49	4.44	4.39	4.34	60
61	3.92	3.88	3.84	3.81	3.77	3.73	3.70	3.66	3.63	3.60	3.56	61
62	2.95	2.93	2.91	2.89	2.87	2.85	2.83	2.81	2.79	2.77	2.75	62
63	1.98	1.97	1.96	1.95	1.94	1.93	1.92	1.91	1.90	1.89	1.88	63
64	0.99	0.99	0.99	0.99	0.98	0.98	0.98	0.98	0.97	0.97	0.97	64

Table 9 Multipliers for loss of earnings to pension age 70 (males)

Age at date of trial	Multiplier calculated with allowance for population mortality and rate of return of											Age at date of trial
	0.0%	0.5%	1.0%	1.5%	2.0%	2.5%	3.0%	3.5%	4.0%	4.5%	5.0%	
16	50.58	44.57	39.53	35.28	31.67	28.60	25.96	23.69	21.73	20.02	18.53	16
17	49.60	43.82	38.94	34.82	31.31	28.31	25.74	23.52	21.59	19.91	18.44	17
18	48.64	43.07	38.36	34.36	30.95	28.03	25.52	23.34	21.45	19.80	18.36	18
19	47.68	42.32	37.77	33.90	30.59	27.74	25.29	23.16	21.31	19.69	18.26	19
20	46.72	41.56	37.17	33.43	30.21	27.45	25.05	22.97	21.16	19.57	18.17	20
21	45.76	40.80	36.57	32.95	29.83	27.14	24.81	22.78	21.00	19.44	18.07	21
22	44.80	40.04	35.96	32.46	29.45	26.83	24.56	22.58	20.84	19.31	17.96	22
23	43.84	39.27	35.35	31.97	29.05	26.52	24.31	22.37	20.67	19.18	17.85	23
24	42.88	38.50	34.73	31.47	28.65	26.19	24.04	22.16	20.50	19.04	17.74	24
25	41.92	37.72	34.10	30.97	28.24	25.86	23.77	21.94	20.32	18.89	17.61	25
26	40.95	36.94	33.47	30.45	27.82	25.51	23.49	21.71	20.13	18.73	17.49	26
27	39.98	36.15	32.83	29.92	27.39	25.16	23.20	21.47	19.93	18.57	17.35	27
28	39.02	35.36	32.18	29.39	26.95	24.80	22.90	21.22	19.73	18.40	17.21	28
29	38.05	34.57	31.52	28.85	26.50	24.43	22.59	20.96	19.51	18.22	17.06	29
30	37.09	33.77	30.86	28.30	26.04	24.05	22.28	20.70	19.29	18.03	16.90	30
31	36.12	32.97	30.19	27.74	25.58	23.66	21.95	20.42	19.06	17.84	16.74	31
32	35.15	32.16	29.52	27.18	25.10	23.26	21.61	20.14	18.82	17.64	16.57	32
33	34.19	31.35	28.83	26.60	24.62	22.85	21.27	19.85	18.57	17.42	16.39	33
34	33.22	30.53	28.15	26.02	24.13	22.43	20.91	19.55	18.32	17.20	16.20	34
35	32.25	29.71	27.45	25.43	23.63	22.00	20.55	19.23	18.05	16.97	16.00	35
36	31.29	28.90	26.75	24.84	23.12	21.57	20.17	18.91	17.77	16.74	15.79	36
37	30.33	28.07	26.05	24.23	22.60	21.12	19.79	18.58	17.48	16.49	15.58	37
38	29.37	27.25	25.34	23.62	22.07	20.67	19.40	18.24	17.19	16.23	15.36	38
39	28.41	26.42	24.63	23.00	21.54	20.20	18.99	17.89	16.88	15.96	15.12	39
40	27.46	25.60	23.91	22.38	20.99	19.73	18.58	17.53	16.57	15.69	14.88	40

Age												Age
41	14.62	15.40	16.24	17.15	18.15	19.24	20.44	21.75	23.18	24.76	26.51	41
42	14.36	15.10	15.90	16.77	17.71	18.75	19.87	21.10	22.45	23.93	25.55	42
43	14.08	14.78	15.55	16.37	17.27	18.24	19.30	20.46	21.72	23.10	24.61	43
44	13.79	14.46	15.18	15.96	16.81	17.72	18.72	19.80	20.98	22.26	23.66	44
45	13.49	14.12	14.81	15.54	16.34	17.20	18.13	19.14	20.23	21.42	22.71	45
46	13.17	13.77	14.42	15.11	15.86	16.66	17.53	18.47	19.48	20.58	21.77	46
47	12.85	13.41	14.02	14.67	15.36	16.11	16.92	17.79	18.73	19.74	20.84	47
48	12.51	13.04	13.61	14.21	14.86	15.56	16.30	17.11	17.97	18.90	19.90	48
49	12.16	12.65	13.18	13.74	14.35	14.99	15.68	16.42	17.21	18.06	18.98	49
50	11.79	12.25	12.74	13.27	13.82	14.42	15.05	15.73	16.45	17.22	18.05	50
51	11.41	11.84	12.29	12.77	13.29	13.83	14.41	15.03	15.68	16.39	17.14	51
52	11.02	11.41	11.83	12.27	12.74	13.23	13.76	14.32	14.92	15.55	16.22	52
53	10.61	10.97	11.35	11.75	12.18	12.63	13.11	13.61	14.14	14.71	15.31	53
54	10.18	10.51	10.86	11.22	11.61	12.01	12.44	12.89	13.37	13.87	14.41	54
55	9.74	10.04	10.35	10.68	11.02	11.39	11.77	12.17	12.59	13.04	13.51	55
56	9.28	9.54	9.82	10.12	10.42	10.75	11.08	11.44	11.81	12.20	12.61	56
57	8.80	9.04	9.28	9.54	9.81	10.10	10.39	10.70	11.03	11.37	11.72	57
58	8.30	8.51	8.73	8.95	9.19	9.44	9.69	9.96	10.24	10.53	10.83	58
59	7.78	7.97	8.15	8.35	8.55	8.76	8.98	9.21	9.45	9.69	9.95	59
60	7.25	7.40	7.56	7.73	7.90	8.08	8.26	8.45	8.65	8.86	9.07	60
61	6.68	6.81	6.95	7.08	7.23	7.37	7.53	7.68	7.85	8.02	8.19	61
62	6.10	6.20	6.31	6.42	6.54	6.66	6.78	6.91	7.04	7.17	7.31	62
63	5.48	5.56	5.65	5.74	5.83	5.92	6.02	6.12	6.22	6.33	6.43	63
64	4.83	4.90	4.96	5.03	5.10	5.17	5.24	5.32	5.39	5.47	5.55	64
65	4.15	4.20	4.25	4.30	4.35	4.40	4.45	4.50	4.55	4.61	4.67	65
66	3.43	3.46	3.49	3.53	3.56	3.59	3.63	3.66	3.70	3.73	3.77	66
67	2.66	2.68	2.70	2.72	2.74	2.76	2.78	2.80	2.82	2.84	2.86	67
68	1.84	1.85	1.86	1.87	1.88	1.89	1.90	1.91	1.91	1.92	1.93	68
69	0.96	0.96	0.96	0.97	0.97	0.97	0.97	0.97	0.98	0.98	0.98	69

Table 10   Multipliers for loss of earnings to pension age 70 (females)

Age at date of trial	Multiplier calculated with allowance for population mortality and rate of return of											Age at date of trial
	0.0%	0.5%	1.0%	1.5%	2.0%	2.5%	3.0%	3.5%	4.0%	4.5%	5.0%	
16	51.98	45.71	40.46	36.04	32.30	29.12	26.40	24.06	22.04	20.28	18.75	16
17	50.99	44.95	39.87	35.59	31.95	28.84	26.18	23.89	21.90	20.18	18.67	17
18	50.01	44.19	39.28	35.12	31.58	28.56	25.96	23.71	21.77	20.07	18.59	18
19	49.03	43.42	38.68	34.65	31.22	28.27	25.73	23.53	21.62	19.96	18.50	19
20	48.04	42.65	38.08	34.18	30.84	27.97	25.50	23.35	21.48	19.84	18.40	20
21	47.06	41.87	37.46	33.69	30.46	27.67	25.25	23.16	21.32	19.72	18.30	21
22	46.07	41.09	36.84	33.20	30.07	27.36	25.00	22.96	21.16	19.59	18.20	22
23	45.09	40.31	36.22	32.70	29.67	27.04	24.75	22.75	21.00	19.45	18.09	23
24	44.10	39.52	35.59	32.20	29.26	26.71	24.48	22.54	20.82	19.31	17.98	24
25	43.11	38.73	34.95	31.68	28.85	26.37	24.21	22.31	20.64	19.17	17.86	25
26	42.13	37.93	34.31	31.16	28.42	26.03	23.93	22.09	20.46	19.01	17.73	26
27	41.14	37.13	33.66	30.63	27.99	25.68	23.64	21.85	20.26	18.85	17.60	27
28	40.16	36.33	33.00	30.10	27.55	25.32	23.35	21.60	20.06	18.69	17.46	28
29	39.17	35.52	32.34	29.55	27.10	24.95	23.04	21.35	19.85	18.51	17.32	29
30	38.19	34.71	31.67	29.00	26.65	24.57	22.73	21.09	19.63	18.33	17.16	30
31	37.21	33.90	31.00	28.44	26.18	24.18	22.40	20.82	19.41	18.14	17.00	31
32	36.22	33.08	30.32	27.87	25.71	23.78	22.07	20.54	19.17	17.94	16.84	32
33	35.24	32.26	29.63	27.30	25.22	23.38	21.73	20.25	18.93	17.74	16.66	33
34	34.26	31.44	28.94	26.71	24.73	22.96	21.38	19.96	18.68	17.52	16.48	34
35	33.28	30.61	28.24	26.12	24.23	22.54	21.02	19.65	18.42	17.30	16.29	35
36	32.30	29.78	27.54	25.53	23.72	22.11	20.65	19.33	18.15	17.07	16.09	36
37	31.33	28.95	26.83	24.92	23.21	21.66	20.27	19.01	17.87	16.83	15.88	37
38	30.35	28.12	26.11	24.31	22.68	21.21	19.88	18.67	17.58	16.58	15.67	38
39	29.38	27.28	25.39	23.69	22.14	20.75	19.48	18.33	17.27	16.32	15.44	39
40	28.41	26.44	24.67	23.06	21.60	20.27	19.07	17.97	16.96	16.04	15.20	40

Age												Age
41	14.95	15.76	16.64	17.60	18.64	19.79	21.04	22.42	23.93	25.60	27.44	41
42	14.70	15.47	16.31	17.22	18.21	19.29	20.48	21.77	23.20	24.75	26.47	42
43	14.42	15.16	15.96	16.82	17.77	18.79	19.90	21.12	22.45	23.91	25.50	43
44	14.14	14.84	15.60	16.42	17.31	18.27	19.32	20.46	21.70	23.06	24.54	44
45	13.85	14.51	15.23	16.00	16.84	17.75	18.73	19.79	20.95	22.21	23.58	45
46	13.54	14.17	14.85	15.57	16.36	17.21	18.12	19.12	20.19	21.35	22.62	46
47	13.22	13.81	14.45	15.13	15.87	16.66	17.51	18.43	19.43	20.50	21.66	47
48	12.88	13.44	14.04	14.68	15.36	16.10	16.89	17.74	18.66	19.64	20.71	48
49	12.54	13.06	13.62	14.21	14.85	15.53	16.26	17.04	17.88	18.79	19.76	49
50	12.17	12.66	13.18	13.73	14.32	14.95	15.62	16.34	17.10	17.93	18.81	50
51	11.79	12.24	12.72	13.23	13.77	14.35	14.97	15.62	16.32	17.07	17.86	51
52	11.39	11.81	12.25	12.72	13.22	13.74	14.30	14.90	15.53	16.20	16.92	52
53	10.98	11.36	11.77	12.19	12.65	13.12	13.63	14.17	14.73	15.34	15.98	53
54	10.55	10.90	11.26	11.65	12.06	12.49	12.94	13.43	13.93	14.47	15.04	54
55	10.10	10.41	10.74	11.09	11.46	11.84	12.25	12.68	13.13	13.60	14.10	55
56	9.62	9.91	10.20	10.51	10.84	11.18	11.54	11.92	12.31	12.73	13.17	56
57	9.13	9.38	9.65	9.92	10.21	10.51	10.82	11.15	11.49	11.86	12.23	57
58	8.62	8.84	9.07	9.31	9.56	9.82	10.09	10.37	10.67	10.98	11.30	58
59	8.08	8.27	8.47	8.68	8.89	9.11	9.35	9.59	9.84	10.10	10.38	59
60	7.52	7.68	7.85	8.03	8.21	8.40	8.59	8.79	9.00	9.22	9.45	60
61	6.93	7.07	7.21	7.35	7.51	7.66	7.82	7.99	8.16	8.34	8.52	61
62	6.31	6.43	6.54	6.66	6.78	6.91	7.04	7.17	7.31	7.45	7.60	62
63	5.67	5.76	5.85	5.94	6.04	6.14	6.24	6.34	6.45	6.56	6.67	63
64	4.99	5.06	5.13	5.20	5.27	5.34	5.42	5.50	5.58	5.66	5.74	64
65	4.27	4.32	4.37	4.42	4.47	4.53	4.58	4.64	4.69	4.75	4.81	65
66	3.52	3.55	3.58	3.62	3.65	3.69	3.72	3.76	3.79	3.83	3.87	66
67	2.72	2.74	2.76	2.78	2.80	2.82	2.84	2.86	2.88	2.90	2.92	67
68	1.87	1.88	1.89	1.90	1.91	1.92	1.92	1.93	1.94	1.95	1.96	68
69	0.97	0.97	0.97	0.97	0.98	0.98	0.98	0.98	0.99	0.99	0.99	69

Table 11   Multipliers for loss of pension commencing age 55 (males)

Age at date of trial	Multiplier calculated with allowance for population mortality and rate of return of											Age at date of trial
	0.0%	0.5%	1.0%	1.5%	2.0%	2.5%	3.0%	3.5%	4.0%	4.5%	5.0%	
0	19.94	14.21	10.17	7.30	5.26	3.80	2.76	2.00	1.46	1.07	0.79	0
1	20.10	14.40	10.35	7.47	5.41	3.93	2.86	2.09	1.53	1.13	0.83	1
2	20.11	14.48	10.46	7.59	5.52	4.03	2.95	2.17	1.60	1.18	0.87	2
3	20.12	14.56	10.57	7.70	5.63	4.13	3.04	2.24	1.66	1.23	0.92	3
4	20.13	14.63	10.68	7.82	5.74	4.23	3.13	2.32	1.73	1.29	0.96	4
5	20.13	14.71	10.79	7.94	5.86	4.34	3.23	2.40	1.80	1.35	1.01	5
6	20.14	14.79	10.90	8.06	5.98	4.45	3.32	2.49	1.87	1.41	1.06	6
7	20.14	14.87	11.01	8.18	6.10	4.56	3.42	2.58	1.94	1.47	1.12	7
8	20.14	14.94	11.12	8.31	6.22	4.68	3.53	2.67	2.02	1.54	1.17	8
9	20.15	15.02	11.24	8.43	6.35	4.80	3.63	2.76	2.10	1.61	1.23	9
10	20.15	15.10	11.35	8.56	6.48	4.92	3.74	2.86	2.19	1.68	1.29	10
11	20.15	15.18	11.47	8.69	6.61	5.04	3.86	2.96	2.28	1.76	1.36	11
12	20.16	15.25	11.58	8.82	6.74	5.17	3.97	3.06	2.37	1.84	1.43	12
13	20.16	15.33	11.70	8.96	6.88	5.30	4.09	3.17	2.46	1.92	1.50	13
14	20.17	15.41	11.82	9.09	7.02	5.43	4.22	3.28	2.56	2.00	1.57	14
15	20.17	15.50	11.94	9.23	7.16	5.57	4.34	3.40	2.66	2.10	1.65	15
16	20.18	15.58	12.07	9.37	7.31	5.71	4.48	3.52	2.77	2.19	1.74	16
17	20.19	15.67	12.19	9.52	7.46	5.86	4.61	3.64	2.88	2.29	1.82	17
18	20.21	15.76	12.32	9.67	7.61	6.01	4.75	3.77	3.00	2.40	1.92	18
19	20.22	15.85	12.46	9.82	7.77	6.16	4.90	3.91	3.13	2.51	2.01	19
20	20.24	15.94	12.59	9.98	7.93	6.32	5.05	4.05	3.25	2.62	2.12	20
21	20.26	16.03	12.73	10.14	8.10	6.49	5.21	4.19	3.39	2.74	2.22	21
22	20.27	16.13	12.87	10.30	8.27	6.65	5.37	4.34	3.52	2.87	2.34	22
23	20.29	16.22	13.01	10.46	8.44	6.83	5.54	4.50	3.67	3.00	2.46	23
24	20.31	16.32	13.15	10.63	8.62	7.00	5.71	4.66	3.82	3.14	2.58	24

25	2.71	3.28	3.98	4.83	5.88	7.18	8.80	10.80	13.29	16.41	20.33	25
26	2.85	3.43	4.14	5.00	6.06	7.37	8.98	10.97	13.44	16.51	20.35	26
27	3.00	3.59	4.31	5.18	6.25	7.56	9.17	11.14	13.58	16.61	20.36	27
28	3.15	3.75	4.48	5.37	6.44	7.76	9.36	11.32	13.73	16.70	20.38	28
29	3.31	3.92	4.67	5.56	6.64	7.96	9.55	11.50	13.88	16.80	20.40	29
30	3.48	4.10	4.86	5.76	6.85	8.16	9.75	11.68	14.03	16.90	20.42	30
31	3.65	4.29	5.06	5.97	7.06	8.37	9.96	11.87	14.19	17.00	20.44	31
32	3.84	4.49	5.26	6.18	7.28	8.59	10.17	12.06	14.34	17.10	20.45	32
33	4.04	4.70	5.48	6.41	7.51	8.82	10.38	12.25	14.50	17.21	20.47	33
34	4.24	4.91	5.70	6.64	7.74	9.04	10.60	12.45	14.66	17.31	20.49	34
35	4.46	5.14	5.94	6.88	7.98	9.28	10.82	12.65	14.82	17.41	20.52	35
36	4.69	5.38	6.18	7.13	8.23	9.52	11.05	12.85	14.99	17.52	20.54	36
37	4.93	5.63	6.44	7.38	8.49	9.77	11.29	13.06	15.16	17.63	20.57	37
38	5.18	5.89	6.71	7.65	8.75	10.03	11.53	13.28	15.33	17.74	20.60	38
39	5.45	6.16	6.98	7.93	9.03	10.30	11.77	13.49	15.50	17.86	20.63	39
40	5.73	6.45	7.28	8.22	9.31	10.57	12.03	13.72	15.68	17.98	20.66	40
41	6.03	6.75	7.58	8.53	9.61	10.86	12.29	13.95	15.87	18.10	20.69	41
42	6.34	7.07	7.90	8.84	9.92	11.15	12.56	14.18	16.06	18.22	20.73	42
43	6.67	7.40	8.23	9.17	10.24	11.45	12.84	14.43	16.25	18.35	20.78	43
44	7.02	7.75	8.58	9.51	10.57	11.76	13.12	14.67	16.45	18.48	20.82	44
45	7.39	8.12	8.94	9.87	10.91	12.09	13.42	14.93	16.55	18.62	20.87	45
46	7.78	8.51	9.33	10.24	11.27	12.42	13.72	15.20	16.87	18.76	20.93	46
47	8.19	8.92	9.73	10.63	11.64	12.77	14.04	15.47	17.08	18.91	20.99	47
48	8.63	9.35	10.15	11.04	12.03	13.13	14.37	15.75	17.31	19.07	21.06	48
49	9.09	9.81	10.60	11.47	12.43	13.51	14.71	16.05	17.55	19.24	21.14	49
50	9.59	10.29	11.06	11.92	12.86	13.91	15.07	16.36	17.80	19.41	21.23	50
51	10.12	10.80	11.56	12.39	13.31	14.32	15.44	16.68	18.06	19.60	21.32	51
52	10.68	11.35	12.09	12.89	13.78	14.75	15.83	17.02	18.34	19.80	21.44	52
53	11.28	11.93	12.64	13.42	14.27	15.21	16.24	17.38	18.63	20.02	21.56	53
54	11.92	12.55	13.23	13.98	14.80	15.69	16.67	17.75	18.94	20.25	21.70	54
55	12.60	13.21	13.86	14.57	15.35	16.20	17.13	18.15	19.26	20.50	21.86	55

Table 12   Multipliers for loss of pension commencing age 55 (females)

Age at date of trial	Multiplier calculated with allowance for population mortality and rate of return of											Age at date of trial
	0.0%	0.5%	1.0%	1.5%	2.0%	2.5%	3.0%	3.5%	4.0%	4.5%	5.0%	
0	24.92	17.58	12.46	8.86	6.33	4.54	3.26	2.36	1.71	1.24	0.91	0
1	25.07	17.78	12.66	9.05	6.50	4.68	3.38	2.46	1.79	1.31	0.96	1
2	25.09	17.88	12.79	9.19	6.63	4.80	3.49	2.54	1.86	1.37	1.01	2
3	25.10	17.97	12.93	9.33	6.76	4.92	3.59	2.63	1.94	1.43	1.06	3
4	25.10	18.07	13.06	9.47	6.90	5.05	3.70	2.73	2.01	1.49	1.11	4
5	25.11	18.16	13.19	9.62	7.04	5.17	3.81	2.82	2.09	1.56	1.17	5
6	25.11	18.25	13.32	9.76	7.18	5.30	3.93	2.92	2.18	1.63	1.22	6
7	25.11	18.35	13.46	9.91	7.33	5.44	4.05	3.02	2.27	1.70	1.29	7
8	25.12	18.44	13.60	10.06	7.47	5.57	4.17	3.13	2.36	1.78	1.35	8
9	25.12	18.54	13.73	10.21	7.62	5.71	4.29	3.24	2.45	1.86	1.42	9
10	25.12	18.63	13.87	10.37	7.78	5.86	4.42	3.35	2.55	1.95	1.49	10
11	25.13	18.73	14.01	10.53	7.94	6.00	4.56	3.47	2.65	2.03	1.56	11
12	25.13	18.82	14.16	10.69	8.09	6.15	4.69	3.59	2.76	2.13	1.64	12
13	25.13	18.92	14.30	10.85	8.26	6.31	4.84	3.72	2.87	2.22	1.72	13
14	25.14	19.02	14.44	11.01	8.42	6.47	4.98	3.85	2.99	2.32	1.81	14
15	25.14	19.12	14.59	11.18	8.59	6.63	5.13	3.99	3.11	2.43	1.90	15
16	25.15	19.22	14.74	11.35	8.77	6.80	5.29	4.13	3.23	2.54	2.00	16
17	25.15	19.32	14.89	11.52	8.95	6.97	5.45	4.27	3.36	2.65	2.10	17
18	25.16	19.42	15.05	11.70	9.13	7.15	5.61	4.42	3.50	2.77	2.20	18
19	25.17	19.52	15.20	11.88	9.31	7.33	5.78	4.58	3.64	2.90	2.31	19
20	25.18	19.63	15.36	12.06	9.50	7.51	5.96	4.74	3.78	3.03	2.43	20
21	25.19	19.73	15.52	12.24	9.70	7.70	6.14	4.91	3.94	3.17	2.55	21
22	25.19	19.84	15.68	12.43	9.89	7.90	6.33	5.08	4.09	3.31	2.68	22
23	25.20	19.94	15.84	12.62	10.09	8.10	6.52	5.26	4.26	3.46	2.82	23
24	25.21	20.05	16.00	12.82	10.30	8.30	6.72	5.45	4.43	3.62	2.96	24
25	25.22	20.16	16.17	13.01	10.51	8.51	6.92	5.64	4.61	3.78	3.11	25

Age												Age
26	25.23	20.26	16.33	13.21	10.72	8.73	7.13	5.84	4.80	3.95	3.26	26
27	25.24	20.37	16.50	13.42	10.94	8.95	7.35	6.05	4.99	4.13	3.43	27
28	25.25	20.48	16.67	13.62	11.16	9.18	7.57	6.26	5.19	4.32	3.60	28
29	25.26	20.59	16.85	13.83	11.39	9.41	7.80	6.48	5.40	4.51	3.78	29
30	25.27	20.70	17.02	14.04	11.62	9.65	8.04	6.71	5.62	4.72	3.97	30
31	25.28	20.82	17.20	14.26	11.86	9.90	8.28	6.95	5.85	4.93	4.17	31
32	25.29	20.93	17.38	14.48	12.10	10.15	8.53	7.20	6.08	5.16	4.38	32
33	25.30	21.05	17.56	14.71	12.35	10.41	8.79	7.45	6.33	5.39	4.61	33
34	25.32	21.16	17.75	14.94	12.61	10.67	9.06	7.72	6.59	5.64	4.84	34
35	25.33	21.28	17.94	15.17	12.87	10.95	9.34	7.99	6.86	5.90	5.08	35
36	25.35	21.40	18.13	15.41	13.13	11.23	9.63	8.28	7.13	6.17	5.34	36
37	25.37	21.53	18.33	15.65	13.41	11.52	9.92	8.57	7.43	6.45	5.61	37
38	25.39	21.65	18.52	15.90	13.69	11.82	10.23	8.88	7.73	6.74	5.90	38
39	25.41	21.78	18.73	16.15	13.97	12.12	10.55	9.20	8.05	7.05	6.20	39
40	25.44	21.91	18.93	16.41	14.27	12.44	10.87	9.53	8.38	7.38	6.52	40
41	25.46	22.04	19.14	16.67	14.57	12.76	11.21	9.87	8.72	7.72	6.85	41
42	25.49	22.18	19.36	16.94	14.87	13.10	11.56	10.23	9.08	8.08	7.20	42
43	25.53	22.32	19.57	17.22	15.19	13.44	11.92	10.60	9.45	8.45	7.57	43
44	25.56	22.46	19.80	17.50	15.52	13.80	12.30	10.99	9.85	8.84	7.96	44
45	25.60	22.61	20.03	17.79	15.85	14.16	12.69	11.39	10.26	9.25	8.37	45
46	25.65	22.76	20.26	18.09	16.20	14.54	13.09	11.81	10.69	9.69	8.80	46
47	25.70	22.92	20.51	18.40	16.56	14.94	13.51	12.25	11.14	10.14	9.26	47
48	25.76	23.09	20.76	18.72	16.92	15.34	13.95	12.71	11.61	10.62	9.75	48
49	25.82	23.26	21.02	19.04	17.30	15.76	14.40	13.18	12.10	11.13	10.26	49
50	25.89	23.44	21.28	19.38	17.70	16.20	14.87	13.68	12.62	11.66	10.80	50
51	25.96	23.62	21.56	19.73	18.10	16.66	15.36	14.20	13.16	12.22	11.37	51
52	26.05	23.82	21.85	20.09	18.53	17.13	15.87	14.75	13.73	12.81	11.98	52
53	26.14	24.03	22.14	20.47	18.96	17.62	16.41	15.32	14.33	13.44	12.63	53
54	26.24	24.24	22.45	20.85	19.42	18.13	16.97	15.92	14.96	14.10	13.31	54
55	26.36	24.47	22.77	21.26	19.89	18.66	17.55	16.54	15.63	14.80	14.03	55

Table 13 Multipliers for loss of pension commencing age 60 (males)

Age at date of trial	Multiplier calculated with allowance for population mortality and rate of return of											Age at date of trial
	0.0%	0.5%	1.0%	1.5%	2.0%	2.5%	3.0%	3.5%	4.0%	4.5%	5.0%	
0	15.48	10.86	7.65	5.40	3.83	2.72	1.94	1.39	0.99	0.71	0.51	0
1	15.61	11.01	7.79	5.53	3.94	2.81	2.01	1.45	1.04	0.75	0.55	1
2	15.61	11.07	7.87	5.62	4.02	2.88	2.08	1.50	1.08	0.79	0.57	2
3	15.62	11.13	7.95	5.70	4.10	2.96	2.14	1.55	1.13	0.82	0.60	3
4	15.63	11.19	8.04	5.79	4.18	3.03	2.20	1.61	1.17	0.86	0.63	4
5	15.63	11.25	8.12	5.88	4.27	3.11	2.27	1.66	1.22	0.90	0.66	5
6	15.63	11.31	8.20	5.97	4.35	3.19	2.34	1.72	1.27	0.94	0.70	6
7	15.64	11.36	8.28	6.06	4.44	3.27	2.41	1.78	1.32	0.98	0.73	7
8	15.64	11.42	8.37	6.15	4.53	3.35	2.48	1.84	1.37	1.03	0.77	8
9	15.64	11.48	8.45	6.24	4.62	3.43	2.56	1.91	1.43	1.07	0.81	9
10	15.64	11.54	8.54	6.34	4.72	3.52	2.63	1.98	1.49	1.12	0.85	10
11	15.65	11.60	8.63	6.43	4.81	3.61	2.71	2.05	1.55	1.17	0.89	11
12	15.65	11.66	8.72	6.53	4.91	3.70	2.80	2.12	1.61	1.22	0.93	12
13	15.65	11.72	8.80	6.63	5.01	3.79	2.88	2.19	1.67	1.28	0.98	13
14	15.66	11.78	8.89	6.73	5.11	3.89	2.97	2.27	1.74	1.34	1.03	14
15	15.66	11.85	8.99	6.84	5.21	3.99	3.06	2.35	1.81	1.40	1.08	15
16	15.67	11.91	9.08	6.94	5.32	4.09	3.15	2.43	1.88	1.46	1.14	16
17	15.68	11.98	9.18	7.05	5.43	4.19	3.25	2.52	1.96	1.53	1.20	17
18	15.69	12.04	9.27	7.16	5.54	4.30	3.35	2.61	2.04	1.60	1.26	18
19	15.70	12.12	9.37	7.27	5.66	4.41	3.45	2.70	2.12	1.67	1.32	19
20	15.71	12.19	9.48	7.39	5.78	4.53	3.56	2.80	2.21	1.75	1.39	20
21	15.73	12.26	9.58	7.51	5.90	4.64	3.67	2.90	2.30	1.83	1.46	21
22	15.74	12.33	9.68	7.63	6.02	4.76	3.78	3.01	2.40	1.91	1.53	22
23	15.76	12.40	9.79	7.75	6.15	4.89	3.90	3.11	2.49	2.00	1.61	23
24	15.77	12.48	9.90	7.87	6.27	5.01	4.02	3.23	2.60	2.09	1.69	24
25	15.78	12.55	10.00	7.99	6.41	5.14	4.14	3.34	2.70	2.19	1.78	25

Age												Age
26	1.87	2.29	2.81	3.46	4.27	5.28	6.54	8.12	10.11	12.62	15.80	26
27	1.96	2.39	2.93	3.59	4.40	5.41	6.68	8.25	10.22	12.70	15.81	27
28	2.06	2.50	3.05	3.71	4.54	5.55	6.81	8.38	10.33	12.77	15.82	28
29	2.17	2.62	3.17	3.85	4.68	5.70	6.96	8.51	10.45	12.85	15.84	29
30	2.28	2.74	3.30	3.99	4.82	5.85	7.10	8.65	10.56	12.92	15.85	30
31	2.39	2.87	3.44	4.13	4.97	6.00	7.25	8.79	10.67	13.00	15.87	31
32	2.52	3.00	3.58	4.28	5.12	6.15	7.40	8.93	10.79	13.07	15.88	32
33	2.65	3.14	3.72	4.43	5.28	6.31	7.56	9.07	10.91	13.15	15.90	33
34	2.78	3.28	3.88	4.59	5.45	6.48	7.72	9.22	11.03	13.23	15.91	34
35	2.92	3.43	4.04	4.76	5.62	6.65	7.88	9.36	11.15	13.31	15.93	35
36	3.07	3.59	4.20	4.93	5.79	6.82	8.05	9.52	11.28	13.39	15.95	36
37	3.23	3.76	4.38	5.11	5.97	7.00	8.22	9.67	11.40	13.48	15.97	37
38	3.40	3.93	4.56	5.29	6.16	7.18	8.39	9.83	11.53	13.56	15.99	38
39	3.57	4.11	4.75	5.49	6.36	7.37	8.57	9.99	11.67	13.65	16.01	39
40	3.76	4.31	4.94	5.69	6.56	7.57	8.76	10.16	11.80	13.74	16.04	40
41	3.95	4.51	5.15	5.90	6.76	7.77	8.95	10.33	11.94	13.84	16.07	41
42	4.16	4.72	5.37	6.12	6.98	7.98	9.15	10.50	12.08	13.93	16.10	42
43	4.37	4.94	5.59	6.34	7.20	8.20	9.35	10.68	12.23	14.03	16.13	43
44	4.60	5.17	5.83	6.58	7.44	8.42	9.56	10.87	12.38	14.13	16.17	44
45	4.84	5.42	6.08	6.83	7.68	8.65	9.77	11.05	12.53	14.23	16.20	45
46	5.10	5.68	6.34	7.08	7.93	8.89	9.99	11.25	12.69	14.34	16.25	46
47	5.37	5.95	6.61	7.35	8.19	9.14	10.22	11.45	12.86	14.46	16.30	47
48	5.66	6.24	6.90	7.64	8.47	9.40	10.46	11.66	13.03	14.58	16.35	48
49	5.96	6.55	7.20	7.93	8.75	9.67	10.71	11.88	13.21	14.71	16.41	49
50	6.29	6.87	7.52	8.24	9.05	9.96	10.97	12.11	13.39	14.84	16.48	50
51	6.63	7.21	7.86	8.57	9.37	10.25	11.24	12.35	13.59	14.99	16.56	51
52	7.00	7.58	8.21	8.92	9.70	10.56	11.53	12.60	13.80	15.14	16.64	52
53	7.39	7.96	8.59	9.28	10.05	10.89	11.83	12.86	14.02	15.30	16.74	53
54	7.81	8.38	8.99	9.67	10.42	11.24	12.14	13.14	14.25	15.48	16.85	54
55	8.26	8.82	9.42	10.08	10.81	11.60	12.47	13.43	14.50	15.67	16.97	55

Table 13   Multipliers for loss of pension commencing age 60 (males)

Age at date of trial	Multiplier calculated with allowance for population mortality and rate of return of											Age at date of trial
	0.0%	0.5%	1.0%	1.5%	2.0%	2.5%	3.0%	3.5%	4.0%	4.5%	5.0%	
56	17.10	15.87	14.76	13.75	12.82	11.99	11.22	10.52	9.88	9.29	8.74	56
57	17.26	16.10	15.04	14.08	13.20	12.40	11.66	10.98	10.36	9.79	9.26	57
58	17.43	16.34	15.34	14.43	13.60	12.83	12.13	11.48	10.89	10.33	9.82	58
59	17.63	16.61	15.67	14.81	14.03	13.30	12.63	12.02	11.45	10.92	10.43	59
60	17.85	16.90	16.03	15.22	14.49	13.81	13.18	12.60	12.06	11.56	11.09	60

Table 14 Multipliers for loss of pension commencing age 60 (females)

Age at date of trial	Multiplier calculated with allowance for population mortality and rate of return of											Age at date of trial
	0.0%	0.5%	1.0%	1.5%	2.0%	2.5%	3.0%	3.5%	4.0%	4.5%	5.0%	
0	20.25	14.08	9.82	6.88	4.83	3.41	2.41	1.71	1.22	0.87	0.62	0
1	20.38	14.24	9.98	7.03	4.96	3.52	2.50	1.78	1.28	0.92	0.66	1
2	20.39	14.32	10.09	7.14	5.06	3.61	2.58	1.85	1.33	0.96	0.69	2
3	20.40	14.39	10.19	7.25	5.17	3.70	2.65	1.91	1.38	1.00	0.73	3
4	20.40	14.47	10.30	7.36	5.27	3.79	2.73	1.98	1.44	1.05	0.76	4
5	20.41	14.54	10.40	7.47	5.38	3.89	2.82	2.05	1.49	1.09	0.80	5
6	20.41	14.62	10.51	7.58	5.49	3.98	2.90	2.12	1.55	1.14	0.84	6
7	20.41	14.69	10.52	7.70	5.60	4.08	2.99	2.20	1.62	1.19	0.88	7
8	20.42	14.77	10.72	7.81	5.71	4.19	3.08	2.27	1.68	1.25	0.93	8
9	20.42	14.85	10.33	7.93	5.82	4.29	3.17	2.35	1.75	1.30	0.98	9
10	20.42	14.92	10.94	8.05	5.94	4.40	3.27	2.43	1.82	1.36	1.02	10
11	20.43	15.00	11.05	8.17	6.06	4.51	3.37	2.52	1.89	1.42	1.08	11
12	20.43	15.08	11.16	8.30	6.18	4.62	3.47	2.61	1.97	1.49	1.13	12
13	20.43	15.15	11.28	8.42	6.31	4.74	3.57	2.70	2.05	1.56	1.19	13
14	20.43	15.23	11.39	8.55	6.44	4.86	3.68	2.80	2.13	1.63	1.25	14
15	20.44	15.31	11.51	8.68	6.57	4.98	3.79	2.89	2.22	1.70	1.31	15
16	20.44	15.39	11.63	8.81	6.70	5.11	3.91	3.00	2.30	1.78	1.37	16
17	20.45	15.47	11.75	8.95	6.83	5.24	4.02	3.10	2.40	1.86	1.44	17
18	20.45	15.55	11.87	9.08	6.97	5.37	4.15	3.21	2.49	1.94	1.52	18
19	20.46	15.64	11.99	9.22	7.11	5.50	4.27	3.32	2.59	2.03	1.59	19
20	20.47	15.72	12.11	9.36	7.26	5.64	4.40	3.44	2.70	2.12	1.67	20
21	20.47	15.80	12.24	9.51	7.41	5.79	4.53	3.56	2.81	2.22	1.76	21
22	20.48	15.89	12.36	9.65	7.56	5.93	4.67	3.69	2.92	2.32	1.84	22
23	20.49	15.97	12.49	9.80	7.71	6.08	4.81	3.82	3.04	2.42	1.94	23
24	20.49	16.06	12.62	9.95	7.87	6.24	4.96	3.95	3.16	2.53	2.04	24
25	20.50	16.14	12.75	10.10	8.03	6.40	5.11	4.09	3.29	2.65	2.14	25

Table 14   Multipliers for loss of pension commencing age 60 (females)

Multiplier calculated with allowance for population mortality and rate of return of

Age at date of trial	0.0%	0.5%	1.0%	1.5%	2.0%	2.5%	3.0%	3.5%	4.0%	4.5%	5.0%	Age at date of trial
26	20.51	16.23	12.88	10.26	8.19	6.56	5.27	4.24	3.42	2.77	2.25	26
27	20.51	16.32	13.02	10.41	8.36	6.72	5.43	4.39	3.56	2.89	2.36	27
28	20.52	16.40	13.15	10.57	8.53	6.90	5.59	4.54	3.70	3.03	2.48	28
29	20.53	16.49	13.29	10.74	8.70	7.07	5.76	4.71	3.85	3.16	2.60	29
30	20.54	16.58	13.43	10.90	8.88	7.25	5.94	4.87	4.01	3.31	2.73	30
31	20.55	16.67	13.57	11.07	9.06	7.43	6.12	5.04	4.17	3.46	2.87	31
32	20.56	16.76	13.71	11.24	9.25	7.62	6.30	5.22	4.34	3.61	3.02	32
33	20.57	16.85	13.85	11.42	9.44	7.82	6.50	5.41	4.52	3.78	3.17	33
34	20.58	16.95	14.00	11.60	9.63	8.02	6.69	5.60	4.70	3.95	3.33	34
35	20.59	17.04	14.15	11.78	9.83	8.22	6.90	5.80	4.89	4.13	3.50	35
36	20.61	17.14	14.30	11.96	10.03	8.44	7.11	6.01	5.09	4.32	3.67	36
37	20.62	17.24	14.45	12.15	10.24	8.65	7.33	6.22	5.30	4.52	3.86	37
38	20.64	17.34	14.61	12.34	10.45	8.88	7.56	6.45	5.51	4.72	4.06	38
39	20.66	17.44	14.77	12.54	10.67	9.11	7.79	6.68	5.74	4.94	4.26	39
40	20.68	17.55	14.93	12.74	10.90	9.34	8.03	6.92	5.97	5.17	4.48	40
41	20.70	17.65	15.10	12.94	11.13	9.59	8.28	7.17	6.22	5.41	4.71	41
42	20.72	17.76	15.27	13.15	11.36	9.84	8.54	7.43	6.48	5.66	4.95	42
43	20.75	17.87	15.44	13.37	11.60	10.10	8.81	7.70	6.74	5.92	5.21	43
44	20.78	17.99	15.61	13.59	11.85	10.36	9.08	7.98	7.02	6.19	5.48	44
45	20.81	18.11	15.80	13.81	12.11	10.64	9.37	8.27	7.32	6.48	5.76	45
46	20.85	18.23	15.98	14.05	12.37	10.93	9.67	8.58	7.62	6.79	6.06	46
47	20.89	18.36	16.17	14.28	12.65	11.22	9.98	8.89	7.94	7.11	6.37	47
48	20.94	18.49	16.37	14.53	12.93	11.53	10.30	9.23	8.28	7.44	6.71	48
49	20.99	18.63	16.58	14.78	13.22	11.84	10.64	9.57	8.63	7.80	7.06	49
50	21.04	18.77	16.79	15.05	13.52	12.17	10.98	9.93	9.00	8.17	7.43	50

51	21.11	18.92	17.00	15.32	13.83	12.51	11.35	10.31	9.39	8.56	7.82	51
52	21.17	19.08	17.23	15.60	14.15	12.87	11.73	10.71	9.79	8.98	8.24	52
53	21.25	19.24	17.46	15.89	14.49	13.24	12.12	11.12	10.22	9.41	8.69	53
54	21.33	19.41	17.71	16.19	14.83	13.62	12.53	11.56	10.67	9.88	9.16	54
55	21.42	19.59	17.96	16.50	15.20	14.02	12.97	12.01	11.15	10.37	9.66	55
56	21.53	19.79	18.23	16.83	15.57	14.44	13.42	12.49	11.65	10.88	10.19	56
57	21.64	19.99	18.51	17.17	15.97	14.88	13.89	13.00	12.18	11.43	10.75	57
58	21.77	20.21	18.81	17.54	16.39	15.34	14.40	13.53	12.74	12.02	11.36	58
59	21.92	20.45	19.12	17.92	16.83	15.83	14.93	14.10	13.34	12.64	12.00	59
60	22.08	20.70	19.45	18.32	17.29	16.35	15.49	14.70	13.98	13.31	12.70	60

Table 15   Multipliers for loss of pension commencing age 65 (males)

Age at date of trial	Multiplier calculated with allowance for population mortality and rate of return of											Age at date of trial
	0.0%	0.5%	1.0%	1.5%	2.0%	2.5%	3.0%	3.5%	4.0%	4.5%	5.0%	
0	11.31	7.81	5.41	3.76	2.62	1.83	1.28	0.90	0.63	0.45	0.32	0
1	11.41	7.92	5.51	3.85	2.69	1.89	1.33	0.94	0.66	0.47	0.34	1
2	11.41	7.96	5.57	3.91	2.75	1.94	1.37	0.97	0.69	0.49	0.35	2
3	11.42	8.00	5.63	3.97	2.81	1.99	1.41	1.01	0.72	0.52	0.37	3
4	11.42	8.05	5.69	4.03	2.86	2.04	1.46	1.04	0.75	0.54	0.39	4
5	11.42	8.09	5.74	4.09	2.92	2.09	1.50	1.08	0.78	0.56	0.41	5
6	11.43	8.13	5.80	4.15	2.98	2.14	1.55	1.12	0.81	0.59	0.43	6
7	11.43	8.17	5.86	4.22	3.04	2.20	1.59	1.16	0.84	0.62	0.45	7
8	11.43	8.22	5.92	4.28	3.10	2.25	1.64	1.20	0.88	0.64	0.47	8
9	11.43	8.26	5.98	4.34	3.16	2.31	1.69	1.24	0.91	0.67	0.50	9
10	11.43	8.30	6.04	4.41	3.23	2.37	1.74	1.28	0.95	0.70	0.52	10
11	11.44	8.34	6.10	4.48	3.29	2.43	1.79	1.33	0.99	0.73	0.55	11
12	11.44	8.39	6.17	4.55	3.36	2.49	1.85	1.38	1.03	0.77	0.57	12
13	11.44	8.43	6.23	4.61	3.43	2.55	1.90	1.42	1.07	0.80	0.60	13
14	11.44	8.48	6.29	4.68	3.50	2.62	1.96	1.47	1.11	0.84	0.63	14
15	11.45	8.52	6.36	4.76	3.57	2.68	2.02	1.53	1.15	0.88	0.67	15
16	11.45	8.57	6.42	4.83	3.64	2.75	2.08	1.58	1.20	0.92	0.70	16
17	11.46	8.61	6.49	4.90	3.71	2.82	2.15	1.64	1.25	0.96	0.73	17
18	11.47	8.66	6.56	4.98	3.79	2.89	2.21	1.69	1.30	1.00	0.77	18
19	11.48	8.71	6.63	5.06	3.87	2.97	2.28	1.76	1.35	1.05	0.81	19
20	11.49	8.76	6.70	5.14	3.95	3.04	2.35	1.82	1.41	1.10	0.85	20
21	11.50	8.82	6.78	5.22	4.03	3.12	2.42	1.88	1.47	1.15	0.90	21
22	11.51	8.87	6.85	5.31	4.12	3.20	2.50	1.95	1.53	1.20	0.94	22
23	11.52	8.92	6.93	5.39	4.20	3.29	2.57	2.02	1.59	1.25	0.99	23
24	11.53	8.97	7.00	5.48	4.29	3.37	2.65	2.09	1.66	1.31	1.04	24
25	11.54	9.03	7.08	5.56	4.38	3.46	2.74	2.17	1.72	1.37	1.09	25

Age												Age
26	1.15	1.43	1.79	2.25	2.82	3.55	4.47	5.65	7.15	9.08	11.55	26
27	1.21	1.50	1.87	2.33	2.91	3.64	4.57	5.74	7.23	9.13	11.56	27
28	1.27	1.57	1.94	2.41	3.00	3.73	4.66	5.83	7.31	9.18	11.57	28
29	1.33	1.64	2.02	2.50	3.09	3.83	4.76	5.92	7.39	9.24	11.58	29
30	1.40	1.72	2.11	2.59	3.19	3.93	4.86	6.02	7.47	9.29	11.59	30
31	1.47	1.79	2.19	2.68	3.28	4.03	4.96	6.11	7.55	9.35	11.60	31
32	1.55	1.88	2.28	2.78	3.39	4.14	5.06	6.21	7.63	9.40	11.61	32
33	1.63	1.96	2.37	2.88	3.49	4.24	5.17	6.31	7.72	9.46	11.62	33
34	1.71	2.05	2.47	2.98	3.60	4.35	5.28	6.41	7.80	9.52	11.63	34
35	1.80	2.15	2.57	3.09	3.71	4.47	5.39	6.52	7.89	9.57	11.64	35
36	1.89	2.25	2.68	3.20	3.83	4.59	5.50	6.62	7.98	9.63	11.66	36
37	1.99	2.35	2.79	3.32	3.95	4.71	5.62	6.73	8.07	9.69	11.67	37
38	2.09	2.46	2.91	3.44	4.07	4.83	5.74	6.84	8.16	9.76	11.69	38
39	2.20	2.58	3.03	3.56	4.20	4.96	5.87	6.95	8.25	9.82	11.70	39
40	2.31	2.70	3.15	3.69	4.33	5.09	5.99	7.07	8.35	9.88	11.72	40
41	2.43	2.82	3.28	3.83	4.47	5.23	6.12	7.19	8.45	9.95	11.74	41
42	2.56	2.96	3.42	3.97	4.61	5.37	6.26	7.31	8.55	10.02	11.77	42
43	2.69	3.09	3.57	4.12	4.76	5.51	6.40	7.43	8.65	10.09	11.79	43
44	2.83	3.24	3.72	4.27	4.91	5.66	6.54	7.56	8.76	10.16	11.82	44
45	2.98	3.39	3.88	4.43	5.07	5.82	6.68	7.69	8.87	10.24	11.84	45
46	3.14	3.56	4.04	4.60	5.24	5.98	6.84	7.83	8.98	10.32	11.88	46
47	3.30	3.73	4.22	4.77	5.41	6.15	6.99	7.97	9.10	10.40	11.91	47
48	3.48	3.91	4.40	4.96	5.59	6.32	7.16	8.12	9.22	10.49	11.95	48
49	3.67	4.10	4.59	5.15	5.78	6.50	7.33	8.27	9.34	10.58	11.99	49
50	3.87	4.30	4.80	5.35	5.98	6.70	7.51	8.43	9.48	10.67	12.04	50
51	4.08	4.52	5.01	5.57	6.19	6.89	7.69	8.59	9.62	10.78	12.10	51
52	4.30	4.74	5.24	5.79	6.41	7.10	7.89	8.77	9.75	10.89	12.16	52
53	4.55	4.99	5.48	6.03	6.64	7.32	8.09	8.95	9.92	11.01	12.23	53
54	4.80	5.25	5.74	6.28	6.88	7.56	8.31	9.14	10.08	11.13	12.31	54
55	5.08	5.52	6.01	6.55	7.14	7.80	8.53	9.35	10.26	11.27	12.40	55

Table 15 Multipliers for loss of pension commencing age 65 (males)

Age at date of trial	Multiplier calculated with allowance for population mortality and rate of return of											Age at date of trial
	0.0%	0.5%	1.0%	1.5%	2.0%	2.5%	3.0%	3.5%	4.0%	4.5%	5.0%	
56	12.50	11.42	10.44	9.56	8.77	8.06	7.41	6.83	6.30	5.82	5.38	56
57	12.61	11.58	10.64	9.79	9.03	8.33	7.70	7.13	6.61	6.13	5.70	57
58	12.74	11.75	10.85	10.04	9.30	8.63	8.02	7.45	6.94	6.47	6.04	58
59	12.88	11.94	11.09	10.31	9.59	8.94	8.35	7.80	7.30	6.84	6.41	59
60	13.05	12.15	11.34	10.59	9.91	9.28	8.71	8.18	7.69	7.24	6.82	60
61	13.23	12.39	11.61	10.90	10.25	9.65	9.10	8.58	8.11	7.67	7.26	61
62	13.44	12.65	11.92	11.24	10.62	10.05	9.52	9.02	8.57	8.14	7.75	62
63	13.68	12.94	12.25	11.61	11.03	10.48	9.98	9.51	9.07	8.66	8.28	63
64	13.95	13.26	12.62	12.02	11.47	10.96	10.48	10.04	9.62	9.23	8.87	64
65	14.27	13.63	13.03	12.48	11.97	11.49	11.04	10.62	10.23	9.86	9.52	65

Table 16 Multipliers for loss of pension commencing age 65 (females)

Age at date of trial	Multiplier calculated with allowance for population mortality and rate of return of											Age at date of trial
	0.0%	0.5%	1.0%	1.5%	2.0%	2.5%	3.0%	3.5%	4.0%	4.5%	5.0%	
0	15.77	10.80	7.42	5.11	3.53	2.45	1.70	1.19	0.83	0.58	0.41	0
1	15.87	10.92	7.54	5.22	3.63	2.53	1.77	1.24	0.87	0.61	0.43	1
2	15.88	10.98	7.62	5.30	3.70	2.59	1.82	1.28	0.91	0.64	0.46	2
3	15.89	11.04	7.70	5.38	3.78	2.66	1.88	1.33	0.94	0.67	0.48	3
4	15.89	11.10	7.78	5.47	3.85	2.72	1.93	1.37	0.98	0.70	0.50	4
5	15.89	11.16	7.86	5.55	3.93	2.79	1.99	1.42	1.02	0.73	0.53	5
6	15.90	11.21	7.93	5.63	4.01	2.86	2.05	1.47	1.06	0.77	0.55	6
7	15.90	11.27	8.02	5.72	4.09	2.94	2.11	1.52	1.10	0.80	0.58	7
8	15.90	11.33	8.10	5.80	4.17	3.01	2.18	1.58	1.15	0.84	0.61	8
9	15.90	11.39	8.18	5.89	4.26	3.09	2.24	1.63	1.19	0.87	0.64	9
10	15.91	11.45	8.26	5.98	4.34	3.16	2.31	1.69	1.24	0.91	0.67	10
11	15.91	11.50	8.35	6.07	4.43	3.24	2.38	1.75	1.29	0.96	0.71	11
12	15.91	11.56	8.43	6.16	4.52	3.32	2.45	1.81	1.34	1.00	0.74	12
13	15.91	11.62	8.52	6.26	4.61	3.41	2.52	1.88	1.40	1.04	0.78	13
14	15.91	11.68	8.60	6.35	4.70	3.49	2.60	1.94	1.45	1.09	0.82	14
15	15.92	11.74	8.69	6.45	4.80	3.58	2.68	2.01	1.51	1.14	0.86	15
16	15.92	11.80	8.78	6.55	4.90	3.67	2.76	2.08	1.57	1.19	0.90	16
17	15.92	11.87	8.87	6.65	5.00	3.76	2.84	2.15	1.64	1.25	0.95	17
18	15.93	11.93	8.96	6.75	5.10	3.86	2.93	2.23	1.70	1.30	1.00	18
19	15.93	11.99	9.05	6.85	5.20	3.96	3.02	2.31	1.77	1.36	1.05	19
20	15.94	12.06	9.15	6.96	5.31	4.06	3.11	2.39	1.84	1.42	1.10	20
21	15.94	12.12	9.24	7.06	5.41	4.16	3.20	2.48	1.92	1.49	1.16	21
22	15.95	12.19	9.34	7.17	5.52	4.27	3.30	2.56	1.99	1.55	1.21	22
23	15.96	12.25	9.43	7.28	5.64	4.37	3.40	2.65	2.07	1.62	1.28	23
24	15.96	12.32	9.53	7.39	5.75	4.48	3.51	2.75	2.16	1.70	1.34	24
25	15.97	12.38	9.63	7.51	5.87	4.60	3.61	2.84	2.24	1.78	1.41	25

Table 16 Multipliers for loss of pension commencing age 65 (females)

Age at date of trial	Multiplier calculated with allowance for population mortality and rate of return of											Age at date of trial
	0.0%	0.5%	1.0%	1.5%	2.0%	2.5%	3.0%	3.5%	4.0%	4.5%	5.0%	
26	15.97	12.45	9.73	7.62	5.99	4.71	3.72	2.94	2.34	1.86	1.48	26
27	15.98	12.51	9.83	7.74	6.11	4.83	3.83	3.05	2.43	1.94	1.55	27
28	15.98	12.58	9.93	7.86	6.23	4.96	3.95	3.16	2.53	2.03	1.63	28
29	15.99	12.65	10.03	7.98	6.36	5.08	4.07	3.27	2.63	2.12	1.71	29
30	15.99	12.72	10.14	8.10	6.49	5.21	4.19	3.38	2.74	2.22	1.80	30
31	16.00	12.79	10.24	8.23	6.62	5.34	4.32	3.50	2.85	2.32	1.89	31
32	16.01	12.86	10.35	8.35	6.76	5.48	4.45	3.63	2.96	2.42	1.99	32
33	16.02	12.93	10.46	8.48	6.90	5.62	4.59	3.76	3.08	2.53	2.09	33
34	16.03	13.00	10.57	8.62	7.04	5.76	4.73	3.89	3.21	2.65	2.19	34
35	16.04	13.07	10.68	8.75	7.18	5.91	4.88	4.03	3.34	2.77	2.30	35
36	16.05	13.15	10.80	8.89	7.33	6.06	5.03	4.17	3.47	2.90	2.42	36
37	16.06	13.22	10.91	9.03	7.49	6.22	5.18	4.32	3.61	3.03	2.54	37
38	16.07	13.30	11.03	9.17	7.64	6.38	5.34	4.48	3.76	3.17	2.67	38
39	16.09	13.38	11.15	9.32	7.80	6.55	5.51	4.64	3.92	3.31	2.81	39
40	16.10	13.46	11.27	9.47	7.97	6.72	5.68	4.81	4.08	3.47	2.95	40
41	16.12	13.54	11.40	9.62	8.13	6.89	5.85	4.98	4.24	3.63	3.10	41
42	16.14	13.62	11.53	9.77	8.31	7.07	6.03	5.16	4.42	3.79	3.26	42
43	16.16	13.71	11.66	9.93	8.48	7.26	6.22	5.35	4.60	3.97	3.43	43
44	16.18	13.80	11.79	10.10	8.66	7.45	6.42	5.54	4.79	4.15	3.60	44
45	16.21	13.89	11.93	10.26	8.85	7.65	6.62	5.75	4.99	4.35	3.79	45
46	16.24	13.98	12.07	10.44	9.04	7.85	6.83	5.96	5.20	4.55	3.99	46
47	16.27	14.08	12.21	10.61	9.24	8.07	7.05	6.18	5.42	4.76	4.20	47
48	16.31	14.18	12.36	10.80	9.45	8.29	7.28	6.41	5.65	4.99	4.41	48
49	16.34	14.29	12.52	10.99	9.66	8.51	7.52	6.65	5.89	5.23	4.65	49
50	16.39	14.40	12.67	11.18	9.88	8.75	7.76	6.90	6.14	5.48	4.89	50

51	16.44	14.51	12.84	11.38	10.11	9.00	8.02	7.16	6.41	5.74	5.15	51
52	16.49	14.63	13.01	11.59	10.34	9.25	8.29	7.44	6.68	6.02	5.43	52
53	16.55	14.76	13.19	11.81	10.59	9.52	8.57	7.72	6.98	6.31	5.72	53
54	16.61	14.89	13.37	12.03	10.84	9.79	8.86	8.03	7.28	6.62	6.03	54
55	16.69	15.03	13.56	12.26	11.11	10.08	9.16	8.34	7.61	6.95	6.36	55
56	16.77	15.18	13.76	12.51	11.38	10.38	9.48	8.68	7.95	7.30	6.71	56
57	16.86	15.33	13.98	12.76	11.67	10.70	9.82	9.03	8.31	7.67	7.08	57
58	16.96	15.50	14.20	13.03	11.98	11.03	10.17	9.40	8.70	8.06	7.48	58
59	17.07	15.68	14.44	13.31	12.30	11.38	10.55	9.79	9.10	8.48	7.90	59
60	17.20	15.88	14.59	13.61	12.64	11.75	10.95	10.21	9.54	8.92	8.36	60
61	17.34	16.09	14.96	13.93	13.00	12.15	11.37	10.66	10.00	9.40	8.85	61
62	17.50	16.32	15.25	14.27	13.38	12.57	11.82	11.13	10.50	9.92	9.38	62
63	17.68	16.57	15.56	14.64	13.79	13.01	12.30	11.64	11.03	10.47	9.95	63
64	17.88	16.85	15.90	15.03	14.23	13.49	12.81	12.18	11.60	11.07	10.57	64
65	18.11	17.15	16.26	15.45	14.70	14.01	13.37	12.77	12.22	11.71	11.24	65

Table 17   Multipliers for loss of pension commencing age 70 (males)

Age at date of trial	Multiplier calculated with allowance for population mortality and rate of return of											Age at date of trial
	0.0%	0.5%	1.0%	1.5%	2.0%	2.5%	3.0%	3.5%	4.0%	4.5%	5.0%	
0	7.61	5.17	3.52	2.40	1.65	1.13	0.78	0.54	0.37	0.26	0.18	0
1	7.68	5.24	3.59	2.46	1.69	1.17	0.81	0.56	0.39	0.27	0.19	1
2	7.68	5.27	3.62	2.50	1.73	1.20	0.83	0.58	0.40	0.28	0.20	2
3	7.68	5.30	3.66	2.54	1.76	1.23	0.86	0.60	0.42	0.30	0.21	3
4	7.69	5.32	3.70	2.58	1.80	1.26	0.88	0.62	0.44	0.31	0.22	4
5	7.69	5.35	3.74	2.61	1.83	1.29	0.91	0.64	0.46	0.32	0.23	5
6	7.69	5.38	3.77	2.65	1.87	1.32	0.94	0.67	0.47	0.34	0.24	6
7	7.69	5.41	3.81	2.70	1.91	1.36	0.97	0.69	0.49	0.35	0.25	7
8	7.69	5.44	3.85	2.74	1.95	1.39	0.99	0.71	0.51	0.37	0.27	8
9	7.69	5.46	3.89	2.78	1.99	1.43	1.02	0.74	0.53	0.39	0.28	9
10	7.70	5.49	3.93	2.82	2.03	1.46	1.06	0.76	0.55	0.40	0.29	10
11	7.70	5.52	3.97	2.86	2.07	1.50	1.09	0.79	0.58	0.42	0.31	11
12	7.70	5.55	4.01	2.91	2.11	1.54	1.12	0.82	0.60	0.44	0.32	12
13	7.70	5.58	4.05	2.95	2.15	1.57	1.15	0.85	0.62	0.46	0.34	13
14	7.70	5.61	4.09	3.00	2.20	1.61	1.19	0.88	0.65	0.48	0.36	14
15	7.70	5.64	4.14	3.04	2.24	1.66	1.23	0.91	0.68	0.50	0.38	15
16	7.71	5.67	4.18	3.09	2.29	1.70	1.26	0.94	0.70	0.53	0.39	16
17	7.71	5.70	4.22	3.14	2.33	1.74	1.30	0.97	0.73	0.55	0.41	17
18	7.72	5.73	4.27	3.19	2.38	1.79	1.34	1.01	0.76	0.58	0.44	18
19	7.72	5.77	4.31	3.24	2.43	1.83	1.38	1.05	0.79	0.60	0.46	19
20	7.73	5.80	4.36	3.29	2.48	1.88	1.42	1.08	0.82	0.63	0.48	20
21	7.74	5.83	4.41	3.34	2.53	1.93	1.47	1.12	0.86	0.66	0.51	21
22	7.74	5.87	4.46	3.39	2.59	1.98	1.51	1.16	0.89	0.69	0.53	22
23	7.75	5.90	4.51	3.45	2.64	2.03	1.56	1.20	0.93	0.72	0.56	23
24	7.76	5.94	4.55	3.50	2.70	2.08	1.61	1.25	0.97	0.75	0.59	24
25	7.76	5.97	4.60	3.56	2.75	2.14	1.66	1.29	1.01	0.79	0.62	25

Age												Age
26	0.65	0.82	1.05	1.34	1.71	2.19	2.81	3.61	4.65	6.01	7.77	26
27	0.68	0.86	1.09	1.39	1.76	2.25	2.87	3.67	4.70	6.04	7.78	27
28	0.72	0.90	1.14	1.44	1.82	2.31	2.93	3.73	4.76	6.08	7.78	28
29	0.75	0.94	1.18	1.49	1.87	2.36	2.99	3.79	4.81	6.11	7.79	29
30	0.79	0.99	1.23	1.54	1.93	2.43	3.05	3.85	4.86	6.15	7.80	30
31	0.83	1.03	1.28	1.60	1.99	2.49	3.12	3.91	4.91	6.19	7.80	31
32	0.87	1.08	1.33	1.65	2.05	2.55	3.18	3.97	4.97	6.22	7.81	32
33	0.92	1.13	1.39	1.71	2.12	2.62	3.25	4.04	5.02	6.26	7.82	33
34	0.96	1.18	1.45	1.77	2.18	2.69	3.32	4.10	5.08	6.30	7.83	34
35	1.01	1.23	1.51	1.84	2.25	2.76	3.39	4.17	5.13	6.34	7.84	35
36	1.07	1.29	1.57	1.91	2.32	2.83	3.46	4.23	5.19	6.37	7.84	36
37	1.12	1.35	1.63	1.97	2.39	2.91	3.53	4.30	5.25	6.41	7.85	37
38	1.18	1.41	1.70	2.05	2.47	2.98	3.61	4.37	5.31	6.46	7.87	38
39	1.24	1.48	1.77	2.12	2.55	3.06	3.69	4.44	5.37	6.50	7.88	39
40	1.30	1.55	1.84	2.20	2.63	3.14	3.77	4.52	5.43	6.54	7.89	40
41	1.37	1.62	1.92	2.28	2.71	3.23	3.85	4.59	5.50	6.58	7.90	41
42	1.44	1.70	2.00	2.36	2.80	3.31	3.93	4.67	5.56	6.63	7.92	42
43	1.52	1.78	2.09	2.45	2.89	3.40	4.02	4.75	5.63	6.68	7.93	43
44	1.60	1.86	2.17	2.54	2.98	3.50	4.11	4.83	5.70	6.72	7.95	44
45	1.68	1.95	2.27	2.64	3.08	3.59	4.20	4.92	5.77	6.77	7.97	45
46	1.77	2.04	2.36	2.74	3.18	3.69	4.30	5.00	5.84	6.83	7.99	46
47	1.86	2.14	2.47	2.84	3.28	3.80	4.39	5.10	5.92	6.88	8.02	47
48	1.96	2.24	2.57	2.95	3.39	3.90	4.50	5.19	6.00	6.94	8.04	48
49	2.07	2.35	2.69	3.07	3.51	4.02	4.60	5.29	6.08	7.00	8.07	49
50	2.18	2.47	2.80	3.19	3.63	4.13	4.72	5.39	6.16	7.06	8.11	50
51	2.30	2.59	2.93	3.31	3.75	4.26	4.83	5.49	6.26	7.13	8.14	51
52	2.43	2.72	3.06	3.45	3.89	4.39	4.95	5.61	6.35	7.21	8.19	52
53	2.56	2.86	3.20	3.59	4.03	4.52	5.08	5.72	6.45	7.28	8.23	53
54	2.71	3.01	3.35	3.74	4.17	4.66	5.22	5.85	6.56	7.37	8.29	54
55	2.86	3.17	3.51	3.90	4.33	4.81	5.36	5.98	6.67	7.46	8.35	55

Table 17   Multipliers for loss of pension commencing age 70 (males)

Age at date of trial	Multiplier calculated with allowance for population mortality and rate of return of											Age at date of trial
	0.0%	0.5%	1.0%	1.5%	2.0%	2.5%	3.0%	3.5%	4.0%	4.5%	5.0%	
56	8.41	7.55	6.79	6.12	5.51	4.97	4.50	4.07	3.68	3.34	3.03	56
57	8.49	7.66	6.92	6.26	5.67	5.15	4.67	4.25	3.86	3.52	3.21	57
58	8.57	7.78	7.06	6.42	5.84	5.33	4.86	4.44	4.06	3.72	3.41	58
59	8.67	7.90	7.21	6.59	6.03	5.52	5.06	4.65	4.27	3.93	3.62	59
60	8.78	8.04	7.38	6.77	6.23	5.73	5.28	4.87	4.50	4.16	3.84	60
61	8.90	8.20	7.55	6.97	6.44	5.96	5.52	5.11	4.74	4.40	4.09	61
62	9.05	8.37	7.75	7.19	6.67	6.20	5.77	5.37	5.01	4.68	4.37	62
63	9.21	8.56	7.97	7.43	6.93	6.47	6.05	5.66	5.30	4.97	4.67	63
64	9.39	8.78	8.21	7.69	7.21	6.77	6.36	5.98	5.63	5.30	5.00	64
65	9.60	9.02	8.48	7.98	7.52	7.09	6.69	6.33	5.98	5.66	5.37	65
66	9.84	9.29	8.78	8.30	7.86	7.45	7.07	6.71	6.38	6.07	5.78	66
67	10.12	9.60	9.11	8.66	8.24	7.85	7.48	7.14	6.82	6.52	6.23	67
68	10.43	9.94	9.49	9.06	8.67	8.29	7.94	7.62	7.31	7.02	6.75	68
69	10.78	10.33	9.91	9.51	9.14	8.79	8.46	8.15	7.86	7.59	7.33	69
70	11.19	10.77	10.38	10.02	9.67	9.35	9.04	8.75	8.48	8.22	7.98	70

Table 18 Multipliers for loss of pension commencing age 70 (females)

Age at date of trial	Multiplier calculated with allowance for population mortality and rate of return of											Age at date of trial
	0.0%	0.5%	1.0%	1.5%	2.0%	2.5%	3.0%	3.5%	4.0%	4.5%	5.0%	
0	11.59	7.81	5.28	3.58	2.43	1.66	1.13	0.78	0.53	0.37	0.25	0
1	11.66	7.90	5.36	3.65	2.50	1.71	1.18	0.81	0.56	0.39	0.27	1
2	11.67	7.94	5.42	3.71	2.55	1.75	1.21	0.84	0.58	0.40	0.28	2
3	11.67	7.98	5.48	3.77	2.60	1.80	1.25	0.87	0.61	0.42	0.30	3
4	11.67	8.02	5.53	3.83	2.65	1.84	1.29	0.90	0.63	0.44	0.31	4
5	11.67	8.07	5.59	3.88	2.71	1.89	1.32	0.93	0.65	0.46	0.33	5
6	11.68	8.11	5.65	3.94	2.76	1.94	1.36	0.96	0.68	0.48	0.34	6
7	11.68	8.15	5.70	4.00	2.82	1.99	1.41	1.00	0.71	0.51	0.36	7
8	11.68	8.19	5.76	4.06	2.87	2.04	1.45	1.03	0.74	0.53	0.38	8
9	11.68	8.23	5.82	4.12	2.93	2.09	1.49	1.07	0.77	0.55	0.40	9
10	11.68	8.27	5.88	4.19	2.99	2.14	1.54	1.11	0.80	0.58	0.42	10
11	11.68	8.32	5.94	4.25	3.05	2.19	1.58	1.14	0.83	0.60	0.44	11
12	11.69	8.36	6.00	4.31	3.11	2.25	1.63	1.18	0.86	0.63	0.46	12
13	11.69	8.40	6.06	4.38	3.17	2.31	1.68	1.23	0.90	0.66	0.48	13
14	11.69	8.45	6.12	4.45	3.24	2.36	1.73	1.27	0.93	0.69	0.51	14
15	11.69	8.49	6.18	4.51	3.30	2.42	1.78	1.31	0.97	0.72	0.53	15
16	11.69	8.53	6.25	4.58	3.37	2.48	1.84	1.36	1.01	0.75	0.56	16
17	11.70	8.58	6.31	4.65	3.44	2.55	1.89	1.41	1.05	0.79	0.59	17
18	11.70	8.63	6.37	4.72	3.51	2.61	1.95	1.46	1.09	0.82	0.62	18
19	11.70	8.67	6.44	4.80	3.58	2.68	2.01	1.51	1.14	0.86	0.65	19
20	11.71	8.72	6.51	4.87	3.65	2.75	2.07	1.56	1.18	0.90	0.68	20
21	11.71	8.76	6.57	4.94	3.73	2.82	2.13	1.62	1.23	0.94	0.72	21
22	11.72	8.81	6.64	5.02	3.80	2.89	2.20	1.68	1.28	0.98	0.75	22
23	11.72	8.86	6.71	5.10	3.88	2.96	2.26	1.73	1.33	1.03	0.79	23
24	11.72	8.90	6.73	5.17	3.96	3.03	2.33	1.80	1.39	1.07	0.83	24
25	11.73	8.95	6.85	5.25	4.04	3.11	2.40	1.86	1.44	1.12	0.87	25

Table 18 Multipliers for loss of pension commencing age 70 (females)

Age at date of trial	Multiplier calculated with allowance for population mortality and rate of return of											Age at date of trial
	0.0%	0.5%	1.0%	1.5%	2.0%	2.5%	3.0%	3.5%	4.0%	4.5%	5.0%	
26	11.73	9.00	6.92	5.33	4.12	3.19	2.48	1.92	1.50	1.17	0.92	26
27	11.73	9.05	6.99	5.42	4.20	3.27	2.55	1.99	1.56	1.22	0.96	27
28	11.74	9.10	7.06	5.50	4.29	3.35	2.63	2.06	1.62	1.28	1.01	28
29	11.74	9.15	7.14	5.58	4.38	3.44	2.71	2.14	1.69	1.34	1.06	29
30	11.75	9.19	7.21	5.67	4.47	3.53	2.79	2.21	1.76	1.40	1.12	30
31	11.75	9.24	7.29	5.76	4.56	3.62	2.88	2.29	1.83	1.46	1.17	31
32	11.76	9.30	7.36	5.85	4.65	3.71	2.96	2.37	1.90	1.53	1.23	32
33	11.76	9.35	7.44	5.94	4.75	3.80	3.05	2.46	1.98	1.60	1.29	33
34	11.77	9.40	7.52	6.03	4.85	3.90	3.15	2.54	2.06	1.67	1.36	34
35	11.78	9.45	7.60	6.12	4.95	4.00	3.24	2.63	2.14	1.75	1.43	35
36	11.79	9.51	7.68	6.22	5.05	4.10	3.34	2.73	2.23	1.83	1.50	36
37	11.80	9.56	7.76	6.32	5.15	4.21	3.45	2.83	2.32	1.91	1.58	37
38	11.81	9.62	7.85	6.42	5.26	4.32	3.55	2.93	2.42	2.00	1.66	38
39	11.82	9.67	7.93	6.52	5.37	4.43	3.66	3.03	2.52	2.09	1.74	39
40	11.83	9.73	8.02	6.62	5.48	4.55	3.78	3.14	2.62	2.19	1.83	40
41	11.84	9.79	8.11	6.73	5.60	4.66	3.89	3.26	2.73	2.29	1.92	41
42	11.85	9.85	8.20	6.84	5.72	4.79	4.01	3.37	2.84	2.39	2.02	42
43	11.87	9.91	8.29	6.95	5.84	4.91	4.14	3.50	2.96	2.50	2.12	43
44	11.89	9.98	8.39	7.07	5.96	5.04	4.27	3.62	3.08	2.62	2.23	44
45	11.91	10.04	8.49	7.18	6.09	5.18	4.41	3.76	3.21	2.74	2.35	45
46	11.93	10.11	8.59	7.30	6.23	5.32	4.55	3.89	3.34	2.87	2.47	46
47	11.95	10.18	8.69	7.43	6.36	5.46	4.69	4.04	3.48	3.01	2.60	47
48	11.98	10.25	8.79	7.56	6.50	5.61	4.84	4.19	3.63	3.15	2.74	48
49	12.01	10.33	8.90	7.69	6.65	5.76	5.00	4.35	3.78	3.30	2.88	49
50	12.04	10.41	9.02	7.82	6.80	5.92	5.16	4.51	3.95	3.46	3.03	50

Age												Age
51	3.19	3.62	4.11	4.68	5.33	6.09	6.96	7.97	9.13	10.49	12.07	51
52	3.36	3.80	4.29	4.86	5.51	6.26	7.12	8.11	9.26	10.58	12.11	52
53	3.54	3.98	4.48	5.05	5.70	6.44	7.29	8.26	9.38	10.67	12.16	53
54	3.74	4.18	4.68	5.25	5.89	6.63	7.46	8.42	9.51	10.77	12.20	54
55	3.94	4.38	4.89	5.45	6.09	6.82	7.65	8.58	9.65	10.87	12.26	55
56	4.16	4.60	5.11	5.67	6.31	7.03	7.84	8.75	9.79	10.97	12.31	56
57	4.39	4.84	5.34	5.90	6.53	7.24	8.04	8.93	9.94	11.09	12.38	57
58	4.63	5.08	5.59	6.14	6.77	7.46	8.24	9.12	10.10	11.21	12.45	58
59	4.90	5.35	5.85	6.40	7.02	7.70	8.47	9.32	10.27	11.34	12.54	59
60	5.18	5.63	6.13	6.68	7.28	7.95	8.70	9.53	10.45	11.48	12.63	60
61	5.49	5.93	6.43	6.97	7.56	8.22	8.95	9.75	10.64	11.63	12.74	61
62	5.81	6.26	6.74	7.28	7.86	8.50	9.21	9.99	10.85	11.80	12.85	62
63	6.17	6.61	7.09	7.61	8.18	8.81	9.49	10.24	11.07	11.98	12.99	63
64	6.55	6.98	7.45	7.97	8.52	9.13	9.79	10.52	11.31	12.18	13.13	64
65	6.96	7.39	7.85	8.35	8.89	9.48	10.12	10.81	11.57	12.40	13.30	65
66	7.42	7.83	8.28	8.77	9.29	9.85	10.46	11.13	11.85	12.64	13.49	66
67	7.91	8.31	8.75	9.21	9.71	10.25	10.84	11.47	12.15	12.89	13.70	67
68	8.45	8.83	9.25	9.70	10.18	10.69	11.24	11.84	12.48	13.18	13.93	68
69	9.03	9.41	9.80	10.22	10.68	11.16	11.68	12.24	12.85	13.50	14.20	69
70	9.68	10.03	10.40	10.80	11.22	11.68	12.16	12.68	13.24	13.84	14.49	70

Table 19   Multipliers for pecuniary loss for life (males)

Age at date of trial	Multiplier calculated with allowance for projected mortality from the 1998-based population projections and rate of return of											Age at date of trial
	0.0%	0.5%	1.0%	1.5%	2.0%	2.5%	3.0%	3.5%	4.0%	4.5%	5.0%	
0	79.84	65.45	54.50	46.07	39.50	34.30	30.14	26.77	24.01	21.72	19.80	0
1	79.24	65.10	54.31	45.99	39.48	34.32	30.18	26.83	24.07	21.79	19.87	1
2	78.26	64.44	53.87	45.69	39.27	34.18	30.08	26.76	24.02	21.75	19.84	2
3	77.27	63.77	53.41	45.37	39.05	34.02	29.98	26.68	23.97	21.71	19.82	3
4	76.28	63.09	52.95	45.05	38.83	33.87	29.87	26.60	23.91	21.67	19.79	4
5	75.28	62.41	52.48	44.72	38.60	33.70	29.75	26.52	23.85	21.63	19.75	5
6	74.28	61.72	52.00	44.39	38.36	33.54	29.63	26.43	23.79	21.58	19.72	6
7	73.27	61.02	51.51	44.04	38.12	33.36	29.51	26.34	23.72	21.53	19.68	7
8	72.27	60.32	51.02	43.70	37.87	33.19	29.38	26.25	23.65	21.48	19.64	8
9	71.27	59.62	50.52	43.34	37.62	33.00	29.24	26.15	23.58	21.42	19.60	9
10	70.26	58.91	50.02	42.99	37.36	32.82	29.11	26.05	23.50	21.37	19.56	10
11	69.26	58.20	49.51	42.62	37.10	32.62	28.97	25.94	23.43	21.31	19.51	11
12	68.25	57.48	49.00	42.25	36.83	32.43	28.82	25.84	23.34	21.24	19.46	12
13	67.25	56.77	48.49	41.88	36.56	32.23	28.67	25.72	23.26	21.18	19.41	13
14	66.24	56.05	47.97	41.50	36.28	32.02	28.52	25.61	23.17	21.11	19.36	14
15	65.25	55.33	47.45	41.12	36.00	31.81	28.36	25.49	23.08	21.04	19.31	15
16	64.25	54.61	46.92	40.74	35.71	31.60	28.20	25.37	22.99	20.97	19.25	16
17	63.26	53.88	46.39	40.35	35.43	31.39	28.04	25.25	22.90	20.90	19.19	17
18	62.28	53.17	45.87	39.96	35.14	31.17	27.88	25.13	22.80	20.83	19.14	18
19	61.31	52.46	45.35	39.57	34.85	30.96	27.72	25.00	22.71	20.76	19.08	19
20	60.34	51.75	44.82	39.18	34.56	30.74	27.55	24.88	22.61	20.68	19.03	20
21	59.37	51.03	44.29	38.79	34.26	30.52	27.39	24.75	22.52	20.61	18.97	21
22	58.40	50.32	43.75	38.39	33.96	30.29	27.21	24.62	22.41	20.53	18.91	22
23	57.43	49.59	43.21	37.98	33.65	30.05	27.03	24.48	22.31	20.45	18.84	23
24	56.45	48.86	42.66	37.56	33.33	29.81	26.84	24.33	22.19	20.36	18.77	24
25	55.48	48.12	42.10	37.13	33.01	29.56	26.65	24.18	22.08	20.26	18.70	25

26	54.50	47.38	41.54	36.71	32.68	29.30	26.45	24.03	21.95	20.17	18.62	26
27	53.53	46.64	40.97	36.27	32.34	29.04	26.25	23.87	21.83	20.07	18.54	27
28	52.55	45.89	40.40	35.83	32.00	28.77	26.04	23.70	21.70	19.96	18.46	28
29	51.57	45.14	39.82	35.38	31.65	28.50	25.82	23.53	21.56	19.86	18.37	29
30	50.59	44.39	39.23	34.92	31.29	28.22	25.60	23.35	21.42	19.74	18.28	30
31	49.61	43.62	38.63	34.45	30.92	27.92	25.37	23.17	21.27	19.62	18.18	31
32	48.62	42.86	38.03	33.98	30.55	27.63	25.13	22.98	21.12	19.50	18.08	32
33	47.64	42.08	37.42	33.49	30.16	27.32	24.88	22.78	20.95	19.36	17.97	33
34	46.65	41.30	36.81	33.00	29.77	27.00	24.63	22.57	20.78	19.23	17.86	34
35	45.66	40.52	36.18	32.50	29.37	26.68	24.36	22.36	20.61	19.08	17.74	35
36	44.66	39.72	35.55	31.99	28.95	26.34	24.09	22.13	20.42	18.93	17.61	36
37	43.67	38.93	34.90	31.47	28.53	26.00	23.81	21.90	20.23	18.77	17.48	37
38	42.67	38.13	34.26	30.95	28.11	25.65	23.52	21.66	20.03	18.60	17.34	38
39	41.68	37.33	33.61	30.42	27.67	25.29	23.22	21.42	19.83	18.43	17.19	39
40	40.70	36.52	32.95	29.88	27.23	24.93	22.92	21.17	19.62	18.25	17.04	40
41	39.71	35.72	32.30	29.34	26.79	24.56	22.62	20.91	19.40	18.07	16.89	41
42	38.73	34.92	31.64	28.80	26.33	24.18	22.30	20.64	19.18	17.88	16.73	42
43	37.75	34.11	30.97	28.25	25.87	23.80	21.98	20.37	18.95	17.69	16.56	43
44	36.77	33.30	30.30	27.69	25.41	23.41	21.65	20.09	18.71	17.49	16.39	44
45	35.80	32.49	29.62	27.12	24.93	23.00	21.31	19.80	18.47	17.27	16.21	45
46	34.82	31.68	28.94	26.54	24.44	22.59	20.96	19.50	18.21	17.05	16.02	46
47	33.84	30.85	28.25	25.96	23.95	22.17	20.59	19.19	17.94	16.82	15.82	47
48	32.86	30.02	27.54	25.36	23.44	21.74	20.22	18.87	17.66	16.58	15.61	48
49	31.87	29.19	26.83	24.76	22.92	21.29	19.84	18.54	17.38	16.33	15.39	49
50	30.89	28.35	26.12	24.14	22.39	20.83	19.44	18.19	17.07	16.07	15.15	50
51	29.91	27.51	25.40	23.52	21.85	20.37	19.03	17.84	16.76	15.79	14.91	51
52	28.93	26.67	24.67	22.90	21.31	19.89	18.62	17.48	16.45	15.51	14.66	52
53	27.96	25.84	23.95	22.27	20.76	19.41	18.20	17.11	16.12	15.22	14.41	53
54	27.00	25.01	23.23	21.64	20.21	18.93	17.78	16.73	15.79	14.93	14.14	54
55	26.06	24.18	22.51	21.01	19.66	18.44	17.34	16.35	15.45	14.62	13.87	55

Table 19   Multipliers for pecuniary loss for life (males)

Age at date of trial	Multiplier calculated with allowance for projected mortality from the 1998-based population projections and rate of return of											Age at date of trial
	0.0%	0.5%	1.0%	1.5%	2.0%	2.5%	3.0%	3.5%	4.0%	4.5%	5.0%	
56	25.12	23.36	21.79	20.37	19.10	17.95	16.91	15.96	15.10	14.31	13.59	56
57	24.20	22.55	21.08	19.75	18.54	17.46	16.47	15.57	14.75	14.00	13.31	57
58	23.30	21.76	20.38	19.13	18.00	16.97	16.03	15.18	14.40	13.68	13.03	58
59	22.42	20.99	19.69	18.52	17.45	16.48	15.60	14.79	14.05	13.37	12.74	59
60	21.56	20.23	19.01	17.91	16.91	16.00	15.16	14.40	13.69	13.05	12.45	60
61	20.72	19.47	18.34	17.31	16.37	15.51	14.72	14.00	13.34	12.72	12.16	61
62	19.88	18.72	17.67	16.71	15.83	15.02	14.28	13.60	12.97	12.39	11.85	62
63	19.05	17.98	17.00	16.10	15.28	14.53	13.83	13.19	12.60	12.05	11.54	63
64	18.22	17.23	16.33	15.49	14.73	14.02	13.37	12.77	12.21	11.70	11.22	64
65	17.40	16.49	15.65	14.88	14.17	13.51	12.91	12.34	11.82	11.34	10.89	65
66	16.58	15.74	14.97	14.26	13.60	12.99	12.43	11.91	11.42	10.97	10.54	66
67	15.76	14.99	14.28	13.63	13.02	12.46	11.94	11.45	11.00	10.58	10.18	67
68	14.94	14.24	13.60	13.00	12.44	11.93	11.44	11.00	10.58	10.18	9.82	68
69	14.14	13.51	12.92	12.37	11.86	11.39	10.95	10.53	10.15	9.78	9.44	69
70	13.36	12.78	12.25	11.75	11.29	10.86	10.45	10.07	9.71	9.38	9.07	70
71	12.60	12.09	11.60	11.15	10.73	10.34	9.96	9.62	9.29	8.98	8.69	71
72	11.89	11.42	10.98	10.57	10.19	9.83	9.49	9.17	8.87	8.59	8.33	72
73	11.20	10.78	10.39	10.02	9.67	9.34	9.04	8.75	8.47	8.21	7.97	73
74	10.56	10.18	9.83	9.49	9.18	8.88	8.60	8.33	8.08	7.85	7.62	74
75	9.95	9.61	9.29	8.99	8.70	8.43	8.18	7.94	7.71	7.49	7.28	75
76	9.37	9.07	8.78	8.50	8.25	8.00	7.77	7.55	7.34	7.14	6.95	76
77	8.81	8.54	8.28	8.04	7.80	7.58	7.37	7.17	6.98	6.80	6.63	77
78	8.28	8.04	7.80	7.58	7.37	7.17	6.98	6.80	6.63	6.47	6.31	78
79	7.78	7.56	7.35	7.15	6.96	6.78	6.61	6.45	6.29	6.14	6.00	79
80	7.29	7.10	6.91	6.73	6.56	6.40	6.25	6.10	5.96	5.83	5.70	80

Age												Age
81	6.83	6.66	6.49	6.33	6.18	6.04	5.90	5.77	5.64	5.52	5.40	81
82	6.39	6.24	6.09	5.95	5.81	5.68	5.56	5.44	5.33	5.22	5.11	82
83	5.98	5.85	5.71	5.59	5.47	5.35	5.24	5.14	5.03	4.93	4.84	83
84	5.60	5.48	5.37	5.25	5.15	5.04	4.94	4.85	4.76	4.67	4.58	84
85	5.25	5.14	5.04	4.94	4.84	4.75	4.66	4.57	4.49	4.41	4.34	85
86	4.92	4.82	4.73	4.64	4.56	4.48	4.40	4.32	4.25	4.17	4.10	86
87	4.62	4.53	4.45	4.37	4.30	4.22	4.15	4.08	4.02	3.95	3.89	87
88	4.34	4.27	4.19	4.12	4.05	3.99	3.92	3.86	3.80	3.75	3.69	88
89	4.08	4.01	3.94	3.88	3.82	3.76	3.71	3.65	3.60	3.54	3.49	89
90	3.81	3.75	3.70	3.64	3.59	3.53	3.48	3.44	3.39	3.34	3.30	90
91	3.54	3.49	3.44	3.39	3.35	3.30	3.26	3.21	3.17	3.13	3.09	91
92	3.29	3.24	3.20	3.16	3.11	3.07	3.03	3.00	2.96	2.92	2.89	92
93	3.05	3.01	2.98	2.94	2.90	2.87	2.83	2.80	2.77	2.74	2.71	93
94	2.83	2.79	2.76	2.73	2.70	2.66	2.63	2.61	2.58	2.55	2.52	94
95	2.62	2.59	2.56	2.53	2.50	2.48	2.45	2.42	2.40	2.37	2.35	95
96	2.42	2.40	2.37	2.35	2.32	2.30	2.28	2.26	2.23	2.21	2.19	96
97	2.25	2.23	2.20	2.18	2.16	2.14	2.12	2.10	2.08	2.07	2.05	97
98	2.09	2.07	2.05	2.03	2.02	2.00	1.98	1.96	1.95	1.93	1.91	98
99	1.94	1.93	1.91	1.90	1.88	1.86	1.85	1.83	1.82	1.81	1.79	99
100	1.81	1.80	1.78	1.77	1.75	1.74	1.73	1.71	1.70	1.69	1.68	100

Table 20 Multipliers for pecuniary loss for life (females)

Multiplier calculated with allowance for projected mortality from the 1998-based population projections and rate of return of

Age at date of trial	0.0%	0.5%	1.0%	1.5%	2.0%	2.5%	3.0%	3.5%	4.0%	4.5%	5.0%	Age at date of trial
0	84.01	68.28	56.45	47.42	40.45	34.97	30.63	27.13	24.27	21.92	19.95	0
1	83.36	67.90	56.24	47.32	40.41	34.98	30.66	27.17	24.33	21.98	20.01	1
2	82.38	67.25	55.81	47.04	40.22	34.85	30.57	27.12	24.29	21.95	19.99	2
3	81.38	66.59	55.37	46.74	40.02	34.72	30.48	27.05	24.24	21.92	19.97	3
4	80.38	65.93	54.92	46.44	39.81	34.58	30.38	26.98	24.20	21.88	19.95	4
5	79.38	65.25	54.47	46.13	39.60	34.43	30.28	26.91	24.14	21.85	19.92	5
6	78.38	64.57	54.00	45.81	39.38	34.28	30.17	26.83	24.09	21.81	19.89	6
7	77.37	63.89	53.54	45.49	39.16	34.12	30.06	26.76	24.03	21.77	19.86	7
8	76.37	63.20	53.07	45.16	38.93	33.96	29.95	26.68	23.98	21.73	19.83	8
9	75.36	62.51	52.59	44.83	38.70	33.80	29.83	26.59	23.92	21.68	19.80	9
10	74.36	61.82	52.11	44.50	38.46	33.63	29.71	26.51	23.85	21.64	19.77	10
11	73.35	61.12	51.62	44.15	38.22	33.46	29.59	26.42	23.79	21.59	19.73	11
12	72.35	60.42	51.13	43.81	37.98	33.28	29.46	26.32	23.72	21.54	19.69	12
13	71.34	59.72	50.64	43.46	37.73	33.10	29.33	26.23	23.65	21.49	19.65	13
14	70.34	59.01	50.14	43.10	37.47	32.92	29.20	26.13	23.58	21.43	19.61	14
15	69.34	58.31	49.63	42.74	37.21	32.73	29.06	26.03	23.50	21.38	19.57	15
16	68.34	57.60	49.13	42.38	36.95	32.54	28.92	25.93	23.43	21.32	19.53	16
17	67.34	56.89	48.62	42.01	36.68	32.34	28.78	25.82	23.35	21.26	19.48	17
18	66.34	56.17	48.10	41.64	36.41	32.14	28.63	25.71	23.26	21.20	19.43	18
19	65.35	55.46	47.58	41.26	36.13	31.94	28.48	25.60	23.18	21.13	19.39	19
20	64.35	54.74	47.06	40.88	35.85	31.73	28.32	25.48	23.09	21.07	19.33	20
21	63.35	54.01	46.53	40.49	35.56	31.52	28.16	25.36	23.00	21.00	19.28	21
22	62.36	53.28	45.99	40.09	35.27	31.30	28.00	25.23	22.90	20.92	19.22	22
23	61.36	52.55	45.45	39.69	34.97	31.07	27.83	25.10	22.80	20.84	19.16	23
24	60.36	51.81	44.90	39.28	34.66	30.84	27.65	24.97	22.70	20.76	19.10	24
25	59.35	51.06	44.35	38.86	34.35	30.60	27.47	24.83	22.59	20.68	19.03	25

Age												Age
26	58.35	50.32	43.79	38.44	34.02	30.35	27.28	24.68	22.48	20.59	18.97	26
27	57.35	49.57	43.22	38.01	33.70	30.10	27.09	24.54	22.36	20.50	18.89	27
28	56.35	48.81	42.65	37.58	33.37	29.85	26.89	24.38	22.24	20.40	18.82	28
29	55.35	48.06	42.08	37.14	33.03	29.59	26.69	24.22	22.12	20.31	18.74	29
30	54.35	47.30	41.49	36.69	32.68	29.32	26.48	24.06	21.99	20.20	18.66	30
31	53.35	46.53	40.91	36.24	32.33	29.05	26.26	23.89	21.85	20.09	18.57	31
32	52.35	45.76	40.32	35.78	31.97	28.76	26.04	23.71	21.71	19.98	18.48	32
33	51.35	44.99	39.72	35.31	31.61	28.48	25.81	23.53	21.57	19.87	18.38	33
34	50.35	44.22	39.11	34.84	31.24	28.18	25.58	23.34	21.42	19.74	18.28	34
35	49.35	43.44	38.50	34.36	30.86	27.88	25.34	23.15	21.26	19.62	18.18	35
36	48.35	42.66	37.89	33.87	30.47	27.57	25.09	22.95	21.10	19.49	18.07	36
37	47.36	41.87	37.27	33.38	30.08	27.26	24.84	22.75	20.93	19.35	17.96	37
38	46.36	41.09	36.54	32.88	29.68	26.94	24.58	22.53	20.76	19.21	17.84	38
39	45.36	40.29	36.01	32.38	29.27	26.61	24.31	22.32	20.58	19.06	17.72	39
40	44.37	39.50	35.38	31.86	28.86	26.27	24.03	22.09	20.39	18.90	17.59	40
41	43.37	38.70	34.73	31.34	28.44	25.93	23.75	21.86	20.20	18.74	17.46	41
42	42.38	37.90	34.09	30.82	28.01	25.57	23.46	21.62	20.00	18.58	17.32	42
43	41.39	37.10	33.43	30.29	27.57	25.21	23.16	21.37	19.80	18.40	17.17	43
44	40.40	36.29	32.78	29.75	27.13	24.85	22.86	21.12	19.58	18.23	17.02	44
45	39.41	35.49	32.11	29.20	26.67	24.47	22.55	20.85	19.36	18.04	16.86	45
46	38.42	34.67	31.44	28.65	26.21	24.09	22.23	20.58	19.13	17.85	16.70	46
47	37.43	33.86	30.77	28.09	25.75	23.70	21.90	20.31	18.90	17.64	16.53	47
48	36.45	33.05	30.09	27.52	25.27	23.30	21.56	20.02	18.65	17.44	16.35	48
49	35.47	32.23	29.41	26.95	24.79	22.89	21.21	19.73	18.40	17.22	16.16	49
50	34.49	31.41	28.72	26.37	24.30	22.48	20.86	19.42	18.14	17.00	15.97	50
51	33.52	30.59	28.03	25.79	23.81	22.05	20.50	19.11	17.88	16.77	15.77	51
52	32.55	29.78	27.34	25.20	23.30	21.62	20.13	18.80	17.60	16.53	15.56	52
53	31.59	28.96	26.65	24.61	22.80	21.19	19.75	18.47	17.32	16.28	15.35	53
54	30.63	28.14	25.95	24.01	22.28	20.74	19.37	18.14	17.03	16.03	15.12	54
55	29.68	27.33	25.25	23.41	21.76	20.29	18.98	17.80	16.73	15.77	14.89	55

Table 20   Multipliers for pecuniary loss for life (females)

Multiplier calculated with allowance for projected mortality from the 1998-based population projections and rate of return of

Age at date of trial	0.0%	0.5%	1.0%	1.5%	2.0%	2.5%	3.0%	3.5%	4.0%	4.5%	5.0%	Age at date of trial
56	28.73	26.51	24.55	22.80	21.24	19.84	18.58	17.45	16.42	15.50	14.66	56
57	27.79	25.70	23.85	22.19	20.71	19.38	18.18	17.09	16.11	15.22	14.41	57
58	26.86	24.90	23.15	21.58	20.18	18.91	17.77	16.73	15.79	14.94	14.16	58
59	25.95	24.11	22.46	20.98	19.65	18.44	17.36	16.37	15.47	14.65	13.91	59
60	25.05	23.32	21.77	20.38	19.12	17.98	16.94	16.00	15.14	14.36	13.64	60
61	24.16	22.54	21.09	19.77	18.58	17.50	16.52	15.63	14.81	14.06	13.38	61
62	23.27	21.76	20.39	19.16	18.04	17.02	16.09	15.24	14.46	13.75	13.10	62
63	22.38	20.97	19.69	18.53	17.48	16.52	15.64	14.84	14.10	13.43	12.80	63
64	21.47	20.17	18.98	17.90	16.91	16.01	15.18	14.43	13.73	13.09	12.50	64
65	20.56	19.35	18.25	17.24	16.32	15.48	14.70	13.99	13.34	12.73	12.17	65
66	19.64	18.53	17.51	16.57	15.72	14.93	14.21	13.54	12.93	12.36	11.83	66
67	18.72	17.69	16.76	15.89	15.10	14.37	13.70	13.08	12.50	11.97	11.47	67
68	17.80	16.86	16.00	15.21	14.48	13.80	13.18	12.60	12.07	11.57	11.10	68
69	16.89	16.04	15.25	14.52	13.85	13.23	12.65	12.12	11.62	11.16	10.73	69
70	16.01	15.23	14.51	13.85	13.23	12.66	12.13	11.64	11.17	10.74	10.34	70
71	15.15	14.44	13.79	13.19	12.62	12.10	11.61	11.16	10.73	10.33	9.96	71
72	14.33	13.69	13.10	12.55	12.03	11.55	11.11	10.69	10.30	9.93	9.58	72
73	13.55	12.98	12.44	11.93	11.46	11.03	10.62	10.23	9.87	9.53	9.21	73
74	12.81	12.29	11.80	11.34	10.91	10.51	10.14	9.79	9.45	9.14	8.85	74
75	12.10	11.63	11.19	10.77	10.38	10.02	9.67	9.35	9.04	8.76	8.49	75
76	11.42	11.00	10.59	10.22	9.86	9.53	9.22	8.92	8.64	8.38	8.13	76
77	10.77	10.38	10.02	9.68	9.36	9.06	8.77	8.50	8.25	8.00	7.77	77
78	10.13	9.79	9.46	9.15	8.86	8.59	8.33	8.08	7.85	7.63	7.42	78
79	9.52	9.21	8.92	8.64	8.38	8.13	7.90	7.67	7.46	7.26	7.07	79
80	8.93	8.65	8.39	8.14	7.91	7.68	7.47	7.27	7.08	6.90	6.72	80

Age											
81	8.36	8.12	7.88	7.66	7.45	7.25	7.06	6.88	6.70	6.54	6.38
82	7.83	7.61	7.40	7.20	7.01	6.83	6.66	6.49	6.34	6.19	6.04
83	7.32	7.12	6.94	6.76	6.59	6.43	6.27	6.13	5.99	5.85	5.72
84	6.85	6.68	6.51	6.35	6.20	6.06	5.92	5.78	5.66	5.54	5.42
85	6.43	6.27	6.12	5.98	5.84	5.71	5.59	5.47	5.35	5.24	5.14
86	6.04	5.90	5.77	5.64	5.52	5.40	5.29	5.18	5.07	4.97	4.88
87	5.70	5.57	5.45	5.34	5.23	5.12	5.02	4.92	4.83	4.73	4.65
88	5.40	5.29	5.18	5.07	4.97	4.88	4.78	4.69	4.61	4.52	4.44
89	5.13	5.03	4.93	4.84	4.74	4.66	4.57	4.49	4.41	4.33	4.26
90	4.88	4.78	4.69	4.61	4.52	4.44	4.36	4.29	4.21	4.14	4.08
91	4.60	4.52	4.44	4.36	4.28	4.21	4.14	4.07	4.01	3.94	3.88
92	4.31	4.24	4.17	4.10	4.03	3.96	3.90	3.84	3.78	3.72	3.67
93	4.02	3.95	3.89	3.83	3.77	3.71	3.65	3.60	3.55	3.50	3.45
94	3.73	3.67	3.61	3.56	3.51	3.46	3.41	3.36	3.31	3.27	3.22
95	3.45	3.40	3.35	3.30	3.26	3.21	3.17	3.13	3.09	3.05	3.01
96	3.18	3.14	3.10	3.06	3.02	2.98	2.94	2.91	2.87	2.84	2.80
97	2.93	2.90	2.86	2.83	2.79	2.76	2.73	2.69	2.66	2.63	2.60
98	2.71	2.68	2.64	2.61	2.58	2.56	2.53	2.50	2.47	2.45	2.42
99	2.51	2.48	2.45	2.43	2.40	2.38	2.35	2.33	2.30	2.28	2.26
100	2.34	2.31	2.29	2.27	2.24	2.22	2.20	2.18	2.16	2.14	2.12

Table 21 Multipliers for loss of earnings to pension age 55 (males)

Multiplier calculated with allowance for projected mortality from the 1998-based population projections and rate of return of

Age at date of trial	0.0%	0.5%	1.0%	1.5%	2.0%	2.5%	3.0%	3.5%	4.0%	4.5%	5.0%	Age at date of trial
16	38.25	34.79	31.75	29.08	26.73	24.65	22.81	21.17	19.70	18.40	17.22	16
17	37.26	33.97	31.07	28.52	26.26	24.26	22.48	20.90	19.48	18.21	17.07	17
18	36.28	33.15	30.39	27.96	25.79	23.87	22.15	20.62	19.25	18.01	16.90	18
19	35.30	32.34	29.71	27.39	25.32	23.47	21.82	20.34	19.01	17.82	16.74	19
20	34.33	31.52	29.03	26.81	24.83	23.06	21.47	20.05	18.77	17.61	16.56	20
21	33.35	30.70	28.34	26.23	24.34	22.64	21.12	19.75	18.51	17.39	16.38	21
22	32.38	29.88	27.64	25.63	23.83	22.22	20.76	19.44	18.25	17.17	16.19	22
23	31.40	29.04	26.93	25.03	23.32	21.77	20.38	19.12	17.97	16.93	15.98	23
24	30.43	28.21	26.21	24.41	22.79	21.32	19.99	18.78	17.69	16.68	15.77	24
25	29.45	27.37	25.49	23.79	22.25	20.86	19.59	18.44	17.39	16.43	15.55	25
26	28.47	26.52	24.76	23.16	21.71	20.39	19.18	18.08	17.08	16.16	15.31	26
27	27.49	25.68	24.02	22.52	21.15	19.90	18.76	17.71	16.76	15.88	15.07	27
28	26.52	24.82	23.28	21.87	20.58	19.40	18.32	17.33	16.42	15.58	14.81	28
29	25.54	23.96	22.52	21.21	20.00	18.89	17.87	16.94	16.07	15.27	14.54	29
30	24.56	23.10	21.76	20.54	19.41	18.37	17.41	16.53	15.71	14.95	14.25	30
31	23.58	22.23	21.00	19.85	18.80	17.83	16.93	16.10	15.33	14.62	13.95	31
32	22.60	21.36	20.22	19.16	18.18	17.28	16.44	15.66	14.94	14.26	13.64	32
33	21.62	20.48	19.43	18.46	17.55	16.71	15.93	15.21	14.53	13.90	13.31	33
34	20.64	19.60	18.64	17.74	16.91	16.13	15.41	14.73	14.10	13.51	12.96	34
35	19.66	18.71	17.84	17.02	16.25	15.54	14.87	14.25	13.66	13.11	12.59	35
36	18.67	17.82	17.02	16.28	15.58	14.93	14.32	13.74	13.20	12.69	12.21	36
37	17.69	16.92	16.21	15.53	14.90	14.30	13.74	13.22	12.72	12.25	11.81	37
38	16.71	16.02	15.38	14.77	14.20	13.66	13.15	12.67	12.22	11.79	11.39	38
39	15.72	15.12	14.54	14.00	13.49	13.01	12.55	12.11	11.70	11.31	10.94	39
40	14.74	14.21	13.70	13.22	12.77	12.34	11.93	11.54	11.17	10.82	10.48	40

Age												Age
41	10.00	10.30	10.61	10.94	11.29	11.65	12.03	12.43	12.86	13.30	13.77	41
42	9.49	9.75	10.03	10.33	10.63	10.95	11.28	11.63	12.00	12.39	12.79	42
43	8.96	9.19	9.43	9.69	9.95	10.23	10.52	10.82	11.14	11.47	11.81	43
44	8.40	8.60	8.81	9.03	9.26	9.49	9.74	10.00	10.27	10.54	10.83	44
45	7.81	7.98	8.16	8.35	8.54	8.74	8.95	9.16	9.38	9.62	9.86	45
46	7.19	7.34	7.49	7.64	7.80	7.97	8.14	8.31	8.49	8.68	8.88	46
47	6.55	6.66	6.79	6.91	7.04	7.17	7.31	7.45	7.59	7.74	7.90	47
48	5.86	5.96	6.05	6.15	6.25	6.36	6.46	6.57	6.68	6.80	6.92	48
49	5.15	5.22	5.29	5.37	5.44	5.52	5.60	5.68	5.76	5.85	5.94	49
50	4.40	4.45	4.50	4.55	4.60	4.66	4.72	4.77	4.83	4.89	4.95	50
51	3.60	3.64	3.67	3.71	3.74	3.78	3.81	3.85	3.89	3.93	3.97	51
52	2.77	2.79	2.81	2.83	2.85	2.87	2.89	2.91	2.94	2.96	2.98	52
53	1.90	1.90	1.91	1.92	1.93	1.94	1.95	1.96	1.97	1.98	1.99	53
54	0.97	0.98	0.98	0.98	0.98	0.99	0.99	0.99	0.99	0.99	1.00	54

Table 22 Multipliers for loss of earnings to pension age 55 (females)

Age at date of trial	Multiplier calculated with allowance for projected mortality from the 1998-based population projections and rate of return of											Age at date of trial
	0.0%	0.5%	1.0%	1.5%	2.0%	2.5%	3.0%	3.5%	4.0%	4.5%	5.0%	
16	38.60	35.09	32.02	29.32	26.94	24.84	22.97	21.32	19.84	18.52	17.33	16
17	37.61	34.27	31.34	28.76	26.48	24.45	22.65	21.05	19.62	18.33	17.18	17
18	36.61	33.45	30.66	28.19	26.00	24.06	22.32	20.77	19.39	18.14	17.02	18
19	35.62	32.62	29.97	27.61	25.52	23.65	21.98	20.49	19.15	17.94	16.85	19
20	34.63	31.79	29.27	27.03	25.03	23.24	21.63	20.19	18.90	17.73	16.67	20
21	33.64	30.95	28.56	26.43	24.52	22.81	21.27	19.89	18.64	17.51	16.48	21
22	32.65	30.11	27.85	25.83	24.01	22.37	20.90	19.57	18.37	17.28	16.29	22
23	31.65	29.27	27.13	25.21	23.48	21.93	20.52	19.24	18.09	17.04	16.08	23
24	30.66	28.42	26.40	24.59	22.95	21.47	20.12	18.90	17.79	16.78	15.86	24
25	29.67	27.57	25.67	23.95	22.40	21.00	19.72	18.55	17.49	16.52	15.63	25
26	28.67	26.71	24.93	23.31	21.85	20.51	19.30	18.19	17.18	16.25	15.40	26
27	27.68	25.85	24.18	22.66	21.28	20.02	18.87	17.81	16.85	15.96	15.15	27
28	26.69	24.98	23.42	22.00	20.70	19.51	18.42	17.43	16.51	15.66	14.88	28
29	25.70	24.11	22.66	21.33	20.11	19.00	17.97	17.02	16.15	15.35	14.61	29
30	24.71	23.24	21.89	20.65	19.51	18.47	17.50	16.61	15.79	15.02	14.32	30
31	23.72	22.36	21.11	19.96	18.90	17.92	17.02	16.18	15.40	14.68	14.02	31
32	22.73	21.48	20.33	19.26	18.28	17.37	16.52	15.74	15.01	14.33	13.70	32
33	21.74	20.59	19.54	18.55	17.64	16.80	16.01	15.28	14.60	13.96	13.36	33
34	20.75	19.71	18.74	17.83	16.99	16.21	15.48	14.80	14.17	13.57	13.02	34
35	19.76	18.81	17.93	17.10	16.33	15.61	14.94	14.31	13.72	13.17	12.65	35
36	18.77	17.92	17.11	16.36	15.66	15.00	14.38	13.80	13.26	12.75	12.26	36
37	17.79	17.01	16.29	15.61	14.97	14.37	13.81	13.28	12.78	12.31	11.86	37
38	16.80	16.11	15.46	14.85	14.27	13.73	13.22	12.74	12.28	11.85	11.44	38
39	15.81	15.20	14.62	14.08	13.56	13.07	12.61	12.18	11.76	11.37	11.00	39
40	14.82	14.29	13.78	13.29	12.83	12.40	11.99	11.59	11.22	10.87	10.53	40

Age												Age
41	10.04	10.35	10.66	10.99	11.34	11.71	12.09	12.50	12.92	13.37	13.84	41
42	9.53	9.80	10.08	10.37	10.68	11.00	11.34	11.69	12.06	12.45	12.85	42
43	8.99	9.23	9.48	9.73	10.00	10.28	10.57	10.87	11.19	11.52	11.87	43
44	8.43	8.63	8.85	9.07	9.30	9.53	9.78	10.04	10.31	10.59	10.88	44
45	7.84	8.01	8.19	8.38	8.57	8.77	8.98	9.20	9.42	9.66	9.90	45
46	7.22	7.36	7.51	7.67	7.83	7.99	8.17	8.34	8.53	8.72	8.91	46
47	6.57	6.68	6.81	6.93	7.06	7.19	7.33	7.47	7.62	7.77	7.93	47
48	5.88	5.97	6.07	6.17	6.27	6.37	6.48	6.59	6.70	6.82	6.94	48
49	5.16	5.23	5.31	5.38	5.46	5.53	5.61	5.69	5.78	5.86	5.95	49
50	4.41	4.46	4.51	4.56	4.62	4.67	4.73	4.78	4.84	4.90	4.96	50
51	3.61	3.65	3.68	3.71	3.75	3.79	3.82	3.86	3.90	3.94	3.98	51
52	2.78	2.80	2.82	2.84	2.86	2.88	2.90	2.92	2.94	2.96	2.99	52
53	1.90	1.91	1.92	1.93	1.94	1.94	1.95	1.96	1.97	1.98	1.99	53
54	0.97	0.98	0.98	0.98	0.98	0.99	0.99	0.99	0.99	1.00	1.00	54

Table 23   Multipliers for loss of earnings to pension age 60 (males)

Multiplier calculated with allowance for projected mortality from the 1998-based population projections and rate of return of

Age at date of trial	0.0%	0.5%	1.0%	1.5%	2.0%	2.5%	3.0%	3.5%	4.0%	4.5%	5.0%	Age at date of trial
16	42.93	38.59	34.85	31.60	28.79	26.33	24.18	22.29	20.62	19.15	17.84	16
17	41.94	37.79	34.20	31.08	28.36	25.98	23.90	22.06	20.43	19.00	17.72	17
18	40.96	36.99	33.55	30.55	27.93	25.63	23.61	21.82	20.24	18.84	17.59	18
19	39.98	36.20	32.91	30.03	27.50	25.28	23.32	21.59	20.05	18.68	17.45	19
20	39.01	35.40	32.25	29.49	27.06	24.92	23.02	21.34	19.84	18.51	17.32	20
21	38.04	34.61	31.60	28.95	26.61	24.55	22.72	21.09	19.63	18.34	17.17	21
22	37.07	33.80	30.93	28.40	26.16	24.17	22.40	20.83	19.42	18.15	17.02	22
23	36.09	32.99	30.26	27.84	25.69	23.78	22.07	20.55	19.19	17.96	16.86	23
24	35.12	32.18	29.58	27.27	25.21	23.38	21.74	20.27	18.95	17.76	16.69	24
25	34.14	31.36	28.89	26.69	24.72	22.97	21.39	19.98	18.70	17.55	16.51	25
26	33.17	30.54	28.19	26.10	24.23	22.55	21.04	19.67	18.45	17.33	16.33	26
27	32.20	29.71	27.49	25.51	23.72	22.12	20.67	19.36	18.18	17.11	16.13	27
28	31.22	28.88	26.79	24.90	23.20	21.67	20.29	19.04	17.90	16.87	15.93	28
29	30.25	28.05	26.07	24.29	22.68	21.22	19.90	18.70	17.61	16.62	15.71	29
30	29.27	27.21	25.35	23.66	22.14	20.76	19.50	18.36	17.31	16.36	15.49	30
31	28.29	26.36	24.62	23.03	21.59	20.28	19.09	18.00	17.00	16.09	15.25	31
32	27.32	25.51	23.88	22.39	21.03	19.79	18.66	17.63	16.68	15.80	15.00	32
33	26.34	24.66	23.13	21.73	20.46	19.29	18.22	17.24	16.34	15.51	14.74	33
34	25.36	23.80	22.38	21.07	19.88	18.78	17.77	16.84	15.98	15.19	14.46	34
35	24.38	22.94	21.61	20.40	19.28	18.25	17.30	16.43	15.62	14.87	14.17	35
36	23.40	22.07	20.84	19.71	18.67	17.71	16.82	16.00	15.24	14.53	13.87	36
37	22.42	21.19	20.06	19.02	18.05	17.15	16.32	15.55	14.84	14.17	13.55	37
38	21.44	20.31	19.27	18.31	17.42	16.59	15.82	15.10	14.43	13.80	13.22	38
39	20.46	19.43	18.48	17.60	16.77	16.01	15.29	14.62	14.00	13.42	12.87	39
40	19.48	18.55	17.69	16.88	16.12	15.42	14.75	14.14	13.56	13.01	12.50	40

Age												Age
41	12.12	12.60	13.10	13.63	14.20	14.81	15.46	16.15	16.88	17.67	18.51	41
42	11.72	12.16	12.62	13.12	13.64	14.19	14.78	15.41	16.07	16.78	17.54	42
43	11.31	11.71	12.13	12.58	13.06	13.56	14.09	14.66	15.25	15.89	16.57	43
44	10.87	11.24	11.62	12.03	12.46	12.91	13.39	13.90	14.43	15.00	15.60	44
45	10.41	10.74	11.09	11.46	11.84	12.25	12.67	13.12	13.60	14.10	14.63	45
46	9.93	10.23	10.54	10.86	11.21	11.57	11.94	12.34	12.76	13.20	13.66	46
47	9.42	9.69	9.96	10.25	10.55	10.87	11.20	11.55	11.91	12.29	12.69	47
48	8.89	9.12	9.37	9.62	9.88	10.15	10.44	10.74	11.05	11.38	11.72	48
49	8.33	8.54	8.74	8.96	9.19	9.42	9.66	9.92	10.18	10.46	10.74	49
50	7.75	7.92	8.10	8.28	8.47	8.67	8.87	9.08	9.30	9.53	9.77	50
51	7.13	7.28	7.42	7.58	7.73	7.90	8.07	8.24	8.42	8.61	8.80	51
52	6.49	6.61	6.73	6.85	6.98	7.11	7.24	7.38	7.53	7.67	7.83	52
53	5.82	5.91	6.00	6.10	6.20	6.30	6.41	6.51	6.52	6.74	6.86	53
54	5.11	5.18	5.25	5.32	5.40	5.47	5.55	5.63	5.71	5.80	5.88	54
55	4.36	4.41	4.46	4.52	4.57	4.62	4.68	4.74	4.79	4.85	4.91	55
56	3.58	3.61	3.65	3.68	3.72	3.75	3.79	3.82	3.36	3.90	3.94	56
57	2.76	2.78	2.80	2.82	2.84	2.86	2.88	2.90	2.92	2.94	2.96	57
58	1.89	1.90	1.91	1.92	1.92	1.93	1.94	1.95	1.96	1.97	1.98	58
59	0.97	0.97	0.98	0.98	0.98	0.98	0.99	0.99	0.99	0.99	1.00	59

Table 24 Multipliers for loss of earnings to pension age 60 (females)

Multiplier calculated with allowance for projected mortality from the 1998-based population projections and rate of return of

Age at date of trial	0.0%	0.5%	1.0%	1.5%	2.0%	2.5%	3.0%	3.5%	4.0%	4.5%	5.0%	Age at date of trial
16	43.38	38.99	35.19	31.90	29.05	26.56	24.38	22.47	20.78	19.29	17.97	16
17	42.39	38.18	34.54	31.38	28.62	26.21	24.10	22.24	20.60	19.14	17.84	17
18	41.40	37.38	33.89	30.85	28.19	25.86	23.81	22.00	20.40	18.98	17.72	18
19	40.41	36.57	33.23	30.31	27.75	25.50	23.52	21.76	20.21	18.82	17.58	19
20	39.42	35.76	32.57	29.77	27.30	25.13	23.21	21.51	20.00	18.65	17.44	20
21	38.43	34.95	31.89	29.21	26.85	24.76	22.90	21.25	19.78	18.47	17.29	21
22	37.43	34.12	31.21	28.65	26.38	24.37	22.58	20.98	19.56	18.28	17.14	22
23	36.44	33.30	30.53	28.08	25.90	23.97	22.25	20.71	19.33	18.09	16.97	23
24	35.45	32.47	29.84	27.50	25.42	23.56	21.90	20.42	19.08	17.88	16.80	24
25	34.46	31.64	29.13	26.91	24.92	23.14	21.55	20.12	18.83	17.67	16.62	25
26	33.46	30.80	28.43	26.31	24.41	22.72	21.19	19.81	18.57	17.45	16.43	26
27	32.47	29.96	27.71	25.70	23.90	22.28	20.81	19.49	18.30	17.21	16.23	27
28	31.48	29.11	26.99	25.09	23.37	21.83	20.43	19.16	18.02	16.97	16.02	28
29	30.49	28.27	26.27	24.47	22.84	21.37	20.03	18.82	17.72	16.72	15.80	29
30	29.50	27.41	25.53	23.83	22.29	20.90	19.63	18.47	17.42	16.46	15.57	30
31	28.51	26.56	24.79	23.19	21.74	20.42	19.21	18.11	17.10	16.18	15.33	31
32	27.52	25.70	24.05	22.54	21.17	19.92	18.78	17.73	16.77	15.89	15.08	32
33	26.53	24.84	23.29	21.88	20.60	19.42	18.34	17.34	16.43	15.59	14.82	33
34	25.55	23.97	22.53	21.21	20.01	18.90	17.88	16.94	16.08	15.28	14.54	34
35	24.56	23.10	21.76	20.54	19.41	18.37	17.41	16.53	15.71	14.95	14.25	35
36	23.57	22.23	20.99	19.85	18.80	17.83	16.93	16.10	15.33	14.61	13.95	36
37	22.59	21.35	20.21	19.15	18.18	17.27	16.43	15.65	14.93	14.26	13.63	37
38	21.60	20.47	19.42	18.44	17.54	16.70	15.92	15.20	14.52	13.89	13.30	38
39	20.62	19.58	18.62	17.73	16.90	16.12	15.40	14.72	14.09	13.50	12.95	39
40	19.63	18.69	17.82	17.00	16.24	15.52	14.86	14.23	13.65	13.10	12.58	40

Age												Age
41	12.20	12.68	13.19	13.73	14.30	14.91	15.57	16.26	17.01	17.80	18.65	41
42	11.80	12.24	12.71	13.20	13.73	14.29	14.88	15.52	16.19	16.91	17.67	42
43	11.38	11.78	12.21	12.66	13.14	13.65	14.19	14.76	15.36	16.01	16.69	43
44	10.94	11.31	11.69	12.11	12.54	13.00	13.48	13.99	14.53	15.10	15.71	44
45	10.47	10.81	11.16	11.53	11.92	12.33	12.76	13.21	13.69	14.20	14.73	45
46	9.99	10.29	10.60	10.93	11.28	11.64	12.02	12.42	12.84	13.28	13.75	46
47	9.48	9.74	10.02	10.31	10.62	10.94	11.27	11.62	11.98	12.37	12.77	47
48	8.94	9.18	9.42	9.67	9.94	10.22	10.50	10.81	11.12	11.45	11.79	48
49	8.38	8.59	8.80	9.01	9.24	9.48	9.72	9.98	10.25	10.52	10.81	49
50	7.80	7.97	8.15	8.33	8.52	8.72	8.93	9.14	9.37	9.60	9.84	50
51	7.18	7.32	7.47	7.63	7.78	7.95	8.12	8.29	8.48	8.66	8.86	51
52	6.53	6.65	6.77	6.89	7.02	7.15	7.29	7.43	7.58	7.73	7.88	52
53	5.85	5.94	6.04	6.14	6.24	6.34	6.45	6.56	6.67	6.78	6.90	53
54	5.14	5.21	5.28	5.35	5.43	5.51	5.59	5.67	5.75	5.84	5.92	54
55	4.39	4.44	4.49	4.54	4.60	4.65	4.71	4.76	4.82	4.88	4.94	55
56	3.60	3.63	3.67	3.70	3.74	3.77	3.81	3.85	3.88	3.92	3.96	56
57	2.77	2.79	2.81	2.83	2.85	2.87	2.89	2.91	2.93	2.95	2.98	57
58	1.90	1.90	1.91	1.92	1.93	1.94	1.95	1.96	1.97	1.98	1.99	58
59	0.97	0.98	0.98	0.98	0.98	0.98	0.99	0.99	0.99	0.99	1.00	59

Table 25   Multipliers for loss of earnings to pension age 65 (males)

Age at date of trial	Multiplier calculated with allowance for projected mortality from the 1998-based population projections and rate of return of											Age at date of trial
	0.0%	0.5%	1.0%	1.5%	2.0%	2.5%	3.0%	3.5%	4.0%	4.5%	5.0%	
16	47.44	42.17	37.69	33.87	30.59	27.76	25.32	23.20	21.35	19.74	18.31	16
17	46.45	41.39	37.07	33.38	30.20	27.45	25.07	23.00	21.20	19.61	18.21	17
18	45.48	40.62	36.46	32.89	29.81	27.14	24.83	22.80	21.03	19.48	18.10	18
19	44.51	39.84	35.84	32.39	29.41	26.83	24.57	22.60	20.87	19.35	18.00	19
20	43.53	39.07	35.22	31.89	29.01	26.50	24.31	22.39	20.70	19.21	17.89	20
21	42.57	38.29	34.59	31.39	28.60	26.17	24.05	22.17	20.53	19.07	17.77	21
22	41.60	37.50	33.96	30.88	28.19	25.84	23.77	21.95	20.34	18.92	17.65	22
23	40.62	36.71	33.32	30.35	27.76	25.49	23.49	21.72	20.15	18.76	17.52	23
24	39.65	35.92	32.67	29.82	27.33	25.13	23.19	21.48	19.95	18.60	17.38	24
25	38.68	35.12	32.01	29.28	26.88	24.76	22.89	21.23	19.75	18.42	17.24	25
26	37.71	34.32	31.35	28.74	26.43	24.39	22.58	20.97	19.53	18.25	17.09	26
27	36.73	33.51	30.68	28.18	25.97	24.01	22.26	20.70	19.31	18.06	16.94	27
28	35.76	32.70	30.01	27.62	25.50	23.61	21.93	20.43	19.08	17.86	16.77	28
29	34.79	31.89	29.32	27.05	25.02	23.21	21.59	20.14	18.84	17.66	16.60	29
30	33.81	31.07	28.64	26.47	24.53	22.80	21.24	19.85	18.59	17.45	16.42	30
31	32.84	30.25	27.94	25.88	24.03	22.37	20.88	19.54	18.32	17.23	16.23	31
32	31.86	29.42	27.23	25.28	23.52	21.94	20.51	19.22	18.05	16.99	16.03	32
33	30.89	28.59	26.52	24.67	23.00	21.49	20.13	18.89	17.77	16.75	15.82	33
34	29.91	27.75	25.80	24.05	22.47	21.03	19.73	18.55	17.48	16.50	15.60	34
35	28.93	26.90	25.07	23.42	21.92	20.56	19.32	18.20	17.17	16.23	15.37	35
36	27.95	26.05	24.34	22.78	21.37	20.08	18.90	17.83	16.85	15.95	15.12	36
37	26.97	25.20	23.60	22.13	20.80	19.58	18.47	17.45	16.52	15.66	14.87	37
38	25.99	24.35	22.85	21.48	20.22	19.08	18.03	17.06	16.17	15.36	14.60	38
39	25.01	23.49	22.09	20.81	19.64	18.56	17.57	16.66	15.82	15.04	14.32	39
40	24.04	22.63	21.33	20.14	19.04	18.03	17.10	16.24	15.45	14.71	14.03	40

Age												Age
41	13.73	14.37	15.07	15.82	16.62	17.50	18.44	19.46	20.57	21.77	23.07	41
42	13.41	14.02	14.67	15.38	16.13	16.95	17.83	18.77	19.80	20.91	22.10	42
43	13.08	13.65	14.27	14.92	15.63	16.39	17.20	18.08	19.02	20.04	21.14	43
44	12.73	13.27	13.84	14.45	15.11	15.81	16.56	17.37	18.24	19.17	20.17	44
45	12.37	12.87	13.40	13.97	14.58	15.22	15.92	16.66	17.45	18.30	19.21	45
46	11.99	12.45	12.95	13.47	14.03	14.62	15.26	15.93	16.65	17.42	18.25	46
47	11.59	12.02	12.47	12.95	13.46	14.01	14.58	15.20	15.85	16.54	17.28	47
48	11.17	11.56	11.98	12.42	12.88	13.37	13.90	14.45	15.03	15.66	16.32	48
49	10.73	11.09	11.46	11.86	12.28	12.73	13.19	13.69	14.21	14.77	15.35	49
50	10.27	10.59	10.93	11.29	11.67	12.06	12.48	12.92	13.38	13.87	14.39	50
51	9.78	10.07	10.38	10.70	11.03	11.38	11.75	12.14	12.54	12.97	13.42	51
52	9.28	9.54	9.80	10.09	10.38	10.69	11.01	11.35	11.70	12.07	12.46	52
53	8.75	8.98	9.21	9.46	9.71	9.98	10.26	10.55	10.85	11.17	11.50	53
54	8.20	8.40	8.60	8.81	9.03	9.26	9.50	9.74	10.00	10.27	10.55	54
55	7.62	7.79	7.96	8.14	8.33	8.52	8.72	8.93	9.14	9.37	9.60	55
56	7.02	7.16	7.31	7.45	7.61	7.77	7.93	8.10	8.28	8.46	8.65	56
57	6.39	6.51	6.62	6.74	6.87	7.00	7.13	7.26	7.40	7.55	7.70	57
58	5.73	5.82	5.92	6.01	6.11	6.21	6.31	6.42	6.53	6.64	6.75	58
59	5.04	5.11	5.18	5.25	5.32	5.40	5.48	5.56	5.64	5.72	5.80	59
60	4.31	4.36	4.41	4.46	4.52	4.57	4.62	4.68	4.74	4.79	4.85	60
61	3.55	3.58	3.61	3.65	3.68	3.72	3.75	3.79	3.82	3.86	3.90	61
62	2.74	2.76	2.77	2.79	2.81	2.83	2.85	2.88	2.90	2.92	2.94	62
63	1.88	1.89	1.90	1.91	1.91	1.92	1.93	1.94	1.95	1.96	1.97	63
64	0.97	0.97	0.97	0.98	0.98	0.98	0.98	0.98	0.99	0.99	0.99	64

Table 26   Multipliers for loss of earnings to pension age 65 (females)

Age at date of trial	Multiplier calculated with allowance for projected mortality from the 1998-based population projections and rate of return of											Age at date of trial
	0.0%	0.5%	1.0%	1.5%	2.0%	2.5%	3.0%	3.5%	4.0%	4.5%	5.0%	
16	48.06	42.69	38.13	34.24	30.91	28.04	25.56	23.41	21.54	19.89	18.45	16
17	47.07	41.91	37.52	33.76	30.52	27.74	25.32	23.22	21.38	19.77	18.35	17
18	46.08	41.13	36.89	33.26	30.13	27.42	25.07	23.02	21.22	19.64	18.25	18
19	45.08	40.34	36.27	32.76	29.73	27.10	24.81	22.81	21.06	19.51	18.14	19
20	44.09	39.54	35.63	32.25	29.32	26.77	24.55	22.60	20.88	19.37	18.03	20
21	43.10	38.75	34.99	31.73	28.90	26.44	24.27	22.38	20.70	19.22	17.91	21
22	42.11	37.95	34.34	31.21	28.48	26.09	23.99	22.15	20.52	19.07	17.79	22
23	41.12	37.14	33.69	30.68	28.04	25.73	23.70	21.91	20.32	18.91	17.65	23
24	40.12	36.33	33.02	30.13	27.60	25.37	23.40	21.66	20.12	18.74	17.52	24
25	39.13	35.52	32.36	29.58	27.15	25.00	23.10	21.41	19.91	18.57	17.37	25
26	38.14	34.70	31.68	29.03	26.69	24.62	22.78	21.15	19.69	18.39	17.22	26
27	37.15	33.88	31.00	28.46	26.22	24.22	22.45	20.87	19.46	18.20	17.06	27
28	36.16	33.05	30.31	27.89	25.74	23.82	22.12	20.59	19.23	18.00	16.89	28
29	35.17	32.22	29.62	27.31	25.25	23.41	21.77	20.30	18.98	17.79	16.72	29
30	34.18	31.39	28.92	26.72	24.75	23.00	21.42	20.00	18.73	17.58	16.54	30
31	33.19	30.56	28.21	26.12	24.25	22.57	21.05	19.69	18.46	17.35	16.34	31
32	32.20	29.72	27.50	25.51	23.73	22.13	20.68	19.37	18.19	17.12	16.14	32
33	31.21	28.88	26.78	24.90	23.21	21.68	20.29	19.04	17.91	16.87	15.93	33
34	30.22	28.03	26.06	24.28	22.67	21.22	19.90	18.70	17.61	16.62	15.71	34
35	29.24	27.18	25.32	23.64	22.12	20.74	19.49	18.35	17.31	16.35	15.48	35
36	28.25	26.33	24.59	23.00	21.57	20.26	19.07	17.98	16.99	16.08	15.24	36
37	27.27	25.47	23.84	22.36	21.00	19.77	18.64	17.61	16.66	15.79	14.99	37
38	26.28	24.61	23.09	21.70	20.43	19.26	18.20	17.22	16.31	15.49	14.72	38
39	25.30	23.75	22.33	21.03	19.84	18.74	17.74	16.81	15.96	15.17	14.44	39
40	24.32	22.88	21.57	20.35	19.24	18.22	17.27	16.40	15.59	14.84	14.15	40

Age												Age
41	23.34	22.01	20.79	19.67	18.63	17.67	16.79	15.97	15.21	14.50	13.85	41
42	22.36	21.14	20.02	18.98	18.01	17.12	16.29	15.53	14.81	14.15	13.53	42
43	21.38	20.27	19.23	18.27	17.38	16.55	15.78	15.07	14.40	13.78	13.20	43
44	20.41	19.39	18.44	17.56	16.74	15.97	15.26	14.60	13.97	13.39	12.85	44
45	19.43	18.51	17.64	16.84	16.08	15.38	14.72	14.11	13.53	12.99	12.48	45
46	18.46	17.62	16.84	16.10	15.42	14.77	14.17	13.60	13.07	12.57	12.10	46
47	17.48	16.73	16.02	15.36	14.74	14.15	13.60	13.08	12.59	12.13	11.70	47
48	16.51	15.84	15.21	14.61	14.05	13.52	13.02	12.55	12.10	11.68	11.28	48
49	15.54	14.94	14.38	13.85	13.34	12.87	12.42	11.99	11.58	11.20	10.84	49
50	14.57	14.04	13.55	13.07	12.63	12.20	11.80	11.42	11.05	10.71	10.38	50
51	13.60	13.14	12.71	12.29	11.90	11.52	11.16	10.82	10.50	10.19	9.89	51
52	12.63	12.24	11.86	11.50	11.16	10.83	10.51	10.21	9.93	9.65	9.39	52
53	11.67	11.33	11.01	10.70	10.40	10.11	9.84	9.58	9.33	9.09	8.86	53
54	10.70	10.42	10.14	9.88	9.63	9.39	9.15	8.93	8.71	8.51	8.31	54
55	9.74	9.50	9.27	9.05	8.84	8.64	8.44	8.25	8.07	7.90	7.72	55
56	8.77	8.58	8.40	8.22	8.04	7.88	7.71	7.56	7.40	7.26	7.12	56
57	7.81	7.66	7.51	7.37	7.23	7.09	6.96	6.84	6.71	6.59	6.48	57
58	6.84	6.73	6.61	6.50	6.39	6.29	6.19	6.09	5.99	5.90	5.81	58
59	5.88	5.79	5.71	5.63	5.55	5.47	5.39	5.32	5.24	5.17	5.10	59
60	4.91	4.85	4.79	4.73	4.68	4.62	4.57	4.51	4.46	4.41	4.36	60
61	3.94	3.90	3.86	3.82	3.79	3.75	3.72	3.68	3.65	3.61	3.58	61
62	2.96	2.94	2.92	2.90	2.88	2.86	2.84	2.82	2.80	2.78	2.76	62
63	1.98	1.97	1.96	1.95	1.94	1.93	1.93	1.92	1.91	1.90	1.89	63
64	1.00	0.99	0.99	0.99	0.99	0.98	0.98	0.98	0.98	0.97	0.97	64

Table 27   Multipliers for loss of earnings to pension age 70 (males)

Age at date of trial	Multiplier calculated with allowance for projected mortality from the 1998-based population projections and rate of return of											Age at date of trial
	0.0%	0.5%	1.0%	1.5%	2.0%	2.5%	3.0%	3.5%	4.0%	4.5%	5.0%	
16	51.72	45.48	40.25	35.85	32.13	28.96	26.26	23.93	21.92	20.18	18.66	16
17	50.73	44.71	39.66	35.39	31.77	28.68	26.04	23.76	21.79	20.07	18.57	17
18	49.75	43.95	39.07	34.93	31.41	28.40	25.82	23.58	21.65	19.96	18.49	18
19	48.78	43.20	38.48	34.47	31.05	28.12	25.59	23.41	21.51	19.85	18.40	19
20	47.81	42.44	37.88	34.00	30.68	27.83	25.36	23.23	21.37	19.74	18.31	20
21	46.84	41.68	37.28	33.53	30.31	27.53	25.13	23.04	21.22	19.62	18.21	21
22	45.87	40.91	36.68	33.05	29.93	27.23	24.89	22.85	21.06	19.50	18.11	22
23	44.90	40.14	36.06	32.56	29.54	26.92	24.64	22.65	20.90	19.37	18.01	23
24	43.93	39.36	35.44	32.06	29.14	26.59	24.38	22.44	20.73	19.23	17.90	24
25	42.96	38.59	34.82	31.56	28.73	26.27	24.11	22.22	20.56	19.09	17.78	25
26	41.99	37.80	34.18	31.05	28.31	25.93	23.84	22.00	20.38	18.94	17.66	26
27	41.02	37.01	33.55	30.53	27.89	25.58	23.56	21.77	20.19	18.78	17.53	27
28	40.04	36.22	32.90	30.00	27.46	25.23	23.27	21.53	19.99	18.62	17.40	28
29	39.07	35.43	32.25	29.46	27.02	24.87	22.97	21.28	19.79	18.45	17.26	29
30	38.10	34.63	31.59	28.92	26.57	24.50	22.66	21.03	19.57	18.27	17.11	30
31	37.12	33.82	30.92	28.37	26.11	24.11	22.34	20.76	19.35	18.09	16.96	31
32	36.15	33.01	30.25	27.81	25.64	23.72	22.01	20.49	19.12	17.90	16.79	32
33	35.17	32.20	29.57	27.23	25.16	23.32	21.68	20.20	18.88	17.69	16.62	33
34	34.20	31.38	28.88	26.65	24.68	22.91	21.33	19.91	18.63	17.48	16.44	34
35	33.22	30.55	28.18	26.07	24.18	22.49	20.97	19.60	18.37	17.26	16.25	35
36	32.24	29.72	27.47	25.47	23.67	22.05	20.60	19.29	18.10	17.03	16.05	36
37	31.26	28.88	26.76	24.86	23.15	21.61	20.21	18.96	17.82	16.78	15.84	37
38	30.28	28.05	26.04	24.24	22.62	21.15	19.82	18.62	17.52	16.53	15.62	38
39	29.30	27.21	25.32	23.62	22.08	20.69	19.42	18.27	17.22	16.27	15.39	39
40	28.33	26.37	24.59	22.99	21.53	20.21	19.01	17.91	16.91	16.00	15.16	40

Age												Age
41	14.91	15.71	16.59	17.54	18.59	19.73	20.98	22.35	23.86	25.53	27.36	41
42	14.65	15.42	16.26	17.17	18.16	19.24	20.42	21.71	23.13	24.69	26.40	42
43	14.38	15.12	15.91	16.78	17.71	18.73	19.85	21.06	22.39	23.84	25.43	43
44	14.10	14.80	15.56	16.37	17.26	18.22	19.27	20.40	21.64	22.99	24.47	44
45	13.81	14.47	15.19	15.96	16.79	17.70	18.67	19.74	20.89	22.14	23.51	45
46	13.50	14.13	14.80	15.53	16.31	17.16	18.07	19.06	20.13	21.29	22.55	46
47	13.18	13.77	14.40	15.09	15.82	16.61	17.46	18.37	19.36	20.43	21.59	47
48	12.84	13.39	13.99	14.63	15.31	16.04	16.83	17.67	18.58	19.57	20.63	48
49	12.48	13.00	13.56	14.15	14.78	15.46	16.19	16.96	17.80	18.70	19.66	49
50	12.11	12.59	13.11	13.66	14.24	14.87	15.53	16.25	17.01	17.83	18.70	50
51	11.72	12.17	12.65	13.15	13.69	14.26	14.87	15.52	16.21	16.95	17.74	51
52	11.32	11.73	12.17	12.63	13.12	13.64	14.20	14.79	15.41	16.08	16.79	52
53	10.90	11.27	11.67	12.10	12.54	13.02	13.52	14.05	14.61	15.21	15.84	53
54	10.46	10.80	11.17	11.55	11.95	12.38	12.83	13.30	13.80	14.33	14.89	54
55	10.00	10.31	10.64	10.98	11.35	11.73	12.13	12.55	12.99	13.46	13.96	55
56	9.53	9.81	10.10	10.41	10.73	11.06	11.42	11.79	12.18	12.59	13.02	56
57	9.04	9.29	9.54	9.81	10.10	10.39	10.70	11.03	11.37	11.72	12.09	57
58	8.53	8.74	8.97	9.21	9.45	9.71	9.98	10.26	10.55	10.86	11.17	58
59	8.00	8.18	8.38	8.58	8.80	9.02	9.25	9.48	9.73	9.99	10.26	59
60	7.44	7.60	7.77	7.94	8.12	8.31	8.50	8.70	8.91	9.12	9.35	60
61	6.86	7.00	7.14	7.28	7.43	7.58	7.74	7.91	8.08	8.25	8.43	61
62	6.26	6.37	6.48	6.60	6.72	6.84	6.97	7.10	7.24	7.38	7.52	62
63	5.62	5.71	5.80	5.89	5.98	6.08	6.18	6.28	6.39	6.50	6.61	63
64	4.95	5.01	5.08	5.15	5.22	5.30	5.37	5.45	5.53	5.61	5.69	64
65	4.24	4.29	4.34	4.39	4.44	4.49	4.54	4.60	4.65	4.71	4.77	65
66	3.49	3.52	3.56	3.59	3.62	3.66	3.69	3.73	3.76	3.80	3.84	66
67	2.70	2.72	2.74	2.76	2.78	2.80	2.82	2.84	2.86	2.88	2.90	67
68	1.86	1.87	1.88	1.89	1.90	1.90	1.91	1.92	1.93	1.94	1.95	68
69	0.96	0.97	0.97	0.97	0.97	0.97	0.98	0.98	0.98	0.98	0.99	69

Table 28 Multipliers for loss of earnings to pension age 70 (females)

Age at date of trial	Multiplier calculated with allowance for projected mortality from the 1998-based population projections and rate of return of											Age at date of trial
	0.0%	0.5%	1.0%	1.5%	2.0%	2.5%	3.0%	3.5%	4.0%	4.5%	5.0%	
16	52.57	46.18	40.84	36.34	32.54	29.31	26.55	24.18	22.14	20.36	18.82	16
17	51.58	45.42	40.25	35.88	32.18	29.03	26.33	24.01	22.01	20.26	18.74	17
18	50.58	44.65	39.65	35.42	31.82	28.75	26.11	23.84	21.87	20.15	18.65	18
19	49.59	43.88	39.05	34.95	31.46	28.46	25.89	23.66	21.73	20.04	18.57	19
20	48.60	43.10	38.44	34.47	31.08	28.17	25.66	23.48	21.58	19.93	18.48	20
21	47.61	42.32	37.83	33.99	30.70	27.87	25.42	23.29	21.43	19.81	18.38	21
22	46.62	41.54	37.21	33.50	30.31	27.56	25.17	23.09	21.28	19.68	18.28	22
23	45.63	40.75	36.58	33.00	29.91	27.24	24.91	22.89	21.11	19.55	18.17	23
24	44.63	39.96	35.95	32.49	29.51	26.91	24.65	22.68	20.94	19.41	18.06	24
25	43.64	39.16	35.31	31.98	29.09	26.58	24.38	22.46	20.76	19.27	17.94	25
26	42.65	38.36	34.66	31.46	28.67	26.23	24.10	22.23	20.58	19.11	17.82	26
27	41.65	37.56	34.01	30.93	28.24	25.88	23.82	22.00	20.39	18.96	17.69	27
28	40.66	36.75	33.35	30.39	27.80	25.52	23.52	21.75	20.19	18.79	17.55	28
29	39.67	35.94	32.69	29.85	27.35	25.16	23.22	21.50	19.98	18.62	17.41	29
30	38.68	35.13	32.02	29.30	26.90	24.78	22.91	21.25	19.77	18.44	17.26	30
31	37.69	34.31	31.35	28.74	26.43	24.40	22.59	20.98	19.54	18.26	17.11	31
32	36.70	33.49	30.67	28.17	25.96	24.00	22.26	20.70	19.31	18.06	16.94	32
33	35.71	32.67	29.98	27.60	25.48	23.60	21.92	20.42	19.07	17.86	16.77	33
34	34.73	31.84	29.28	27.01	24.99	23.19	21.57	20.13	18.82	17.65	16.59	34
35	33.74	31.01	28.58	26.42	24.49	22.76	21.22	19.82	18.57	17.43	16.41	35
36	32.76	30.18	27.88	25.82	23.98	22.33	20.85	19.51	18.30	17.20	16.21	36
37	31.77	29.34	27.17	25.22	23.47	21.89	20.47	19.19	18.02	16.97	16.01	37
38	30.79	28.50	26.45	24.60	22.94	21.44	20.08	18.85	17.73	16.72	15.79	38
39	29.81	27.66	25.72	23.98	22.40	20.98	19.68	18.51	17.44	16.46	15.57	39
40	28.83	26.81	24.99	23.35	21.86	20.50	19.27	18.15	17.13	16.19	15.33	40

Age												Age
41	15.09	15.91	16.81	17.78	18.85	20.02	21.30	22.71	24.26	25.96	27.85	41
42	14.83	15.62	16.47	17.40	18.42	19.52	20.74	22.06	23.51	25.11	26.87	42
43	14.57	15.32	16.13	17.01	17.97	19.02	20.16	21.40	22.77	24.26	25.89	43
44	14.29	15.00	15.77	16.61	17.52	18.50	19.57	20.74	22.01	23.40	24.92	44
45	13.99	14.67	15.40	16.19	17.05	17.97	18.98	20.07	21.25	22.54	23.95	45
46	13.69	14.33	15.02	15.76	16.57	17.43	18.37	19.39	20.48	21.68	22.97	46
47	13.37	13.97	14.62	15.32	16.07	16.88	17.75	18.69	19.71	20.81	22.00	47
48	13.03	13.60	14.21	14.86	15.56	16.32	17.13	18.00	18.93	19.94	21.04	48
49	12.68	13.21	13.78	14.39	15.04	15.74	16.49	17.29	18.15	19.07	20.07	49
50	12.31	12.81	13.34	13.91	14.51	15.15	15.84	16.57	17.36	18.20	19.10	50
51	11.93	12.39	12.88	13.40	13.96	14.55	15.18	15.85	16.56	17.33	18.14	51
52	11.53	11.96	12.41	12.89	13.39	13.93	14.51	15.11	15.76	16.45	17.18	52
53	11.12	11.51	11.92	12.36	12.82	13.31	13.82	14.37	14.95	15.57	16.23	53
54	10.68	11.04	11.41	11.81	12.22	12.66	13.13	13.62	14.14	14.69	15.27	54
55	10.22	10.55	10.89	11.24	11.62	12.01	12.42	12.86	13.32	13.81	14.32	55
56	9.75	10.04	10.34	10.66	10.99	11.34	11.71	12.09	12.50	12.92	13.37	56
57	9.25	9.51	9.78	10.06	10.35	10.66	10.98	11.32	11.67	12.04	12.42	57
58	8.73	8.96	9.19	9.44	9.69	9.96	10.24	10.53	10.33	11.15	11.48	58
59	8.19	8.38	8.59	8.80	9.02	9.25	9.48	9.73	9.99	10.26	10.54	59
60	7.62	7.79	7.96	8.14	8.33	8.52	8.72	8.92	9.14	9.36	9.59	60
61	7.02	7.16	7.31	7.46	7.61	7.77	7.93	8.10	8.28	8.46	8.65	61
62	6.40	6.51	6.63	6.75	6.87	7.00	7.14	7.27	7.41	7.56	7.71	62
63	5.74	5.83	5.92	6.02	6.12	6.22	6.32	6.42	6.53	6.65	6.76	63
64	5.05	5.12	5.19	5.26	5.33	5.41	5.48	5.56	5.64	5.73	5.81	64
65	4.32	4.37	4.42	4.47	4.52	4.57	4.63	4.68	4.74	4.80	4.86	65
66	3.55	3.58	3.61	3.65	3.68	3.72	3.75	3.79	3.83	3.86	3.90	66
67	2.74	2.76	2.77	2.79	2.81	2.83	2.85	2.88	2.90	2.92	2.94	67
68	1.88	1.89	1.90	1.90	1.91	1.92	1.93	1.94	1.95	1.96	1.97	68
69	0.97	0.97	0.97	0.98	0.98	0.98	0.98	0.98	0.99	0.99	0.99	69

Table 29   Multipliers for loss of pension commencing age 55 (males)

| Age at date of trial | Multiplier calculated with allowance for projected mortality from the 1998-based population projections and rate of return of | | | | | | | | | | | Age at date of trial |
	0.0%	0.5%	1.0%	1.5%	2.0%	2.5%	3.0%	3.5%	4.0%	4.5%	5.0%	
0	25.94	18.26	12.90	9.16	6.53	4.67	3.35	2.42	1.75	1.27	0.93	0
1	26.07	18.44	13.10	9.34	6.69	4.81	3.47	2.52	1.83	1.33	0.98	1
2	26.07	18.53	13.23	9.48	6.83	4.93	3.58	2.60	1.90	1.39	1.03	2
3	26.07	18.63	13.36	9.63	6.96	5.06	3.68	2.70	1.98	1.46	1.08	3
4	26.07	18.72	13.50	9.77	7.10	5.18	3.80	2.79	2.06	1.52	1.13	4
5	26.07	18.81	13.63	9.92	7.24	5.31	3.91	2.89	2.14	1.59	1.19	5
6	26.06	18.90	13.76	10.06	7.39	5.44	4.03	2.99	2.23	1.66	1.25	6
7	26.06	18.99	13.90	10.21	7.53	5.58	4.15	3.09	2.31	1.74	1.31	7
8	26.05	19.08	14.03	10.36	7.68	5.72	4.27	3.20	2.41	1.82	1.37	8
9	26.05	19.17	14.17	10.52	7.83	5.86	4.40	3.31	2.50	1.90	1.44	9
10	26.04	19.26	14.31	10.67	7.99	6.00	4.53	3.43	2.60	1.98	1.51	10
11	26.03	19.35	14.45	10.83	8.15	6.15	4.66	3.54	2.70	2.07	1.59	11
12	26.03	19.45	14.59	10.99	8.31	6.30	4.80	3.67	2.81	2.16	1.67	12
13	26.02	19.54	14.73	11.15	8.47	6.46	4.94	3.80	2.92	2.26	1.75	13
14	26.01	19.63	14.88	11.31	8.64	6.62	5.09	3.93	3.04	2.36	1.84	14
15	26.01	19.73	15.02	11.48	8.81	6.78	5.24	4.06	3.16	2.47	1.93	15
16	26.00	19.82	15.17	11.65	8.98	6.95	5.40	4.21	3.29	2.58	2.03	16
17	26.00	19.92	15.32	11.83	9.16	7.13	5.56	4.35	3.42	2.69	2.13	17
18	26.00	20.02	15.47	12.00	9.35	7.30	5.73	4.51	3.56	2.81	2.23	18
19	26.00	20.12	15.63	12.19	9.54	7.49	5.90	4.66	3.70	2.94	2.35	19
20	26.01	20.23	15.79	12.37	9.73	7.68	6.08	4.83	3.85	3.08	2.47	20
21	26.01	20.33	15.95	12.56	9.93	7.87	6.26	5.00	4.00	3.22	2.59	21
22	26.02	20.44	16.12	12.75	10.13	8.07	6.45	5.18	4.17	3.36	2.72	22
23	26.02	20.54	16.28	12.95	10.33	8.28	6.65	5.36	4.33	3.51	2.86	23
24	26.03	20.65	16.44	13.14	10.54	8.48	6.85	5.55	4.51	3.67	3.00	24
25	26.03	20.75	16.61	13.34	10.75	8.70	7.06	5.74	4.69	3.84	3.15	25

Age												Age
26	3.31	4.01	4.88	5.95	7.27	8.92	10.97	13.54	16.78	20.86	26.03	26
27	3.48	4.19	5.07	6.16	7.49	9.14	11.19	13.75	16.95	20.97	26.03	27
28	3.65	4.38	5.28	6.37	7.72	9.37	11.42	13.96	17.12	21.07	26.03	28
29	3.83	4.58	5.49	6.60	7.95	9.61	11.65	14.17	17.29	21.18	26.03	29
30	4.03	4.79	5.71	6.83	8.19	9.85	11.88	14.38	17.46	21.28	26.03	30
31	4.23	5.00	5.94	7.07	8.43	10.09	12.12	14.60	17.64	21.39	26.03	31
32	4.44	5.23	6.18	7.32	8.69	10.35	12.36	14.81	17.81	21.49	26.02	32
33	4.66	5.47	6.42	7.57	8.95	10.60	12.61	15.04	17.99	21.60	26.02	33
34	4.90	5.71	6.68	7.84	9.22	10.87	12.86	15.26	18.17	21.70	26.01	34
35	5.14	5.97	6.95	8.11	9.49	11.14	13.11	15.48	18.34	21.80	26.00	35
36	5.40	6.24	7.23	8.39	9.77	11.42	13.37	15.71	18.52	21.90	25.99	36
37	5.67	6.52	7.51	8.68	10.07	11.70	13.64	15.94	18.70	22.00	25.98	37
38	5.95	6.81	7.81	8.99	10.37	11.99	13.90	16.18	18.88	22.11	25.97	38
39	6.25	7.12	8.13	9.30	10.68	12.29	14.18	16.42	19.06	22.21	25.96	39
40	6.56	7.44	8.45	9.63	11.00	12.59	14.46	16.66	19.25	22.31	25.95	40
41	6.89	7.78	8.79	9.97	11.33	12.91	14.75	16.91	19.44	22.42	25.95	41
42	7.24	8.13	9.15	10.32	11.67	13.23	15.05	17.16	19.54	22.53	25.94	42
43	7.61	8.50	9.52	10.68	12.02	13.57	15.35	17.42	19.33	22.65	25.94	43
44	7.99	8.89	9.90	11.06	12.39	13.91	15.66	17.69	20.03	22.76	25.94	44
45	8.40	9.29	10.30	11.46	12.77	14.26	15.98	17.96	20.24	22.88	25.94	45
46	8.82	9.72	10.72	11.86	13.16	14.63	16.31	18.23	20.44	22.99	25.94	46
47	9.27	10.16	11.16	12.28	13.56	15.00	16.64	18.51	20.65	23.11	25.94	47
48	9.74	10.62	11.61	12.72	13.97	15.38	16.98	18.79	20.36	23.22	25.94	48
49	10.24	11.11	12.08	13.17	14.40	15.77	17.32	19.08	21.07	23.34	25.94	49
50	10.76	11.62	12.58	13.64	14.84	16.17	17.68	19.37	21.29	23.46	25.93	50
51	11.31	12.16	13.09	14.13	15.29	16.59	18.04	19.67	21.51	23.58	25.94	51
52	11.89	12.72	13.63	14.65	15.77	17.02	18.42	19.98	21.74	23.72	25.95	52
53	12.51	13.32	14.21	15.19	16.27	17.47	18.81	20.31	21.98	23.86	25.97	53
54	13.17	13.95	14.81	15.75	16.79	17.95	19.22	20.65	22.24	24.01	26.01	54
55	13.87	14.62	15.45	16.35	17.34	18.44	19.66	21.01	22.51	24.18	26.06	55

Table 30   Multipliers for loss of pension commencing age 55 (females)

Multiplier calculated with allowance for projected mortality from the 1998-based population projections and rate of return of

Age at date of trial	0.0%	0.5%	1.0%	1.5%	2.0%	2.5%	3.0%	3.5%	4.0%	4.5%	5.0%	Age at date of trial
0	29.68	20.74	14.56	10.27	7.27	5.17	3.70	2.65	1.91	1.38	1.00	0
1	29.80	20.93	14.76	10.46	7.45	5.33	3.82	2.76	1.99	1.45	1.06	1
2	29.81	21.03	14.91	10.62	7.60	5.46	3.94	2.85	2.07	1.51	1.11	2
3	29.81	21.14	15.06	10.78	7.75	5.60	4.06	2.95	2.16	1.58	1.17	3
4	29.80	21.24	15.21	10.94	7.90	5.74	4.18	3.06	2.24	1.65	1.22	4
5	29.80	21.35	15.36	11.10	8.06	5.88	4.30	3.16	2.33	1.73	1.28	5
6	29.80	21.45	15.51	11.27	8.22	6.02	4.43	3.27	2.43	1.81	1.35	6
7	29.79	21.55	15.66	11.44	8.38	6.17	4.56	3.39	2.52	1.89	1.42	7
8	29.79	21.66	15.82	11.61	8.55	6.33	4.70	3.51	2.62	1.97	1.49	8
9	29.78	21.76	15.97	11.78	8.72	6.48	4.84	3.63	2.73	2.06	1.56	9
10	29.77	21.86	16.13	11.95	8.89	6.64	4.98	3.75	2.84	2.15	1.64	10
11	29.77	21.97	16.29	12.13	9.07	6.81	5.13	3.88	2.95	2.25	1.72	11
12	29.76	22.07	16.45	12.31	9.25	6.98	5.29	4.02	3.07	2.35	1.81	12
13	29.75	22.18	16.61	12.49	9.43	7.15	5.44	4.16	3.19	2.45	1.90	13
14	29.75	22.29	16.77	12.68	9.62	7.33	5.61	4.30	3.32	2.56	1.99	14
15	29.74	22.39	16.94	12.86	9.81	7.51	5.77	4.45	3.45	2.68	2.09	15
16	29.74	22.50	17.10	13.05	10.00	7.70	5.95	4.61	3.59	2.80	2.19	16
17	29.73	22.61	17.27	13.25	10.20	7.89	6.12	4.77	3.73	2.93	2.30	17
18	29.73	22.72	17.44	13.45	10.41	8.09	6.31	4.94	3.88	3.06	2.42	18
19	29.73	22.83	17.62	13.65	10.61	8.29	6.50	5.11	4.03	3.19	2.54	19
20	29.72	22.94	17.79	13.85	10.83	8.49	6.69	5.29	4.19	3.34	2.67	20
21	29.72	23.06	17.96	14.06	11.04	8.71	6.89	5.47	4.36	3.49	2.80	21
22	29.71	23.17	18.14	14.26	11.26	8.92	7.10	5.66	4.54	3.65	2.94	22
23	29.70	23.28	18.32	14.48	11.48	9.14	7.31	5.86	4.72	3.81	3.08	23
24	29.70	23.39	18.50	14.69	11.71	9.37	7.53	6.07	4.91	3.98	3.24	24
25	29.69	23.50	18.68	14.91	11.94	9.60	7.75	6.28	5.10	4.16	3.40	25

Age											Age
26	3.57	4.34	5.30	6.50	7.98	9.84	12.18	15.13	18.86	23.61	29.68	26
27	3.75	4.54	5.51	6.72	8.22	10.09	12.42	15.35	19.04	23.72	29.67	27
28	3.93	4.74	5.73	6.96	8.46	10.34	12.66	15.58	19.23	23.83	29.66	28
29	4.13	4.96	5.96	7.20	8.72	10.59	12.91	15.81	19.42	23.95	29.65	29
30	4.34	5.18	6.20	7.45	8.98	10.85	13.17	16.04	19.61	24.06	29.64	30
31	4.55	5.41	6.45	7.71	9.24	11.12	13.43	16.28	19.80	24.17	29.63	31
32	4.78	5.65	6.70	7.98	9.52	11.40	13.70	16.52	19.99	24.29	29.62	32
33	5.02	5.91	6.97	8.25	9.80	11.68	13.97	16.76	20.18	24.40	29.61	33
34	5.27	6.17	7.25	8.54	10.10	11.97	14.24	17.01	20.38	24.51	29.60	34
35	5.53	6.45	7.54	8.84	10.40	12.27	14.52	17.26	20.58	24.63	29.59	35
36	5.81	6.74	7.84	9.15	10.71	12.57	14.81	17.51	20.78	24.74	29.58	36
37	6.10	7.04	8.15	9.47	11.03	12.88	15.11	17.77	20.98	24.86	29.57	37
38	6.40	7.36	8.48	9.80	11.36	13.21	15.40	18.03	21.18	24.98	29.56	38
39	6.72	7.69	8.82	10.14	11.70	13.53	15.71	18.30	21.39	25.09	29.55	39
40	7.06	8.04	9.17	10.50	12.05	13.87	16.02	18.57	21.60	25.21	29.54	40
41	7.42	8.40	9.54	10.86	12.41	14.22	16.34	18.85	21.81	25.33	29.53	41
42	7.79	8.78	9.92	11.24	12.78	14.57	16.67	19.13	22.03	25.45	29.53	42
43	8.18	9.18	10.32	11.64	13.17	14.94	17.00	19.41	22.24	25.58	29.52	43
44	8.59	9.59	10.74	12.05	13.56	15.31	17.34	19.71	22.47	25.70	29.52	44
45	9.02	10.03	11.17	12.47	13.97	15.70	17.69	20.00	22.69	25.83	29.51	45
46	9.48	10.48	11.62	12.92	14.40	16.10	18.05	20.30	22.92	25.96	29.51	46
47	9.96	10.96	12.09	13.37	14.83	16.50	18.42	20.61	23.15	26.09	29.51	47
48	10.47	11.46	12.58	13.85	15.29	16.92	18.79	20.93	23.39	26.23	29.51	48
49	11.00	11.99	13.10	14.35	15.76	17.36	19.18	21.25	23.63	26.37	29.52	49
50	11.56	12.54	13.63	14.86	16.24	17.80	19.57	21.59	23.88	26.51	29.53	50
51	12.16	13.12	14.20	15.40	16.75	18.27	19.98	21.93	24.14	26.66	29.54	51
52	12.78	13.73	14.78	15.96	17.27	18.75	20.41	22.28	24.40	26.81	29.57	52
53	13.45	14.37	15.40	16.54	17.82	19.24	20.84	22.64	24.67	26.98	29.59	53
54	14.15	15.05	16.05	17.16	18.39	19.76	21.29	23.02	24.96	27.15	29.63	54
55	14.89	15.77	16.73	17.80	18.98	20.29	21.76	23.41	25.25	27.33	29.68	55

Table 31   Multipliers for loss of pension commencing age 60 (males)

Age at date of trial	Multiplier calculated with allowance for projected mortality from the 1998-based population projections and rate of return of											Age at date of trial
	0.0%	0.5%	1.0%	1.5%	2.0%	2.5%	3.0%	3.5%	4.0%	4.5%	5.0%	
0	21.29	14.76	10.28	7.18	5.04	3.54	2.50	1.77	1.26	0.90	0.64	0
1	21.39	14.91	10.43	7.32	5.16	3.65	2.59	1.84	1.32	0.94	0.68	1
2	21.39	14.99	10.54	7.44	5.27	3.74	2.67	1.91	1.37	0.99	0.71	2
3	21.39	15.06	10.64	7.55	5.37	3.84	2.75	1.98	1.43	1.03	0.75	3
4	21.39	15.13	10.75	7.66	5.48	3.93	2.83	2.05	1.48	1.08	0.79	4
5	21.39	15.21	10.85	7.77	5.59	4.03	2.92	2.12	1.54	1.13	0.83	5
6	21.38	15.28	10.96	7.89	5.70	4.13	3.00	2.19	1.60	1.18	0.87	6
7	21.38	15.35	11.07	8.00	5.81	4.23	3.09	2.27	1.67	1.23	0.91	7
8	21.37	15.43	11.17	8.12	5.93	4.34	3.18	2.35	1.73	1.28	0.95	8
9	21.37	15.50	11.28	8.24	6.04	4.44	3.28	2.43	1.80	1.34	1.00	9
10	21.36	15.57	11.39	8.36	6.16	4.55	3.38	2.51	1.87	1.40	1.05	10
11	21.36	15.65	11.50	8.49	6.28	4.67	3.48	2.60	1.95	1.46	1.10	11
12	21.35	15.72	11.61	8.61	6.41	4.78	3.58	2.69	2.03	1.53	1.16	12
13	21.34	15.79	11.73	8.74	6.53	4.90	3.69	2.78	2.11	1.60	1.22	13
14	21.34	15.87	11.84	8.87	6.66	5.02	3.80	2.88	2.19	1.67	1.28	14
15	21.33	15.94	11.96	9.00	6.79	5.15	3.91	2.98	2.28	1.74	1.34	15
16	21.32	16.02	12.07	9.13	6.93	5.27	4.03	3.08	2.37	1.82	1.41	16
17	21.32	16.09	12.19	9.27	7.06	5.40	4.15	3.19	2.46	1.90	1.48	17
18	21.32	16.18	12.31	9.41	7.21	5.54	4.27	3.30	2.56	1.99	1.55	18
19	21.32	16.26	12.44	9.55	7.35	5.68	4.40	3.42	2.66	2.08	1.63	19
20	21.33	16.34	12.57	9.69	7.50	5.82	4.53	3.54	2.77	2.17	1.71	20
21	21.33	16.43	12.69	9.84	7.65	5.97	4.67	3.66	2.88	2.27	1.80	21
22	21.33	16.51	12.82	9.99	7.81	6.12	4.81	3.79	3.00	2.38	1.89	22
23	21.33	16.59	12.95	10.14	7.96	6.27	4.96	3.93	3.12	2.48	1.98	23
24	21.33	16.68	13.08	10.29	8.12	6.43	5.10	4.06	3.24	2.60	2.08	24
25	21.33	16.76	13.21	10.45	8.29	6.59	5.26	4.21	3.37	2.71	2.19	25

Age												Age
26	2.30	2.84	3.51	4.35	5.42	6.76	8.45	10.60	13.34	16.84	21.33	26
27	2.41	2.96	3.65	4.51	5.58	6.93	8.62	10.76	13.48	16.93	21.33	27
28	2.53	3.10	3.80	4.66	5.75	7.10	8.79	10.92	13.61	17.01	21.33	28
29	2.66	3.24	3.95	4.83	5.92	7.28	8.97	11.09	13.75	17.09	21.32	29
30	2.79	3.38	4.11	5.00	6.10	7.46	9.15	11.25	13.88	17.18	21.32	30
31	2.93	3.53	4.27	5.17	6.28	7.64	9.33	11.42	14.02	17.26	21.32	31
32	3.08	3.69	4.44	5.35	6.47	7.83	9.51	11.59	14.16	17.34	21.31	32
33	3.23	3.86	4.62	5.54	6.66	8.03	9.70	11.76	14.29	17.42	21.30	33
34	3.39	4.03	4.80	5.73	6.86	8.22	9.89	11.93	14.43	17.50	21.29	34
35	3.56	4.21	4.99	5.93	7.06	8.43	10.09	12.10	14.57	17.58	21.28	35
36	3.74	4.40	5.19	6.13	7.27	8.63	10.28	12.28	14.70	17.66	21.27	36
37	3.92	4.60	5.39	6.35	7.48	8.85	10.48	12.46	14.84	17.74	21.25	37
38	4.12	4.80	5.61	6.57	7.70	9.06	10.69	12.64	14.98	17.81	21.24	38
39	4.32	5.02	5.83	6.79	7.93	9.29	10.90	12.82	15.12	17.89	21.23	39
40	4.54	5.24	6.06	7.03	8.17	9.51	11.11	13.01	15.27	17.97	21.21	40
41	4.77	5.48	6.30	7.27	8.41	9.75	11.33	13.20	15.42	18.05	21.20	41
42	5.01	5.72	6.56	7.53	8.66	9.99	11.55	13.39	15.57	18.14	21.19	42
43	5.26	5.98	6.82	7.79	8.92	10.24	11.78	13.59	15.72	18.22	21.19	43
44	5.52	6.25	7.09	8.06	9.19	10.50	12.02	13.79	15.87	18.31	21.18	44
45	5.80	6.53	7.38	8.35	9.47	10.76	12.26	14.00	16.02	18.39	21.17	45
46	6.09	6.83	7.67	8.64	9.75	11.03	12.50	14.20	16.18	18.48	21.16	46
47	6.39	7.14	7.98	8.94	10.04	11.30	12.75	14.41	16.34	18.56	21.15	47
48	6.71	7.46	8.30	9.25	10.34	11.58	13.00	14.62	16.49	18.65	21.14	48
49	7.05	7.79	8.63	9.58	10.65	11.87	13.26	14.84	16.65	18.73	21.13	49
50	7.41	8.15	8.98	9.91	10.97	12.16	13.52	15.06	16.81	18.82	21.12	50
51	7.78	8.52	9.34	10.26	11.30	12.47	13.79	15.28	16.98	18.91	21.11	51
52	8.17	8.90	9.72	10.63	11.64	12.79	14.07	15.51	17.15	19.00	21.10	52
53	8.59	9.32	10.12	11.01	12.00	13.11	14.36	15.75	17.33	19.10	21.11	53
54	9.04	9.75	10.54	11.41	12.38	13.46	14.66	16.01	17.51	19.21	21.12	54
55	9.51	10.21	10.98	11.83	12.77	13.82	14.98	16.27	17.71	19.33	21.14	55

Table 31   Multipliers for loss of pension commencing age 60 (males)

Age at date of trial	Multiplier calculated with allowance for projected mortality from the 1998-based population projections and rate of return of											Age at date of trial
	0.0%	0.5%	1.0%	1.5%	2.0%	2.5%	3.0%	3.5%	4.0%	4.5%	5.0%	
56	21.18	19.46	17.92	16.55	15.31	14.20	13.19	12.28	11.45	10.70	10.01	56
57	21.23	19.61	18.16	16.85	15.67	14.60	13.63	12.75	11.95	11.22	10.56	57
58	21.32	19.79	18.42	17.18	16.05	15.03	14.11	13.26	12.49	11.79	11.14	58
59	21.43	20.00	18.70	17.53	16.47	15.50	14.62	13.81	13.07	12.39	11.77	59
60	21.56	20.23	19.01	17.91	16.91	16.00	15.16	14.40	13.69	13.05	12.45	60

Table 32 Multipliers for loss of pension commencing age 60 (females)

Multiplier calculated with allowance for projected mortality from the 1998-based population projections and rate of return of

Age at date of trial	0.0%	0.5%	1.0%	1.5%	2.0%	2.5%	3.0%	3.5%	4.0%	4.5%	5.0%	Age at date of trial
0	24.92	17.16	11.87	8.24	5.74	4.02	2.82	1.99	1.41	1.00	0.71	0
1	25.02	17.31	12.03	8.40	5.88	4.14	2.92	2.07	1.47	1.05	0.75	1
2	25.02	17.40	12.15	8.52	6.00	4.24	3.01	2.14	1.53	1.10	0.79	2
3	25.02	17.49	12.28	8.65	6.12	4.35	3.10	2.22	1.59	1.15	0.83	3
4	25.02	17.57	12.40	8.78	6.24	4.46	3.19	2.29	1.66	1.20	0.87	4
5	25.01	17.66	12.52	8.91	6.37	4.57	3.29	2.38	1.72	1.25	0.91	5
6	25.01	17.74	12.64	9.04	6.49	4.68	3.39	2.46	1.79	1.31	0.96	6
7	25.00	17.83	12.77	9.18	6.62	4.80	3.49	2.54	1.86	1.37	1.01	7
8	25.00	17.92	12.89	9.31	6.75	4.92	3.59	2.63	1.94	1.43	1.06	8
9	24.99	18.00	13.02	9.45	6.89	5.04	3.70	2.72	2.01	1.49	1.11	9
10	24.99	18.09	13.15	9.59	7.02	5.16	3.81	2.82	2.09	1.56	1.17	10
11	24.98	18.17	13.27	9.73	7.16	5.29	3.92	2.92	2.18	1.63	1.22	11
12	24.97	18.26	13.40	9.88	7.30	5.42	4.04	3.02	2.26	1.70	1.28	12
13	24.97	18.35	13.53	10.02	7.45	5.56	4.16	3.12	2.35	1.78	1.35	13
14	24.96	18.43	13.67	10.17	7.60	5.69	4.28	3.23	2.45	1.86	1.42	14
15	24.96	18.52	13.80	10.32	7.75	5.83	4.41	3.34	2.54	1.94	1.49	15
16	24.95	18.61	13.94	10.47	7.90	5.98	4.54	3.46	2.65	2.03	1.56	16
17	24.95	18.70	14.07	10.63	8.06	6.13	4.68	3.58	2.75	2.12	1.64	17
18	24.94	18.79	14.21	10.79	8.22	6.28	4.82	3.71	2.86	2.21	1.72	18
19	24.94	18.88	14.35	10.95	8.38	6.44	4.96	3.84	2.97	2.31	1.81	19
20	24.93	18.97	14.49	11.11	8.55	6.60	5.11	3.97	3.09	2.42	1.90	20
21	24.93	19.06	14.63	11.27	8.72	6.76	5.26	4.11	3.22	2.53	1.99	21
22	24.92	19.16	14.78	11.44	8.89	6.93	5.42	4.25	3.34	2.64	2.09	22
23	24.92	19.25	14.92	11.61	9.06	7.10	5.58	4.40	3.48	2.76	2.19	23
24	24.91	19.34	15.07	11.78	9.24	7.28	5.75	4.55	3.62	2.88	2.30	24
25	24.90	19.43	15.21	11.95	9.42	7.46	5.92	4.71	3.76	3.01	2.42	25

Table 32   Multipliers for loss of pension commencing age 60 (females)

Age at date of trial	Multiplier calculated with allowance for projected mortality from the 1998-based population projections and rate of return of											Age at date of trial
	0.0%	0.5%	1.0%	1.5%	2.0%	2.5%	3.0%	3.5%	4.0%	4.5%	5.0%	
26	24.89	19.52	15.36	12.13	9.61	7.64	6.09	4.87	3.91	3.14	2.54	26
27	24.88	19.61	15.51	12.31	9.80	7.83	6.27	5.04	4.06	3.29	2.66	27
28	24.87	19.70	15.66	12.49	9.99	8.02	6.46	5.22	4.23	3.43	2.80	28
29	24.86	19.79	15.81	12.67	10.19	8.22	6.65	5.40	4.39	3.59	2.93	29
30	24.85	19.88	15.96	12.86	10.39	8.42	6.85	5.59	4.57	3.75	3.08	30
31	24.84	19.97	16.11	13.04	10.59	8.63	7.05	5.78	4.75	3.91	3.23	31
32	24.83	20.06	16.27	13.24	10.80	8.84	7.26	5.98	4.94	4.09	3.39	32
33	24.82	20.16	16.42	13.43	11.01	9.06	7.48	6.19	5.13	4.27	3.56	33
34	24.81	20.25	16.58	13.62	11.23	9.28	7.70	6.40	5.34	4.46	3.74	34
35	24.79	20.34	16.74	13.82	11.45	9.51	7.93	6.62	5.55	4.66	3.93	35
36	24.78	20.43	16.90	14.03	11.68	9.75	8.16	6.85	5.77	4.87	4.12	36
37	24.77	20.52	17.06	14.23	11.90	9.99	8.40	7.09	6.00	5.09	4.33	37
38	24.76	20.62	17.23	14.44	12.14	10.23	8.65	7.34	6.24	5.32	4.54	38
39	24.74	20.71	17.39	14.65	12.38	10.49	8.91	7.59	6.49	5.56	4.77	39
40	24.73	20.80	17.56	14.86	12.62	10.75	9.18	7.86	6.74	5.80	5.01	40
41	24.72	20.90	17.73	15.08	12.87	11.01	9.45	8.13	7.01	6.06	5.26	41
42	24.71	21.00	17.90	15.30	13.12	11.28	9.73	8.41	7.29	6.34	5.52	42
43	24.70	21.09	18.07	15.53	13.38	11.56	10.02	8.71	7.58	6.62	5.80	43
44	24.69	21.19	18.24	15.76	13.65	11.85	10.32	9.01	7.89	6.92	6.09	44
45	24.68	21.29	18.42	15.99	13.92	12.15	10.63	9.33	8.20	7.23	6.39	45
46	24.67	21.39	18.60	16.23	14.19	12.45	10.95	9.65	8.53	7.56	6.71	46
47	24.66	21.49	18.79	16.47	14.48	12.76	11.28	9.99	8.88	7.90	7.05	47
48	24.66	21.60	18.97	16.72	14.77	13.08	11.62	10.34	9.23	8.26	7.40	48
49	24.66	21.70	19.16	16.97	15.07	13.41	11.97	10.71	9.61	8.64	7.78	49
50	24.66	21.82	19.36	17.23	15.37	13.75	12.34	11.09	10.00	9.03	8.17	50

51	24.66	21.93	19.56	17.49	15.69	14.11	12.71	11.49	10.40	9.44	8.59	51
52	24.67	22.05	19.77	17.77	16.01	14.47	13.11	11.90	10.83	9.88	9.03	52
53	24.68	22.18	19.98	18.05	16.35	14.85	13.52	12.33	11.28	10.34	9.49	53
54	24.71	22.31	20.20	18.34	16.70	15.24	13.94	12.78	11.75	10.82	9.99	54
55	24.73	22.45	20.43	18.64	17.06	15.64	14.38	13.25	12.24	11.33	10.51	55
56	24.77	22.59	20.67	18.95	17.43	16.07	14.84	13.75	12.76	11.86	11.06	56
57	24.81	22.75	20.92	19.28	17.82	16.51	15.33	14.26	13.30	12.43	11.64	57
58	24.87	22.92	21.18	19.62	18.23	16.97	15.84	14.81	13.88	13.04	12.27	58
59	24.95	23.11	21.47	19.99	18.66	17.46	16.37	15.39	14.49	13.68	12.93	59
60	25.05	23.32	21.77	20.38	19.12	17.98	16.94	16.00	15.14	14.36	13.64	60

Table 33 Multipliers for loss of pension commencing age 65 (males)

Age at date of trial	Multiplier calculated with allowance for projected mortality from the 1998-based population projections and rate of return of											Age at date of trial
	0.0%	0.5%	1.0%	1.5%	2.0%	2.5%	3.0%	3.5%	4.0%	4.5%	5.0%	
0	16.79	11.47	7.86	5.41	3.73	2.58	1.79	1.25	0.87	0.61	0.43	0
1	16.87	11.58	7.98	5.51	3.82	2.66	1.86	1.30	0.91	0.64	0.45	1
2	16.87	11.64	8.06	5.60	3.90	2.73	1.91	1.34	0.95	0.67	0.48	2
3	16.87	11.70	8.14	5.68	3.98	2.79	1.97	1.39	0.99	0.70	0.50	3
4	16.87	11.75	8.22	5.76	4.06	2.86	2.03	1.44	1.03	0.73	0.52	4
5	16.86	11.81	8.30	5.85	4.14	2.93	2.09	1.49	1.07	0.76	0.55	5
6	16.86	11.87	8.38	5.94	4.22	3.01	2.15	1.54	1.11	0.80	0.58	6
7	16.86	11.92	8.46	6.02	4.30	3.08	2.21	1.60	1.15	0.84	0.61	7
8	16.85	11.98	8.54	6.11	4.39	3.16	2.28	1.65	1.20	0.87	0.64	8
9	16.85	12.04	8.63	6.20	4.47	3.24	2.35	1.71	1.25	0.91	0.67	9
10	16.84	12.09	8.71	6.29	4.56	3.32	2.42	1.77	1.30	0.95	0.70	10
11	16.83	12.15	8.79	6.39	4.65	3.40	2.49	1.83	1.35	0.99	0.74	11
12	16.83	12.20	8.88	6.48	4.74	3.48	2.56	1.89	1.40	1.04	0.77	12
13	16.82	12.26	8.96	6.57	4.84	3.57	2.64	1.96	1.46	1.09	0.81	13
14	16.82	12.32	9.05	6.67	4.93	3.65	2.72	2.03	1.51	1.13	0.85	14
15	16.81	12.38	9.14	6.77	5.03	3.75	2.80	2.10	1.57	1.18	0.89	15
16	16.81	12.43	9.23	6.87	5.13	3.84	2.88	2.17	1.64	1.24	0.94	16
17	16.80	12.49	9.32	6.97	5.23	3.93	2.97	2.24	1.70	1.29	0.99	17
18	16.80	12.55	9.41	7.07	5.33	4.03	3.06	2.32	1.77	1.35	1.03	18
19	16.80	12.62	9.50	7.18	5.44	4.13	3.15	2.40	1.84	1.41	1.09	19
20	16.80	12.68	9.60	7.29	5.55	4.24	3.24	2.49	1.91	1.48	1.14	20
21	16.80	12.75	9.70	7.40	5.66	4.34	3.34	2.58	1.99	1.54	1.20	21
22	16.80	12.81	9.80	7.51	5.77	4.45	3.44	2.67	2.07	1.61	1.26	22
23	16.80	12.87	9.89	7.62	5.89	4.56	3.54	2.76	2.15	1.69	1.32	23
24	16.80	12.94	9.99	7.74	6.01	4.68	3.65	2.86	2.24	1.76	1.39	24
25	16.80	13.00	10.09	7.85	6.13	4.79	3.76	2.96	2.33	1.84	1.46	25

Age												Age
26	1.53	1.92	2.42	3.06	3.87	4.91	6.25	7.97	10.19	13.06	16.80	26
27	1.61	2.01	2.52	3.17	3.99	5.03	6.37	8.09	10.29	13.13	16.79	27
28	1.69	2.10	2.62	3.28	4.11	5.16	6.50	8.21	10.39	13.19	16.79	28
29	1.77	2.19	2.72	3.39	4.23	5.29	6.63	8.33	10.49	13.25	16.78	29
30	1.86	2.29	2.83	3.51	4.36	5.42	6.76	8.45	10.59	13.31	16.78	30
31	1.95	2.39	2.95	3.63	4.48	5.55	6.89	8.57	10.70	13.38	16.77	31
32	2.05	2.50	3.06	3.76	4.62	5.69	7.03	8.70	10.80	13.44	16.76	32
33	2.15	2.61	3.18	3.89	4.75	5.83	7.16	8.83	10.90	13.50	16.75	33
34	2.26	2.73	3.31	4.02	4.89	5.97	7.30	8.95	11.00	13.55	16.74	34
35	2.37	2.85	3.44	4.16	5.04	6.12	7.44	9.08	11.10	13.61	16.73	35
36	2.48	2.98	3.57	4.30	5.19	6.27	7.59	9.21	11.21	13.67	16.71	36
37	2.61	3.11	3.72	4.45	5.34	6.42	7.73	9.34	11.31	13.73	16.70	37
38	2.74	3.25	3.86	4.60	5.49	6.57	7.88	9.47	11.41	13.78	16.68	38
39	2.87	3.39	4.01	4.76	5.65	6.73	8.03	9.61	11.52	13.84	16.67	39
40	3.01	3.54	4.17	4.92	5.82	6.90	8.19	9.74	11.62	13.90	16.65	40
41	3.16	3.70	4.34	5.09	5.99	7.06	8.35	9.88	11.73	13.95	16.64	41
42	3.32	3.86	4.51	5.27	6.17	7.24	8.51	10.03	11.84	14.01	16.63	42
43	3.48	4.04	4.69	5.45	6.35	7.41	8.67	10.17	11.95	14.07	16.61	43
44	3.66	4.22	4.87	5.64	6.54	7.59	8.84	10.31	12.06	14.13	16.60	44
45	3.84	4.40	5.06	5.83	6.73	7.78	9.01	10.46	12.17	14.19	16.59	45
46	4.03	4.60	5.26	6.03	6.93	7.97	9.19	10.61	12.28	14.25	16.57	46
47	4.23	4.81	5.47	6.24	7.13	8.16	9.36	10.76	12.40	14.31	16.56	47
48	4.44	5.02	5.69	6.45	7.34	8.36	9.54	10.92	12.51	14.37	16.54	48
49	4.66	5.24	5.91	6.68	7.55	8.56	9.73	11.07	12.62	14.42	16.52	49
50	4.89	5.48	6.14	6.91	7.78	8.77	9.91	11.22	12.74	14.48	16.50	50
51	5.13	5.72	6.39	7.14	8.00	8.98	10.10	11.38	12.85	14.54	16.48	51
52	5.39	5.98	6.64	7.39	8.24	9.20	10.30	11.55	12.97	14.60	16.47	52
53	5.66	6.25	6.91	7.65	8.49	9.43	10.50	11.72	13.10	14.67	16.46	53
54	5.94	6.53	7.19	7.92	8.75	9.67	10.72	11.89	13.23	14.74	16.45	54
55	6.25	6.83	7.48	8.21	9.01	9.92	10.94	12.08	13.36	14.82	16.46	55

Table 33   Multipliers for loss of pension commencing age 65 (males)

Age at date of trial	Multiplier calculated with allowance for projected mortality from the 1998-based population projections and rate of return of											Age at date of trial
	0.0%	0.5%	1.0%	1.5%	2.0%	2.5%	3.0%	3.5%	4.0%	4.5%	5.0%	
56	16.47	14.90	13.51	12.27	11.17	10.18	9.30	8.51	7.79	7.15	6.57	56
57	16.50	15.00	13.67	12.48	11.42	10.46	9.60	8.83	8.13	7.49	6.92	57
58	16.55	15.13	13.85	12.71	11.69	10.76	9.92	9.17	8.48	7.86	7.30	58
59	16.62	15.27	14.06	12.96	11.98	11.08	10.27	9.54	8.87	8.26	7.70	59
60	16.71	15.43	14.28	13.23	12.29	11.43	10.65	9.93	9.28	8.68	8.14	60
61	16.82	15.61	14.52	13.52	12.62	11.80	11.04	10.35	9.72	9.14	8.61	61
62	16.94	15.81	14.77	13.83	12.97	12.19	11.47	10.81	10.20	9.64	9.12	62
63	17.08	16.02	15.05	14.16	13.35	12.60	11.92	11.28	10.70	10.16	9.66	63
64	17.23	16.24	15.34	14.51	13.75	13.04	12.39	11.80	11.24	10.73	10.25	64
65	17.40	16.49	15.65	14.88	14.17	13.51	12.91	12.34	11.82	11.34	10.89	65

Table 34 Multipliers for loss of pension commencing age 65 (females)

Age at date of trial	Multiplier calculated with allowance for projected mortality from the 1998-based population projections and rate of return of											Age at date of trial
	0.0%	0.5%	1.0%	1.5%	2.0%	2.5%	3.0%	3.5%	4.0%	4.5%	5.0%	
0	20.26	13.75	9.36	6.40	4.39	3.02	2.09	1.45	1.01	0.70	0.49	0
1	20.34	13.87	9.49	6.52	4.50	3.11	2.16	1.50	1.05	0.74	0.52	1
2	20.34	13.94	9.59	6.62	4.59	3.19	2.23	1.56	1.09	0.77	0.54	2
3	20.34	14.01	9.69	6.72	4.68	3.27	2.29	1.61	1.14	0.80	0.57	3
4	20.33	14.08	9.78	6.82	4.77	3.35	2.36	1.67	1.18	0.84	0.60	4
5	20.33	14.15	9.88	6.92	4.87	3.43	2.43	1.73	1.23	0.88	0.63	5
6	20.33	14.21	9.97	7.02	4.96	3.52	2.50	1.79	1.28	0.92	0.66	6
7	20.32	14.28	10.07	7.13	5.06	3.61	2.58	1.85	1.33	0.96	0.69	7
8	20.32	14.35	10.17	7.23	5.16	3.70	2.66	1.91	1.38	1.00	0.73	8
9	20.31	14.42	10.27	7.34	5.26	3.79	2.73	1.98	1.44	1.05	0.76	9
10	20.31	14.49	10.37	7.45	5.37	3.88	2.82	2.05	1.49	1.09	0.80	10
11	20.30	14.56	10.47	7.56	5.47	3.98	2.90	2.12	1.55	1.14	0.84	11
12	20.30	14.62	10.57	7.67	5.58	4.08	2.99	2.19	1.62	1.19	0.88	12
13	20.29	14.69	10.68	7.78	5.69	4.18	3.07	2.27	1.68	1.25	0.93	13
14	20.29	14.76	10.78	7.90	5.81	4.28	3.17	2.35	1.75	1.30	0.98	14
15	20.28	14.83	10.89	8.01	5.92	4.39	3.26	2.43	1.82	1.36	1.02	15
16	20.28	14.90	10.99	8.13	6.04	4.50	3.36	2.51	1.89	1.42	1.07	16
17	20.27	14.97	11.10	8.25	6.16	4.61	3.46	2.60	1.96	1.49	1.13	17
18	20.27	15.05	11.21	8.38	6.28	4.72	3.56	2.69	2.04	1.55	1.18	18
19	20.26	15.12	11.32	8.50	6.40	4.84	3.67	2.79	2.12	1.62	1.24	19
20	20.26	15.19	11.43	8.63	6.53	4.96	3.78	2.88	2.21	1.70	1.31	20
21	20.25	15.26	11.54	8.75	6.66	5.08	3.89	2.98	2.30	1.77	1.37	21
22	20.25	15.33	11.65	8.88	6.79	5.21	4.00	3.09	2.39	1.85	1.44	22
23	20.24	15.41	11.76	9.01	6.92	5.33	4.12	3.19	2.48	1.93	1.51	23
24	20.23	15.48	11.88	9.14	7.06	5.47	4.24	3.31	2.58	2.02	1.59	24
25	20.22	15.55	11.99	9.28	7.20	5.60	4.37	3.42	2.68	2.11	1.66	25

Table 34   Multipliers for loss of pension commencing age 65 (females)

Age at date of trial	Multiplier calculated with allowance for projected mortality from the 1998-based population projections and rate of return of											Age at date of trial
	0.0%	0.5%	1.0%	1.5%	2.0%	2.5%	3.0%	3.5%	4.0%	4.5%	5.0%	
26	20.21	15.62	12.11	9.41	7.34	5.74	4.50	3.54	2.79	2.20	1.75	26
27	20.20	15.69	12.22	9.55	7.48	5.88	4.63	3.66	2.90	2.30	1.83	27
28	20.19	15.76	12.34	9.69	7.63	6.02	4.77	3.79	3.01	2.41	1.92	28
29	20.18	15.83	12.46	9.83	7.78	6.17	4.91	3.92	3.13	2.51	2.02	29
30	20.17	15.90	12.58	9.97	7.93	6.32	5.06	4.05	3.26	2.63	2.12	30
31	20.16	15.98	12.69	10.12	8.09	6.48	5.21	4.19	3.39	2.74	2.23	31
32	20.15	16.05	12.81	10.26	8.24	6.64	5.36	4.34	3.52	2.86	2.34	32
33	20.14	16.12	12.94	10.41	8.40	6.80	5.52	4.49	3.66	2.99	2.45	33
34	20.13	16.19	13.06	10.56	8.57	6.97	5.68	4.64	3.81	3.13	2.57	34
35	20.12	16.26	13.18	10.72	8.73	7.14	5.85	4.80	3.96	3.26	2.70	35
36	20.10	16.33	13.30	10.87	8.90	7.31	6.02	4.97	4.11	3.41	2.83	36
37	20.09	16.40	13.43	11.03	9.08	7.49	6.20	5.14	4.27	3.56	2.97	37
38	20.07	16.47	13.56	11.18	9.25	7.67	6.38	5.32	4.44	3.72	3.12	38
39	20.06	16.54	13.68	11.35	9.43	7.86	6.57	5.50	4.62	3.89	3.28	39
40	20.05	16.62	13.81	11.51	9.62	8.05	6.76	5.69	4.80	4.06	3.44	40
41	20.03	16.69	13.94	11.67	9.80	8.25	6.96	5.89	4.99	4.24	3.61	41
42	20.02	16.76	14.07	11.84	9.99	8.45	7.17	6.09	5.19	4.43	3.79	42
43	20.00	16.83	14.20	12.01	10.19	8.66	7.38	6.30	5.39	4.63	3.98	43
44	19.99	16.91	14.34	12.19	10.39	8.87	7.60	6.52	5.61	4.83	4.17	44
45	19.98	16.98	14.47	12.36	10.59	9.09	7.82	6.75	5.83	5.05	4.38	45
46	19.96	17.05	14.61	12.54	10.80	9.31	8.05	6.98	6.06	5.28	4.60	46
47	19.95	17.13	14.75	12.73	11.01	9.54	8.29	7.22	6.30	5.51	4.83	47
48	19.94	17.21	14.89	12.91	11.22	9.78	8.54	7.47	6.56	5.76	5.07	48
49	19.93	17.29	15.03	13.10	11.45	10.02	8.80	7.74	6.82	6.02	5.33	49
50	19.92	17.37	15.18	13.30	11.67	10.27	9.06	8.01	7.09	6.29	5.59	50

51	19.92	17.45	15.33	13.49	11.91	10.53	9.33	8.29	7.38	6.58	5.88	51
52	19.92	17.54	15.48	13.70	12.15	10.80	9.62	8.58	7.68	6.88	6.17	52
53	19.92	17.63	15.64	13.91	12.40	11.07	9.91	8.89	7.99	7.19	6.49	53
54	19.93	17.73	15.81	14.13	12.65	11.36	10.22	9.21	8.32	7.52	6.82	54
55	19.94	17.83	15.98	14.35	12.92	11.65	10.54	9.54	8.66	7.87	7.17	55
56	19.95	17.93	16.15	14.58	13.19	11.96	10.87	9.89	9.02	8.24	7.54	56
57	19.98	18.05	16.34	14.83	13.48	12.28	11.21	10.26	9.40	8.63	7.93	57
58	20.02	18.17	16.54	15.08	13.78	12.62	11.58	10.64	9.80	9.04	8.35	58
59	20.07	18.32	16.75	15.35	14.10	12.98	11.97	11.05	10.23	9.48	8.80	59
60	20.14	18.47	16.98	15.64	14.44	13.35	12.37	11.49	10.68	9.95	9.28	60
61	20.22	18.64	17.22	15.95	14.79	13.75	12.80	11.94	11.16	10.45	9.80	61
62	20.31	18.82	17.47	16.26	15.16	14.16	13.25	12.42	11.67	10.97	10.34	62
63	20.39	19.00	17.73	16.58	15.54	14.59	13.72	12.92	12.20	11.53	10.91	63
64	20.48	19.17	17.99	16.91	15.92	15.03	14.20	13.45	12.75	12.11	11.52	64
65	20.56	19.35	18.25	17.24	16.32	15.48	14.70	13.99	13.34	12.73	12.17	65

Table 35 Multipliers for loss of pension commencing age 70 (males)

Age at date of trial	Multiplier calculated with allowance for projected mortality from the 1998-based population projections and rate of return of											Age at date of trial
	0.0%	0.5%	1.0%	1.5%	2.0%	2.5%	3.0%	3.5%	4.0%	4.5%	5.0%	
0	12.53	8.43	5.68	3.85	2.61	1.78	1.21	0.83	0.57	0.39	0.27	0
1	12.59	8.51	5.77	3.92	2.67	1.83	1.25	0.86	0.60	0.41	0.29	1
2	12.59	8.55	5.83	3.98	2.73	1.88	1.29	0.89	0.62	0.43	0.30	2
3	12.59	8.59	5.88	4.04	2.78	1.92	1.33	0.92	0.64	0.45	0.31	3
4	12.59	8.64	5.94	4.10	2.84	1.97	1.37	0.96	0.67	0.47	0.33	4
5	12.59	8.68	6.00	4.16	2.89	2.02	1.41	0.99	0.70	0.49	0.35	5
6	12.58	8.72	6.06	4.22	2.95	2.07	1.45	1.02	0.72	0.51	0.36	6
7	12.58	8.76	6.12	4.28	3.01	2.12	1.50	1.06	0.75	0.54	0.38	7
8	12.57	8.80	6.18	4.35	3.07	2.17	1.54	1.10	0.78	0.56	0.40	8
9	12.57	8.84	6.24	4.41	3.13	2.23	1.59	1.13	0.81	0.58	0.42	9
10	12.56	8.88	6.30	4.48	3.19	2.28	1.63	1.17	0.85	0.61	0.44	10
11	12.56	8.92	6.36	4.54	3.25	2.34	1.68	1.21	0.88	0.64	0.46	11
12	12.55	8.96	6.42	4.61	3.32	2.39	1.73	1.26	0.91	0.67	0.49	12
13	12.55	9.00	6.48	4.67	3.38	2.45	1.78	1.30	0.95	0.70	0.51	13
14	12.54	9.05	6.54	4.74	3.45	2.51	1.84	1.35	0.99	0.73	0.54	14
15	12.54	9.09	6.60	4.81	3.52	2.58	1.89	1.39	1.03	0.76	0.56	15
16	12.53	9.13	6.67	4.88	3.59	2.64	1.95	1.44	1.07	0.79	0.59	16
17	12.53	9.17	6.73	4.95	3.66	2.70	2.00	1.49	1.11	0.83	0.62	17
18	12.53	9.22	6.80	5.03	3.73	2.77	2.06	1.54	1.15	0.87	0.65	18
19	12.53	9.26	6.87	5.10	3.80	2.84	2.13	1.60	1.20	0.91	0.68	19
20	12.53	9.31	6.94	5.18	3.88	2.91	2.19	1.65	1.25	0.95	0.72	20
21	12.53	9.36	7.00	5.26	3.96	2.98	2.26	1.71	1.30	0.99	0.75	21
22	12.53	9.40	7.07	5.34	4.04	3.06	2.32	1.77	1.35	1.03	0.79	22
23	12.52	9.45	7.14	5.42	4.12	3.14	2.39	1.83	1.40	1.08	0.83	23
24	12.52	9.49	7.21	5.50	4.20	3.21	2.47	1.90	1.46	1.13	0.87	24
25	12.52	9.54	7.28	5.58	4.28	3.29	2.54	1.96	1.52	1.18	0.92	25

Age												Age
26	0.96	1.23	1.58	2.03	2.61	3.37	4.36	5.66	7.36	9.58	12.51	26
27	1.01	1.29	1.64	2.10	2.69	3.46	4.45	5.74	7.43	9.63	12.51	27
28	1.06	1.34	1.71	2.17	2.77	3.54	4.54	5.83	7.50	9.67	12.51	28
29	1.11	1.40	1.77	2.25	2.85	3.63	4.63	5.91	7.57	9.72	12.50	29
30	1.17	1.47	1.85	2.33	2.94	3.72	4.72	6.00	7.64	9.76	12.49	30
31	1.23	1.53	1.92	2.41	3.02	3.81	4.81	6.08	7.71	9.80	12.48	31
32	1.29	1.60	1.99	2.49	3.11	3.90	4.90	6.17	7.79	9.84	12.48	32
33	1.35	1.67	2.07	2.57	3.20	4.00	5.00	6.26	7.86	9.89	12.47	33
34	1.42	1.74	2.15	2.66	3.30	4.09	5.09	6.35	7.93	9.93	12.45	34
35	1.49	1.82	2.24	2.75	3.39	4.19	5.19	6.44	8.00	9.97	12.44	35
36	1.56	1.90	2.32	2.85	3.49	4.29	5.29	6.53	8.07	10.00	12.43	36
37	1.64	1.99	2.42	2.94	3.59	4.40	5.39	6.62	8.14	10.04	12.41	37
38	1.72	2.07	2.51	3.04	3.70	4.50	5.49	6.71	8.21	10.08	12.40	38
39	1.80	2.16	2.61	3.15	3.80	4.61	5.59	6.80	8.29	10.12	12.38	39
40	1.89	2.26	2.71	3.25	3.91	4.72	5.70	6.89	8.36	10.16	12.37	40
41	1.98	2.36	2.81	3.36	4.03	4.83	5.81	6.99	8.43	10.19	12.35	41
42	2.08	2.46	2.92	3.48	4.14	4.95	5.92	7.09	8.51	10.23	12.34	42
43	2.18	2.57	3.04	3.60	4.26	5.06	6.03	7.19	8.58	10.27	12.32	43
44	2.29	2.68	3.16	3.72	4.39	5.19	6.14	7.28	8.66	10.31	12.30	44
45	2.40	2.80	3.28	3.84	4.51	5.31	6.26	7.38	8.73	10.35	12.29	45
46	2.52	2.93	3.41	3.97	4.64	5.44	6.37	7.49	8.81	10.39	12.27	46
47	2.64	3.05	3.54	4.11	4.78	5.56	6.49	7.59	8.88	10.42	12.25	47
48	2.77	3.19	3.68	4.25	4.91	5.70	6.61	7.69	8.96	10.46	12.23	48
49	2.90	3.33	3.82	4.39	5.05	5.83	6.73	7.79	9.03	10.49	12.21	49
50	3.04	3.47	3.96	4.54	5.20	5.97	6.86	7.90	9.11	10.52	12.18	50
51	3.19	3.62	4.12	4.69	5.35	6.10	6.98	8.00	9.18	10.56	12.16	51
52	3.35	3.78	4.28	4.85	5.50	6.25	7.11	8.11	9.26	10.59	12.14	52
53	3.51	3.95	4.45	5.01	5.66	6.40	7.25	8.22	9.34	10.63	12.12	53
54	3.69	4.12	4.62	5.18	5.82	6.55	7.39	8.34	9.43	10.67	12.11	54
55	3.87	4.31	4.80	5.36	6.00	6.71	7.53	8.46	9.51	10.72	12.10	55

Table 35 Multipliers for loss of pension commencing age 70 (males)

Multiplier calculated with allowance for projected mortality from the 1998-based population projections and rate of return of

Age at date of trial	0.0%	0.5%	1.0%	1.5%	2.0%	2.5%	3.0%	3.5%	4.0%	4.5%	5.0%	Age at date of trial
56	12.09	10.77	9.61	8.58	7.68	6.88	6.18	5.55	5.00	4.50	4.07	56
57	12.10	10.83	9.71	8.72	7.84	7.06	6.37	5.75	5.20	4.71	4.28	57
58	12.13	10.91	9.83	8.87	8.02	7.26	6.58	5.97	5.43	4.94	4.50	58
59	12.17	11.00	9.96	9.03	8.21	7.47	6.80	6.20	5.67	5.18	4.75	59
60	12.22	11.10	10.11	9.21	8.41	7.69	7.04	6.45	5.92	5.44	5.01	60
61	12.28	11.22	10.26	9.40	8.63	7.93	7.29	6.72	6.20	5.72	5.29	61
62	12.36	11.35	10.43	9.61	8.86	8.18	7.56	7.00	6.49	6.02	5.60	62
63	12.44	11.48	10.61	9.82	9.10	8.45	7.85	7.30	6.80	6.34	5.92	63
64	12.53	11.62	10.80	10.04	9.36	8.73	8.15	7.62	7.13	6.68	6.27	64
65	12.63	11.78	11.00	10.28	9.62	9.02	8.47	7.96	7.49	7.05	6.65	65
66	12.74	11.94	11.20	10.53	9.91	9.33	8.80	8.31	7.86	7.44	7.05	66
67	12.86	12.11	11.43	10.79	10.21	9.67	9.16	8.70	8.26	7.86	7.48	67
68	12.99	12.30	11.67	11.08	10.53	10.02	9.55	9.11	8.70	8.32	7.96	68
69	13.15	12.52	11.94	11.39	10.89	10.41	9.97	9.56	9.18	8.82	8.48	69
70	13.36	12.78	12.25	11.75	11.29	10.86	10.45	10.07	9.71	9.38	9.07	70

Table 36   Multipliers for loss of pension commencing age 70 (females)

Age at date of trial	Multiplier calculated with allowance for projected mortality from the 1998-based population projections and rate of return of											Age at date of trial
	0.0%	0.5%	1.0%	1.5%	2.0%	2.5%	3.0%	3.5%	4.0%	4.5%	5.0%	
0	15.76	10.53	7.06	4.75	3.21	2.17	1.48	1.01	0.69	0.47	0.32	0
1	15.82	10.63	7.16	4.84	3.29	2.24	1.53	1.05	0.72	0.49	0.34	1
2	15.82	10.68	7.24	4.92	3.35	2.29	1.57	1.08	0.75	0.52	0.36	2
3	15.82	10.73	7.31	4.99	3.42	2.35	1.62	1.12	0.78	0.54	0.38	3
4	15.82	10.79	7.38	5.07	3.49	2.41	1.67	1.16	0.81	0.56	0.40	4
5	15.82	10.84	7.45	5.14	3.56	2.47	1.72	1.20	0.84	0.59	0.42	5
6	15.81	10.89	7.53	5.22	3.63	2.53	1.77	1.24	0.87	0.62	0.44	6
7	15.81	10.94	7.60	5.29	3.70	2.59	1.82	1.28	0.91	0.64	0.46	7
8	15.80	10.99	7.67	5.37	3.77	2.66	1.88	1.33	0.94	0.67	0.48	8
9	15.80	11.05	7.75	5.45	3.85	2.72	1.93	1.38	0.98	0.70	0.50	9
10	15.80	11.10	7.82	5.53	3.92	2.79	1.99	1.42	1.02	0.73	0.53	10
11	15.79	11.15	7.90	5.61	4.00	2.86	2.05	1.47	1.06	0.77	0.56	11
12	15.79	11.20	7.98	5.69	4.08	2.93	2.11	1.52	1.10	0.80	0.58	12
13	15.78	11.26	8.05	5.78	4.16	3.00	2.17	1.58	1.15	0.84	0.61	13
14	15.78	11.31	8.13	5.86	4.24	3.08	2.24	1.63	1.19	0.87	0.64	14
15	15.77	11.36	8.21	5.95	4.32	3.15	2.30	1.69	1.24	0.91	0.67	15
16	15.77	11.42	8.29	6.04	4.41	3.23	2.37	1.75	1.29	0.95	0.71	16
17	15.76	11.47	8.37	6.13	4.50	3.31	2.44	1.81	1.34	1.00	0.74	17
18	15.76	11.52	8.45	6.22	4.59	3.39	2.51	1.87	1.39	1.04	0.78	18
19	15.75	11.58	8.53	6.31	4.68	3.48	2.59	1.93	1.45	1.09	0.82	19
20	15.75	11.63	8.62	6.40	4.77	3.56	2.67	2.00	1.51	1.14	0.86	20
21	15.74	11.69	8.70	6.49	4.86	3.65	2.75	2.07	1.57	1.19	0.90	21
22	15.74	11.74	8.78	6.59	4.96	3.74	2.83	2.14	1.63	1.24	0.95	22
23	15.73	11.79	8.87	6.69	5.05	3.83	2.91	2.22	1.69	1.30	0.99	23
24	15.72	11.85	8.95	6.78	5.15	3.93	3.00	2.29	1.76	1.35	1.04	24
25	15.72	11.90	9.04	6.88	5.25	4.02	3.09	2.37	1.83	1.41	1.10	25

Table 36   Multipliers for loss of pension commencing age 70 (females)

Age at date of trial	Multiplier calculated with allowance for projected mortality from the 1998-based population projections and rate of return of											Age at date of trial
	0.0%	0.5%	1.0%	1.5%	2.0%	2.5%	3.0%	3.5%	4.0%	4.5%	5.0%	
26	15.71	11.95	9.12	6.98	5.36	4.12	3.18	2.46	1.90	1.48	1.15	26
27	15.70	12.01	9.21	7.08	5.46	4.22	3.27	2.54	1.98	1.54	1.21	27
28	15.69	12.06	9.30	7.19	5.57	4.32	3.37	2.63	2.06	1.61	1.27	28
29	15.68	12.11	9.38	7.29	5.68	4.43	3.47	2.72	2.14	1.68	1.33	29
30	15.67	12.17	9.47	7.39	5.79	4.54	3.57	2.81	2.22	1.76	1.39	30
31	15.66	12.22	9.56	7.50	5.90	4.65	3.67	2.91	2.31	1.84	1.46	31
32	15.65	12.27	9.65	7.61	6.01	4.76	3.78	3.01	2.40	1.92	1.54	32
33	15.64	12.33	9.74	7.72	6.13	4.88	3.89	3.11	2.49	2.00	1.61	33
34	15.62	12.38	9.83	7.83	6.25	5.00	4.01	3.22	2.59	2.09	1.69	34
35	15.61	12.43	9.92	7.94	6.37	5.12	4.12	3.33	2.69	2.18	1.77	35
36	15.60	12.48	10.01	8.05	6.49	5.24	4.24	3.44	2.80	2.28	1.86	36
37	15.59	12.53	10.10	8.16	6.61	5.37	4.37	3.56	2.91	2.38	1.95	37
38	15.57	12.58	10.20	8.28	6.74	5.50	4.50	3.68	3.02	2.49	2.05	38
39	15.56	12.64	10.29	8.40	6.87	5.63	4.63	3.81	3.14	2.60	2.15	39
40	15.54	12.69	10.38	8.52	7.00	5.77	4.76	3.94	3.27	2.71	2.26	40
41	15.53	12.74	10.48	8.64	7.13	5.91	4.90	4.07	3.39	2.83	2.37	41
42	15.51	12.79	10.57	8.76	7.27	6.05	5.04	4.21	3.53	2.96	2.49	42
43	15.49	12.84	10.67	8.88	7.41	6.20	5.19	4.36	3.67	3.09	2.61	43
44	15.48	12.89	10.76	9.01	7.55	6.35	5.34	4.51	3.81	3.23	2.74	44
45	15.46	12.94	10.86	9.13	7.70	6.50	5.50	4.66	3.96	3.37	2.87	45
46	15.45	13.00	10.96	9.26	7.84	6.66	5.66	4.82	4.11	3.52	3.01	46
47	15.43	13.05	11.06	9.39	7.99	6.82	5.82	4.99	4.28	3.67	3.16	47
48	15.42	13.10	11.16	9.53	8.15	6.98	5.99	5.16	4.44	3.84	3.32	48
49	15.40	13.16	11.26	9.66	8.30	7.15	6.17	5.33	4.62	4.01	3.48	49
50	15.39	13.21	11.37	9.80	8.46	7.33	6.35	5.52	4.80	4.19	3.66	50

Age												Age
51	15.38	13.27	11.47	9.94	8.63	7.51	6.54	5.71	4.99	4.37	3.84	51
52	15.37	13.33	11.58	10.08	8.80	7.69	6.73	5.91	5.19	4.57	4.03	52
53	15.36	13.39	11.69	10.23	8.97	7.88	6.94	6.11	5.40	4.78	4.23	53
54	15.36	13.45	11.81	10.39	9.15	8.08	7.15	6.33	5.62	4.99	4.44	54
55	15.35	13.52	11.93	10.54	9.34	8.28	7.36	6.55	5.85	5.22	4.67	55
56	15.36	13.59	12.05	10.71	9.53	8.50	7.59	6.79	6.08	5.46	4.91	56
57	15.37	13.67	12.18	10.88	9.73	8.72	7.82	7.03	6.33	5.71	5.16	57
58	15.38	13.75	12.32	11.06	9.94	8.95	8.07	7.29	6.60	5.98	5.43	58
59	15.42	13.85	12.47	11.25	10.16	9.20	8.34	7.57	6.88	6.27	5.72	59
60	15.46	13.96	12.63	11.45	10.40	9.46	8.62	7.86	7.18	6.57	6.02	60
61	15.51	14.08	12.81	11.67	10.65	9.73	8.91	8.17	7.50	6.90	6.35	61
62	15.56	14.20	12.98	11.89	10.90	10.01	9.21	8.49	7.83	7.24	6.70	62
63	15.62	14.32	13.16	12.11	11.16	10.31	9.53	8.82	8.18	7.60	7.06	63
64	15.66	14.44	13.33	12.33	11.43	10.60	9.85	9.17	8.54	7.97	7.45	64
65	15.70	14.55	13.51	12.56	11.69	10.90	10.18	9.52	8.92	8.36	7.85	65
66	15.74	14.66	13.68	12.78	11.96	11.21	10.53	9.90	9.31	8.78	8.28	66
67	15.78	14.78	13.86	13.02	12.25	11.54	10.89	10.28	9.73	9.21	8.74	67
68	15.83	14.90	14.05	13.27	12.55	11.88	11.27	10.70	10.17	9.68	9.23	68
69	15.90	15.05	14.26	13.54	12.87	12.25	11.68	11.14	10.65	10.19	9.76	69
70	16.01	15.23	14.51	13.85	13.23	12.66	12.13	11.64	11.17	10.74	10.34	70

Table 37   Discounting factors for term certain

Factor to discount value of multiplier for a period of deferment

Term	0.5%	1.0%	1.5%	2.0%	2.5%	3.0%	3.5%	4.0%	4.5%	5.0%	Term
1	0.9950	0.9901	0.9852	0.9804	0.9756	0.9709	0.9662	0.9615	0.9569	0.9524	1
2	0.9901	0.9803	0.9707	0.9612	0.9518	0.9426	0.9335	0.9246	0.9157	0.9070	2
3	0.9851	0.9706	0.9563	0.9423	0.9286	0.9151	0.9019	0.8890	0.8763	0.8638	3
4	0.9802	0.9610	0.9422	0.9238	0.9060	0.8885	0.8714	0.8548	0.8386	0.8227	4
5	0.9754	0.9515	0.9283	0.9057	0.8839	0.8626	0.8420	0.8219	0.8025	0.7835	5
6	0.9705	0.9420	0.9145	0.8880	0.8623	0.8375	0.8135	0.7903	0.7679	0.7462	6
7	0.9657	0.9327	0.9010	0.8706	0.8413	0.8131	0.7860	0.7599	0.7348	0.7107	7
8	0.9609	0.9235	0.8877	0.8535	0.8207	0.7894	0.7594	0.7307	0.7032	0.6768	8
9	0.9561	0.9143	0.8746	0.8368	0.8007	0.7664	0.7337	0.7026	0.6729	0.6446	9
10	0.9513	0.9053	0.8617	0.8203	0.7812	0.7441	0.7089	0.6756	0.6439	0.6139	10
11	0.9466	0.8963	0.8489	0.8043	0.7621	0.7224	0.6849	0.6496	0.6162	0.5847	11
12	0.9419	0.8874	0.8364	0.7885	0.7436	0.7014	0.6618	0.6246	0.5897	0.5568	12
13	0.9372	0.8787	0.8240	0.7730	0.7254	0.6810	0.6394	0.6006	0.5643	0.5303	13
14	0.9326	0.8700	0.8118	0.7579	0.7077	0.6611	0.6178	0.5775	0.5400	0.5051	14
15	0.9279	0.8613	0.7999	0.7430	0.6905	0.6419	0.5969	0.5553	0.5167	0.4810	15
16	0.9233	0.8528	0.7880	0.7284	0.6736	0.6232	0.5767	0.5339	0.4945	0.4581	16
17	0.9187	0.8444	0.7764	0.7142	0.6572	0.6050	0.5572	0.5134	0.4732	0.4363	17
18	0.9141	0.8360	0.7649	0.7002	0.6412	0.5874	0.5384	0.4936	0.4528	0.4155	18
19	0.9096	0.8277	0.7536	0.6864	0.6255	0.5703	0.5202	0.4746	0.4333	0.3957	19
20	0.9051	0.8195	0.7425	0.6730	0.6103	0.5537	0.5026	0.4564	0.4146	0.3769	20
21	0.9006	0.8114	0.7315	0.6598	0.5954	0.5375	0.4856	0.4388	0.3968	0.3589	21
22	0.8961	0.8034	0.7207	0.6468	0.5809	0.5219	0.4692	0.4220	0.3797	0.3418	22
23	0.8916	0.7954	0.7100	0.6342	0.5667	0.5067	0.4533	0.4057	0.3634	0.3256	23
24	0.8872	0.7876	0.6995	0.6217	0.5529	0.4919	0.4380	0.3901	0.3477	0.3101	24
25	0.8828	0.7798	0.6892	0.6095	0.5394	0.4776	0.4231	0.3751	0.3327	0.2953	25
26	0.8784	0.7720	0.6790	0.5976	0.5262	0.4637	0.4088	0.3607	0.3184	0.2812	26
27	0.8740	0.7644	0.6690	0.5859	0.5134	0.4502	0.3950	0.3468	0.3047	0.2678	27
28	0.8697	0.7568	0.6591	0.5744	0.5009	0.4371	0.3817	0.3335	0.2916	0.2551	28
29	0.8653	0.7493	0.6494	0.5631	0.4887	0.4243	0.3687	0.3207	0.2790	0.2429	29
30	0.8610	0.7419	0.6398	0.5521	0.4767	0.4120	0.3563	0.3083	0.2670	0.2314	30

Age											Age
31	0.8567	0.7346	0.6303	0.5412	0.4651	0.4000	0.3442	0.2965	0.2555	0.2204	31
32	0.8525	0.7273	0.6210	0.5306	0.4538	0.3883	0.3326	0.2851	0.2445	0.2099	32
33	0.8482	0.7201	0.6118	0.5202	0.4427	0.3770	0.3213	0.2741	0.2340	0.1999	33
34	0.8440	0.7130	0.6028	0.5100	0.4319	0.3660	0.3105	0.2636	0.2239	0.1904	34
35	0.8398	0.7059	0.5939	0.5000	0.4214	0.3554	0.3000	0.2534	0.2143	0.1813	35
36	0.8356	0.6989	0.5851	0.4902	0.4111	0.3450	0.2898	0.2437	0.2050	0.1727	36
37	0.8315	0.6920	0.5764	0.4806	0.4011	0.3350	0.2800	0.2343	0.1962	0.1644	37
38	0.8274	0.6852	0.5679	0.4712	0.3913	0.3252	0.2706	0.2253	0.1878	0.1566	38
39	0.8232	0.6784	0.5595	0.4619	0.3817	0.3158	0.2614	0.2166	0.1797	0.1491	39
40	0.8191	0.6717	0.5513	0.4529	0.3724	0.3066	0.2526	0.2083	0.1719	0.1420	40
41	0.8151	0.6650	0.5431	0.4440	0.3633	0.2976	0.2440	0.2003	0.1645	0.1353	41
42	0.8110	0.6584	0.5351	0.4353	0.3545	0.2890	0.2358	0.1926	0.1574	0.1288	42
43	0.8070	0.6519	0.5272	0.4268	0.3458	0.2805	0.2278	0.1852	0.1507	0.1227	43
44	0.8030	0.6454	0.5194	0.4184	0.3374	0.2724	0.2201	0.1780	0.1442	0.1169	44
45	0.7990	0.6391	0.5117	0.4102	0.3292	0.2644	0.2127	0.1712	0.1380	0.1113	45
46	0.7950	0.6327	0.5042	0.4022	0.3211	0.2567	0.2055	0.1646	0.1320	0.1060	46
47	0.7910	0.6265	0.4967	0.3943	0.3133	0.2493	0.1985	0.1583	0.1263	0.1009	47
48	0.7871	0.6203	0.4894	0.3865	0.3057	0.2420	0.1918	0.1522	0.1209	0.0961	48
49	0.7832	0.6141	0.4821	0.3790	0.2982	0.2350	0.1853	0.1463	0.1157	0.0916	49
50	0.7793	0.6080	0.4750	0.3715	0.2909	0.2281	0.1791	0.1407	0.1107	0.0872	50
51	0.7754	0.6020	0.4680	0.3642	0.2838	0.2215	0.1730	0.1353	0.1059	0.0831	51
52	0.7716	0.5961	0.4611	0.3571	0.2769	0.2150	0.1671	0.1301	0.1014	0.0791	52
53	0.7677	0.5902	0.4543	0.3501	0.2702	0.2088	0.1615	0.1251	0.0970	0.0753	53
54	0.7639	0.5843	0.4475	0.3432	0.2636	0.2027	0.1560	0.1203	0.0928	0.0717	54
55	0.7601	0.5785	0.4409	0.3365	0.2572	0.1968	0.1508	0.1157	0.0888	0.0683	55
56	0.7563	0.5728	0.4344	0.3299	0.2509	0.1910	0.1457	0.1112	0.0850	0.0651	56
57	0.7525	0.5671	0.4280	0.3234	0.2448	0.1855	0.1407	0.1069	0.0814	0.0620	57
58	0.7488	0.5615	0.4217	0.3171	0.2388	0.1801	0.1360	0.1028	0.0778	0.0590	58
59	0.7451	0.5560	0.4154	0.3109	0.2330	0.1748	0.1314	0.0989	0.0745	0.0562	59
60	0.7414	0.5504	0.4093	0.3048	0.2273	0.1697	0.1269	0.0951	0.0713	0.0535	60
61	0.7377	0.5450	0.4032	0.2988	0.2217	0.1648	0.1226	0.0914	0.0682	0.0510	61
62	0.7340	0.5396	0.3973	0.2929	0.2163	0.1600	0.1185	0.0879	0.0653	0.0486	62
63	0.7304	0.5343	0.3914	0.2872	0.2111	0.1553	0.1145	0.0845	0.0625	0.0462	63
64	0.7267	0.5290	0.3856	0.2816	0.2059	0.1508	0.1106	0.0813	0.0598	0.0440	64
65	0.7231	0.5237	0.3799	0.2761	0.2009	0.1464	0.1069	0.0781	0.0572	0.0419	65

Table 37   Discounting factors for term certain

Factor to discount value of multiplier for a period of deferment

Term	0.5%	1.0%	1.5%	2.0%	2.5%	3.0%	3.5%	4.0%	4.5%	5.0%	Term
66	0.7195	0.5185	0.3743	0.2706	0.1960	0.1421	0.1033	0.0751	0.0547	0.0399	66
67	0.7159	0.5134	0.3688	0.2653	0.1912	0.1380	0.0998	0.0722	0.0524	0.0380	67
68	0.7124	0.5083	0.3633	0.2601	0.1865	0.1340	0.0964	0.0695	0.0501	0.0362	68
69	0.7088	0.5033	0.3580	0.2550	0.1820	0.1301	0.0931	0.0668	0.0480	0.0345	69
70	0.7053	0.4983	0.3527	0.2500	0.1776	0.1263	0.0900	0.0642	0.0459	0.0329	70
71	0.7018	0.4934	0.3475	0.2451	0.1732	0.1226	0.0869	0.0617	0.0439	0.0313	71
72	0.6983	0.4885	0.3423	0.2403	0.1690	0.1190	0.0840	0.0594	0.0420	0.0298	72
73	0.6948	0.4837	0.3373	0.2356	0.1649	0.1156	0.0812	0.0571	0.0402	0.0284	73
74	0.6914	0.4789	0.3323	0.2310	0.1609	0.1122	0.0784	0.0549	0.0385	0.0270	74
75	0.6879	0.4741	0.3274	0.2265	0.1569	0.1089	0.0758	0.0528	0.0368	0.0258	75
76	0.6845	0.4694	0.3225	0.2220	0.1531	0.1058	0.0732	0.0508	0.0353	0.0245	76
77	0.6811	0.4648	0.3178	0.2177	0.1494	0.1027	0.0707	0.0488	0.0337	0.0234	77
78	0.6777	0.4602	0.3131	0.2134	0.1457	0.0997	0.0683	0.0469	0.0323	0.0222	78
79	0.6743	0.4556	0.3084	0.2092	0.1422	0.0968	0.0660	0.0451	0.0309	0.0212	79
80	0.6710	0.4511	0.3039	0.2051	0.1387	0.0940	0.0638	0.0434	0.0296	0.0202	80

Table 38 Multipliers for pecuniary loss for term certain

Multiplier for regular frequent payments for a term certain at rate of return of

Term	0.5%	1.0%	1.5%	2.0%	2.5%	3.0%	3.5%	4.0%	4.5%	5.0%	Term
1	1.00	1.00	0.99	0.99	0.99	0.99	0.98	0.98	0.98	0.98	1
2	1.99	1.98	1.97	1.96	1.95	1.94	1.93	1.92	1.91	1.91	2
3	2.98	2.96	2.93	2.91	2.89	2.87	2.85	2.83	2.81	2.79	3
4	3.96	3.92	3.88	3.85	3.81	3.77	3.74	3.70	3.67	3.63	4
5	4.94	4.88	4.82	4.76	4.70	4.65	4.59	4.54	4.49	4.44	5
6	5.91	5.82	5.74	5.66	5.58	5.50	5.42	5.35	5.27	5.20	6
7	6.88	6.76	6.65	6.54	6.43	6.32	6.22	6.12	6.02	5.93	7
8	7.84	7.69	7.54	7.40	7.26	7.12	6.99	6.87	6.74	6.62	8
9	8.80	8.61	8.42	8.24	8.07	7.90	7.74	7.58	7.43	7.28	9
10	9.75	9.52	9.29	9.07	8.86	8.66	8.46	8.27	8.09	7.91	10
11	10.70	10.42	10.15	9.88	9.63	9.39	9.16	8.93	8.72	8.51	11
12	11.65	11.31	10.99	10.68	10.39	10.10	9.83	9.57	9.32	9.08	12
13	12.59	12.19	11.82	11.46	11.12	10.79	10.48	10.18	9.90	9.63	13
14	13.52	13.07	12.64	12.23	11.84	11.46	11.11	10.77	10.45	10.14	14
15	14.45	13.93	13.44	12.98	12.54	12.12	11.72	11.34	10.98	10.64	15
16	15.38	14.79	14.24	13.71	13.22	12.75	12.30	11.88	11.48	11.11	16
17	16.30	15.64	15.02	14.43	13.88	13.36	12.87	12.41	11.97	11.55	17
18	17.22	16.48	15.79	15.14	14.53	13.96	13.42	12.91	12.43	11.98	18
19	18.13	17.31	16.55	15.83	15.17	14.54	13.95	13.39	12.87	12.38	19
20	19.03	18.14	17.30	16.51	15.78	15.10	14.46	13.86	13.30	12.77	20
21	19.94	18.95	18.03	17.18	16.39	15.65	14.95	14.31	13.70	13.14	21
22	20.84	19.76	18.76	17.83	16.97	16.17	15.43	14.74	14.09	13.49	22
23	21.73	20.56	19.48	18.47	17.55	16.69	15.89	15.15	14.46	13.82	23
24	22.62	21.35	20.18	19.10	18.11	17.19	16.34	15.55	14.82	14.14	24
25	23.50	22.13	20.87	19.72	18.65	17.67	16.77	15.93	15.16	14.44	25
26	24.38	22.91	21.56	20.32	19.19	18.14	17.18	16.30	15.48	14.73	26
27	25.26	23.68	22.23	20.91	19.71	18.60	17.59	16.65	15.80	15.01	27
28	26.13	24.44	22.90	21.49	20.21	19.04	17.97	16.99	16.09	15.27	28
29	27.00	25.19	23.55	22.06	20.71	19.47	18.35	17.32	16.38	15.52	29
30	27.86	25.94	24.20	22.62	21.19	19.89	18.71	17.64	16.65	15.75	30

Table 38   Multipliers for pecuniary loss for term certain

Multiplier for regular frequent payments for a term certain at rate of return of

Term	0.5%	1.0%	1.5%	2.0%	2.5%	3.0%	3.5%	4.0%	4.5%	5.0%	Term
31	28.72	26.67	24.83	23.17	21.66	20.30	19.06	17.94	16.91	15.98	31
32	29.58	27.41	25.46	23.70	22.12	20.69	19.40	18.23	17.16	16.19	32
33	30.43	28.13	26.07	24.23	22.57	21.08	19.73	18.51	17.40	16.40	33
34	31.27	28.85	26.68	24.74	23.01	21.45	20.04	18.78	17.63	16.59	34
35	32.12	29.56	27.28	25.25	23.43	21.81	20.35	19.04	17.85	16.78	35
36	32.95	30.26	27.87	25.74	23.85	22.16	20.64	19.28	18.06	16.96	36
37	33.79	30.95	28.45	26.23	24.26	22.50	20.93	19.52	18.26	17.13	37
38	34.62	31.64	29.02	26.70	24.65	22.83	21.20	19.75	18.45	17.29	38
39	35.44	32.32	29.58	27.17	25.04	23.15	21.47	19.97	18.64	17.44	39
40	36.26	33.00	30.14	27.63	25.42	23.46	21.73	20.19	18.81	17.58	40
41	37.08	33.67	30.69	28.08	25.78	23.76	21.97	20.39	18.98	17.72	41
42	37.89	34.33	31.23	28.52	26.14	24.06	22.21	20.59	19.14	17.86	42
43	38.70	34.98	31.76	28.95	26.49	24.34	22.45	20.78	19.30	17.98	43
44	39.51	35.63	32.28	29.37	26.83	24.62	22.67	20.96	19.44	18.10	44
45	40.31	36.27	32.80	29.78	27.17	24.88	22.89	21.13	19.58	18.21	45
46	41.10	36.91	33.30	30.19	27.49	25.15	23.10	21.30	19.72	18.32	46
47	41.90	37.54	33.80	30.59	27.81	25.40	23.30	21.46	19.85	18.43	47
48	42.69	38.16	34.30	30.98	28.12	25.64	23.49	21.62	19.97	18.53	48
49	43.47	38.78	34.78	31.36	28.42	25.88	23.68	21.77	20.09	18.62	49
50	44.25	39.39	35.26	31.74	28.72	26.11	23.86	21.91	20.20	18.71	50
51	45.03	40.00	35.73	32.10	29.00	26.34	24.04	22.05	20.31	18.79	51
52	45.80	40.60	36.20	32.47	29.28	26.56	24.21	22.18	20.42	18.87	52
53	46.57	41.19	36.66	32.82	29.56	26.77	24.37	22.31	20.51	18.95	53
54	47.34	41.78	37.11	33.17	29.82	26.97	24.53	22.43	20.61	19.03	54
55	48.10	42.36	37.55	33.51	30.08	27.17	24.69	22.55	20.70	19.10	55
56	48.86	42.93	37.99	33.84	30.34	27.37	24.83	22.66	20.79	19.16	56
57	49.61	43.50	38.42	34.17	30.59	27.56	24.98	22.77	20.87	19.23	57
58	50.36	44.07	38.84	34.49	30.83	27.74	25.12	22.88	20.95	19.29	58
59	51.11	44.63	39.26	34.80	31.06	27.92	25.25	22.98	21.03	19.34	59
60	51.85	45.18	39.67	35.11	31.29	28.09	25.38	23.07	21.10	19.40	60

Age											Age
61	52.59	45.73	40.08	35.41	31.52	28.26	25.50	23.17	21.17	19.45	61
62	53.33	46.27	40.48	35.70	31.74	28.42	25.62	23.26	21.24	19.50	62
63	54.06	46.81	40.88	36.00	31.95	28.58	25.74	23.34	21.30	19.55	63
64	54.79	47.34	41.26	36.28	32.16	28.73	25.85	23.42	21.36	19.59	64
65	55.52	47.86	41.65	36.56	32.36	28.88	25.96	23.50	21.42	19.64	65
66	56.24	48.39	42.02	36.83	32.56	29.02	26.07	23.58	21.47	19.68	66
67	56.95	48.90	42.40	37.10	32.75	29.16	26.17	23.65	21.53	19.72	67
68	57.67	49.41	42.76	37.36	32.94	29.30	26.27	23.73	21.58	19.75	68
69	58.38	49.92	43.12	37.62	33.13	29.43	26.36	23.79	21.63	19.79	69
70	59.09	50.42	43.48	37.87	33.31	29.56	26.45	23.86	21.68	19.82	70
71	59.79	50.91	43.83	38.12	33.48	29.68	26.54	23.92	21.72	19.85	71
72	60.49	51.41	44.17	38.36	33.65	29.80	26.63	23.98	21.76	19.88	72
73	61.19	51.89	44.51	38.60	33.82	29.92	26.71	24.04	21.80	19.91	73
74	61.88	52.37	44.85	38.83	33.98	30.03	26.79	24.10	21.84	19.94	74
75	62.57	52.85	45.18	39.06	34.14	30.15	26.87	24.15	21.88	19.97	75
76	63.26	53.32	45.50	39.29	34.30	30.25	26.94	24.20	21.92	19.99	76
77	63.94	53.79	45.82	39.51	34.45	30.36	27.01	24.25	21.95	20.02	77
78	64.62	54.25	46.14	39.72	34.60	30.46	27.08	24.30	21.99	20.04	78
79	65.29	54.71	46.45	39.93	34.74	30.56	27.15	24.35	22.02	20.06	79
80	65.97	55.16	46.75	40.14	34.88	30.65	27.21	24.39	22.05	20.08	80

390 *Appendix II*

ACTUARIAL FORMULAE AND BASIS

The functions tabulated are:

Tables 1, 2, 19 and 20	$\bar{a}_x$
Tables 3, 4, 21 and 22	$\bar{a}_{x:\overline{55-x}|}$
Tables 5, 6 , 23 and 24	$\bar{a}_{x:\overline{60-x}|}$
Tables 7, 8 , 25 and 26	$\bar{a}_{x:\overline{65-x}|}$
Tables 9, 10 , 27 and 28	$\bar{a}_{x:\overline{70-x}|}$
Tables 11, 12, 29 and 30	$(55-x)|\,\bar{a}_{55}$
Tables 13, 14, 31 and 32	$(60-x)|\,\bar{a}_{60}$
Tables 15, 16, 33 and 34	$(65-x)|\,\bar{a}_{65}$
Tables 17, 18, 35 and 36	$(70-x)|\,\bar{a}_{70}$
Table 37:	$1/(1+i)^n$
Table 38:	$\bar{a}_{\overline{n}|}$

- Mortality: English Life Tables No. 15 (Tables 1 to 18)
- Mortality assumptions for 1998-based official population projections for England & Wales (Tables 19 to 36)
- Loadings: None
- Rate of return: As stated in the Tables

Index

All references are to paragraph number.